A LINE IN THE TAR SANDS

"The story of Greenhouse Goo is global. But so is its resistance: beautiful, complex, and rich. *A Line in the Tar Sands* is drawn with hope and righteous anger, celebrating the cosmologies that the tar sands industry—and its politicians—would destroy."
　　—Raj Patel, author of *Stuffed and Starved*

"Opposition to the tar sands of Alberta and the pipelines that would carry their deadly crude has created one of the most potent civil society movements in our history. Led by grassroots and First Nations communities and fuelled by anger at the gutting of our freshwater heritage by the Harper government, this movement has the potential to change politics in Canada forever. Rich in detail and filled with hope, *A Line in the Tar Sands* tells the story of this movement and inspires a whole new generation to action."
　　—Maude Barlow, Council of Canadians

"Alberta tar sands oil, if fully exploited, will add enough carbon dioxide to the earth's atmosphere to break the planetary carbon budget, unleashing untold, irreversible, worldwide ecological destruction. A massive, diverse people's movement has arisen in response, drawing 'a line in the sand' before the fossil fuel juggernaut. *A Line in the Tar Sands* is the indispensable guide to this frontline struggle on behalf of humanity and the earth."
　　—John Bellamy Foster, co-author of *What Every Environmentalist Needs to Know about Capitalism*

"*A Line in the Tar Sands* weaves a holistic story of the history of the tar sands, the growth of the environmental movement, and Indigenous peoples determined to stop this insidious development."
　　—Katsi'tsakwas Ellen Gabriel, Indigenous human rights activist, Turtle Clan from Kanehsatà:ke Mohawk Territory

"The battle over Alberta bitumen pits malignant Petro-Capital against an inspiring and growing ensemble of activists. It has the feel of a Stalingrad in the war for a livable world: the stakes are that high. *A Line in the Tar Sands* tells this story superbly and with quiet passion. Here is a book for everyone who cares about the future."

—Joel Kovel, author of *The Enemy of Nature*

"Grounded learning comes from a cycle of action and reflection: we make change in the world, step back and assess our efforts, revise them, and then come back with more powerful and focused action. This is how our movements learn from one another and become more strategic and visionary. This book captures that action and reflection—it starts with organizers from different parts of struggle, offering their insights and learnings. They're woven together in this anthology to offer new ways of understanding the interconnected crises we face and to build a tool for solidarity."

—Sharon Lungo, The Ruckus Society

"In northern Alberta, the petroleum industry is engaged in the worst environmental crime in history. If business as usual continues in the tar sands, the world's fast-warming climate will be pushed over the edge to disaster. *A Line in the Tar Sands* is essential reading about that crime, and about the growing movement to stop the tar sands criminals before they stop us."

—Ian Angus, editor of ClimateAndCapitalism.com, co-author
of *Too Many People? Population, Immigration, and the
Environmental Crisis*

"*A Line in the Tar Sands* elegantly connects migrant rights, human rights, rights of nature, indigenous sovereignty, and corporate concentration, and broadcasts a vision for ecological justice rooted in a healing movement of resistance, resilience, and restoration."

—Gopal Dayaneni, Movement Generation Justice and Ecology Project

"*A Line in the Tar Sands* brings us powerful stories and strategic insights from the organizers who are turning the multi-pronged frontlines of the problem into the frontlines of the solution. Tap into the momentum of the movement that is making the defusing of the tar sands bomb an international priority. Whether you are new to the fight or a veteran organizer, this book is for anyone who is part of building a sane, just, hopeful future from the ground up."

—Patrick Reinsborough and Christine Cordero,
Center for Story-based Strategy

A LINE IN
THE TAR SANDS

STRUGGLES FOR ENVIRONMENTAL JUSTICE

EDITED BY
TOBAN BLACK
TONY WEIS
STEPHEN D'ARCY
JOSHUA KAHN RUSSELL

A Line in the Tar Sands: Struggles for Environmental Justice

First published in Canada in 2014 by Between the Lines
401 Richmond Street West, Studio 277, Toronto, Ontario, M5V 3A8, Canada
1-800-718-7201
www.btlbooks.com

First published in the United States and the United Kingdom in 2014 by PM Press
PO Box 23912, Oakland, CA 94623
www.pmpress.org

Library and Archives Canada Cataloguing in Publication

D'Arcy, Steve, 1968-, author
    A line in the tar sands : struggles for environmental justice / Stephen D'Arcy, Tony Weis, Toban Black, Joshua Kahn Russell.
Includes index.
Co-published by: PM Press.
Issued in print and electronic formats.
ISBN 978-1-77113-109-4 (pbk.).--ISBN 978-1-77113-110-0 (epub).--ISBN 978-1-77113-111-7 (pdf)
    1. Oil sands industry--Environmental aspects--Alberta. 2. Oil sands--Environmental aspects--Alberta. 3. Environmental justice--Canada. I. Title.

Library of Congress Control Number: 2014908063

ISBN 978 1 77113 109 4   Between the Lines paperback
ISBN 978 1 6296 3039 7   PM Press paperback
ISBN 978 1 77113 110 0   Between the Lines epub
ISBN 978 1 77113 111 7   Between the Lines pdf

Interior design by David Vereschagin/Quadrat Communications
Back cover photo: Hereditary Chief Toghestiy of the Likhts'amisyu Clan and Wet'suwet'en Nation, at the Royal Bank of Canada shareholder meeting to confront them on their tar sands investments, 2010. Toghestiy is a supporter and organizer for the Unist'ot'en Camp.

10 9 8 7 6 5 4 3 2 1

Printed in the USA by the Employee Owners of Thomson-Shore in Dexter, Michigan.
www.thomsonshore.com

Between the Lines gratefully acknowledges assistance for its publishing activities from the Canada Council for the Arts, the Ontario Arts Council, the Government of Ontario through the Ontario Book Publishers Tax Credit program, and the Government of Canada through the Canada Book Fund.

Canada Council for the Arts   Conseil des Arts du Canada   Canadä

ONTARIO ARTS COUNCIL
CONSEIL DES ARTS DE L'ONTARIO
an Ontario government agency
un organisme du gouvernement de l'Ontario

To those defending their communities from the tar sands industry, whose struggle for liberation helps liberate the entire planet.

To those working to build bridges and to un-build walls and borders, in service of broad-based multiracial mass movements.

To our elders and mentors, who remind us that the struggle has *always* been urgent, and that justice is a journey, not a destination.

To everyone doing their part to co-create a better world, which the tar sands industry has no place in.

The editors' proceeds from this book will be donated to front-line grassroots environmental justice groups and campaigns.

Table of Contents

Part II: Communities and Resistance

Part III: Future Prospects

List of Contributors

Greg Albo is an Associate Professor in the Department of Political Science at York University. He is co-author of *In and Out of Crisis: The Global Financial Meltdown and Left Alternatives* (PM Press), and a co-editor of the *Socialist Register*. He is also on the executive of the Toronto-based Centre for Social Justice.

Sâkihitowin Awâsis is a Two-Spirited Didikai Métis spoken-word artist and community organizer living in London, Ontario, who has been active in the struggle against the Line 9 pipeline reversal in Ontario.

Toban Black is a community organizer and an associate editor for *Upping the Anti*. As an activist, he has focused on extreme energy projects and community-based alternatives.

Rae Breaux is from California and is an organizer with the Rising Tide North America. She is also the Grassroots Actions Campaigner for 350.org.

Jeremy Brecher is the author of more than a dozen books on labour and social movements, including *Strike!* (PM Press) and *Global Village or Global Pillage* (South End Press). He currently works with the Labor Network for Sustainability.

Linda Capato is a queer climate activist in the San Francisco Bay Area who works to support communities directly affected by climate change and extractive industries, and currently serves as the Fracking Campaign Coordinator for 350.org.

Jesse Cardinal is the Coordinator of Keepers of the Athabasca, and a co-organizer and spokesperson in the Healing Walk.

Angela V. Carter is an Assistant Professor in the Department of Political Science at the University of Waterloo. Her research focuses on comparative environmental regulatory and policy regimes surrounding oil developments in key oil-dependent Canadian and American cases.

Emily Coats is a campaigner with the UK Tar Sands Network, and has been involved in a number of climate justice campaigns in the UK. Her MSc thesis was about tar sands resistance.

Stephen D'Arcy is an Associate Professor and Chair in the Department of Philosophy at Huron University College. He is the author of *Languages of the Unheard: Why Militant Protest is Good for Democracy* (Between the Lines). He is also a climate justice and economic democracy activist.

Yves Engler is a Montreal-based activist and author. He has published several books with RED/Fernwood, including *The Ugly Canadian: Stephen Harper's Foreign Policy*; *Lester Pearson's Peacekeeping: The Truth May Hurt*; and *The Black Book of Canadian Foreign Policy*.

Cherri Foytlin is a freelance journalist, author, advocate, speaker, and mother of six who lives in South Louisiana—an area inundated with industrial pollution. She is the co-author of the e-book *Spill It! The Truth About the Deep Water Horizon Oil Rig Explosion*, and regularly contributes to www.BridgetheGulfProject.org, the *Huffington Post*, *Daily Kos*, and several local newspapers.

Sonia Grant is an environmental justice organizer and a PhD student in Anthropology at the University of Chicago. While based in Toronto, Sonia was active in the grassroots movement against the Enbridge Line 9 reversal.

Harjap Grewal is an anti-authoritarian organizer based in Vancouver, Coast Salish Territories. He works with the No One Is Illegal Collective and various local campaigns. He organizes within the local South Asian community, with communities of colour, and in solidarity with Indigenous sovereignty struggles, focusing primarily on migrant, trade, and environmental justice rooted in an anti-capitalist and anti-colonial analysis.

Randolph Haluza-DeLay is an Associate Professor of Sociology at King's University College in Edmonton. He teaches and has published widely in sociology, environmental education, geography, and leisure studies, and co-edited *How the World's Religions are Responding to Climate Change: Social Scientific Investigations* (Routledge).

Ryan Katz-Rosene is a PhD candidate in Geography at Carleton University in Ottawa. His research interests include critical perspectives on growth, energy, and transportation, and environmental political economy.

Naomi Klein is an award-winning journalist, syndicated columnist, and author of the international bestsellers *The Shock Doctrine* and *No Logo* (both with Picador).

Melina Laboucan-Massimo is a member of the Lubicon Cree First Nation in Alberta, Canada, and an Indigenous and environmental activist. She has worked with Redwire Media Society, the Indigenous Environmental Network, and, most recently, as a tar sands, climate, and energy campaigner with Greenpeace.

Winona LaDuke is an Ojibwe economist working on issues of sustainable development, renewable energy, and food systems. She lives and works on the White Earth reservation, and writes extensively on Indigenous and environmental issues.

Crystal Lameman is a member of Beaver Lake Cree Nation in Alberta, Canada, and is an Indigenous rights and tar sands campaigner.

Christine Leclerc is a Communications Manager, author of *Counterfeit* (Capilano University Editions) and *Oilywood* (Nomados Editions), and an Editorial Collective Member for *The Enpipe Line* (Creekstone Press).

Kerry Lemon raised two children with her husband in their off-the-grid home in East Texas. Kerry is committed to social justice and community-building, and her involvement with grassroots organizing is fuelled by her family's personal experience with the detrimental impacts of petroleum extraction practices.

Matt Leonard is a long-time direct action coordinator and climate activist based in the San Francisco Bay Area. He currently serves as the Director of Special Projects for 350.org.

Martin Lukacs is a journalist and environmental blogger with *The Guardian*, and an editor-at-large with the *Media Co-op*.

Tyler McCreary is a post-doctoral fellow in Geography at the University of British Columbia with research interests in Indigenous studies, post-colonial theory, critical geography, cultural geography, and political ecology. He is also a contributor for rabble.ca and a member of the editorial collective of *Canadian Dimension*.

Bill McKibben is a founder of 350.org and the Schumann Distinguished Professor in Residence at Middlebury College. He has written a dozen books about the environment, including *The End of Nature* (Random House), *Eaarth: Making a Life on a Tough New Planet* (Holt), and *Oil and Honey:*

The Education of an Unlikely Activist (Holt). In 2011, he was elected a Fellow of the American Academy of Arts and Sciences.

Yudith Nieto was born in Mexico and grew up in the fence-line refining community of Manchester in Houston, Texas, which helped inspire her to become involved in the environmental justice movement. Yudith has worked with Texas Environmental Justice Advocacy Services, and has also been involved in organizing direct actions with the Tar Sands Blockade.

Joshua Kahn Russell is a core trainer with the Wildfire Project and the Ruckus Society. He is the co-author of *Organizing Cools the Planet* (PM Press) and co-editor of *Beautiful Trouble* (O/R Books), and is currently working as the Global Trainings Manager of 350.org.

Macdonald Stainsby is a freelance writer, journalist, and social justice activist currently based in his hometown of Burnaby, British Columbia. He has worked on tar sands in particular since 2006, both in Canada and internationally, and is the coordinator of the international tar sands information portals OilSandsTruth.org and TarSandsWorld.com.

Clayton Thomas-Muller is a member the Mathias Colomb Cree Nation in Manitoba, Canada. He has worked with the Indigenous Environmental Network and is currently the campaign director for the Polaris Institute's Indigenous Tar Sands Campaign.

Brian Tokar is the Director of the Institute for Social Ecology and a Lecturer in Environmental Studies at the University of Vermont. He has written and edited many books, including *Toward Climate Justice* (New Compass Press) and *Earth for Sale: Reclaiming Ecology in an Age of Corporate Greenwash* (South End Press).

Dave Vasey is a grassroots activist in Toronto who has been active in Environmental Justice Toronto, Occupy Toronto, the Mining Injustice Solidarity Network, and anti–tar sands campaigning.

Harsha Walia is a South Asian activist, writer, and popular educator rooted in migrant justice, Indigenous solidarity, Palestinian liberation, anti-racist, feminist, anti-imperialist, and anti-capitalist movements and communities for over a decade. She is the author of *Undoing Border Imperialism* (AK Press).

Tony Weis is an Associate Professor in Geography at Western University. He is the author of *The Global Food Economy: The Battle for the Future of Farming* and *The Ecological Hoofprint: The Global Burden of Industrial Livestock* (both Zed Books).

Rex Weyler is a journalist, writer, and ecologist, and a co-founder of Greenpeace International. His books include *Blood of the Land* (New Society), *Song of the Whale* (Doubleday), and *Greenpeace: The Inside Story* (Raincoast Books).

Will Wooten is an online organizer with the Tar Sands Blockade, a progressive political activist, and a freelance writer based in Texas.

Jess Worth is a co-founder of the UK Tar Sands Network. She is a former co-editor of the award-winning magazine *New Internationalist*, and was a member of the campaign organization *People & Planet*.

Lilian Yap is a doctoral student in Political Science at York University, analyzing the nature of "green work" and the recycling sectors in Toronto and Buenos Aires.

Foreword

NAOMI KLEIN AND BILL McKIBBEN

The fight over the tar sands is among the epic environmental and social justice battles of our time, and one of the first that managed to marry quite explicitly concern for frontline communities and immediate local hazards with fear for the future of the entire planet.

It began, of course, with many years of resistance from Indigenous people in the Athabasca region to the destruction of their ancestral landscapes and to the calamitous health conditions they faced. The destruction is so thorough, and on such an enormous scale, that Oil Sands Truth calls it "the largest industrial project in human history and likely also the most destructive."[1] But because of the remoteness of this vast landscape, and the failure by governments and industry to take the rights of Indigenous people seriously, the global magnitude of what was at stake was not entirely clear until 2011, when NASA scientist James Hansen calculated how much carbon the tar sands contained. He arrived at some eye-popping numbers. In essence, he found that if you could burn all the oil in Alberta tonight, the atmospheric concentration of CO_2 would go from its present Arctic-melting level of 400 parts per million to 540 parts per million. This conclusion led him to say that the continuing exploitation of the tar sands amounted to "game over" for the climate, as it promised to ensure a range of very dangerous feedback loops would kick in—the so-called "runaway" climate change scenario.[2]

Happily for advocates, there was a good way to attack the expansion of the tar sands. The Keystone XL (KXL) pipeline, slated to be the biggest straw sucking oil out of this toxic mess and atmospheric disaster, needed a presidential permit from one Barack Obama. And so ranchers, farmers, students, Indigenous leaders, campaigners, and others in the US went to work, staging one of the largest civil disobedience actions in thirty years in the US. Their work to cut the fuse to the continent's largest carbon bomb helped to slow down the KXL approval process, and helped spur and highlight similar resistance efforts from Canada's Pacific Coast to movements making inroads into the backrooms of the EU. The effort to stop the tar sands had become a beautifully sprawling international movement, without any central leadership but with remarkable coordination, passion, and energy.

As this fascinating book makes clear, that sprawling effort has managed to unite a wide variety of actors. Some are traditional environmental organizations, which have worked hard to pressure legislators and financiers; the US Sierra Club was even inspired by local activists to drop its 120-year-old ban on civil disobedience! But perhaps even more powerful have been less traditional efforts, stretching across various parts of North America and all the way across the Atlantic. Faith groups have played a large role, and even some mainstream politicians have become strong advocates. Through it all, and above all, Indigenous communities have been the motor that kept the fight rolling forward.

It's unclear, of course, how the battle will end. The world's biggest fossil fuel companies are heavily invested in the tar sands, along with an array of very powerful players, and they're unlikely to walk away from trillions of dollars in potential profits. But that beautiful sprawling resistance movement is now heavily invested in this fight too: emotionally and personally invested, with a deep sense of justice and solidarity that gives it strength. The tar sands has become a key front in the fight against climate change, and the fight for a better future, and it's hard to overstate the importance of the struggles it has inspired.

Introduction

Drawing a Line in the Tar Sands

●

TONY WEIS, TOBAN BLACK, STEPHEN D'ARCY,
AND JOSHUA KAHN RUSSELL

●

Stories of Resistance

This book offers stories of sadness and pain, visions of hope, and reflections on strategy. It explores the consequences of a system of global capitalism that has pushed our planet and those who live on it to the brink of collapse. Taken together, the chapters examine key impacts of the largest industrial project on earth—and they point ways towards a new world. They are about the tar sands specifically, but they are also about the human spirit, struggling to push through centuries of colonialism and standing on the edge of a new era. Of all possible futures, the least likely is one in which business as usual continues unabated. Peoples' movements will either succeed in transforming our economic and political systems to build a new world, or we will burn with the old one.

We hope this book will be useful in classrooms, in activist strategy sessions, and anywhere that people are struggling for a more just and sustainable world. It includes contributions from locally grounded community members and activists on the frontlines[1] of tar sands destruction, alongside academic analyses of the global consequences of this industry. It offers insights into organizing and activist missteps, as well as lessons learned. Many of these stories are central to movement strategy, and all too often go unheard. They need to be screamed from the rooftops for anyone who will listen.

Who We Are

We see our role as editors as being similar to that of facilitators: this is not our story to tell, and this book is an effort to support others who are speaking for themselves and their own communities. Like all environmental injustices, tar sands impacts hit Indigenous communities, low-income people, and communities of colour first and hardest.[2] While everyone who breathes air and drinks water has a stake in this fight, those on the frontlines of the tar sands have been resisting for decades, and their experiences shine light and leadership for the rest of us.

As editors, the four of us have different relationships to tar sands struggles. We're a mixture of academics and activists. Our team includes individuals who have spent some or all of our adult lives engaged in solidarity work or national-level campaigning.[3] None of us comes from frontline communities. Therefore, we have approached our contribution in editing this book as a way of using our access and relative privilege *to co-create a platform*. We have prioritized supporting activists whose primary focus is serving their communities, as opposed to the behind-the-scenes mechanics of editing and publishing. There are many streams of resistance to the tar sands, and we have looked to the book's contributors to define their contours and how they flow into a single river. Aligning diverse tributaries of resistance is the work of interdependent solidarity, and requires nuance in giving explicit attention to the streams of frontline campaigns. Much of the content in this book emerged from a process of consultation with people living in the communities hit hardest by the industry, as well as with activists, journalists, and scholars. It reflects an attempt to balance insights on impacts and organizing from frontline communities with technical and theoretical analysis from people working at other scales. Creating a platform that centres a frontline lens presents similar challenges and contradictions to those present in the messy complexity of real-world organizing. Therefore, the process of facilitating this collection reflects the politics articulated within the book itself. Acknowledging and navigating limitations and contradictions is central to the praxis of solidarity and common struggle described in this volume. We believe there is great value in bringing this range of perspectives together, and are guided by a politic that *those directly affected by injustice are best positioned to determine appropriate strategies and offer visionary solutions*. This book therefore centres women and Indigenous authors.

These motivations are reflected in how the chapters are organized. The first group provides analyses about the broader impacts and politics of the tar sands. The heart of the book beats in the second section, which focuses on a range of oppositional struggles occurring on different fronts and includes visions that articulate some of the ways towards a better world. The third group picks up on this challenge of moving forward, and provides insights into how struggles against the tar sands relate to the need for wider social transformations. Our ultimate hope is that the various pieces of this book add up to both a penetrating picture of the tar sands and a useful tool for social movements, which can help to strengthen resistance.

Themes and the Line in the Sand

The title of this book is a metaphor of uncompromising resistance, because the tar sands are an environmental injustice of the highest order. A "line in the sand" means: *it has gone this far, but no further*. We are confronting an industry that is worth trillions of dollars and is driven by some of the largest corporations on earth, which have no goals any nobler than maximizing short-term profits and growth. The fight to stop this industry is clearly one of the epic challenges of our age, and only a serious and sustained mobilization can turn the tide.

One key theme that runs through many chapters is that, while the implications of the tar sands extend up to the scale of the whole planet, the movement to stop them fundamentally demands solidarity with the Indigenous communities struggling to defend their land, water, and sovereignty. Another key theme is that there are many possible points of intervention, but struggles around pipelines appear to have distinct significance as a point of weakness for the tar sands industry. Thus, to use another metaphor, the spreading tentacles of the tar sands industry extend with them the seams of resistance in a wider continental upsurge.

In facilitating this book, we did not expect anything resembling a blueprint or single programmatic response to emerge, and we recognized that an all-inclusive reporting of the impacts, injustices, risks, and fronts of resistance is simply not possible. The magnitude and scope of the tar sands industry precludes any one collection of essays from covering everything. We hope that any gaps and limitations in this book do not detract from the analytical, tactical, and strategic insights it brings to readers. We also hope that this book will help open further conversations about the tar sands, and that the resulting dialogue will be fortified by the many stories and intersections that were not covered here.

Next, we will provide some background about the tar sands industry and the growing movement against it.

The Race to Extend the Age of Fossil Fuels: Profits, Power, and Claims of Inevitability

The Athabasca River Basin in western Canada contains one of the world's largest reserves of fossil energy in the form of bitumen, a tar-like substance that must be heavily refined to separate oil from sand and clay—hence the name *tar sands*.[4] The world's largest industrial landscape now sits atop the Athabasca tar sands, where the industry is wreaking devastation on the homelands of Cree, Dene, and Métis peoples, on immense tracts of boreal forest, and on the habitat of many animal species.

The tar sands landscape is marked by vast deforestation, strip mines, wastewater "ponds," and freshwater diversions; an expanding network of pipelines and roads; massive refineries and energy-generation facilities; and the world's largest earth-moving machines. In addition to its physical size, the tar sands are regularly identified as the world's biggest energy project and site of capital investment. In a major 2008 report, Environmental Defence called it simply "the most destructive project on earth."[5] If this industrial expansion across the Athabasca Basin continues in the coming decades, the tar sands extraction landscape will span an area the size of England.

While the Athabasca River Basin constitutes the heart of the tar sands industry, its infrastructure is increasingly continental in scope. Pipelines are the vital arteries of the industry, bringing bitumen to refineries and ultimately to markets, and they already stretch over thousands of kilometres across North America. At least fifty refineries have been handling blends of tar sands and conventional oil.[6] Still, this is not enough to satisfy investors' voracious appetite for growing profits, which is driving an aggressive push to expand, construct, or repurpose a series of pipelines in order to increase rising volumes of production and transport. Several thousand more kilometres of pipelines are planned. These projects include: TransCanada's attempt to expand and reroute the Keystone pipeline in the US to feed refineries around the Gulf of Mexico; Enbridge's efforts to build the Northern Gateway pipeline across British Columbia to enable shipping on the Pacific Ocean; and TransCanada's plans to establish an Energy East corridor to the eastern seaboard, where Atlantic shipping and refining may occur. The appetite for growth is plainly reflected in the words of Alberta's finance minister, who claims that the industry soon will require "two or three Enbridge-Keystones" to handle the glut of unprocessed bitumen and continue expanding at the pace sought by investors.[7] At the other end of these pipeline arteries, there is a push for expanded upgrading and refining capacity, port facilities, and ocean-going tankers to widen distribution on a global scale.

This colossal enterprise is driven by a confluence of transnational energy corporations and finance capital. The world's largest oil and gas companies all have tar sands projects; banks and investment funds from around the world have increasingly joined capital based in Canada and the US. In addition, the industry has been relentlessly subsidized and promoted by the Canadian and Albertan governments in a range of ways: decades of direct and indirect subsidies; lax regulations and a reliance on "self-regulation"; deep cuts to environmental monitoring capacities;[8] the failure to make serious, multilateral commitments to climate change mitigation; aggressive lobbying in the Canadian press and international policy forums; and missions to lock in trade and investment in the tar sands through bilateral and multilateral agreements.[9] Taken together, it is hard to overstate the magnitude of the economic and political power at hand.

Yet, pilot operations began in the late 1960s and the quantity of bitumen in the Athabasca tar sands has long been known, so an obvious question is: why has the industry heated up so much since the 1990s, after decades of far slower expansion? The answer relates in part to the fact that bitumen is much more difficult and costly to extract and refine into usable end products than conventional oil reserves. This means that *returns on investment are much lower* in the tar sands than in places with cheaper production costs (such as the Middle East, historically.) *At the same time, enormous capital investment is needed* to enable the extraction, transport, and refining of bitumen. So it was not until world oil prices began to rise quickly in the face of growing limits to conventional supplies—reflecting the dynamics of "peak oil"[10]—that the tar sands industry became sufficiently profitable for many large-scale energy and financial corporations to ramp up their investments. Here, it is also helpful to remember that oil, coal, and natural gas account for roughly four-fifths of the world's net primary energy supply (that is, the sum of energy used in all production, transportation, and households).[11] Of these, oil is the most crucial, as both the greatest source of energy generation and the overwhelming source of liquid fuel that powers global transportation systems. The centrality of oil in global capitalism is reflected in the fact that oil-centred giants, like ExxonMobil, Royal Dutch Shell, BP, Chevron, and Sinopec, consistently rank among the largest and most profitable corporations in the world. The geopolitical dimension of this push is plainly apparent in the Harper government's attempts to promote Canada as a world "energy superpower," which is capable of enhancing the "energy security" for its friends, most notably the US.

It is clear that the race to expand the production of unconventional reserves like bitumen is tied to the decline of conventional oil and gas reserves. In addition to tar sands, this general pressure is also central to the rise of hydraulic fracturing (more commonly known as "fracking") for "tight" oil and natural gas and the mining of kerogen shale (a bitumen-like substance), as well as increasing offshore drilling in deeper water and higher latitudes for conventional reserves. This overall shift is increasingly being described in terms of a turn towards "extreme fossil energy," because of the heightened difficulty, costs, risks, and pollution burden it entails.[12] The Athabasca tar sands are the world's largest "extreme energy" frontier, both because of the size of the area and the scale of its bitumen deposits, and because the growth and technological development of the industry there is now helping to stoke the expansion of extraction in similar—though smaller—reserves around the world, in countries such as Venezuela and the United States.

To hear it from corporate and government elites, this turn towards extreme extraction is more or less inevitable. Their basic argument is that fossil fuels are the lifeblood of modern economies, so further extraction of unconventional reserves in the Athabasca tar sands and elsewhere is needed to enable continued growth. The basic mantra is that more extraction means more wealth and more jobs. Some industry champions, such as the Canadian Association of Petroleum Producers, take the claim of necessity a step further and celebrate the determination of investors who sink billions of dollars into the technology and infrastructure needed to make harder-to-use materials usable.

These claims of necessity contain a certain degree of truth combined with a greater mistruth. The basic truth starts with the fact that fossil fuels permeate nearly every aspect of global capitalism and have a central function in powering the relentless pursuit of growth and profits. Thus, the race to expand the tar sands and other forms of extreme fossil energy is indeed necessary to perpetuate the current order of things and, at least in the near term, the success in this has been reflected in the diminished talk of peak oil. (Here, along with the tar sands, the explosive rise of fracking for oil and gas is especially notable.) Of course, extreme energy projects can mean great earnings for financiers from Wall Street to Bay Street, and for energy corporations from Calgary to Texas to Europe—though we must be clear that these industries also relate to jobs for ordinary people in countless ways, from the tar sands themselves, to automobile assembly lines, to a food system that runs on oil. However, the greater mistruth in the claim of necessity for the tar sands lies in the assumption that a growth-dependent, fossil fuel–addicted economic system can and must continue. The reality is that this course is far from inevitable, and that it guarantees disastrous outcomes.

The next section provides some background on the tar sands industry, concentrating on environmental impacts but also identifying other social injustices it has intensified.

The Human and Ecological Costs of the Tar Sands

To be sure, there is no such thing as "clean" fossil fuels, and extraction has always been marked by uneven impacts, as it has generated immense wealth and immense damage. However, vastly more land, freshwater diversions, and energy are all required to extract and refine a barrel of usable oil from bitumen as compared to conventional crude. This translates into immensely more deforestation, habitat destruction, toxic wastewater, and greenhouse gas emissions per barrel.

Though it is not possible to distinguish all of the interrelated costs associated with the tar sands industry, it is possible to draw these along five principal contours: the ecological damage and public health risks associated with tar sands extraction in the Athabasca River Basin; the environmental and public health risks associated with the transport and refining of bitumen; the assaults on Indigenous communities in the Athabasca region and in the path of actual or proposed pipeline and shipping routes; the role the industry plays in reinforcing right-wing agendas, while intensifying social injustices in North America; and the impact of the industry on climate change.[13]

The Ecological Devastation of Extraction

Many have likened the tar sands to Mordor, the ominous and deathly landscape depicted in J.R.R. Tolkien's *Lord of the Rings* series.[14] Such imagery helps to visualize the ruination of land on a scale that is hard to comprehend. Some stunning photojournalism in recent years has also helped to make the scale of ecological transformation hit home (see Box 1).

• •

Box 1: Visualizing the Mordor Landscape

National Geographic: Scraping Bottom: The Canadian Oil Boom
> ngm.nationalgeographic.com/2009/03/canadian-oil-sands/
> essick-photography

Scientific American: Pay Dirt: How to Turn Tar Sands into Oil. Slide Show
> www.scientificamerican.com/slideshow/how-to-turn-tar-sands-
> into-oil-slideshow/

Greenpeace International's Tar Sands Photo Set
> www.flickr.com//photos/greenpeaceinternational/sets/
> 72157622250648761/show/

Tar Sands Oil Extraction—The Dirty Truth
> www.youtube.com/watch?v=YkwoRivP17A

• •

Bitumen extraction occurs in two ways. The first method is strip mining, which happens where the bitumen is relatively close to the earth's surface (at a depth equivalent to the expanse of a soccer field or less). This means ripping away boreal forests—what the industry euphemistically describes as "overburden." Wetlands are also drained to make way for gas-guzzling equipment, such as earth diggers and three-storey heavy hauling trucks. Most of the industry's plans for the Athabasca River Basin involve a second method, which is known as "in situ extraction." This technique is used where bitumen is deeper and impossible to strip mine. In situ extraction works by injecting heated, high-pressure water to melt the earth so that the bitumen can be pushed to the surface. This also requires a tremendous amount of energy, which has been drawn mainly from natural gas (which ties the industry to the expansion of hydraulic fracturing). In the future, nuclear power plants may be constructed in the area to satisfy these immense energy demands.[15]

Tar sands companies also have a voracious thirst for water. Great volumes are used in the process of separating oil from the clay and sand, and the magnitude of these withdrawals is dramatically altering the water cycle of the vast Athabasca River Basin. Making matters much worse is the water pollution that results from extraction—including the release of steamed bitumen from in situ extraction into surrounding water tables.[16] Because of the chemical additives that are used, the wastewater from the processes of mining and refining contains a stew of pollutants, including corrosive naphthenic acid and cancer-causing alkyl-substituted polycyclic aromatic hydrocarbon, along with clay and sand. A generally accepted estimate is that three to five cubic metres of polluted wastewater sludge, or "tailings," is generated for every cubic metre of bitumen extracted. Waste tailings are then stored in what are euphemistically called "ponds," which are visible to the naked eye from outer space.[17] These ponds are one of the most notorious features of the Athabascan Mordor landscape.

The leaching and runoff from tailings ponds are extremely hazardous for surrounding ecosystems and communities, especially since some of the pollutants have been found to be toxic even at very low concentrations.[18] Further, a 2014 study concluded that previous estimates of the polycyclic aromatic hydrocarbons—many of which are highly carcinogenic and pose great risks to surrounding people and wildlife—emitted from tailings ponds have been seriously underestimated to date.[19] The combination of deforestation, wetland destruction, water diversions, and persistent toxins and bioaccumulation (i.e., the tendency of persistent chemicals to concentrate as they move up food webs through fish and wildlife) together have a huge impact on ecosystem health and wildlife habitat. Species of wildlife and fish have been found to have sores and deformities, which, as we note below, bears heavily on nearby Indigenous people. After tailings ponds were shown to have caused thousands of migratory bird deaths, an infamous response from the tar sands industry was to install airguns to discourage landing and nesting. Yet, in spite of the tremendous risks, provincial and federal governments have failed to conduct adequate independent monitoring of this pollution for decades, as a number of eminent environmental scientists have emphasized.[20]

To encapsulate the extent to which power brokers are willing to destroy the homelands and livelihoods of the Indigenous people of the region, Clayton Thomas-Muller likens the Athabasca River Basin to a "national sacrifice zone," and argues that the net result is nothing less than an "industrial genocide."[21] As more pipelines extend across the continent and refinery capacity is increased, other communities are being rendered sacrifice zones as well.

The Environmental and Health Risks in Mining, Transporting, and Refining Bitumen

As noted, the tar sands industry is pushing hard to expand pipeline and shipping projects in order to enable bitumen to be refined in more processing facilities, thereby accessing a wider range of markets. Pumping tar sands through pipelines increases spill risks relative to conventional crude. This is because pipelines carrying bitumen contain higher concentrations of acid and sulphur, which causes more corrosion, and because increased pressure is needed to move this tarry substance (which some have compared to a mixture of peanut butter and sandpaper) through pipelines, generating more heat.[22] When the inevitable spills do occur, tar sands pipelines also release toxins, such as cancer-causing benzene and fumes from gas condensate, which are needed to dilute and pump bitumen. These toxic additives also magnify the environmental health risks from spills, which are made worse by the fact that bitumen that spills into water bodies settles quickly into sediment and cannot be skimmed off.

When piped bitumen does reach its intended targets, it is either transformed into synthetic oil at upgrading facilities, or it is mixed with oil in refineries that make petroleum products. Each of these options intensifies pollution and waste. Again, it is important to emphasize that the process of refining bitumen is more energy intensive than processing conventional crude. The amplified pollution burdens include not only additional greenhouse gas emissions, but also sulphur dioxide emissions, which cause acid rain and are a health hazard in surrounding regions.[23] To date, upgrading has been concentrated in northern and central Alberta, in cities like Fort McMurray and Fort Saskatchewan. Many of the refineries that process tar sands are located outside of Alberta, particularly around the Great Lakes in the upper Midwest, where the impacts from refining include the accumulation of piles of petroleum coke soot, a black, rock-like substance that is left behind after refining. In Detroit, a three-storey stockpile of petroleum coke spanned a city block until local protests caused authorities to relocate these wastes.

If proposed pipelines and pipeline expansions to the Pacific (via British Columbia or Pacific Northwestern states) or Atlantic coasts (via New Brunswick and Maine) were to be accepted, these would intensify shipping traffic, while bringing new pollution threats to coastal regions. In British Columbia, the proposed Northern Gateway pipeline not only runs through one of the world's largest remaining temperate rainforests, the Great Bear Rainforest, but it would also involve especially treacherous tanker shipping routes out of its terminus near Kitimat, weaving through coastal inlets and around the Haida Gwaii archipelago and territory of the Haida First Nation. At the same time, companies are attempting to increase the flow of tar sands bitumen through Kinder Morgan's Trans Mountain pipeline in southern British Columbia, where Vancouver likewise may serve as a port for tar sands tanker traffic. The Exxon Valdez disaster is a forewarning of the potential risks of these plans.

Although rail shipments are more expensive than pipelines, the tar sands industry has increasingly been utilizing railways in response to the limits of existing pipeline capacity, which lags behind the scale of extraction. As increasing pipeline capacity is taken up to pump tar sands, greater volumes of conventional oil are now being moved by rail, and it is ominous to note that there has been a dramatic surge in spills and accidents around US rail cars carrying oil since 2009.[24]

A further aspect of transport impacts relates to the attempt to establish a "megaload" corridor through the US Northwest and the northern Rocky Mountains. This would enable massive modules manufactured in Asia—some as tall as three-storey buildings and weighing close to 300 metric tons—to be brought to northern Alberta for use in constructing facilities there. The transport of these modules entails significant wear and tear on existing public infrastructure, and the further expansion of highways.[25]

As many upcoming chapters make clear, a range of struggles is bound to follow wherever further tar sands refining occurs.

The Assault on Indigenous Communities

The *United Nations Declaration on the Rights of Indigenous Peoples* is a major reference point in struggles for Indigenous self-determination in the face of past and ongoing colonization. The Declaration enshrines the right to "free, prior and informed consent" in relation to any projects that may affect Indigenous homelands and livelihoods. Such rights are increasingly being trampled on by the expansion of the tar sands landscape and the extension of pipelines across North America, as objections on the basis of health, culture, and livelihoods are routinely ignored or dismissed by both corporations and governments. While Indigenous rights to self-determination remain just as crucial in areas where treaty agreements do not exist, it is also crucial to recognize how extraction, refining, and pipeline operations violate a series of treaty agreements that should provide legal protection against ongoing colonial activities.

The assaults on Indigenous sovereignty and autonomy are especially acute in the First Nations of the Athabasca River Basin, where large parts of traditional territories have been invaded by strip mines, in situ well pads, upgraders, pipelines, highways and truck traffic, and huge, hazardous tailings ponds. These disrupt cultural traditions, livelihoods, and food security practices, including hunting and fishing, while posing serious health risks. A major aspect of these impacts is the leaching and runoff of toxins from tailings ponds, which contaminate the drinking-water supplies of downstream communities, like Fort Chipewyan of the Athabasca Chipewyan First Nation. There, residents have experienced a well-documented spike in health problems, including rare cancers, in recent years.

Indigenous peoples are also disproportionately affected by the path of pipelines, and the threats to ecological and human health these entail. Across North America, pipeline routes wantonly cut through numerous traditional territories. For example, in Oklahoma alone, the Keystone XL extension would cross the jurisdictions of the Sac and Fox, Muscogee, and Choctaw tribal governments. Several other tribal lands are immediately beside the pipeline route, and infrastructure such as pumping stations would operate on these territories.

Fuelling the Political Right and Social Injustice

As a number of chapters in this book stress, the economic power of the tar sands industry is closely tied to right-wing political agendas in North America, and the industry and its allies in government are aggressively bracing themselves against criticism by lashing out at opponents. Part of their defence of the industry revolves around grossly exaggerated promises of efficiency, ecological restoration, and carbon capture and storage. Defenders also trumpet the alleged security and human rights benefits of producing oil in "friendly" Canada instead of countries that are portrayed as despotic and oppressive (as in the so-called "ethical oil" argument). At the same time, the erosion of environmental monitoring and regulatory capacity in Canada is part of a much broader assault on democratic processes and institutions, including the muzzling of government scientists and the concealment of ostensibly public hearings.[26]

Although the tar sands industry is supported, to varying degrees, by the three primary political parties in Canada, neo-conservatives are its most aggressive champions. Journalists have exposed links between the "ethical oil" media campaign and the Conservative Party,[27] and it is no coincidence that the electoral district of Prime Minister Harper is in Calgary—where Canada's oil and gas industry is headquartered. Since the Conservatives took power in 2006, federal support for the tar sands industry has dramatically increased in a variety of ways—including subsidies, lobbying, and advertising. For instance, in 2013-14, $40 million was allocated to Natural Resources Canada to promote Canada's oil and gas sector.[28] Other unseemly connections lurk, such as the fact that a former Conservative cabinet minister was appointed to oversee Canada's spy agency (CSIS) while still employed by Enbridge, a tie that is even more alarming in light of evidence that spies and police were assigned to monitor opposition towards the company's Northern Gateway project. (Not surprisingly, the Conservative-appointed conflict of interest and ethics commissioner dismissed concerns.)[29] Another tactic in the growing clampdown on dissent has been to portray tar sands opponents as misguided or "foreign-inspired" enemies of Canada.

While the tar sands landscape is certainly awash in money, and tar sands profits permeate the economy in many ways, the greatest beneficiaries, by far, are the energy and financial sector executives and large shareholders—while Indigenous people in the Athabasca Basin bear the brunt of the industry's negative effects. In addition to the tar sands industry's environ-mental impacts, it is also notorious for unsafe and unhealthy working condi-tions, exorbitant living costs in industry boom towns like Fort McMurray, and stark and widening inequalities spilling over into various parts of the province. The high wages in the industry have contributed to labour short-ages in the other low-paying sectors, leaving many people to struggle with rising prices of necessities, such as housing.

As criticisms of these social costs grow,[30] the government of Canada has helped to brace the tar sands industry by expanding the number of "tempor-ary foreign workers" in Alberta, in step with lobbying by the government of Alberta. In 2012, the population of "temporary foreign workers" in Alberta reached nearly seventy thousand—more than any other province. The Alberta Federation of Labour has documented the deplorable conditions that many of these workers face,[31] and their increasing place in the tar sands industry is concentrated in lower-paid, lower-skilled, and lower-status jobs[32]—labour inequalities that have not yet received adequate attention from tar sands researchers and campaigners.

Closing the Door on Climate Change Mitigation

The carbon dioxide (CO_2) emitted from burning fossil fuels is the most fun-damental factor causing the earth's climate to warm, and climate science is clear that annual emissions must be drastically reduced if there is any chance to mitigate the worst impacts of climate change. Since the onset of the indus-trial revolution, the combustion of fossil fuels has emitted billions of tons of CO_2 into the earth's atmosphere, increasing CO_2 concentrations from around 280 parts per million (ppm) to over 400 ppm in 2014. This has enhanced the heat-trapping capacity of the atmosphere, and average surface temperatures are already more than 0.8°C higher than pre-industrial levels.[33]

This warming is bringing major changes, such as rising sea levels, increasing heat waves, thawing permafrost, dramatic declines in Arctic sea ice, and melting glaciers from Greenland to low-latitude mountain ranges. A prevailing target is that we must keep average surface temperatures from rising more than 2°C above pre-industrial averages, though many climate scientists suggest that even less warming than this will initiate a dangerous, if not catastrophic, series of positive feedbacks and runaway changes.[34]

Failure to rapidly mitigate the severity of future warming would spell catastrophe for large parts of the world, and the impacts are bound to hit many poorer countries most immediately and most severely. Threats include flooding and saltwater intrusion with sea-level rise, heightened aridity and drought, intensified tropical storms, declining seasonal runoff from mid- and low-latitude glaciers, and changing disease vectors.[35] In order to have any hope of keeping levels of warming within ostensibly "safe" levels, a well-established estimate from climate models is that atmospheric CO_2 concentrations must be brought down to *at least* 350 ppm in the coming decades.

Many changes are needed to reduce the amount of CO_2 in the atmosphere, but none is more important than drastically cutting consumption of oil, coal, and natural gas. So, while the tar sands and other forms of extreme fossil fuels might help to prop up the current economic order for a little while longer, extracting and burning this carbon is quite literally a pathological endeavour. Nothing reflects this pathology more than the tar sands, which was dubbed "Greenhouse Goo" in *Scientific American* to indicate its extraordinary contribution to climate change.[36]

There are 1.8 trillion barrels of bitumen in the Athabasca Basin, and the Alberta government estimates that 315 billion barrels can be extracted.[37] Not only is this a motherlode of carbon, but the energy intensity of tar sands extraction and refining makes the effective emissions per barrel far greater than with conventional oil reserves. This heightened energy budget stems from the running of huge machines, the heating of great volumes of water, the pumping of bitumen, and massive increases in petroleum coke by-products (which, when they are used in energy generation, are even worse than coal in terms of relative CO_2 emissions).[38] In 2012, the extraction and burning of bitumen in Alberta was estimated to have released more CO_2 than the combined emissions of 100 nations,[39] and the atmospheric impact is worsened by the methane emitted from the tailings ponds and by the CO_2 released from deforestation and the destruction of carbon-rich peatland.[40]

Renowned US NASA climate scientist James Hansen has calculated that the tar sands contain twice the amount of CO_2 emitted by global oil use in our entire history, and concluded that their continuing exploitation would be a "game-over" scenario for climate change.[41] In other words, the tar sands industry alone could shatter any hope of mitigating extremely dangerous levels of warming.

The Line in the Tar Sands: The Growing Resistance

The stakes are rising as the tar sands industry pushes ever harder to expand production, pipelines, and export markets. Fortunately, a growing push-back is mounting against the mighty nexus of corporate and political power on a multitude of fronts. This opposition is grounded in the struggles of Indigenous communities in the Athabasca River Basin and along existing and planned pipeline corridors, who have borne the brunt of the ecological devastation and adverse health impacts as their sovereignty has been undermined by both governments and corporations. Indigenous resistance has taken many forms, with community-based efforts to protect their land, water, and autonomy providing the foundation for broader initiatives like the Unist'ot'en Camp,[42] the Yinka Dene Alliance, Moccasins on the Ground gatherings, the Healing Walk, and the Idle No More movement.[43]

As proposals for new and extended pipelines have radiated outwards across the continent, opposition to the tar sands industry has also grown among various non-Indigenous communities and organizations. Movement strategists have often seen pipelines as a strategic vulnerability for the tar sands industry, for two major reasons. First, as suggested earlier, the industry is extremely fearful of how bottlenecks can constrain expansion, and hence both increased pipeline capacity and access to a wider set of refineries are deemed to be essential to continuing growth and investments. At present, much of the tar sands processing capacity is concentrated in the US Midwest, and a glut of bitumen in the region has contributed to falling prices.[44] Tapping into further refinery capacity elsewhere would increase profits by avoiding such regional gluts, and by sparing the industry from the costs of building new upgrading facilities in northern Alberta, where these are particularly expensive due to the limits of existing infrastructure in this remote region. While such bottlenecks remain in place, campaigns against new and expanded pipelines have been able to slow investment in the industry, as investors have become wary of delays with additional pipelines (though it seems that some unfortunately are opting to invest in US shale oil instead). Rail shipments are growing, but these are more expensive, and cannot substitute for pipelines in terms of the scale of the expansion sought by investors.[45]

The second reason that pipelines are such a strategic vulnerability for the industry is that they provoke resistance by projecting serious eco-health risks onto ever more regions. These threats have been put on stark display in a number of recent spills, including those in the Kalamazoo River in 2010, and in Mayflower, Arkansas, in 2013. The risks of toxic pollution on land and in water bodies have repeatedly served to galvanize frontline mobilizations against pipelines and refineries, and these have grown into a major part of the struggles against the tar sands.

The most well-known pipeline battle has surrounded the Keystone XL proposal, but many other confrontations—ranging from direct actions to court cases—have been intensifying across the US and Canada. (Such battles are discussed in several of the upcoming chapters.) For instance, the Northern Gateway proposal has been met with mounting resistance for the hazards it would pose on land and with soaring tanker traffic moving in coastal waters and around the Haida Gwaii islands. In Ontario and Quebec, there have been a range of mobilizations in different communities to oppose the reversal of the flow of the Enbridge Line 9 pipeline, which could enable the company to ship bitumen through southern Ontario and Montreal to the Atlantic coast. Mobilizations have arisen to challenge Enbridge's Flanagan South Pipeline plan, which would flow from the Chicago area to the Gulf Coast. After environmental organizations were unsuccessful in filing an injunction against the project, other strategies have been explored by the Great Plains Tar Sands Resistance network, among others in the region. Anishinaabe communities in Minnesota have staged protests against the Alberta Clipper pipeline that already runs across their land (stretching from Alberta to Superior, Wisconsin) and Enbridge's plans to dramatically increase the volume of bitumen being pumped through it. In addition, frontline opposition has emerged in response to megaload shipments through the US Northwest, and to stop new tar sands mining in Utah.[46]

Frontline mobilizations from the Athabasca River Basin to sites for existing and proposed pipeline corridors and tar sands refining can be viewed as an extension of decades of environmental justice campaigning in North America, which emerged out of the disproportionate siting of polluting industries, dumps, and resource extraction among poor and often racially marginalized groups.[47] And just as many environmental justice campaigns have become better connected over time, building solidarity based on shared forms of oppression and aspirations, so too are the struggles of frontline communities becoming more entwined.

As the network of resistance has grown, it has increasingly intersected with the efforts of environmental activists and organizations fighting for action on climate change, who recognize how pivotal stopping the tar sands is to any hope of preventing disastrous levels of warming. The unifying element in these global and local struggles—the proverbial *line in the tar sands*—is a refusal to accept the legitimacy of the industry and a demand that the bitumen be left in the ground.[48]

But beneath this broad goal, there are a diversity of targets and a multiplicity of tactics. The primary targets are, of course, the energy corporations at the helm of the tar sands industry, the Mordor landscape they are creating, and the infrastructure projects they are planning. Secondary targets include things like: government review processes, which promise at least a modicum of public participation; pension funds and financial institutions like the Royal Bank of Canada, which have a crucial role in capitalizing extraction, transport, and refining operations; and campaigns to affect fuel policies in the European Union, which would forbid tar sands imports.

Many activists and organizations have converged in mass demonstrations, such as the rally to stop Keystone XL in the US. Indigenous communities and environmental organizations have presented critical evidence and arguments to the public hearings and environmental impact assessments surrounding pipeline and shipment plans, or present rearguard legal challenges. In Alberta, the tar sands industry is facing various legal challenges from the Beaver Lake Cree, the Athabasca Chipewyan First Nation, and the Fort McKay First Nation. Land defence struggles and direct action have ranged from attempts to physically disrupt production, to establishing blockades and encampments on key sites, to spectacular banner drops in the tar sands and on Canadian Parliament buildings. Public education has taken a range of forms, such as speaking tours and the creation of a range of Internet resources (see Box 2 for some examples).

The struggles against the tar sands industry are also intertwined with an even wider set of movements striving towards urgent social, political, and economic change, as they work to build hopeful transitions away from

● ●

Box 2: Selected Web-Based Resources

All Against the Haul — www.allagainstthehaul.org

Defenders of the Land — www.defendersoftheland.org

Great Plains Tar Sands Resistance — gptarsandsresistance.org

Greenpeace — www.greenpeace.org/canada/en/campaigns/Energy/tarsands

Healing Walk — www.healingwalk.org

Honor the Earth — www.honorearth.org/stop-tar-sands

Indigenous Environmental Network — www.ienearth.org/what-we-do/
tar-sands

Keepers of the Athabasca — www.keepersofthewater.ca/athabasca

MI CATS — www.michigancats.org

NRDC Pipeline and Tanker Trouble — www.nrdc.org/international/
pipelinetrouble.asp

Oil Sands Reality Check — oilsandsrealitycheck.org

Oil Sands Truth — oilsandstruth.org

Pipe Up Against Enbridge — pipeupagainstenbridge.ca

Rising Tide North America — risingtidenorthamerica.org

Tar Sands Action — tarsandsaction.org

Tar Sands Blockade — www.tarsandsblockade.org

Tar Sands Solutions Network — tarsandssolutions.org

Tar Sands Watch — www.tarsandswatch.org

Tar Sands World — www.tarsandsworld.com

UK Tar Sands Network — www.no-tar-sands.org

Unist'ot'en Camp — unistotencamp.com

Utah Tar Sands Resistance — www.tarsandsresist.org

Yinka Dene Alliance — yinkadene.ca

● ●

a ruinous addiction to fossil fuels and the pursuit of endless growth. The corporate behemoths driving the tar sands are implicated in myriad injustices around the world, and they—along with their political minions—are among the most powerful forces in the world forestalling such transitions. Challenging these forces also entails a vast range of efforts to organize our societies more democratically, equitably, and sustainably, from our food systems to the design of our cities to the way we heat and power our homes.

It is hard to assess the degree to which different efforts and even victories in the short term might ultimately contribute to the big, long-term objective of keeping the bitumen in the ground. But at the very least, the resistance has already succeeded in making it clear that the continuation of the tar sands industry and other extreme energy projects are *far from inevitable*, as more and more people come to understand that these can and must be stopped.

Community members expose Canada's extraction and climate policies during a "Toxic Tour" in the lead-up to the 2010 G20 Summit in Toronto, Ontario.

I

Tar Sands Expansionism

1

Petro-Capitalism and the Tar Sands

●

ANGELA V. CARTER

●

How do we make sense of the overwhelming complexity, contradictions, and magnitude of Alberta's tar sands?[1] Daily media stories track stunning private investment and looming public deficits, vast profits and shocking environmental and health problems, technological feats and labour shortfalls, all involving some of the world's largest transnational corporations (TNCs), powerful governments, First Nations and other affected frontline communities, international non-governmental organizations, and a growing social movement in resistance. The enormity of this industry was encapsulated in very clear terms by Prime Minister Harper early in his administration:

> Digging the bitumen out of the ground, squeezing out the oil and converting it into synthetic crude is a monumental challenge. It requires vast amounts of capital, Brobdingnagian technology, and an army of skilled workers. In short, it is an enterprise of epic proportions, akin to the building of the pyramids or China's Great Wall. Only bigger.[2]

The impact of this epic endeavour extends to nearly every corner of Canada as the industry draws precarious labour from across the country; attempts to extend pipelines south, west, and east; spreads pollution into neighbouring communities, provinces, and territories; and drives up national CO_2 emissions. At the same time, the industry is contingent on volatile global price fluctuations in response to the vagaries of international reserves and far-off geopolitics. In short, what happens in Alberta doesn't stay in Alberta—and the fate of Alberta is entangled in a far broader global context.

This chapter uses petro-capitalism as a lens to capture the scale and complexity of the tar sands industry. Petro-capitalism places oil centre stage in understanding political economic systems, as well as foregrounding the economic, political, and environmental costs of fossil fuel dependence. In this, it helps to focus our attention on:

- the dizzying rates of capitalist growth made possible by oil;
- the ensuing political transformations that reinforce the oil-dependent economy and block transitions to a safer and fairer way of organizing economic life; and
- the perpetual state of crisis that is induced by the imperative of expansion, one that simultaneously undermines the supply of non-renewable fuel and—more importantly—the earth's life-support systems.

Ultimately, this conceptual framework helps us understand not only how Alberta is intimately connected to global oil crises, and the United States energy market in particular, but also how Canada and especially Alberta are riven with political, economic, and environmental problems in attempts to expand tar sands extraction.

Petro-Capitalism

At the centre of the analysis of capitalism's relation to nature is its inherent and unavoidable dependence on fossil fuels, and particularly on oil.
    —Elmar Altvater[3]

From the nineteenth century onwards, fossil fuels (starting with coal) have increasingly come to power capitalist expansion. The transportability and energy density of fossil fuels brought a great shift, from the waxing and waning rhythms of biotic energy from the sun, wind, or muscles, to around-the-clock and around-the-globe production and distribution. Fossil fuels allowed the continuous expansion of manufacturing, as their great energy density was both abundant and relatively cheap in relation to the productivity it stoked. This served to expand the geographic scope of production, permitting the long-distance transportation of raw materials and goods throughout the global economy.[4]

Current critical scholarship on energy has begun to explore how capitalism could only grow and flourish with fossil energy and steep environmental costs. From research in critical geography and radical political economy to more popular publications on environmental problems, an increasing number of writers are now highlighting how capitalism is not only about the growth and expansion of enterprise, private property, profits, and capital accumulation, but that this is also fundamentally premised upon the rapid growth and development of hydrocarbon consumption. The concept of "petro-capitalism" helps to indicate just how dependent this political economic system is on fossil energy, particularly oil.

The economic logic of petro-capitalism is grounded in the proposition that efforts to expand profit growth through mass production and mass consumption have hinged on the mass extraction of fossil fuels. With the development of fossil fuels, annualized economic growth rates on a world scale jumped from 0.2 per cent in the early 1800s to more than 2 per cent at the end of the twentieth century. Similarly, the globalization of production and consumption patterns over the past four decades has only come about with the development of extremely energy-intensive systems of production and transportation. Newly industrializing countries have recently crowded into markets and added to the already insatiable demand of the industrialized countries, and now consume nearly one-fourth of global oil production.[5]

But petro-capitalism has not just evolved economically: it has required a great deal of *political* intervention at every turn. From the beginning, oil production has been a highly centralized process, controlled by major corporations and powerful governments, with access dependent upon intrigue, corruption, innumerable episodes of imperial intervention, and military might alongside economic power. As Altvater notes, fossil fuels have never been "distributed through a democratic, solidaristic rationing."[6]

Indeed, in examining the scope of long-run political problems associated with oil development, some scholars have claimed that countries tied to oil commonly suffer from a "resource curse," another key aspect of petro-capitalism. This essentially implies that oil-dependent governments are frequently vulnerable to long-term economic volatility and decline, as well as democratic stagnation or deterioration due to growing political conservatism and authoritarianism, with the costs and benefits of extraction often distributed unfairly, leading to increased class, regional, sectoral, ethnic, and gender inequalities. Countries suffering under the resource curse may also experience *policy* deterioration due to the institutional "molding" effect of oil revenue dependence, as governments tend to become rentier states where oil rent collection comes to dominate government financing and planning, "thereby weakening state capacity."[7] Under such conditions, petro-states lose the broader notion of public good and come to act ever more strategically to maintain power and protect the oil industry. This leads to long-term institutional inertia, which keeps ruling governments focused on privileging and expanding the oil industry above all else.

A final fundamental aspect of petro-capitalism is the inevitable environmental damage, in particular through its contribution to greenhouse gas emissions. Since capitalism needs infinite economic growth and ever-expanding consumption, its logic essentially compels increasing CO_2 emissions that threaten the global ecological system—and indeed life itself.[8] The growth imperative drives the continual global search for new (though ultimately finite) oil supplies in ways that often have high energy and resource demands (as in the tar sands, and in hydraulic fracturing for shale oil and gas) and carry a large ecological burden.

In sum, the conceptual framework of petro-capitalism centres oil as the lifeblood of global capitalism, with the power to fundamentally reshape political institutions from global to national to provincial levels. Yet it is also a system in permanent crisis due to its intractable role in climate change and environmental degradation, alongside inevitable challenges to oil supplies.

Global Petro-Capitalist Crises

The contradictory nature of petro-capitalism, which depends upon incessant expansion at ever-higher economic and environmental costs, is coming into sharper focus with the global access to a steady supply of conventional crude oil now in question, and threatening to create a global energy crisis. From 1971 to 2010, world oil consumption nearly doubled, driven in great part by the need for transportation fuels in rich-world economies. Roughly one-fifth of the world's population consumes two-thirds of global oil. Within the OECD, the US clearly dominates oil demand, consuming over 20 per cent of total global oil production with less than 5 per cent of the world's population. Yet fast-growing demand is coming from non-OECD countries— nearly half from China,[9] which now surpasses total American oil consumption (albeit with much lower levels of per capita consumption due to its very large population).

Global oil supply is just barely meeting this rising global demand. Data from the International Energy Agency (IEA) showed that the world's supply of oil in 2012 was 91.1 million barrels per day (bpd), slightly above world demand at 89.8 million bpd, which is forecasted to keep increasing.[10] The uncertainty over whether oil supply can keep up with this rising demand is contributing to a range of dynamics, including:

- the intensifying race by governments and TNCs alike to control and militarize oil reserves in the Middle East, the former USSR, South America, and Western Africa;
- the surge in the exploration of secondary fields at the margins of major "mature" fields; and
- attempts to squeeze the last drops out of old fields using enhanced oil recovery technologies.

However, the greatest hope for petro-capitalism lies in finding new supplies from "frontier" regions, including ultra-deep offshore wells and high latitudes, and even more so by exploiting so-called "unconventional" reserves, such as those found in the tar sands and in shale formations.

Yet even as TNCs pour billions of dollars into attempts to discover new sources of fossil fuels, the reality is that global climate stability cannot withstand the CO_2 emissions this would entail. Just as capitalist economic growth has mirrored fossil fuel consumption, so too have world CO_2 emissions mirrored world GDP growth.[11] However, climate scientists are warning in ever-stronger terms that the window to radically reduce annual CO_2 emissions to a level that might mitigate dangerous levels of climate instability is fast closing. The result is that petro-capitalism on a world scale is currently running out of cheap and easy oil supplies at the same time that it is running up against its climatic limits.

Petro-Capitalism at the National Scale

Canada is the world's only growing producer of this strategic com-modity with a secure, stable government. Canada is, as I have said, an emerging energy superpower. It is one reason why Canada will increasingly be a leader and why Alberta is a leader within it.
      —Stephen Harper in 2006[12]

Since coming to power in 2006, arguably the most important pillar of Stephen Harper's economic plan for Canada has been to take advantage of the global decline in conventional oil reserves and the ensuing increase in demand for "unconventional" fossil fuels, aspiring to make Canada a global (fossil) "energy superpower." Such aspirations are not mere polit-ical swagger, as Canada has sizable conventional reserves and even larger unconventional ones, centred on the tar sands. According to the National Energy Board, Canada produced over 3.3 million bpd in 2012, which, based on IEA data, placed Canada as the world's sixth-largest global oil producer. However, this is poised to grow, as a recent OECD report noted that "Canada has the second-largest proven oil reserves in the world, most of which are in oil sands."[13] Along with this large volume, the IEA has also flagged the important fact that Canada is the leading global *non*-OPEC (Organization of the Petroleum Exporting Countries) oil supplier.[14]

Fossil energy has become Canada's most valuable export, driven by the tar sands. In the space of a mere decade, from 1999 to 2008, Canada's energy exports grew in value more than fourfold: from $28 billion to $128 billion.[15] According to Statistics Canada, energy exports as a percentage of total exports grew from 10 per cent in 1990, to 13 per cent in 2000, to over 25 per cent in 2011. Canada's economic reliance on fossil fuel exports is now to an extent that oil prices are widely recognized to be linked to the strength of the Canadian dollar, and in particular the exchange rate with the US dollar, giving rise to the "petro-loonie" neologism. The value of traded energy and metal shares account for approximately half of the total shares traded on the Toronto Stock Exchange.[16]

This dramatic growth has been fostered by the policy framework established by the Canadian federal government geared to ramping up oil development. While this has centred on promoting tar sands extraction and its associated pipeline projects, it has also sought to promote offshore exploration and drilling in other frontiers, like the Arctic and the Gulf of St. Lawrence. Meanwhile, the Harper government has weakened environmental policies and monitoring capacities in order to facilitate oil and gas development and other resource extraction, most notably through amendments to the *Canadian Environmental Assessment Act* contained in Bill C-38, the 2012 omnibus budget bill (the latter acting as an important trigger in the Idle No More insurgence). Further, the Harper government has demonstrated a paltry commitment to developing clean energy technologies and facilitating energy efficiency and conservation, and reneged on the country's international commitment to reduce GHG emissions, making Canada the first country to withdraw from the Kyoto Protocol in late 2011.

Another glaring aspect of the federal government's scramble to expand oil production is its utter failure to manage this growth for the national long-term interest, a problem reflected most notably in the lack of a national energy policy. In contrast to other developed industrial states, including the US, Canada has no strategic petroleum reserves, nor is there a policy to save the revenue of this one-time resource or invest it in renewable forms of energy. A 2009 report on international oil wealth funds starkly contrasted the mega-funds of Norway ($512 billion) and the UAE ($875 billion) with the meagre Canadian oil savings, with just $14.4 billion in Alberta's Heritage Fund.[17] Nor does Canada have a plan to wisely invest this revenue in long-term public goods, instead focusing this windfall largely on tax cuts to corporations and individuals.[18]

Another distinguishing feature of the policy framework facilitating the expansion of oil extraction is that instead of being managed for the national public interest, resources are made extremely accessible to international players. While 80 per cent of the world's remaining oil reserves are formally held by national governments, Canadian policy has facilitated a private and often foreign-led industry, forgoing national ownership and development since the privatization and free-trade frenzy of the early 1990s. Canada's "more accommodating attitude towards foreign investment" than many oil-rich countries[19] has resulted in about half of the Canadian oil industry's capital and oil production today being foreign-owned, with foreign direct investment having risen particularly sharply since 2006.[20]

To date, the only state-owned development of Canada's oil reserves is being undertaken by *other* countries, such as through Norway's Statoil and

China's CNOOC. Canadian government investments have mainly focused on indirect and direct public subsidies (e.g., infrastructure, research support, tax breaks) to the benefit of private corporations. In recent years, this has been augmented by government assistance lobbying and marketing the tar sands abroad, promoting Canada as a secure, reliable, and geographically proximate supplier of oil resources to other countries, especially the US. Gary Doer, the Canadian ambassador to the US, summarizes the essential pitch in the context of the Keystone XL pipeline debate:

> We don't think it's that complicated to have oil from Canada flow to the United States to replace oil from Venezuela [or] the Middle East—we actually don't think this is a complicated decision.... It's actually not just jobs versus the environment. It's also the whole issue of whether the United States grabs this opportunity to establish energy independence in North America through oil from Canada.[21]

Canada's combination of large reserves, rapid growth, and openness to transnational investment has not been lost on the US, Canada's number-one export partner. American oil analysts have long identified Canadian oil as a key part of the solution to US energy security. Over a decade ago, the US National Energy Policy Development Group stressed the importance of securing geographically closer oil reserves from more politically stable supplies in North America, with Canada's tar sands specifically identified.[22] US-based TNCs have been prominent players in the expansion of tar sands extraction, as American foreign investment now accounts for roughly one-third of all tar sands production, while fast-rising Chinese investment has recently risen to a comparable share.[23]

Canadian oil exports to the US have more than tripled since the 1990s, and in 2004 Canada surpassed Saudi Arabia as the leading foreign supplier of oil to the US. In 2010, Canada supplied over 20 per cent of the US's total oil imports.[24] While foreign investment in the tar sands has become increasingly diversified between US, Chinese, and European interests, the US remains the primary export market: in 2011, 98.5 per cent of Canada's oil and gas exports went to the US. NAFTA's "proportionality" clause ensures this dramatic southbound oil flow, although (as discussed elsewhere in this book) the Harper administration is actively seeking the diversification of export markets through west or eastbound pipeline projects.

One irony of this export boom to the US is that most of Canada's eastern provinces continue to rely heavily on foreign imports. Remarkably, eastern Canada imported 90 per cent of its oil in 2008, about 1.2 million bpd, primarily from Algeria, Norway, the UK, Saudi Arabia, and Iraq in recent years. These supplies pose varying risks, including security and political instability and declining production—to say nothing of the various other concerns.[25]

Both industry and government are seeking to develop new oil and gas reserves across the country, but to date Canada's oil export boom remains overwhelmingly based on the tar sands. Canadian conventional oil production has peaked (new frontier discoveries in the Arctic or the Gulf of St. Lawrence notwithstanding), and 170 of Canada's 175 billion barrels of proven oil reserves—a whopping 97 per cent—are in the tar sands.[26] In short, projections of increasing Canadian oil production are based squarely on the tar sands, and the Canadian Association of Petroleum Producers (CAPP) anticipates that total production will increase by roughly two-thirds between 2009 and 2025.[27] This is also reflected in resource-centred business investment in Canada, which is again driven by the tar sands more than any other sector in the country.

Petro-Capitalism at the Provincial Scale

In the late 1970s, extraction in Alberta's tar sands was limited to projects run by Suncor and Syncrude and averaged only 55,000 bpd, constrained by technological problems and high costs. However, rising investment, technological innovation, and generous government subsidies enabled this production to nearly quadruple in the 1980s and double again in the 1990s. Average production reached almost 1 million bpd in the 2000s and hit 1.5 million bpd in 2010.[28] The Government of Alberta has ambitious projections for future growth, having already approved projects that are expected to result in a production level of over 5 million bpd, with some early projections anticipating production as high as 11 million bpd by 2050.[29]

This dramatic expansion has literally remade Alberta, reflected in the 2010 CAPP campaign branding the province as energy incarnate: "Alberta *is* Energy" (developed further in the following chapter). This has led to an extreme dependence of the Alberta economy and government on oil and gas revenues. From 1971 to 2004, the oil and gas industry is estimated to have contributed both directly and indirectly to over two-fifths of the provincial GDP, and has regularly accounted for between 30 and 50 per cent of provincial government revenues.[30]

Yet, as the discussion of petro-capitalism at the outset of this chapter underscores, this economic windfall must also be understood in light of its high environmental and human costs. For instance, it is estimated that over 700 square kilometres of land—roughly equivalent to the size of Calgary, one of North America's largest cities by area—has been directly disrupted by tar sands mining since the start of the industry in the late 1960s. But this is merely the beginning; this footprint will grow dramatically if approved projects proceed as planned, with some 84,000 square kilometres of land having already been leased for tar sands expansion. The ecological devastation, particularly in terms of deforestation and the pollution of streams, rivers, and lakes, has contributed to the decline of numerous species in the region, including some endangered and threatened species.[31] While corporate public relations campaigns boast about the industry's capacity to reclaim damaged sites, the notion that original ecosystems can be reconstructed is questionable at best, and to date a mere 0.1 per cent of mined land has been certified as reclaimed. This fundamental contradiction was stated most plainly by a consultation participant, who noted that "development is going along at hyperspeed but reclamation is going along at geological speed."[32]

The voracious thirst for freshwater in tar sands extraction has altered the flow of the Athabasca River in an already drought-prone province, and this is expected to continue, with yearly industry freshwater withdrawals from the Athabasca forecast to soon triple the volume withdrawn by the city of Calgary (and its more than one million citizens).[33] At the other end of the pipe, the tar sands' toxic tailings "ponds" now cover more than 170 square kilometres and pose a risk to local ecosystems due to the millions of litres of pollution water that leaches into the ground every day.[34] The extraction and upgrading projects also generate staggering air emissions of CO_2, nitrogen oxides, sulphur dioxide, and volatile organic compounds. As has been documented by the Pembina Institute, the tar sands constitute the "fastest growing and most significant source of emissions across Canadian economic subsectors," and the industry is expected to grow to over 14 per cent of the country's emissions by 2020.[35]

The toxic wastes have inflicted much damage to human health, wildlife, and traditional foods in surrounding Indigenous communities, degradation that is in turn implicated in the destruction of traditional livelihoods, a major issue discussed elsewhere in this book. Farther downstream, water pollutants are flowing into the fragile inland Peace-Athabasca Delta and through the Mackenzie Basin to the Arctic Ocean.[36] In addition to the role of GHGs worsening climate change, other airborne pollutants increase soil and lake acidification in Alberta as well as neighbouring Saskatchewan and Manitoba.[37]

In spite of this enormous and wide-ranging environmental toll, only very weak efforts have been made to enhance environmental monitoring and management capacities. Alberta's environmental policy regime is marked by delayed and ineffective regulatory consideration of impacts and serious regulatory gaps for CO_2 emissions, freshwater extraction, reclamation, and authentic public consultation. Instead, typifying the politics associated with petro-capitalism, the provincial government (in tandem with the federal government) has consistently downplayed or denied the environmental and human impacts of the industry while aggressively promoting its expansion.

Although G20 leaders committed in 2009 to phase out fossil fuel subsidies, direct support to the industry remains substantial: recent estimates of annual provincial and federal subsidies (heavily skewed towards Alberta) range between approximately $2.3 billion[38] and $2.8 billion.[39] In addition to the explicit subsidies, the low royalty rates charged by the province (which were originally intended to attract investment, given the high costs and slow early development) can be seen to represent an additional implicit subsidy. In 2006, Alberta's Royalty Review Panel compared international unconventional oil developments and found that the provincial government's share of resource benefits were well below that of Norway, Venezuela, and American states such as California and Alaska.[40]

Moreover, as discussed in subsequent chapters, the provincial government—again in tandem with the federal government—is further supporting the tar sands with a communications strategy to legitimize the industry at home and abroad. Sometimes this is through rosy imagery of reclaimed lands and improved efficiency; sometimes it is by attempting to criminalize opposition, with a few elected officials having gone so far as to liken it to terrorist activity.[41] This came to the forefront of a political debate in the winter of 2012, when Natural Resources Minister Joe Oliver went on the offensive against the interference of "foreign"-funded "radical groups," including environmental groups challenging the Northern Gateway pipeline review process.[42] By the spring, a counterterrorism unit was in place in Alberta, justified by claims that it was needed to defend "a strong economy supported by the province's natural resources and the need to protect critical infrastructure."[43]

In sum, Alberta has become extremely dependent upon an environmentally disastrous industry, and the government is clearly coming to embody many of the darker aspects of a petro-state. However, the lens of petro-capitalism helps us to recognize that however aggressive the promotion of the tar sands may be at this scale, this is but one dynamic among many that is driving the industry forward.

Beyond Petro-Capitalism

There is nothing to celebrate in Canada's emerging place as a world "energy superpower." This growth is premised on the especially "ugly, difficult and tough stuff at the bottom of the barrel," as Andrew Nikiforuk puts it, which has only become feasible for extraction as conventional reserves decline—and carries with it exorbitant social, economic, and environmental costs.[44] The decline in conventional oil supplies has now made it rational to invest previously unthinkable amounts of capital, energy, and resources into the tar sands while discounting the value of both current and future ecosystem services. In contrast to Harper's imagery of the tar sands as a heroic or mythical feat, cited at the outset of this chapter, this expansion is an act of socio-ecological hubris and a reflection of a pathological economic system.

The concept of petro-capitalism provides more than a critique of what is—it also poses questions about the politics associated with organizing non-fossil-fuel-dependent societies. Petro-capitalism involves, at root, concentrated ownership and control and a highly uneven distribution of benefits and costs. In contrast, sustainable, renewable energy offers greater possibility for more decentralized, localized, small-scale, diverse, community-based energy production, with more equitable sharing of development's costs and benefits and greater attention to negative socio-environmental consequences. As

Altvater argues, "The transition to renewable energy requires appropriate technologies, but requires even more appropriate social institutions and economic forms"—perhaps a *"solar revolution"* that could remake how we work, produce, consume, and relate to each other.[45] If energy struggles and transformations are in fact political, transitioning beyond oil implies a shift to a new political-economic system, away from one dependent upon incessant growth and accumulation and towards more environmentally sustainable and socially just ways of organizing how we produce, distribute, and consume.

2

Assembling Consent in Alberta

Hegemony and the Tar Sands

●

RANDOLPH HALUZA-DeLAY

●

Tar Sands as a Landscape of Hegemony

"Do you drive?" the politician asked. So did the tar sands engineer. And the mechanic. Even many Albertans with no connection to the oil and gas industry ask it. "How can you criticize the tar sands if you drive?" they sometimes say outright. Most of the time it is implied. Despite the glaring problems with tar sands development, as identified throughout this book, everyday life in the petro-dominated province of Alberta is captured by the pernicious and faulty notion that "there is no alternative" to exploiting the tar sands. The implication is that to have a problem with the tar sands is to be a hypocrite, and that tar sands extraction is the only "realistic" choice.

Fossil energy extraction has been powerfully woven into the fabric of Alberta's identity, often through the very deliberate efforts of political and economic actors. The dominance of the fossil fuel sector in the economy is what some characterize as "petro-capitalism." The perceived inevitability of tar sands expansion can be seen to have infiltrated the "common sense" in Alberta, and indeed much of Canada. As the expansion of the tar sands is normalized in popular perception and becomes the effective status quo, attempts to challenge it are then framed in terms of impossible and unacceptable economic risks. And yet, tremendous private profits are made even larger by public subsidies, extremely low royalty rates, and limited regulation.[1] At the same time, the enormous social and ecological consequences get deflected.

In short, there is a prevailing language and set of assumptions behind the public life of the tar sands in Alberta, and it plays out in governance, other institutions, and everyday life for Albertans. The term *hegemony* represents this situation. Hegemony, as explained by Antonio Gramsci, means the ongoing acceptance by the populace of a social arrangement that has greatest benefits for particular elites rather than for the public.[2] Hegemony is inscribed across the landscape of Alberta. It has not been accidental. It has been carefully crafted.

Recognizing this strategic imperative, the Canadian Association of Petroleum Producers (CAPP) concluded a two-year public relations campaign at the end of 2012, in which they exhorted Albertans to "have a conversation with your neighbours." "Alberta is Energy," the campaign was called. CAPP's marketing positioned energy extraction and production as being inextricable from Albertan self-identity: "Energy is what makes us Albertan." This connection was welded tighter by a purportedly self-evident presumption that "the world needs energy; lots of it."[3] Once again, the message is communicated that there is no alternative to the insatiable extraction of more fossil fuels, and the tar sands are a bounty that we are obligated to develop as rapidly as possible. After all, this is what Albertans do, the marketing asserts.

Social theory can at times appear obscure and jargon-laden, but its insights can help uncover taken-for-granted and hidden social processes, illuminate systems of power, and help to create more effective movement strategies. Among the most pressing needs for the political culture of Alberta is to recognize how discourses shape people's abilities to think about their sociopolitical world and environmental issues. This is the first step to seeing how these discourses and the social and political arrangements they legitimate might be changed. Discourse—whether hegemonic or counter-hegemonic—shapes our ability to imagine our world, and even whether or not we see or desire alternatives. Hegemony plays a crucial role in the failure to respond to environmental problems. Despite all the science, environmental issues are profoundly social. That is, the environmental degradation that we see is the result of how societies organize themselves, build their infrastructure, and use resources, energy, and the rest of nature. Environmental issues are also about who—in government and otherwise—has power over these decisions.

Hegemony refers to the mystification of this domination, so that we consent to the way things are without carefully scrutinizing who gets more of the benefits and who pays more of the costs.

Of course, in liberal democracies like ours, corporate executives and government actors never use the language of "domination" and "exploitation" about Alberta's citizens—the ordinary "Marthas and Henrys," as former premier Ralph Klein once famously referred to them.[4] Rather, elite discursive practices tend to be much more subtle. Activists, citizens, and scholars must pay heed to the different ways that discourse can contribute to hegemony. For instance, the issues might be disguised so as to make them appear beyond questioning. They might be obfuscated in technical detail or jargon, allowing debates to be claimed as the territory of "experts" rather than citizens. The overall debate might be deliberately polarized, framed as the exclusive choice between competing desires for wealth accumulation versus environmental and social protection. Given the extensive environmental and social effects of the tar sands, and the long-term consequences— such as their contribution to climate change and the toxification of the Albertan landscape—petro-capitalism needs cultural machinery to maintain its existing popular support.

When this fails, states use physical violence, but for the most part domination works by the failure to recognize the extent of power structures on the part of those who are being dominated. Gramsci's concept of hegemony indicates the importance of understanding how structures of thought and practice can lead people to tacitly or overtly give consent to their domination, thereby helping to perpetuate the status quo. Contemporary theories of hegemony explain it in terms of the ways capitalism is built into the everyday patterns of living, thinking, talking, and feeling. The hegemonic patterns then become "common sense." "Alberta is Energy" says that this is what we do; nothing else makes sense. "Do you drive?" places the moral onus on individuals rather than on collective decisions, say, to make public transit so effective no one needs to drive but can still fully participate in modern society. The hegemonic ideology of market-driven politics, as if the market were a self-existing entity and "free," ignores how our choices are already constrained by past decisions, creating the current structures and corresponding options. Hegemony is internalized, so that it becomes relatively impervious to counter-hegemonic critique.[5] Yet this analysis is not bleak. We must also keep in mind that none of this is fixed and immutable. On the contrary, hegemony is something that is "continually to be renewed, recreated, defended, and modified,"[6] which is why it is so useful to examine the marketing that promotes tar sands hegemony.

This chapter is motivated by the growing recognition that social movements, as well as scholars studying and supporting them, need to pay more attention to cultural representations and outcomes.[7] In order to confront a hegemonic system like the tar sands in Alberta, there is a need to identify the cultural machinery used to manufacture popular consent. Critical scholarship can have a useful role to play in this. This includes working to deconstruct prevailing discourses, which is a key part of what Gramsci termed the "war of position"—the long-term effort to dismantle the authority of the hegemon. Shifting the language—and built-in assumptions—with which issues are framed and discussed is ultimately part of the process of building counter-narratives and fertilizing the soil for alternatives to take root.[8]

This chapter summarizes some of the key methods used to represent the tar sands and build public consent to the continuing destruction they entail, based on an ongoing research project. Central to building public consent are the ways the tar sands industry and its government allies speak to Alberta's citizens. This industry-government alliance helps to cultivate a narrative of provincial citizenship that is wrapped into the unmitigated exploitation of energy resources. Albertans become *Homo energeticus.*[9] The chapter then turns to some of the ways that this has been contested and then countered again by the powerful capital-state partnership that not only dominates Alberta's economy and politics but is also a major force shaping its culture.

Creating Hegemonic Representations of the Tar Sands

Both industry and government have very active roles in constructing positive representations of the tar sands in Alberta, and of the need for incessant expansion. Of course, we should expect this of industry, and the associated network of industry-funded think tanks and associations, spokespersons, and CEOs. More disconcerting is the common language and positioning that the government shares with the special interests of industry, in direct contrast to other interests and citizen coalitions that are questioning the trajectory of tar sands development.

Chief among the industry advocates is CAPP. In launching the public relations campaign noted earlier, CAPP demonstrates its awareness of strategic objectives, as its press release plainly asserts the "need to *draw a line of sight* between our industry and the revenue flowing from it to education [and] health care" (emphasis added). No comparable clarity of vision was drawn to the high corporate revenues and low public royalties achieved in rapaciously exploiting the tar sands.[10]

Similar discursive features are even more apparent in presentations of industry actors, which openly play on the notion of "common sense" (recall how the idea of common sense is an important aspect of how hegemony is secured—and yet we rarely ask how what seems to "make sense" came to be so commonly held). For instance, the Alberta Enterprise Group, another industry advocacy group, describes its mission as being to "challenge all levels of government to make *common-sense* decisions in the interest of all Albertans" (emphasis added), while its website declared that energy is "common sense" and "It's what makes us Albertans."[11] The Alberta Enterprise Group had a notable role in coordinating the January 2008 trade mission to promote the tar sands in Washington, DC, at a time when the U.S. National Mayors were beginning to express increasing concern about their growing dependence upon Canada's "dirty oil." There, again mobilizing Albertan identity, AEG's vice-president of communications stated: "Advocating for the oilsands isn't just about preserving the resource's commercial value. It speaks to *who Albertans are as a people*" (emphasis added).[12] Such strategies resonate with well-established provincial narratives, and how Leduc #1 (the first major crude oil discovery in Alberta)[13] as well as other energy booms have been used to forge Alberta's identity. This energy-producer narrative is writ into Alberta's public education system, as even the Grade 4 Social Studies curriculum focuses upon the province's resource abundance, without any word of environmental consequences.[14]

From several places on its website, CAPP linked directly to another website that prominently displayed a video produced by the Ministry of Environment.[15] One might presume that this government department is charged with protecting the environment, and an early interviewee comments in the video, "I'm one of *them*," claiming a positive association with environmentalists. Shortly thereafter, another government environmental scientist scornfully disassociates himself and his agency from the "negative" environmentalists: "Let *them* throw rocks at us," he says scornfully, referring to those who oppose tar sands extraction on environmental grounds.[16] A good illustration of the manner in which both industry and government have tended to relate to their critics is the fact that it took legal proceedings to force the latter scientist to retract an industry-publicized attack on the scientific rigour of independent and peer-reviewed research showing the harmful effects of the tar sands.[17]

In short, a strong capital-state partnership is aligned to promote tar sands expansion and oppose any resistance to it,[18] and it seems clear that the provincial identity is being strategically represented by both industry and government as a means of manufacturing popular consent. It is onto this hegemonic cultural landscape that social movement actors must not only work to present criticisms, but also convey alternatives capable of resonating with the wider population. Such alternatives cannot be merely technical reports; they and their communication are cultural politics.

Contesting Hegemonic Representations

Opposition to the tar sands within Alberta has come mainly from Indigenous communities and a range of environmental organizations, church-based groups, and labour unions. Early advocacy strategies of these groups often involved participating in the lengthy consultation processes, usually to reduce the environmental consequences of tar sands projects. Some groups have largely stayed at the consultative and lobbying level, refusing to go beyond modest targets of enhanced royalties, improved technologies, and promises about using tar sands revenues to build a "new green economy." However, others have found the processes of consultation and dialogue to be time consuming and largely ineffective at influencing government decisionmaking,[19] and this has led some groups to increasingly favour more direct forms of action. Another response to the stifled political dialogue on the tar sands at the provincial and national levels has been for oppositional groups to seek out new coalitions. Pipeline battles—the Northern Gateway and Keystone XL being only two examples—have mobilized all these strategies and more. They also illustrate how the terrain of battle is constantly shifting.

To date, the most effective oppositional coalitions within Alberta have involved alliances between Indigenous communities and environmental

NGOs. These efforts have increasingly extended networks of organizations from local levels across provincial and national borders all the way to international arenas. This transnational "scale-jumping" reflects an attempt to leverage more resources and voices to bring rational arguments and moral objections to the media and to a range of constituencies, from the European Union to the United States to the United Nations.

Not surprisingly, this has induced a range of counter-responses from the capital-state partnership in Alberta. As detailed elsewhere in this book, both provincial and federal governments have responded to the escalating contestation abroad by embarking on multimillion-dollar public relations campaigns and extensive political lobbying for the tar sands in the US and Europe. Within Alberta, responses to opponents have been varied. With respect to the demands for environmental justice from Indigenous communities in the region,[20] the industry and the government have largely sought to evade or narrow the scope of their responsibility by focusing on things like remediating some health concerns and ignoring unceded treaty rights.

Environmental protests have, on the other hand, typically been met with vociferous criticism. Elected government officials have strategically invoked the label of "eco-terrorism" in order to discredit certain opponents. This tag has even been used to encompass nonviolent action by environmental organizations (media stunts like unfurling a banner at a political event may cause laughter, but probably caused no terror!). Even church officials have been chastised. Father Luc Bouchard, the former Roman Catholic bishop of St. Paul, Alberta, whose diocese included the Fort McMurray area, received numerous demands (polite and otherwise) to "stay out of their oil sands business" following his widely read 2009 pastoral letter, which argued that the level and type of tar sands development "cannot be morally justified."[21] A year later, in a speech, Bouchard described how the industry and government reactions to his letter were "like they were reading from the same page," using similar responses and common language while ignoring the questions he raised.[22] Diverting the essence of his concerns, they instead emphasized the technical efforts to reduce the impact of tar sands extraction while increasing production—a sort of technocratic closure of debate that should be understood as a form of cultural politics, narrowing the terms in which the "environment" and its management can be discussed.[23]

Oppositional forces have barely dented the hegemonic representations of *Homo energeticus* and unending tar sands expansion within Alberta, and have had relatively little effect on environmental governance either provincially or federally. However, there is a possibility that the success in raising international awareness may yet swing back and serve to enhance public legitimacy for critique of the tar sands in Alberta—a sort of "boomerang effect."[24]

Conclusion

Insights from social theorists like Gramsci suggest that environmental and social justice movements should think of themselves as engaging in cultural politics as well as legislative reform because of the need to contest the cultural legitimation, norms, and worldviews that support the political status quo. While we must be cautious that this contest does not supplant the actions to win political influence or power, it is important to recognize that culture is not peripheral to environmental and social justice struggles— rather, it lies at the heart of counter-hegemonic political action. This has great relevance to the struggles to oppose the tar sands because, in addition to its war on the environment and on frontline communities, the tar sands also involve the ongoing normalization of the petro-domination of politics and everyday lifestyles.

In Alberta, the continuing expansion of the tar sands industry is deeply embedded not only in the provincial economy and politics, but also in the common-sense consciousness, social discourse, and lifestyle practices of ordinary citizens. The hegemony of the tar sands industry stems not only from the scale of profits, the power of transnational energy corporations, and the support of the state, but also the way a particular narrative of identity has been manufactured, sold, and ultimately internalized by ordinary Albertans. Once such narratives are widely entrenched, any attempt to contest the unfettered expansion of the tar sands can then be decried as contrary to the interests of the people of Alberta. In addition to the mobilization of identity, other key discursive tactics used to prop up the hegemonic status quo are to project its inevitability ("there is no alternative") and to place the entirety of the discussion on technical grounds, thereby displacing wide-reaching moral questions about Indigenous rights, social justice, and the protection of nature with narrowly defined technological and managerial "solutions."[25]

In sum, it is important for the forces opposing the tar sands to pay more attention to the nature of cultural politics, and how the prevailing powers are working to shape the discourse, "common sense," and identity narratives within Alberta and Canada. Critical social researchers can complement these efforts through research that sheds light on the symbolic violence that accompanies the real violence of the tar sands, and the cultural machinery bent on manufacturing hegemonic consent. In addition to exposing this, activists and scholars alike will have to develop compelling alternative narratives about what Alberta *could be*, and work to effectively communicate these to the "Marthas and Henrys" of the province.

3

The Rise of Reactionary Environmentalism in the Tar Sands

●

RYAN KATZ-ROSENE

●

*Canada is the environmentally responsible choice for the U.S. to
meet its energy needs in oil for years to come.*
—Joe Oliver, Canada's minister of natural resources, in 2013[1]

*Unfortunately, there are environmental and other radical groups
that would seek to block this opportunity to diversify our trade.*
—Joe Oliver, Canada's minister of natural resources, in 2012[2]

In a recent open letter to Canadians, Minister of Natural Resources Joe
Oliver warned that "radical" environmentalists with anti-expansionist views
of the tar sands were putting corporate profits at peril. Ironically, the tar
sands industry and its supporting politicians have responded to the "radical"
threat by increasingly attempting to drape the incessant expansion of bitumen production in the guise of environmentalism and sustainability. This
includes claims about "responsible resource development" (in contrast to the
"unrealistic" anti-growth agenda of the radicals), the "ethical" superiority of
Canadian oil (in contrast to tyrannical regimes elsewhere), the increasing
efficiency of extraction processes, and the wonders of land reclamation.[3]

This chapter examines how a combination of federal and provincial governments, industry, and high-profile apologists has attempted to construct these narratives by co-opting and discursively reframing environmental concerns. I argue that this approach, which is best understood as a form of *reactionary environmentalism*, is designed to reassure investors, neutralize criticism, and placate both apathetic and concerned citizens. Its Achilles heel, however, lies in claims to be engaging in a rational conversation, despite lacking evidence, in order to defend the unsustainable proposition of endless growth.

Reactionary Environmentalism in the Tar Sands

Reactionary environmentalism is, in essence, an extreme right-wing philosophy tied to the political economic ideology of neo-liberal capitalism. It goes under various guises, such as "ecological modernization," "market ecology," and "green neo-liberalism," with the fundamental premise being a "business-as-usual" approach to environmental problems that largely places the onus on technological innovation and corporate self-management.[4] In this messianic vision of enlightened corporations operating benignly within ever-freer markets, the best thing for the environment—it is claimed—is to turn *everything* into a commodity, from the water we drink to the air we breathe, as this supposedly yields uncoerced behavioural reform and promotes investment in innovation and efficiency. Yet regardless of whether adherents truly believe such promises, reactionary environmentalism must also be seen in light of its primary objective: to oppose socio-political change and defend the status quo.

Reactionary environmentalism has taken many different forms in relation to the tar sands. It can be seen as a sort of double-headed beast: on one hand, in attack mode, seeking to condemn environmental science and neuter environmental regulations; on the other hand, portraying a "softer" side, with a feel-good message of "progress" in industry's efforts to reduce the intensity of ecological damage from bitumen production and restore disrupted forests and wetlands. I will focus my attention here on five main examples of reactionary environmentalism in the tar sands.

I. Co-opting Environmental Concepts

Not long ago, the main marketing strategy for Alberta Synthetic Crude Oil (SCO) was purely and simply to convince potential producers that it was worth the capital investment, whereas in recent years, industry has had to dress up the entire megaproject in green clothing. Years ago, efforts to reduce ecological impacts were seldom trumpeted, mostly because they were seldom practiced. It is important to recall that it was not until 2003 that the US Energy Information Administration even recognized Alberta's vast bituminous deposits as an economically viable source of oil.[5] So while the production of SCO had already been wreaking havoc upon the landscapes and communities of northern Alberta for decades, up to this time serious attention to questions of the environment overwhelmingly took a backseat to SCO's main selling points—economic growth and energy security—in order to secure further investment and exports.

However, in recent years, the industry has made its efforts to enhance the efficiency of extraction and minimize the per-barrel impact a primary selling point. Former Alberta premier Alison Redford clearly admitted this shift after a 2011 trip to Washington, going so far as to suggest that marketing SCO to Americans would thereafter hinge on reframing the environmental image of the tar sands: "We heard very quickly that [Americans] don't want to hear anymore the security argument or the jobs argument. We get that.... Really, this is about environmental stewardship and sustainable development of the oil sands. We were quite happy to talk about that, [but] that was a shift in the kinds of conversations that Alberta was having."[6]

Although this has been a marked turn in some ways, it did not come entirely out of the blue. As early as the mid-1990s, industry and government together began thinking about how to placate environmental concerns, which was reflected in the National Task Force on Oil Sands Strategies. The task force's final report cryptically acknowledged the significant environmental risks of developing the tar sands, and suggested that these will have to be minimized—at least perceptively—in order to garner enough public consent: "Oil sands development will not proceed unless the environmental consequences are mitigated to a degree acceptable to regulators and the public."[7]

It is interesting to note how this strategic approach to environmental management originally took shape as a *response* to the risks posed to the expansion of tar sands production by genuine ecological concerns, as interpreted through a financial lens. That is, ecological critiques posed clear threats to profitability, and the response was to co-opt and thereby neutralize them. The adoption of a cumulative environmental approach to monitoring

Children wear masks to protect themselves from the toxic fumes that surround their community during the fourth annual Healing Walk, 2013.

the ecological impacts of development illustrates this well. This concept was raised long ago by ecologists who were critical of the consistent failure of large-scale developments to consider impacts holistically. In the tar sands, the response was to set up the Cumulative Environmental Management Agency (CEMA) in 2001, which government authorities claimed would take the varying viewpoints of industry, environmental, and Indigenous groups into account. Yet the rhetoric of a cumulative approach fell flat, as industry dominated CEMA to such an extent that a number of First Nations communities and environmental organizations withdrew participation in 2008, claiming that it had "lost all legitimacy as an organization and process for environmental management in the oil sands."[8]

In the wake of this blow to CEMA's legitimacy, critics put out a renewed call for a moratorium on new tar sands project approvals until the cumulative impacts of development were better understood, to which authorities responded with attempts to co-opt the very image of a moratorium in the first place. In 2009, in the wake of the global financial crisis, the Canadian minister of the environment tried to dispel the need for government intervention because "there has been a *de facto* moratorium on oil sands developments because of the nature of the economy."[9] The hollowness of this claim was subsequently exposed when a spokesperson for the Oil Sands Developers Group said: "There isn't a de facto moratorium. In fact, the Oil Sands [Developers Group] is continuing to invest significant amounts of dollars in growth."[10] Much like earlier attempts to co-opt the cumulative approach concept, the imagery of a "de facto moratorium" amounts to a cursory attempt to appease critics, spinning the *idea* of slowing down the pace and scale of development without actually doing anything to affect it.

Another example of how environmental criticisms have been spun into a counter-narrative occurred in 2005, when a dozen environmental organizations in Alberta issued a joint declaration stating that the tar sands were expanding too fast.[11] These claims were, of course, nothing new, but thanks to the growing activism and media coverage surrounding the tar sands, they had become harder to brush aside. Unfortunately, this declaration also came with a gift, as it set out conditions by which further expansion would be acceptable, including the implementation of: a sound regulatory regime that would facilitate the transition to a sustainable energy economy by *decreasing the demand* for synthetic crude oil; a new fiscal regime to ensure long-term sustainable prosperity in Alberta by *reducing dependence* on the energy industry; and the adoption of an adequate and independent *cumulative approach* to environmental management. Rather than deny the validity of the declaration, authorities reacted to it by simply co-opting its rhetoric. As a result, we hear about industry having adopted a cumulative approach and slowing down the pace of development, while in reality production has continued to grow year after year.

2. Reframing: From Unsustainable to "Sustainable" Development

Both Big Oil and its backers in the Albertan and Canadian governments have increasingly attempted to challenge the label of unsustainability with respect to the tar sands, in part by simply reframing the discourse. Although fossil fuels are by their very nature non-renewable and unsustainable, the tar sands are now being sold as a "sustainable" megaproject. The provincial government of Alberta has some experience in this regard, having faced a crisis of legitimacy in the 1990s over its dependency on natural resource extraction. The response then, as now, has been to construct new ecological subjectivities rather than enact substantive regulations. As Davidson and MacKendrick effectively put it, the "close relations between natural resource industrial interests and the Alberta administration, combined with Alberta's neo-liberal political ideology, limited opportunities for significant environmental reform. The province consequently opted for a process of discursive reframing rather than institutional restructuring."[12] In other words, industry is simply changing its lingo, not its behaviour.

This attempt at discursive reframing has resulted in the creation of dubiously titled agencies, such as the Oil Sands Sustainable Development Secretariat, and produced reams of documents that claim, in defiance of the laws of physics, that tar sands operations are "sustainable."[13] The federal government has also gotten into the act, as exemplified by a report entitled *The Oil Sands: Toward Sustainable Development*, produced by the House of Commons Standing Committee on Natural Resources shortly after the Harper Conservatives came to power.[14]

The rhetoric of reactionary environmentalism has increasingly been exported in the face of mounting resistance from US and EU environmental groups (as discussed at various other points in this book). This includes using public resources to hire high-priced lobbyists tasked with convincing American and European policy-makers of the positive impact of technological and regulatory measures taken,[15] repeatedly invoking terms like "environmentally responsible" and "sustainable development" in reference to tar sands production. Thus, rather than address the unsustainable nature of production at a material level, the response of reactionary environmentalism has been to discursively rebrand the production process.

3. The Trope of "Ethical Oil"

One of the most vivid examples of reactionary environmentalism in the tar sands can be found in the so-called "ethical oil" argument. This was first put forward in a popular book by right-wing pundit Ezra Levant and was subsequently promoted via the website EthicalOil.org, run by neo-conservative lawyer Alykhan Velshi.[16] Both Levant and Velshi have very strong, well-established ties to the Conservative Party of Canada, and Levant clearly positioned his book as an attempt to deflect attention from Andrew Nikiforuk's award-winning 2008 book, *Tar Sands: Dirty Oil and the Future of a Continent*.[17]

The "ethical oil" narrative couples a highly selective use of facts with a reliance on nasty personal attacks to create a classic straw man geared towards making the tar sands look benign. The part it does get right is the fact that petroleum production is very dirty business—this is, after all, an industry rife with examples of coercion, deceit, and gross corporate negligence. Yet where Levant and Velshi go wrong is in assuming that because extraction elsewhere has often been very bad, this makes the tar sands somehow good, as though it is exempted from the toxicity, CO_2 emissions, corrupt politics, and other negative aspects of the petroleum business.

The trope of "ethical oil" rests in large measure on Alberta's place in an affluent, Western, democratic, capitalist nation, which ensures that transnational corporations (including many of the same players who have been implicated in crimes elsewhere) are welcome to purchase their extraction "rights" and can be entrusted to be responsible, law-abiding corporate citizens. Former premier Ralph Klein helped convert Alberta into a "capitalist paradise,"[18] and this political and regulatory environment of neo-liberal capitalism is the crux of Levant's claim that "the oil sands are cleaner than any other competing jurisdiction."[19] After all, the companies are just doing what they are allowed to do by law!

Levant attempts to build his case further through a hodgepodge of relativist claims, and some patently absurd ones. For instance, at one point he goes so far as to liken the extraction of bitumen to "the largest cleanup of an oil spill in the history of the world."[20] He also casts doubt on the science of climate change as a mere "theory," while celebrating the industry's tremendous efforts to reduce the intensity of pollution per barrel produced and its impacts on water, wildlife, and downstream communities—all the while heaping scorn upon dirty industries abroad. Ultimately, like other examples of reactionary environmentalism, the "ethical oil" argument amounts to an attempt to divert the attention of citizens, policy-makers, and investors, both in Canada and abroad.

4. The Fixation on Technological Innovation

In recent years, the tar sands industry has developed an aggressive public relations complex, headed by the Canadian Association of Petroleum Producers (CAPP) and Natural Resources Canada. This involves a range of advertising platforms (e.g., prominent billboards in cities and along highways, television commercials, and bus stop posters) touting such things as reclamation areas and the economic benefits to all of Canada. The essential goal of these advertisements is to reassure Canadians that the tar sands are being developed responsibly and bring many economic benefits, while adverse impacts are carefully mitigated.

A central theme in the CAPP advertisements is the portrayal of technological innovation as something capable of largely solving the environmental degradation associated with tar sands extraction. Of course, improved technologies aimed at reducing pollution levels are not in themselves negative, but focusing on such "fixes" can distract the public from the more fundamental demands being made by environmental scientists and advocates. That is, while climate scientists demand that net greenhouse gas emissions be reduced, and ecologists demand that the production of tailings ponds and the practices of clear-cutting and open pit mining be stopped altogether, the tar sands public relations complex meets these with promises to reduce the pollution burden per barrel produced, reduce CO_2 emissions through carbon capture and storage technologies, slow the growth of toxic tailings ponds through tailings reductions operations, and reclaim degraded ecosystems through sophisticated engineering strategies.

So while new technologies can indeed decrease the relative impacts of production, this focus fails to mention how efficiency gains are often offset by the growth in overall production, a well-established tendency in the history of resource exploitation in capitalism that is referred to as the Jevons paradox. The point is that technological innovations are being driven with the goal of *enabling* both increasing profitability and increasing volumes of bitumen extraction. The imagery of technological solutions is also coupled with a portrayal of the tar sands as a highly regulated industry, when regulations have in fact been limited, geared towards facilitating expansion, and often gone unenforced.[21] For example, a recent television advertisement by the federal government claims that it is "protecting the environment with new fines for companies that break the law, returning developed land to its natural state, increasing pipeline inspections by 50 percent, [and] requiring double hulls for tankers,"[22] claims that are very clearly designed to neutralize some of the criticisms associated with the Northern Gateway pipeline proposal by appealing to innovations in technology and legislation.

5. Silencing the Rest

Where environmental problems prove difficult to spin, one tactic has been to attack the messenger—firing whistleblowers and slandering critics,[23] with environmental organizations that are critical of the tar sands regularly portrayed as "outsiders" and "foreigners." A stark illustration of this vilification occurred when Conservative politicians tried to discredit renowned environmental journalist Andrew Nikiforuk and Dr. John O'Connor when they testified at a parliamentary committee, implicitly accusing them of treason for having travelled to Norway to notify Statoil investors about the impacts of investment in the tar sands.[24]

These efforts to tarnish the reputation of Dr. O'Connor followed an incident some years earlier, in which his medical license was revoked by Health Canada after he raised concerns about potential correlations between bituminous developments and cancer in a First Nations community downstream. Health Canada accused O'Connor of causing undue alarm, hiding medical information, and overbilling patients—charges that would years later be dropped as baseless.[25] Astoundingly, such intimidation was not without precedent: Dr. David Swann, the former medical officer of health for the Palliser Health Authority in southeastern Alberta, was fired in 2002 for making public statements in support of the Kyoto Protocol—a stance the health board condemned because it was seen as something that would hurt Alberta's fossil fuel–reliant economy.[26] Adam Albright sums it up well:

> Today those who speak the truth [about the tar sands] are discredited and banished. Openly criticize and your job will disappear. Write a story and your services will no longer be needed. Publicize a health threat and you will be run out of the province. Try to enact a Climate Law and the Minister of Environment will go to the far reaches of the continent to make sure it does not pass. The Giant Machine just rolls along as million dollar PR campaigns are trotted out at the first sign of dissent.[27]

Conclusion

For Big Oil and their loyal politicians, environmental concerns raised by scientists, organizations, doctors, and citizens represent a real threat to exponential growth and corporate earnings. All they can see is a reservoir worth trillions of dollars, with proven reserves (extractable with current technology) that amount to more than two centuries' worth of production at 2011 levels. The economic motivation for creating an alternative eco-narrative could not be clearer. But as this chapter has shown, reactionary environmentalism is exposed as a flimsy shield without any substance. The tar sands public relations machinery has repeatedly sought to neuter the implications of any environmental criticism in order to justify continuing expansion. Struggles to confront the tar sands must take heed of these strategies and continue working to expose them for the hollow and misleading promises they are.

4

Canadian Diplomatic Efforts to Sell the Tar Sands

●

YVES ENGLER

•

Growing International Attention

The rapid growth of the tar sands has unleashed an important international political battle, pitting the Canadian government, a plethora of right-wing think tanks, and some of the richest companies in the world against a growing mass of individuals, First Nations, and environmental organizations. In November 2011, I got an unexpected taste of this battle while in London, England. My first glimpse was a public discussion focused on how, in the words of organizers, "the UK government has recently bowed to Canadian government and industry pressure and are trying to undermine the European Fuel Quality Directive"[1]—something that would have effectively banned tar sands exports from Europe by forcing suppliers to privilege lower-emission fuels. Next, I came across a King's College newspaper story about how a speech given by Joe Oliver, Canada's natural resources minister, at the London School of Economics was interrupted by a group called People and Planet, presenting him with an award for "Greenwash Propagandist of the Year."[2]

I later learned that these were but a few episodes of the growth in grassroots activism in England opposing the tar sands. For instance, in January

2011, protesters gathered outside the Canadian High Commission when Alberta energy minister Ron Liepert visited London, and in June 2013 a number of speeches Prime Minister Stephen Harper made in Britain were protested by environmentalists. In October 2012, activists interrupted a speech by Canada's minister of the environment at Chatham House, rejecting his professed concern about responding to climate change. One activist even took the stage to call him "a member of a dangerous anti-environment group called the Canadian government who are committed to wrecking the climate."[3]

This international attention is not confined to England. In May 2012, dozens of cities in thirteen countries participated in the third annual "Stop the Tar Sands" day of action. In late 2011, several prominent South Africans, including anti-apartheid hero Archbishop Desmond Tutu, criticized Alberta's dirty oil in a full-page *Globe and Mail* advertisement. The ad stated that: "For us in Africa, climate change is a life and death issue. By dramatically increasing Canada's global warming pollution, tar sands mining and drilling makes the problem worse, and exposes millions of Africans to more devastating drought and famine today and in the years to come."[4]

In Norway, the tar sands became an election issue in 2009 during political debates because of widespread public opposition to the fact that Norway's state-owned energy company, Statoil, has significant investments in Alberta. Jim Prentice, Canada's minister of the environment at the time, visited Norway around this election period and was struck by the extent of public hostility towards Statoil's investment in the tar sands. According to a diplomatic cable released by Wikileaks, Prentice later told US ambassador David Jacobsen that the experience "heightened his awareness of the negative consequences to Canada's historically 'green' standing on the world stage."[5] Prentice also told the US ambassador in Ottawa that the Conservatives were "too slow" in responding to the dirty oil label and "failed to grasp the magnitude of the situation." A confidential August 2010 email from London-based Canadian diplomat Sushma Gera echoed this sentiment, noting that "the oil sands are posing a growing reputational problem, with the oil sands defining the Canadian brand," and warning that "with [a] recent increase in the NGO campaigns targeting [the European] public, we anticipate increased risk to Canadian interests much beyond the oil sands."[6]

The Government of Canada Fights Back in Europe

In the face of this growing international opposition, the Canadian government has responded with intensive lobbying efforts, to the extent that Martin Lukacs has rightly described it as having "become the foreign branch of the Tar Sands industry."[7] A few months after Prentice's 2009 European tour, Foreign Affairs laid out a Pan-European Oil Sands Advocacy Strategy that was designed to "protect and advance Canadian interests related to the oil sands," and reframe "the European debate on oil sands."[8] According to internal documents, Canadian embassies tailored messages for each country "based on lines from Ottawa," which would focus on government efforts to reduce the industry's environmental and social impacts.[9]

As part of the strategy, Canadian diplomats were: offered trips to Alberta and industry-sponsored conferences; instructed to monitor environmental activism; told to engage in public relations geared at combatting "significant negative media coverage"; and instructed to share "intelligence" with "likeminded allies," including BP, Statoil, TOTAL, and Shell, which have "huge investments" in Alberta.[10] In August 2010, the Pan-European Oil Sands team reported that:

- the Canadian embassy in Norway "holds regular meetings with Statoil to update on each other's activities and coordinate where appropriate";
- the Canadian embassy in the Netherlands "is enhancing its engagement with the private sector and met with Shell recently";
- the Canadian embassy in France "has regular meetings with Total"; and
- the Canadian embassy in Britain "is also in regular contact with the private sector including meetings with Shell, BP and Royal Bank of Scotland as well as Canadian oil companies."[11]

This strategic alliance with the oil industry reaches up to the highest levels. For instance, in June 2010, Stephen Harper met TOTAL's chief executive Christophe de Margerie when he visited Paris, which one can only assume was part of the prescribed "engagement with the private sector."[12]

The Canadian government has also trained its diplomats to promote the tar sands. A February 2011 retreat brought diplomats from thirteen different European offices together with a number of federal government departments, Alberta's energy minister, and representatives from TOTAL, Shell, Statoil, and the Canadian Association of Petroleum Producers.[13] At this "training" session, diplomats were given "an industry perspective" as well as information on the official positions of both the Canadian and Albertan governments. An email to officials from Foreign Affairs, Environment Canada, and Natural Resources Canada summarizing this meeting explained that "two key messages from day one were: oil sands advocacy in Europe is now recognized as a priority for all concerned; and there is a clear need for regular in-house training to equip those of us on the ground with the expertise to deal with this highly technical file."[14]

Another central goal of the Pan-European Oil Sands Advocacy Strategy has been to oppose the designation of the tar sands in the EU's proposed Fuel Quality Directive, as noted at the outset. To this end, diplomats were tasked with "targeting" and lobbying key European politicians, "especially from the ruling and influential parties."[15] Here, it is important to recognize that since Europe does not import tar sands oil, the legislation would have little direct effect on exports, but the worry has been that this could set a precedent to be copied elsewhere. London-based Canadian diplomat Kumar Gupta summarized this fear clearly in an April 2011 email released through access to information legislation: "While Europe is not an important market for oil sands-derived products, Europe legislation/regulation, such as the EU Fuel Quality Directive, has the potential to impact the industry globally."[16]

To give an indication of the extent of the lobbying efforts, Friends of the Earth Europe found that Canadian officials met British and European representatives 110 times between September 2009 and July 2011 in a bid to derail the Fuel Quality Directive and ensure what the Canadian government calls "non-discriminatory market access" for tar sands exports.[17] Two comments from European parliamentarians in 2012 are especially revealing. Chris Davies, a UK representative to the EU, described Canada's lobbying campaign as having "been stunning in its intensity," while Satu Hassi, a Finnish representative, noted that she had seen "massive lobbying campaigns by the car industry, by the chemicals industry, banks, food giants, etc. But so far I have not seen such a lobbying campaign by any state" that could compare with that of the Canadian government on behalf of the tar sands industry.[18]

As the EU debated the Fuel Quality Directive, the Conservatives issued stern warnings in their bid to have the tar sands exempted. In early 2012,

David Plunkett, Canada's ambassador to the EU, addressed a letter stating that: "If the final measures single out oil sands crude in a discriminatory, arbitrary or unscientific way, or are otherwise inconsistent with the EU's international trade obligations, I want to state that Canada will explore every avenue at its disposal to defend its interests, including at the World Trade Organization."[19] The *Ottawa Citizen* summed this up plainly: "Canada threatens trade war with EU ahead of oilsands vote."[20] Canada has also issued warnings to the EU that its support for action on climate change risks disrupting world oil supplies.

The Conservatives' strategy seems to have borne some fruit. In February 2012, *The Globe and Mail* described an EU vote as having "given the Canadian government a win in its battle to preserve international markets for oil sands producers against an environmental lobbying effort, which wants refiners worldwide to pay financial penalties for using the carbon intensive Alberta crude as well as other sources of 'dirty' fuel."[21] After the vote, Friends of the Earth Europe spokesperson Darek Urbaniak lamented this influence, insisting that "some European governments have given in to Canadian and oil lobby pressure, instead of saying no to climate-hostile Tar Sands."[22]

At the start of 2014, the European Union looked set to drop the Fuel Quality Directive after 2020.[23]

The Crucial US Theatre

While the EU stance on the tar sands remains politically sensitive due to the fear of a dangerous precedent being set, it is opposition to the tar sands in the US that most concerns the Conservatives—as the US is the predominant export market. For instance, an internal March 2009 Natural Resources Canada PowerPoint presentation expressed fears that "US legislation at both federal and state levels potentially target oil sands production," while a November 2010 Foreign Affairs memo described how the tar sands industry "is under ferocious attack by the US environmental movement."[24]

To combat this opposition, the Conservative government has worked feverishly to lobby against any US legislation that might curtail tar sands expansion, guided by the US Oil Sands Advocacy Strategy. According to *Embassy*, "some suggest that the energy file is by far the biggest issue that the Canadian-US diplomatic network deals with, and consumes the most personnel and resources."[25] In August 2010, *Embassy* made a request to the Department of Foreign Affairs for a breakdown of the resources devoted to tar sands lobbying, which was rebuffed, with a department spokesperson noting: "What I can tell you is that numerous employees in the Canadian Embassy's Washington Advocacy Secretariat, which includes the Province of Alberta's office, are engaged in various aspects of energy advocacy, as is the Ambassador and other sections within the Embassy."[26]

Both *Maisonneuve* magazine and *The Tyee* have published articles detailing the extensive lobbying efforts that Gary Doer, Canada's ambassador to the US, has made on behalf of the tar sands industry. In a series dubbed "The War for the Oil Sands in Washington," *Tyee* reporter Geoff Dembicki examined how "Doer has devoted much of his professional energy to promoting the oil sands industry, flying to industry roundtables, meeting with US policymakers, and speaking to national magazines."[27]

On the legislative front, the Conservative government's first target was a law established at the end of 2007: Section 526 of the *Energy Security and Independence Act*, which is often referred to as the Waxman bill, having been introduced by Democratic congressman Henry Waxman. The Waxman bill effectively forbids government agencies—including the US military, by far the largest government purchaser—from buying oil with a larger than average carbon footprint. In response, Canadian embassy officials began strategic communications with the American Petroleum Institute and its offshoot, the Center for North American Energy Security, as well as with companies such as Exxon Mobil, BP, Chevron, Marathon, Devon, and Encana.[28] The goal was to ensure that the Waxman bill would not apply to the tar sands, as Waxman had intended. In addition to helping build a coalition of domestic oil lobbyists, the Canadian government protested the Waxman bill through diplomatic channels that stretched upwards to the US Secretary of Defense.[29]

The larger fear, as Canadian energy advisor Paul Connors put it, was that the Waxman bill "would grow into a larger debate in which the US would consider a wider LCFS [Low Carbon Fuel Standard] for transportation fuels."[30] These perceived risks grew as Barack Obama campaigned with a promise to consider just such a thing. The Conservatives lobbied against this during the election campaign, including at the Democratic National Convention. Canadian officials threatened that Canada would build a pipeline to the

Pacific Coast and sell to China and India if the US enacted legislation that impeded the importation of tar sands products.[31]

In spite of these efforts, President Obama initially appeared determined to enact legislation to measure the emissions associated with producing different types of fuel, which continued to scare both the Conservatives and the tar sands industry—who teamed up for further lobbying efforts. In December 2011, a Salon.com article detailed their success in watering down Obama's legislation, particularly the LCFS, concluding that "Canadian embassy officials worked closely with the planet's wealthiest oil companies to weaken the section's language, and in some cases, to repeal the bill entirely... helping to blunt President Obama's climate change agenda. And few outside of the Canadian embassy were any wiser."[32]

Canadian lobbying efforts in the US have extended beyond the federal government and taken aim at state policies designed to reduce carbon emissions from fuel. To the chagrin of Ottawa, in 2007 California governor Arnold Schwarzenegger signed the world's first LCFS into law. The bill mandated California's Air Resources Board to assign carbon footprints to different fuels in a bid to deter oil suppliers from using high-carbon fuel sources. According to Geoff Dembicki, Canadian officials attempted to intervene at least five times to affect how California defined its LCFS.[33] In April 2009, Canada's minister of natural resources, Lisa Raitt, wrote to Governor Schwarzenegger expressing a fear that "your LCFS regulation ... could serve as a model for other states and perhaps the US federal government," and urging "that the LCFS regulation should assign all mainstream crude oil fuel pathways the same CI [carbon intensity] rather than distinguish among different sources of crude oil."[34]

The pressure did not stop there. The Center for North American Energy Security, an organization that has worked closely with the Canadian embassy in promoting the tar sands, sued California to repeal the LCFS in conjunction with two other groups, arguing that the policy would "harm [US] energy security by discouraging the use of Canadian crude oil."[35] The first phase of the lawsuit was successful, forcing California to postpone its LCFS policy in late 2011 until it could be adjudicated at a higher court.

In 2010, the state of Wisconsin proposed an LCFS similar to California's as part of its *Clean Energy Jobs Act*, and again Canadian officials formally intervened. Appearing before Wisconsin's Senate Select Committee on Clean Energy, Canadian consul Georges Rioux appealed to US geopolitical anxieties, asking legislators to consider whether tougher fuel standards would "result in Wisconsin becoming more dependent on oil from Saudi Arabia, Iraq and Venezuela" if they cut off the supply from their "friends and allies" to the North.[36] Three months later, Wisconsin abandoned its LCFS proposal. Canadian diplomats have also lobbied state governors in opposition to LCFSs even before they had been tabled. As with the Waxman bill, the underlying fear is that any movement towards an LCFS on transportation fuel could someday develop at a national level, which could have a devastating impact on US imports of tar sands oil.

The Conservatives' lobbying efforts in the US have focused most heavily on supporting Calgary-based TransCanada's plan to build the $7 billion Keystone XL pipeline from Alberta to US refineries on the Gulf of Mexico. Much to their dismay, momentous social and environmental struggles against Keystone XL have forestalled the pipeline, as discussed elsewhere in this collection, forcing redoubled efforts. In January 2013, Canadian foreign minister John Baird said the top issue on his agenda in the US was getting Keystone XL approved. The Canadian government (as well as those of Alberta and Saskatchewan) has spent tens of millions of dollars pushing Keystone XL in a campaign that's included hiring lobbying firms, taking journalists to dinner, and purchasing ads.[37] In April 2013, Natural Resources Canada began a major advertising campaign in Washington newspapers and on public spaces near Capitol Hill. They also launched a new website targeting US audiences, which emphasized Canada as a reliable energy supplier and "world environmental leader" on energy issues. To pay for its "responsible resource development" campaign, Natural Resources Canada requested $12 million in new cash, and between 2010-11 and 2013-14, Natural Resources Canada's advertising budget increased 7,000 per cent.[38]

An important part of this campaign is lobbying visits by top Canadian officials, which cost up to $45,000 each. An April 2013 *Hill Times* article titled "Canada's Keystone XL pitch goes into overdrive" listed twenty-five visits to Washington and other US cities by Canadian ministers, deputy ministers, and provincial premiers since July 2011. This has included Prime Minister Harper directly lobbying President Obama to approve Keystone XL on a number of separate occasions. The federal government has also devoted innumerable hours of public servants' salaries to Keystone XL lobbying. In April 2013, a Foreign Affairs spokesperson told the *National Post* that a "couple dozen" staff members at the Canadian Embassy in Washington were pushing the pipeline.[39]

Outside of Washington, the twenty-two Canadian consulates in the US have also worked aggressively to secure a permit for TransCanada's pipeline. Among various other efforts, the consuls have written letters to local papers, spoken to state legislators, and accompanied governors on visits to Alberta and the tar sands. Lobbying for Keystone has been at the forefront of Ambassador Gary Doer's agenda, to the extent that TransCanada sent him a personalized thank-you note in August 2011, which expressed appreciation to Doer and his team "for all of the hard work and perseverance in helping get us this far ... it has made a big difference."[40] Doer regularly responded to critical commentary in the media and lobbied at both the national and state levels. For instance, Doer flew to Nebraska to visit the state's governor after he had come out against the pipeline (efforts that were accompanied by an extensive lobbying campaign by TransCanada). In response to the twenty-eight members of Congress who jointly expressed serious concerns about the "major environmental and health hazards" associated with Keystone XL,[41] Doer trumpeted Canada's promise to reduce overall greenhouse gas emissions 17 per cent by 2020 from the 2005 level, in blatant disregard of the fact that Canada's emissions have steadily risen, and that the sort of tar sands expansion he is advocating would make this objective impossible to reach.

Conclusion

With the tar sands industry planning to more than double total production by 2030, the Canadian government has worked hard to make sure the world accepts this carbon-heavy oil. This has entailed tens of millions of dollars in public resources spent on combatting opposition in a range of settings. In so doing, Canadian diplomacy should be seen to have become a very important lobbying arm for the tar sands industry.

5

The Environmental NGO Industry and Frontline Communities

●

DAVE VASEY

●

Introduction

There have been many calls for direct action against the tar sands. I heard my first of these during a gathering of grassroots Indigenous and non-Indigenous allies in the fall of 2008 at the Everyone's Downstream conference in Edmonton. Since then, calls for direct action have been repeated by scientists, Hollywood celebrities, and respected leftists, among many others. There has been a growing consciousness of what the tar sands really are: ecocide and industrial genocide. Tar sands activism has helped create national debates, while bringing international attention towards environmental, political, and economic conditions in the nation-state of Canada. Given the scale of the global ecological crisis unfolding around Canada, it has been heartening to witness the tar sands move from an obscure "Alberta" issue to an international one. While it is impossible to quantify the effect tar sands activism has had, a sobering reality is clear: the tar sands had expanded approximately 0.6 million barrels per day (bpd) within five years of the gathering in 2008, and the Canadian state's leadership is firmly entrenched in supporting further expansion from 1.9 million bpd in 2013 to 6.2 million bpd by 2030. Opposition is needed more than ever before.

Taking action is both a personal and political choice: people take action for different reasons. For some, this results from witnessing a family or community member die from pollution. Others are challenging the roots of capital expansion, colonialism, empire, migrant injustice, climate change, and undemocratic process. Some also seek to preserve endangered species, support Indigenous rights, and protect spiritual relationships with the land. The "why" behind direct action is infinitely complex, and so too are the "how" and "with whom." But these questions are critical in translating any reluctance into collective action.

These also are grounds for much infighting among activists. In taking action, "how" and "with whom" often reflect resources, opportunities, locations, depths of impact, socio-economic status, and preferred tactics. The current activist culture is also significantly shaped by a history of uprisings, community organizing, civil disobedience, art, and popular and political education. My personal priority is to support community struggles and recognize how organizing reflects a deep historical narrative, in which tactics are in tune with the needs of people and the planet. I do not subscribe to the idea that there is any one path to achieving change; rather, I recognize the influence of a diverse history of activism.

In the nation-state of Canada, the complex terrain of environmental activism is heavily influenced by both capital and popular movements for change. Understanding the history of relationships within environmental organizing can help build the proverbial bridges required to create a movement that stops the expansion of tar sands, and protects people and the planet. Much has been much written by Macdonald Stainsby, Dru Oja Jay, Sandra Cuffe, Dawn Paley, and others about the influence of foundational funding on environmental non-governmental organizations (ENGOs) and tar sands campaigns.[1] This chapter is an effort to contribute to a historical understanding of ENGOs and grassroots relationships by looking at outcomes of those relationships for communities and larger movement building.

There is some speculation that a deal similar to the Canadian Boreal Forest Agreement may be struck regarding the tar sands. ENGOs maintain that the tar sands are a "line in the sand" and that no deal will be struck with industry. Given the stakes involved for the climate and for people—particularly future generations—it is encouraging to hear ENGOs take such a stand on the tar sands. At the same time, it is important to recognize how, in 2010, ENGOs accepted and endorsed the logging of vast tracts of land when they signed the Canadian Boreal Forest Agreement with industrial logging companies. In addition, they agreed to work with industry to "bridge the gap" between activists and industry, which involved opposing community struggles. Some bridges don't need to be built, and prioritizing relationships with industry over frontline communities was a critical mistake for ENGOs. This helped industry create the social consent required for public relations, despite widespread opposition by many grassroots and First Nations activists.[2]

While Greenpeace and Canopy withdrew from the agreement, many saw the move as too little too late, and held that, had voices from the frontlines of the environmental justice (EJ) movement been included in decision-making, the agreement would not have been signed in the first place. In this chapter, I look at tensions and spaces of shared interest between the ENGOs and grassroots EJ models of organizing against ecological destruction. After a brief explanation of each model, I will sketch a path towards a renewal of the relationship between established ENGOs and grassroots activism.

Two Models of Environmental Organizing

Traditional environmental organizing tended to seek the protection of wilderness and endangered species, largely by courting support from white, upper- and middle-class conservationists. In conservation narratives, landscapes would be protected for recreation, biodiversity, and heritage, though the land-based relationships of Indigenous peoples were rarely considered in the heritage narratives. In contrast, EJ organizers have often attempted to integrate anti-colonial and anti-capitalist principles into their efforts, while ENGOs have maintained distance from these radical critiques.[3] A grassroots social justice orientation has also distinguished EJ mobilizations from the lobbying orientation of conservation groups. Such divisions are part of a wider gulf between EJ activists and ENGOs.

To understand these tensions, we need to look at some of the changes in environmental organizing over the past few decades. In the late 1970s and early 1980s, a fundamentally different concept of environmental threats came to popular consciousness under the term *environmental racism*. In the early 1980s, the struggle of community members in Warren County, North

Carolina, against the North Carolina government's decision to locate a poly-chlorinated biphenyl dumpsite next to a predominantly black neighbour-hood highlighted the relationship between environmental risk and race.[4] Warren County residents merged tactics from the civil rights movement with environmental discourse as they responded to environmental hazards in their community as a form of racial injustice. These efforts helped to alert researchers to the pattern—soon to be widely documented—of disproportion-ate environmental burdens being imposed on the neighbourhoods of people of colour and low-income residents.[5] This pattern has included the siting of toxic waste dumps and high-pollution industries. In 1983, the United Church of Christ commissioned the *Fauntroy* report, and in 1987, the *Toxic Wastes and Race in the United States* report.[6] Both reports observed how race was the single largest factor in relation to the locations of hazardous waste sites in the US. These reports—with the subsequent *Environmental Justice Principles* at the First National People of Color Environmental Leadership Summit in Washington, DC, in 1991—became the basis for environmental justice movements in the US.[7]

This activism demonstrated how grassroots EJ organizing could be grounded in local communities. It also indirectly revealed a gulf between established ENGOs and people of colour. In 1990, grassroots EJ organizers confronted the largest and most well-funded environmental organizations, known as the "Group of Ten," regarding the exclusion of people of colour from staff positions in ENGOs. They also highlighted how some groups relied on funds from extractive industries that were having a direct impact on communities of colour. And they chastised ENGOs for participating in the annexation of Indigenous lands for conservation initiatives. The letter demanded that these organizations cease their organizing or fundraising in communities of colour:

> Although environmental organizations calling themselves the "Group of Ten" often claim to represent our interests, in observing your activities it has become clear to us that your organizations play an equal role in the disruption of our communities. There is a clear lack of accountability by the Group of Ten environmental organizations towards Third World communities in the Southwest, in the United States as a whole, and internationally.[8]

In response to the EJ-based critique of the Group of Ten organizations, many ENGOs attempted to make changes to their approach. For instance, they began to talk about environmental racism, and, increasingly, they began to highlight Indigenous concerns as well as narrowly conservationist ones. In some cases, they began to seek partnerships with Indigenous organizations. A standing critique is that these changes were superficial: they were more a matter of updating their rhetoric, without necessarily becoming any less distant from grassroots struggles and frontline communities.

One side of the limitations of the dominant ENGO approach is the failure of mainstream environmentalism to challenge neo-liberal capitalism. Neo-liberalism is a type of capitalism with extensive government support, in the form of deregulation, privatization, and reducing government intervention, while expanding the role of markets in economic life. The logic of neo-liberalism holds that the free market will respond to the environmental and social needs of the public by creating new technologies or services. Both Rodriguez and McMichael contend that what they describe as the "NGO industrial complex" reinforces neo-liberal capitalism, as ENGOs fill a market role of assuaging public guilt for social or environmental destruction without challenging the root issue of capitalism.[9] Simply put, many ENGOs profit from selling stories of environmental destruction and token reforms to the public. Rodriguez further notes that the appropriation of frontline voices reinforces colonial frameworks, where largely white actors dictate and influence campaigns, and frontline voices at times become campaign props.

Recognizing the significance of these ENGOs, Gereffi and colleagues associate the rise of environmentalism with increased corporate influence over regulatory frames, given how policy changes have been strongly influenced by industry lobbyists and business-friendly politicians.[10] By grassroots standards, ENGOs can seem well resourced, yet they have little capacity to compete with big business for influence within the confines of lobbying efforts inside the official political process. When they buy into the lobbying process as the only game in town, ENGOs, in effect, allow corporate advocacy groups and industry lobbyists, with their massive budgets and unmatched capacity to buy influence with politicians, to shift the location of the debate over policy onto terrain that is especially favourable for corporations.

Health or environmental hazards are measured against "cost-benefit" models, and a heavy focus on generating profit allows for the sacrifice of communities and lands whenever doing so is deemed "economically neces-sary." Hence, ENGO campaigns for renewable energies have been classified as "unprofitable," while anti–wind turbine campaigns—organized by a vocal minority who are supported by the oil industry—have had more suc-cess lobbying governments about the health concerns of wind than anti–tar᾿ sands activists have done in the face of the ongoing ecocide and industrial genocide for downstream communities. It seems out of place for ENGOs to promote green energy in the face of long-term neo-liberal policy reform, and these organizations have failed to compete with fossil fuel industry lobbies. Moreover, when positive policy gains have been made, government and industry have largely abdicated responsibility for enforcement (even for weak targets), or they have treated pollution fines as a cost of doing business.

Today, ENGO campaigns have retained key features that are at the root of the tensions with grassroots campaigning: the bureaucratic and top-down organizing style; accountability to campaign funders rather than affected communities; the narrow focus on the official policy-making process; and the single-issue (non-systemic) approach to popular education. Below, I will discuss the case of the Great Bear Rainforest campaign in British Columbia. Throughout this chapter, I indicate how ENGOs have, for the most part, shied away from anything that might smack of anti-capitalism, and even from identifying corporate power and profit maximization as central to the prob-lems that they claim to address. On the contrary, many have embraced the frameworks of "green capitalism" or "ethical consumerism"—no doubt, in part, to appease funders and reassure policy-makers of their respectability.

ENGOs' Failure to Address Colonialism and Environmental Racism

In Canada, ENGOs have begun to recognize how resource extraction is a racialized issue, in which business priorities outweigh concerns about the pollution and destruction wrought on First Nations communities. In 2001, the Ministry of Natural Resources estimated that over twelve hundred Indigenous communities lived within two hundred kilometres of mining operations.[11] Furthermore, the Assembly of First Nations reported that 36 per cent of First Nations communities lived within fifty kilometres of mining developments and associated pollution zones in 2001.[12] As Haluza-DeLay and colleagues note, Indigenous peoples are the most oppressed group in

Canada, and they have faced pressure to assimilate into capitalist economies and "develop" resources in ways that are antithetical to traditional values.[13] Haluza-DeLay and colleagues discuss the complexity of issues facing Indigenous communities:

> The specific history of resource development and its place in regional and national economies also makes for specifically Canadian forms of environmental justice issues.... Aboriginal peoples are faced with systemic environmental injustice in terms of treaty and land claims processes; ... energy projects ...; air, water and land pollution; ... deplorable drinking water issues [and] resource extraction by outsiders on unceded territory by government sanctioned contracts ... ; the failure by the Canadian state to recognize underlying and unalienable Aboriginal title and rights; and the unwillingness of the Canadian state to right historical wrongs to First Peoples.[14]

Despite increased awareness and the incorporation of EJ frames and community concerns into their messaging, ENGOs have been criticized for the appropriation of community voices and accountability to funders that are linked to Big Oil, among other questionable industries.[15] At the community level, First Nations motivations for resisting resource developments tend to be highly differentiated from ENGOs. Given how traditional Indigenous lifestyles have been undercut or eliminated, many communities require consideration of socio-economic needs, and at times, associated dependency on industry funds. There are few resources for community activists, and many at the grassroots in tar sands–affected communities have questioned why the millions of dollars that ENGOs spend on tar sands campaigns have not been put towards mobilizing frontline and impacted FN communities, or advocating treaty rights, basic health studies, or reparations for ecological destruction.

During the 1980s and 1990s "war in the woods" in British Columbia, FN communities encountered difficulties when engaging with ENGOs to amplify their campaigns to protect forests from industrial logging.[16] These campaigns succeeded in receiving international attention; however, during that time, local voices felt manipulated to fit ENGO narratives, which often positioned Indigenous peoples as spokespersons to press but not as organizers, and failed to recognize the socio-economic needs FN communities articulated.[17] Stainsby and Oja Jay characterize ENGO organizing with FN people during the Great Bear Rainforest campaign as damaging, given how ENGOs, in collaboration with industry and the provincial government, negotiated settlements without community input or consent.[18] Several ENGOs had been involved in blockading roads with First Nations, yet, in 2000, these same organizations were part of an about-face negotiation with government that excluded grassroots and First Nations activists, effectively terminating direct action capacity. The abdication of democratic process upset many community members, who felt they had been alienated from power and decision-making, and quite literally were left alone on the road.

Following the negotiated settlement between the BC government, industry, and ENGOs—known as the Great Bear Rainforest Agreement (GBRA)— some BC First Nations became involved in proposals for "decentralized governance."[19] A series of co-management projects was created to reconcile Indigenous-government relations throughout BC (and indeed, Canada). The earliest project created was the Interim Measurements Agreement (IMA) with the Nuu-chah-nulth First Nation and the BC government. ENGOs worked closely with the Nuu-chah-nulth community during the "war in the woods" in BC in the 1980s and 1990s. Prior to the IMA, the Central Regional Board was created as a "consensus-based" decision-making body representing both government and the Nuu-chah-nulth peoples to determine co-management recommendations. Decentralization ostensibly facilitates shared decision-making between communities, ENGOs, government, and industry interests. However, resources and structures to support communities through this process were extremely limited. Moreover, reaching "consensus" between industry and FN communities created scenarios in which industry simply withheld support for solutions until bottom-line economic objectives were met.

The term *procedural injustice* helps to explain how communities are marginalized in decentralized governance processes. Procedural injustice refers to the inequities of access to the resources and knowledge needed to participate fully in decision-making processes, where underfunded and under-staffed communities are expected to keep pace with industry and government timelines. Often, discussions are framed in highly academic language, and community participation requires a "learn as you go" approach, with a further burden of translating academic discussions for community members.[20] Mabee and Hoberg characterized the aforementioned decentralized governance in

Nuu-chah-nulth territory as a failed strategy for FN political goals, reporting that "when asked whether First Nations were equal partners in *decision-making*, the majority of First Nations and government interviewees answered with a qualified 'no'"[21] (emphasis added). However, the GBRA has been heralded as a "model" for settling resource disputes by ENGOs, government, and industry.[22] Despite widespread critique of the GBRA, the Canadian Boreal Forest Agreement reinforced models of decentralized governance in a similar collaboration between ENGOs, industry, and government.

The aforementioned patterns can be expected to recur if ENGOs do not pose enough of a challenge to industries, or to capitalist economics more broadly. When operating within the structures of capital, there has been little incentive for ENGOs to challenge wealth accumulation. Instead, many have emulated "growth through profit" models. Many ENGOs working on tar sands campaigns derive substantial funding from Pew Charitable Trusts, a foundation with explicit links to tar sands giant Suncor.[23] To expand ENGO budgets, campaign pitches must ultimately entice Pew board members—who include former oil executives—and there is a great paradox as Big Oil funds its own dissent. Thus, when they compete for funding, ENGOs are often limited to the terms set by funders, rather than the needs of larger social movements or frontline communities.

Even direct action has remained largely focused on media attention and accountability to funders, rather than community empowerment. Despite widespread environmental concerns in civil society, ENGOs have failed to advance a vision to structurally reorient the Canadian state's economy away from ecologically destructive capitalism. Rather, ENGO mitigation strategies for tar sands tend to involve green energy, much as they did in the 1970s.[24] Repeating this narrative for over forty years has done little to shift government or industry decisions away from resource extraction in Canada, or indeed globally. Moreover, the full scope of these issues is usually not recognized by ENGOs or messaged to ENGO supporters.

Reorienting ENGOs: Potential Collaborations

Mistrust and hostility between ENGOs and grassroots activists have been part of a rift between highly competent organizers, while expansion of the tar sands has continued under one of the most far-right governments in the world. In May 2012, David Suzuki suggested that environmentalism had failed because the "environment" has been framed as a special lobby pitted against economic interests. Suzuki notes that:

> In creating dedicated departments, we made the environment another special interest, like education, health, and agriculture. The environment subsumes every aspect of our activities, but we failed to make the point that our lives, health, and livelihoods absolutely depend on the biosphere—air, water, soil, sunlight, and biodiversity. Without them, we sicken and die. This perspective is reflected in spiritual practices that understand that everything is inter-connected, as well as traditional societies that revere "Mother Earth" as the source of all that matters in life.[25]

The structures of capitalism are so violent and irrational that attempts to gain appeal within them exclude advocacy for the dissolution of the state and financial system, despite how these core values are required to stop "growth" models and empower self-determining bioregional communities. Indeed, ENGOs generally are proposing "green capitalist" alternatives to the tar sands (such as industrial solar farms), which would not overcome the macro issues of wealth polarization, racism, sexism, food insecurity, or health issues (both mental and physical) that are products of both capitalism generally, and the destruction caused by the tar sands industry specifically. Moreover, by not responding to these issues, and failing to integrate them into their analysis, ENGOs have failed to tap into an array of motivations that could mobilize the public to take action for land defence and community autonomy.

Yet, while it is important to hold ENGOs accountable, it is also import-ant to seek common ground with them. The scale of the ecological crisis necessitates that our collective focus remain on stopping industry and gov-ernment from committing further ecocide and genocide, and not on tearing each other apart. ENGOs have contributed significantly to public education on the tar sands, and many have worked with community members seeking to bring attention to environmental injustice. Several ENGOs have had staff and volunteers on the frontlines of direct action, and others have adopted the principle that communities should tell their own story. Given that the Harper regime has eliminated most of the past legislative environmental victories in a few short years, arguments for maintaining credibility through participating in lobbying efforts are increasingly recognized as hollow. So where do we go from here?

Drawing from centuries of resistance, many FN activists frame their campaigns with an analysis of colonialism, capitalism, and environmental justice. Importantly, rather than excluding ENGOs, some First Nations and grassroots activists have sought to reorient relationships so that these organizations might recognize community self-determination and sovereignty. Clayton Thomas-Muller, of the Mathias Colomb Cree Nation (Pukatawagan) in northern Manitoba and co-director of the Indigenous Tar Sands Campaign, observes:

> There is a potential now for a broad social movement that issues a challenge to Canadian capitalism, colonialism, and ecological destruction that is as profound as the broadest social movements of the past 40 years. Part of developing this movement is creating spaces for Indigenous communities to share experiences with each other and strategize together outside of government created bureaucracies. Also important is the creation of a large body of supporters who are able to articulate and understand the issues, and intervene in ways that support, rather than bar, the formation of a broader movement.[26]

Such synergies can be seen as part of the more radical and grassroots EJ critiques and mobilizing. In this chapter, I have focused on the orientation of the more promising forms of EJ organizing. However, one should not oversimplify the contrast between the two models I have focused on here. We should recognize how environmental justice language has sometimes been co-opted by bureaucratic ENGOs, as well as governments. For instance, in the early 1990s, documents from the Clinton administration in the US included nods to environmental justice language.[27] Nevertheless, the EJ movement's original community-based organizing has remained active and intact.

But we can also look to other promising examples of movement building in so-called Canada. The Toronto G20 mobilization, Occupy, Quebec's student strike, and Idle No More movements have been consistent with radical grassroots EJ organizing principles, in that these mobilizations have favoured community-led decision-making, direct action, and popular education focused on issues of capitalism and colonialism (among many others). What was achieved by these movements in terms of raising consciousness has yet to be determined. These networks and campaigns have collectively mobilized hundreds of thousands against neo-liberalism (most strongly in Quebec), and have gained attention from millions. For example, the student strike opposed tuition increases, which amount to remaking students into consumers. It is also noteworthy that a significant portion of the supporters of these movements believes that direct action is necessary. Moreover, many supporters view police repression, deregulation, and corporate influence on policy and economics as attacks on democracy—politically, legally, and in terms of human rights. Tactically, grassroots organizers have engaged social and economic disruption in the spirit of the civil rights movement, as they have placed strong pressures on government to deal with crisis issues of poverty, treaty rights, and environmental destruction (among other issues) within the Canadian state through diverse tactics.

Popular movements, such as Occupy and Idle No More, have at times articulated explicitly anti-capitalist and anti-colonial goals and concerns, and they have often prioritized the inclusion of those who are most affected by neo-liberalism and neo-colonialism in both their messaging and decision-making. In addition, these movements have engaged in actions that have captured the popular imagination through complex frames that, at their best, seek the emancipation of all peoples regardless of race, class, ability, gender, and orientation, while contributing significantly to discussions about capitalism and colonialism. Moreover, strong stands taken in Elsipogtog in eastern Canada, and from many other First Nations in the wake of Idle No More, all have demonstrated that resolve, courage, and networks of support can stop projects.

However, in the face of state repression, grassroots movements have also been unable to overcome systemic conditions, even when they have attempted to challenge them. Nevertheless, it is still possible for us to collectively move towards the threshold of change. Integrating ENGO resources, experience, and knowledge with grassroots ideology, organizing structures, and narratives could provide the synergy needed to do the long-term organizing required to shut down tar sands projects. If ENGOs can bring their activities into alignment with popular movements mobilizing for environmental justice, we can better directly challenge and confront business and government. As Antonio Machado wrote, "Wanderer, your footsteps are the road, and nothing more; wanderer, there is no road, the road is made by walking."[28] To stop the tar sands, let's walk together.

6

Canada's Eastward Pipelines

A Corporate Export Swindle, Confronted by Cross-Country Resistance

●

MARTIN LUKACS

•

Introduction

The defeat went barely noticed by the media. Amid the rolling hills of Quebec's lush farm and wine region, the small town of Dunham had beaten back oil giants.

Companies like Enbridge and the owners of Portland-Montreal Pipe Line—namely Imperial Oil, Suncor, and Shell—have been trying to construct a pumping station to pipe heavy crude over a nearby mountain range. The infrastructure is integral to Enbridge's plans to ship Alberta tar sands, via Quebec, to the eastern coast of the United States. But when Enbridge quietly initiated this project in 2008, a coalition of local farmers, residents, and environmentalists formed in opposition. They marched, launched legal challenges, and organized Canada's first UK-inspired climate camp, which culminated in promises of civil disobedience.[1]

The oil companies fought back in court. Enbridge dropped the project's initial name—"Trailbreaker"—in an attempt to fool residents into thinking they had abandoned their wider plans to ship Alberta tar sands eastward. The federal government even dispatched spies to intimidate community organizers. But, ground down by Dunham's efforts, the companies withdrew in July 2013. They still want a pumping station in Quebec; they just won't be able to build it in this town.

The triumph may herald the fate of two massive tar sands pipeline projects that loom over central and eastern Canada. The first is Enbridge's now-unnamed plan, which involves reversing a network of pipelines that currently carry African and European oil from the East Coast to western Canada. This could bring up to three hundred thousand barrels of Alberta tar sands oil daily to the US seaboard, via the Enbridge Line 9 pipeline in Ontario and western Quebec, as well as the Portland-Montreal Pipe Line, which runs between Montreal and the coast of Maine.[2] The other plan is TransCanada's recently announced Energy East project, a $12 billion investment to convert a natural gas pipeline and build an extension in the provinces of Quebec and New Brunswick. It could ship as many as 1.1 million barrels per day to Canada's coast. Covering 4,400 kilometres, it would require the construction of 1,400 kilometres of new pipeline.[3] Both projects would traverse some of the most densely populated areas in the country.

False Promises

Business leaders, politicians, and the mainstream media have intoned patriotically about the potential boost these projects will bring to the prosperity and energy security of Canadians. "This is truly a nation-building project that will diversify our economy and create new jobs here in Alberta and across the country," Alberta's then-premier Alison Redford declared about Energy East.[4] "Each of these enterprises required innovative thinking and a strong belief that building critical infrastructure ties our country together, making it stronger and more in control of our own destiny," added TransCanada CEO Russ Girling.[5]

The exercise in flag-waving is intended to sell a single idea: that the interests of oil companies are the same as those of the population at large. But if the soaring rhetoric is an indication of anything, it is the growing desperation of Alberta's oil barons and their allies in government. With a protest movement having (so far) blocked the construction of TransCanada's Keystone XL pipeline south to the Gulf Coast, and Enbridge's Gateway pipeline west to the Pacific, Alberta's oil companies are sitting on top of a lot of landlocked bitumen. And as their crude sells at a reduced price, they are losing billions in profit.[6]

Thus, the frantic drive for an eastern ocean distribution route has nothing to do with the needs of ordinary Canadians: it is an export plan to serve the corporate bottom line. Once the crude reaches the coast, it will fetch higher prices on the world market and go to the highest bidder—the United States, Europe, India, or China. Nor will these tar sands solve Canadians' need for energy security: as Canada's oil prices align with the world's, consumers at the pump may pay even more.

If the oil companies will capture the benefits, everyone else will carry the risks. To start with, tar sands crude is much more corrosive. An international expert on pipeline safety has concluded that there is a "high risk" that Enbridge's pipeline will rupture because of cracking and corrosion.[7] TransCanada's pipeline, built in the 1950s, is even older. The Gulf of St. Lawrence and the Bay of Fundy, rich ecosystems on which fishing and tourism depend, would be threatened by toxic bitumen. These waters should be protected as a public trust, not exploited as a tanker transit route.

The economic consequences are just as drastic. Every pipeline that is built will further lock Canada into a state of dependency on the export of bitumen, a classic "staples trap" that will weaken an economy that relies on extractive industries. Canada's petro-dollar has already hollowed out its manufacturing core, destroying hundreds of thousands of jobs. And new pipelines will also lock Canada into carbon-intensive production, at exactly the moment when other countries are transitioning to low-carbon energy and preparing to mitigate the impacts of climate change.[8]

In other words, these are not pipelines to build a nation. They are a scheme by which to swindle it.

The flimsiness of their case has forced the oil barons to resort to other tactics. To split labour unions away from the opposition, TransCanada and Enbridge have taken to making inflated claims about the jobs that might be created. Their template is being drawn from the fight over Keystone XL in the United States, during which TransCanada promised as many as twenty thousand to forty thousand jobs. When economists crunched the figures, they landed on a different total: as few as a thousand temporary jobs, and only twenty permanent ones.[9]

Neither company appears to be shying away from conflicts of interest— they seem, in fact, to depend on them. The media has reported that Enbridge is handing out "donations" to municipalities along the path of its Line 9 pipeline, including $44,000 to a police station in Hamilton, Ontario.[10] This practice is better described by a simpler term: bribery. And TransCanada has hired a company to lead their lobbying charge in Quebec. Who else have they worked for? The same municipalities they intended to lobby.

Prospects for Opposition

Those opposed to the pipelines must do a better job of countering business proponents, who have suggested that if the Enbridge pipeline is not approved, it would be a "clear signal" that "no economic development [is] possible in Quebec."[11] Such fear mongering about how action on climate change would bring about an economic Armageddon have become common, though no less effective. A local of the Communications, Energy, and Paperworkers (CEP) union in Quebec—now a branch of the new union Unifor—joined a business coalition in supporting the pipeline, hoping that a few hundred refining jobs in Montreal will be revived.[12] CEP has argued for the refining of bitumen in Canada instead of exporting abroad, and thus joined the movement against Keystone XL and the Northern Gateway pipeline. But both labour and other voices must do better at highlighting the importance of building economic alternatives into the movement against pipelines, an omission that marked the battle against the Keystone XL, and allowed some US labour leaders to stridently attack the environmentalists leading that campaign.

In Quebec and elsewhere, the movement needs to confront the right-wing narrative on these issues by arguing the facts: investment in a green industrial transition will bring far more jobs—secure, ecological, and socially useful jobs—relative to investment in the infrastructure needed to develop the tar sands.[13] Pipelines will create only a few jobs and huge private-sector profits, while burdening the public with long-term environmental damage. The movement must demand loudly that the same workers who shouldn't be building pipelines or staffing refineries should instead receive good, high-paying jobs, albeit jobs that simultaneously address climate change: retrofitting homes and buildings, erecting high-speed rail and public transit, and building infrastructure to protect against the storms ahead.[14]

Whatever the limitations of existing campaigns, the pipeline struggles have had an electrifying impact on organizing across Canada. As pipelines have become the most visible—and vulnerable—instruments disfiguring the country's environment, economy, and democracy, they have spawned an unprecedented development: wherever they have been proposed, their path traces the outlines of a new resistance. Through the summer months of 2013 alone, there were protests in Winnipeg, an occupation in southern Ontario, mobilizations in Ottawa and Toronto, and blockades in New England. The only "nation-building" occurring appears to be a coast-to-coast movement of opposition.

While the resistance in Dunham, Quebec, was the earliest to appear against Enbridge's eastern pipeline project, it was soon followed by organizing among cities and First Nations communities in southern Ontario. More specifically, organizing has been underway in different boroughs of Toronto, in cities such as Guelph and Kingston, and on Six Nations territory. The regional campaigning against the project has consisted of a set of local campaigns. When locals initiated a six-day blockade of an Enbridge pumping station along the Line in Hamilton in 2013, they were actively supported by activists across southern Ontario. At the western end of Enbridge Line 9, Aamjiwnaang First Nation has been at the centre of other regional protest efforts. This Native community is located within Sarnia in the middle of so-called "Chemical Valley," one of the most toxic industrial zones in North America (see chapter

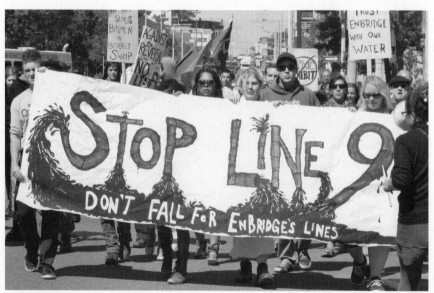

A Swamp Line 9 rally in Hamilton, Ontario, 2013.

13). In 2013, non-Native organizers were drawn to Sarnia for two regional strategy sessions and protests. Campaigners opposing Enbridge's plans for Line 9 have often stressed the importance of treaty and Aboriginal rights in opposing the shipment of tar sands crude. Indigenous rights pose the biggest obstacle to Canada's reckless resource extraction agenda—and organizing that prioritizes these rights offers a model for organizers elsewhere.

Across the US border, in New England, opposition has also been mounting, building off a rich and varied tradition of environmental and anti-nuclear organizing.[15] The Portland-Montreal pipeline, constructed in the 1950s, currently pumps about 400,000 barrels of overseas oil a day from Portland, Maine, and then up through Canada—but it will be reversed as part of Enbridge's plans to bring oil from the West in Alberta. Environmentalists have closely tracked these plans, and organizing was catalyzed by meetings between activists from Dunham, Quebec, and Vermont and Maine. In February 2013, some two thousand people marched out onto the pier in Portland from where the tar sands would be shipped. A month later, almost thirty Vermont towns became "tar sands–free zones," passing resolutions against the transport of tar sands through the state in town-hall meetings that are part of a storied, direct democratic tradition dating back hundreds of years. (In the early 1980s, close to two hundred towns in the state passed resolutions for a nuclear weapons freeze, boosting the national anti-nuclear movement.)

But it is the movement simmering in Quebec that may ultimately be the most fiery, and decisive. In the spring and summer of 2011, Quebec residents mobilized for one of the world's only moratoriums on shale gas exploitation. On Earth Day in April 2013, nearly fifty thousand people marched through Montreal, with a main demand of rejecting the transport of tar sands through the province. Polls regularly indicate that a majority of Quebecers have serious objections to the idea.[16] And in the summer of 2013, Quebec's population was still reeling from the explosion of a train carrying fracked shale oil through the town of Lac-Mégantic. The incident left forty-seven people dead—casualties of deregulation and a boom in dirty, unconventional energy. Quebecers may have to pay the $200 million cleanup costs themselves, after the US company responsible declared bankruptcy to avoid liability.

The former Parti Québécois (PQ) government extended a moratorium on shale gas projects, but their stance on tar sands shipments was in keeping with the close links between top party members and the oil and gas industry.

Environment minister Daniel Breton briefly made waves when he harshly criticized the idea of shipping tar sands through Quebec and promised to closely scrutinize the plan. But a few weeks later—the same day that Enbridge filed an application for their pipeline with Canada's federal energy regulatory body—Quebec's premier, Pauline Marois, booted Breton out of her cabinet. "A total coincidence," insisted an Enbridge spokesman.[17]

In the face of mounting opposition, the Quebec government initially promised a public consultation on the Enbridge pipeline, though not on TransCanada. But it proved to be a charade, as Quebec's parliamentary commission gave a green light to the reversal of Line 9 in early 2014 (which was soon followed by the National Energy Board's approval of the reversal of Line 9 in Ontario and Quebec).[18] The fact that a Quebec nationalist premier has rarely caved in such a brazen way to the interests of oil corporations and the federal government will no doubt rile much of the Quebec sovereigntist population.[19] Unfortunately, the two parties to the PQ's right—the Liberal Party and Coalition Avenir Québec—are worse on the question of the pipelines, supporting both Enbridge and TransCanada's projects.

The movement in Quebec has the chance to achieve more than just blocking tar sands pipeline projects in the province. It could set an inspiring international precedent by winning a moratorium on the exploitation and shipment of all extreme fossil fuels, extending the existing moratorium on shale gas by adding to it both tar sands and oil shale, which companies are exploring on Anticosti Island in the Gulf of St. Lawrence. It is a positive sign that the Regroupement interrégional gaz de schiste de la vallée du St-Laurent—the anti–shale gas coalition that includes more than a hundred citizen groups—has changed its mandate to actively oppose all extreme energy sources, including the tar sands pipelines.

For now, the anti–tar sands movement in the province awaits the kind of proactive strategy that was provided for the anti–shale gas movement by the grassroots group Moratoire d'une génération (One-Generation Moratorium). That group issued an ultimatum to the government, completed a six-hundred-kilometre walk across the province, and trained for and promised sustained civil disobedience—galvanizing the movement and prompting the government to respond with a moratorium.[20]

While mainstream Quebec environmental organizations like Équiterre have laid important educational and media groundwork in the campaign against the tar sands pipelines, a lot will depend on grassroots and rural groups who could generate a plan for coordinated, escalating direct action, much like the campaign against Dunham's pumping station, on a province-wide scale.

If that can happen, the victory over the oil barons that has been celebrated in the little Quebec farm and wine town will not be the last.

7

Migrant Justice and the Tar Sands Industry

●

INTERVIEW WITH HARSHA WALIA BY
JOSHUA KAHN RUSSELL

●

Can you provide background and context to migrant worker struggles in the tar sands?

In recent decades, Canada has shifted from something of a mixed manufacturing and extraction economy to one almost entirely driven by resource exploitation through oil, gas, coal, fracking, mineral mining, and logging industries. This happens locally within its borders on Indigenous lands—for example, the Alberta tar sands—as well as across its borders throughout the Global South. For example, 75 per cent of global exploration and mining projects are headquartered in Canada.[1]

As manufacturing jobs were outsourced to the Global South to find cheaper pools of labour, resource-extractive industries required an "insourcing" of cheap labour to work in the dangerous production of dirty energy and the economy around it. This led to a drastic surge in Canada's temporary foreign worker program, bringing in hundreds of thousands of migrant workers. Migrant workers are the flipside of outsourcing; they are essentially the same labour pool as those who are working in sweatshops, call centres, and factories across the Global South to fill the consumption needs of the Global North and the global elite. They work without health and safety protections, their pay is less than minimum wage, they are often forced to live in dangerous and isolated work camps, they are legally tied down and indentured to a single employer, and their legal immigration status is temporary and precarious. They are perpetually displaceable and deportable, living in the shadows and invisible to most Canadians.

In Canada, there is an overwhelming public belief that most people who come here have the right to permanent residency—that it's a "country of immigrants." This benevolent multicultural myth erases both the reality of settler-colonialism and the genocide of Indigenous peoples, as well as the long and ongoing history of indentured stolen labour. This is particularly true in the current context. For the past few years, Canada has accepted more migrant workers than permanent residents. This shift is most pronounced in resource-extractive economies, such as in the provinces of British Columbia and Alberta, where an entire petro-economy relies on the exploitable labour of migrant workers both in oil fields and in the associated service sector.

Temporary workers are therefore a state-sanctioned federal program of indentured labour. They are similar to the US's "guest worker programs." In a number of bilateral meetings, US representatives have looked to Canada's long-standing migrant worker program as the model to follow because it is a perfect way to contain and manage migration—commodify a certain class of migrants for their labour, use them, exploit them, bleed them, grant them no basic services, enforce conditions of servitude, and then remove them. And because the workers are essentially tied to and tracked by their employer, there is less chance of mobility, and of building community and resistance.

What are some ways the exploitation and invisibility of migrant workers operate in the tar sands?

The number of temporary workers in Alberta is skyrocketing. In 2008, there was more than a 55 per cent jump from the year before.[2] The structural invisibility and isolation of migrant worker communities, combined with the lack of monitoring and data from the companies that employ them, makes it very difficult to know in detail what the conditions of migrant workers in the tar sands are. If migrant workers speak out against their horrendous working or living conditions, they can be deported immediately without the ability to return, or put on blacklists.

Yet, even in the context of this reprisal and intimidation, there were over eight hundred complaints from migrant workers in a single year in Alberta, signalling how pervasive and endemic the abuse is.[3] This situation of migrant workers in the tar sands garnered some national attention in 2007, when four migrants were critically injured and two Chinese workers died in an SSEC Canada facility.[4] There was a record of over fifty workplace charges laid, but the company got away with pleading guilty to only three of the charges. Only a few weeks after the workers' deaths, at the very same worksite, another tanker collapsed, despite there being a "no work order" due to the deaths. It is illustrative of the political conditions in which these companies operate: people die, and there are no meaningful repercussions. We know that the fossil fuel and extractive industries generally operate with impunity. Yet migrant worker programs allow this level of impunity to skyrocket because companies can hire an inherently exploitable seasonal labour pool without rights and support systems and who labour under conditions of transient servitude.

These structural dynamics make it important to clarify the politics of environmental and labour movements with relation to migrant workers. In the labour movement, many unions are speaking out against migrant worker programs because they see migrant workers as "stealing Canadian jobs." Their analysis and practice is less focused on the exploitation of migrant workers or organizing with them, and more concerned with the loss of employment for "real Canadians." The Alberta Federation of Labour, for example, has fluctuated on the issue of migrant workers in the tar sands. Generally, they are opposed to migrant worker programs and have done commendable, extensive work to highlight the deplorable working conditions. But recently, in at least two high-profile incidents,[5] they also spoke out against the "displacement" of Canadian workers by migrant workers in the tar sands.

This approach needs to be challenged, because it signals a "race to the bottom": laying off union workers to bring in precarious labour is a way for the government and big business to dismantle workers' rights across the board. If we don't recognize the economic and social conditions that make migrant workers vulnerable in the first place, we further marginalize and isolate them with divisive rhetoric, which is also, frankly, quite entitled and

ALLAN LISSNER

Mining justice activists from Papua New Guinea and Canada demonstrate in Toronto, Ontario, 2010.

racist. Union politics of "protectionism" in this era of austerity and scarcity mean that migrant workers of colour, rather than the state and capital, get scapegoated as the problem.

Many people within the mainstream environmental movement simply portray workers as "apathetic" or "greedy," happy to make money off the destruction their work involves them in, in the tar sands and elsewhere. At the same time, many environmentalists pay little attention to the fact that it is CEOs and other executives, who do not work in the most toxic sites in the tar sands, who are the culprits—not the workers they exploit to fuel their operations. The failure to understand the intersection of the state, colonialism, labour, capital, and impoverishment contributes to a massive gap in concrete data about the toxic conditions these workers face, and further perpetuates structural divisions between movements and communities. In the case of migrant workers in the tar sands, it is not as if they do not care about the toxic or climate impacts of the industry; instead, we must recognize that they are forced into working conditions where they are brought in for brief periods of time, restricted from knowledge about the impacts on their own health and on the land, and left isolated. A clear illustration of the need to confront divisions between environmentalists and workers can be seen in my experience on the Healing Walk in 2013 (see chapter 12). As we proceeded down the highway, we passed two buses of all people of colour—so presumably, migrant workers—banging on the windows in a show of support.

While environmental activists seeking out alliances with labour unions is generally a positive shift, there has to be caution about whom these unions represent and whether migrant workers are included within the framework of "labour-environmental alliances." I would argue that they overwhelmingly are not, which further perpetuates the hegemony of large environmental NGOs and union bureaucracies to frame the narrative around climate change in narrow ways that leave out the voices of those affected on various frontlines.

How can the labour and climate justice movements support migrant workers?

The best way for the labour and climate justice movements to address these gaps is to explicitly support the migrant justice movement around the demand that migrant workers should be given full legal status and permanent residency immediately upon arrival. This is a direct counter to unions that are calling for the deportation or prohibition of migrant workers. I agree with the mainstream labour movement that migrant workers should not be working in deplorable conditions for less than minimum wage, but I disagree with their racism and protectionism around "saving Canadian jobs" that is decontextualized from the dynamics of global political economy. Instead of the logic of "divide and conquer" that pits Canadian workers against migrant workers, we should be organizing to lift up the wage floor for all. If the climate justice and labour movements support this call, it can be a unifying moral demand that supports migrant worker communities.

Beyond "support," migrant justice fits into the heart of a climate justice framework. Some groups have been making these links, but how can the politics of climate justice develop to incorporate this in a deeper way?

The demand for permanent residency fits clearly within a climate justice framework of place-based resiliency to ensure that people are not deportable or disposable. Environmental justice principles demand that we stand with people who are displaced—or are made displaceable. Nobody should be forced off their land; we all should have the right to live in our communities without environmental degradation, and we should reject the logic of displacement and disposability that is at the core of capitalism and colonialism. Legal status and permanent residency for migrant workers, therefore, is a concrete demand that is central to an environmental justice framework and illuminates a dignified way forward for people to build homes and community with one another.

Finally, migrant workers need to be at the centre of a climate justice analysis because so many migrant workers are actually displaced as a direct result of environmental injustices in a wide range of settings. Just as free-trade agreements, such as NAFTA, have created mass poverty in Mexico and forced migration to the United States, the consequences of point-source pollution, rising sea levels, and extreme weather are already now displacing people across the Global South, and this is bound to increase in the future. It is painful, and nothing short of cruel irony, to hear stories of migrant workers who have been displaced from their homelands due to Canadian mining companies or Western imperialist land grabs, and who are now forced to work in extractive industries within Canada that are harmful to them, to the land, and to the surrounding communities.

Despite massive climate-induced displacement and migrations and the creation of "climate refugees," the number of which is estimated to reach fifty million by the year 2020,[6] countries like the US and Canada don't even recognize climate refugees as a legal category. This is not surprising, since neither state even meaningfully acknowledges climate change as a reality! The impact on migrants, however, is that many migrants who are climate refugees cannot make an asylum or refugee claim based on that experience, since the state does not recognize or accept climate refugees. Instead, hundreds of climate refugees end up coming as migrant workers or become undocumented, and are then subject to further exploitation and racism.

North American environmentalists need to realize that extreme climate impacts in the Global South are not just things that happen "over there," but have consequences for those displaced and arriving "over here," making solidarity with climate refugees and migrants even more urgent. For example, one of the largest groups of migrant workers in Canada, including in Alberta, are those coming from the Philippines, a country that is being extremely adversely affected by climate change. Yet, instead of acknowledging and recognizing Western complicity in climate change—or the history of Western occupation and World Bank structural adjustment in the Philippines—we end up with Canadians slipping easily into forms of racist protectionist discourse like "Filipinos are taking over Canada."

And so again I return to the necessity of the labour and climate justice movements, and other related social movements, to support the migrant justice movement, because low-income migrant workers are the human face of environmental degradation, colonial displacements, and labour exploitation at a local and global scale. Global solidarity calls on us to envision an expansive ethical orientation of the world, to enact and embody an understanding of the interdependence of communities, and to centre the voices and experiences of those living at the nexus of multiple systems of oppression and invisibility.

8

Responding to Chinese Investments in the Tar Sands

HARJAP GREWAL

Before and after Barack Obama's 2014 State of the Union address on US television, an advertisement was played that opposed the Keystone XL pipeline. It did not highlight the ways in which this project endangers ecosystems, dispossesses Indigenous people, and intensifies climate change. Instead, it opposed the pipeline because of ties between the tar sands industry and China. After alluding to partnerships between the Canadian and Chinese governments, the advertisement focused on Chinese tar sands investments. The ad suggested that "*they*" want the Keystone XL project to send tar sands "to foreign countries like theirs." This particular ad was paid for by the NextGen Climate Group, a foundation that was established and directed by a billionaire.[1] Although the ad should not be viewed as a product of the movement against the tar sands, there are grounds to worry that its xenophobic and anti-Chinese sentiments might have resonated with some environmentalists.

This same framework sometimes has been part of campaigns against new and expanded pipelines in British Columbia, where campaigners have regularly referred to tar sands being shipped to China and Asian markets via the Northern Gateway and Trans Mountain pipelines. In these campaigns, suggestions that "China wants Canada's oil" or "China is taking over the world" not only miss the opportunity to present a more sophisticated analysis of both the goals of governments and the harms that fossil fuel and petrochemical industries bring to communities in both places—they also foster racist anti-Asian attitudes. Any influence of these dangerous ideas within the environmental movement must be exposed and challenged.

In this chapter, I focus on Canadian responses to Chinese investments in the tar sands, and in the Canadian economy more broadly, to illustrate some of the dangers of accepting xenophobic attitudes in our campaigns. This chapter focuses on international trade agreements that protect investments in extractive industries because it is crucial to address these agreements in campaigns around the tar sands.

The Foreign Investment Promotion and Protection Agreement (FIPA) negotiated with China is one of the latest in a long line of trade deals pursued by the Canadian state to allow investor-state arbitration in order to bully communities into accepting corporate demands. When these deals go into effect, local community control and environmental regulations will be weakened as international capital investments pour into industrial infrastructure, mining, pipelines, and associated extractive industries. Since the North American Free Trade Agreement (NAFTA) came into force in 1994, international trade agreements have protected investments in enterprises in Canada. The transnational investments in Athabasca tar sands operations are major cases in point. Once a mining project has been established, NAFTA ensures that federal and provincial governments in Canada can be sued if restrictions are subsequently applied to companies with US or Mexican investors. The Chapter 11 clause in this agreement provides such protections for investors, and these provisions have only been strengthened in the latest agreements. The Canada-China FIPA is one such agreement that should be addressed. It is important for critics of the tar sands industry to oppose these deals, but the basis of this opposition is crucial.

The China-Canada FIPA Deal

As transnational investments drive Athabasca tar sands extraction, there has been an exceptional amount of attention in Canada towards financing from China. For instance, there was a major controversy when China National Offshore Oil Corporation was acquiring Nexen, a Calgary-based oil and gas company.[2] Anti-Asian prejudices are sometimes subtle but unmistakable in the heightened concern about Chinese investors and companies in the tar sands. Some of this scrutiny towards China has come from the corporate press, as well as politicians who hope to capitalize on the anxieties of some voters about the perceived "threat" of "foreign" takeover.[3] However, the same xenophobia has also been part of campaigns opposing the bilateral negotiations for a FIPA investment agreement between the Canadian and Chinese governments. Environmental NGOs were among the campaigners raising such objections, which were reiterated by the Green Party.[4]

This strategy was not successful, however. Negotiations for this FIPA deal were concluded in September of 2012, though legal and procedural obstacles have slowed implementation. This opposition has included a legal challenge from Hupacasath First Nation, which was rejected by a federal court in Canada's legal system in early 2014. Indigenous self-determination should have been a central feature of previous campaigns against the agreement. These campaigns are worth revisiting to address how they often involved a flawed strategy that may have prevented the public from seeing the full picture.

In some campaigning and journalism,[5] the claim was made that Canada was "selling out," or being put up "for sale." There were suggestions that only China would benefit from this agreement, while Canada would not. The reality is that the Canadian state and corporations, as well as the Chinese state and its corporations, would both benefit from this agreement. Agreements like the FIPA with China can only be understood if the broader politics and economics that surround them are considered. Negotiations for such FIPA agreements have been a key plank of Canadian capitalism and foreign policy for the past several years, and many of these agreements have been brokered already.

In recent years, to name only a few examples, Canada has renewed one of its oldest bilateral trade agreements with Israel, completed a bilateral agreement with Colombia, and pursued an investment agreement with India. In 2013, after four years of negotiations, Canada reached a Comprehensive Economic and Trade Agreement (CETA) with the EU. In all of these cases, corporations—both state-run and privately owned—are working together with governments to protect and advance financial investments, while undermining grassroots democracy.

Canada has signed forty FIPAs, and is negotiating another ten. The government has been signing FIPAs since 1991, but a new framework was designed in 2004 that was first used in an agreement with Peru in 2006. At the time, we did not see a major national campaign in Canada opposing this agreement. Canadian corporations, particularly mining companies that have been facing popular opposition from peasant and Indigenous communities throughout Latin America, were the most prominent beneficiaries of the agreement.

Canada established the FIPA model to strengthen the rights of Canadian multinational corporations. The FIPA is a Made in Canada agreement—and not a model proposed and imposed by China. To suggest that the FIPA "does not benefit Canada" misses the mark. With this new agreement, Canadian corporations will be beneficiaries of investment protections for their operations in China, and vice versa. As Maude Barlow has pointed out, this FIPA "will give Canadian corporations investing in China the right to sue the Chinese government if there is an attempt to improve existing human rights, labour or environmental standards."[6] Within Canada, the agreement will also privilege foreign investment the Harper government badly wants to speed up resource projects, while disciplining or rendering harmless fight-backs from Indigenous peoples and other communities, in much the same way the FIPAs have done for Canadian capital abroad. For instance, trade agreements like NAFTA prevent a movement from seeking a moratorium or ban that would provide some room for further mobilizing towards change while extraction is halted. Although lobbying to strengthen or defend policies such as environmental protections is a very limited approach to resistance—even in the absence of such trade agreements—these efforts can be part of much deeper revolutionary movement strategies. Such possibilities are being closed off, in Canada and abroad.

Given that Canada is negotiating and has entered into a range of agreements with a series of national governments, it seems that the agreement with China received greater attention because of Canada's rarely held role as the potentially more vulnerable state party. Hypocritically, this kind of outrage is largely nonexistent when Canada pursues agreements with some countries of the Global South. When Canada completed a FIPA with Tanzania in early 2012, there were only two news stories, and no public campaigns.[7] If the FIPA with China is put into force, it is possible that more capital will flow from China to Canada rather than the other way around, but the fear of losing the relationship of Western domination over the Global South seems, at least in part, to have motivated this frenzied response, rather than a principled analysis and mobilization about the impact of the agreement on people and the environment. As a result, the vulnerabilities of peasants, workers, and Indigenous communities in China have remained absent from these campaigns.

The Broader Context

Even as there has been an emphasis on tar sands exports to China, the environmental movement has some awareness of the refining capacity on the West Coast of the US. There has been a grassroots campaign against the Richmond refinery in California, where Chevron has refined tar sands.[8] The Kinder Morgan Trans Mountain pipeline also delivers bitumen south of the border to Washington State. It seems that the real goal of these pipeline projects is to get tar sands oil to international waters, where an international bidding process will drive up their price. And while the Chinese government is certainly attempting to secure energy supplies by investing in the tar sands, the list of profiteers extracting bitumen is full of the names of US, Canadian, and European corporations, like Suncor/PetroCanada, Syncrude, Shell, Chevron, ConocoPhillips, Imperial Oil, TOTAL, and ExxonMobil, that receive Western state support. All of these companies are driving tar sands projects.

China, Canada, and much of the rest of the world are in the grip of market fundamentalism—the promotion of economic growth, and the relentless pursuit of profits. This has led corporations to secure ideal investment climates by any means necessary. When the Free Trade Area of the Americas was defeated, national governments pursued bilateral trade agreements on behalf of their corporate sponsors. And when bilateral agreements were not enough, Special Economic Zones (SEZs) have been established, where corporations write their own labour laws, environmental regulations, and taxation regimes.

The proliferation of SEZs and more conventional corporate land grabs in China has resulted in popular uprisings. In 2010, there were an estimated 180,000 mass incidents—that is, protests, riots, and group petitioning.[9] In 2011, farmers in Guangdong province protested for months due to land disputes and government land confiscations. Entering a FIPA with Canada will provide one more instrument for multinational corporations to grab land from under the feet of farmers in China.

These efforts are receiving legislative support from the Chinese and Canadian governments—while providing minimal support to people, and making everything available to multinational corporations. Everything must be commodified. Everything is for sale.

It is a shame that a majority of opposing voices in previous campaigns have chosen to homogenize China and the Chinese as convenient bogey-men. This is somewhat similar to how the campaign against NAFTA was led in Canada, which was portrayed by many critics as the victim and a "colony" of the US, and the US was the bully. This messaging masked the fact that both states are imperial powers and products of colonialism.[10] However, a lively anti-globalization movement eventually reframed these debates to identify the real victims and beneficiaries of international trade and invest-ment agreements: multinational corporations benefit from agreements signed by politicians, who then impose these investment and trade regimes onto communities without their consent. The Canada-China agreement is no different.

Racist attitudes factor into trade instruments that guarantee exploitative labour for corporations. Migrant worker programs and outsourcing rely on the construction of "competing" workforces, based on racial and national identities, to provide the social license to justify dramatically lower wages and horrific working conditions for the "foreign worker." The lives of two Chinese migrant workers who died working in the tar sands in 2007 serve as a stark reminder of how the demonization of people of colour and other national-ities assists in creating brutally unsafe working environments that would be deemed unsuitable for Canadian workers. With the economic recession and a documented rise in white supremacist and neo-Nazi organizations through-out the West, any legitimacy given to these polarizing attitudes is extremely worrying. It seems that market fundamentalism and extreme racism have been making inroads together.

How should we understand statements about how Canada is for sale? Public institutions, such as the health care system and water infrastructure, are threatened with privatization; international investors want in. While people resist the dictates of global finance to privatize the public, we must also recognize that the establishment of the Canadian state itself is based on one of the largest acts of violence and land grabs. As Indigenous lands were settled, a legal regime of Crown and private property was established, and

Indigenous people were killed and displaced in order to sell land and natural resources to the highest bidder. This model of imposition and exploitation has been used by Canada since long before the first investment agreement was ever established. Centuries ago, furs and cod were the major commodities sought in these lands. Even before Canada was officially founded, it was always in the business of taking and selling off Indigenous lands. Now there are just different buyers. A campaign suggesting that Stephen Harper is suddenly "selling Canada" to China hides this history.

The links between modern free trade agreements, North American fossil fuel export pipelines, and the history of colonization must be made visible. Some of this analysis can be found in a publication entitled *Colonization Redux: New Agreements, Old Games*, which argues that "while some may see the bewildering proliferation of bilateral FTAs (Free Trade Agreements) and BITs (Bilateral Investment Treaties) throughout the world as a relatively new phenomenon," in fact this mania "has deep roots," which "lie in a long history of colonial exploitation, capitalism and imperialism. The classic colonial state was structured for the exploitation and extraction of resources."[11]

An Alternative Approach

Considering the limitations of previous campaigns against the FIPA with China can help us to achieve more effective analysis and resistance in the future. We need an alternative approach to these campaigns around transnational investments. Of course, messages about defending "Canada" from "China" have had campaign traction. But, strategically and tactically speaking, choosing a more limited but convenient analysis may also limit the effectiveness of the campaign. In 2000, labour activists Kent Wong and Elaine Bernard raised principled and tactical concerns about a US labour-led campaign against China's attempt to gain "permanent normal" trade relations status. They wrote: "While the campaign was launched with the intent of promoting internationalism and avoiding China-bashing, we fear that the ultimate impact of the campaign has been to fuel cold war politics, encourage an unholy alliance with the right wing, and has resulted in racially offensive messages. As well, the campaign has weakened the strong anti-corporate and international solidarity focus coming out of the anti-WTO protests in Seattle."[12] A more principled and effective path that avoids the reinforcement of racist attitudes and the complete invisibilization of colonial history is possible.

Like the history of nations, the history of people's movements shapes our present reality. Many committed organizers have struggled for years to reorient the impulse to "protect Canada" towards building solidarity between communities affected by FTAs around the world. The proliferation of this work has created diverse movements united all over the globe—especially those led by rural, Indigenous, and peasant communities. These movements recognize how legal, trade, and investment regimes are used to divide, rule, exploit, and oppress communities.

A way to begin articulating an alternative approach is to speak about defending communities and the land, rather than defending Canada. We must reject anti-Chinese racism, and affirm Aboriginal title and Indigenous self-determination, without casting Canada as a helpless victim. But the 1 per cent—the elites, and their political friends—tell us that investment is good for Canada, for Canadian interests, for Canadian jobs, and for the Canadian economy. If the goal is to protect communities and lands across Canada, we need to play from a different script.

The argument that "we will lose popular support if we are too radical" is circular and self-fulfilling. Anti-Asian racism may mobilize people if it continues to be promoted—while Indigenous solidarity and other crucial bases for resistance may not mobilize people until these are actively prioritized. Just as the movements against tar sands and fracking have sometimes rallied alongside Indigenous communities and prioritized Indigenous voices, trade justice campaigns should be building genuine solidarity—locally and globally—to strengthen community power.

The goals of a movement that rejects trade agreements that support transnational investment in the tar sands should be: no government should have the capacity to promise investment certainty or security to international capital, because people's uprisings will continue to create uncertainty for elites; governments may sign agreements and issue permits, but the people will remain in the way; and we will organize in solidarity with directly affected frontline communities both locally and globally to support another 180,000 mass incidents of resistance.

9

New Beginnings
Tar Sands Prospecting Abroad

●

MACDONALD STAINSBY

●

The Rise of "Extreme" Fossil Energy Extraction

The revolution to spread extreme forms of fossil fuel extraction has unfortunately begun. As global conventional oil extraction either will soon peak or has already peaked (having reached the highest level of extraction possible, followed by a decline in production numbers), there is a race on to find new ways of extracting ever-dirtier forms of fossil energy through unconventional, increasingly expensive, and dangerous methods. These methods are what I refer to here as "extreme" extraction, from turning coal into liquid forms of energy, to hydraulic fracturing (or "fracking") to open huge swaths of natural gas and trapped "tight" oil in the US and Russia, and the net result threatens to add years of life to the dying fossil fuel economy. While some industry champions celebrate this extreme extraction as having put questions of "peak oil" behind us, it in fact illustrates a central pillar: the fossil fuel industry is now turning its attention to scraping the proverbial bottom of the barrel.

Of the various forms of extreme extraction, the tar sands in Canada are quite likely the most well known, a gigaproject that is slowly metastasizing into a teraproject, now widely recognized as the largest industrial project in human history. The reasons are much the same ones we have known since the vast expansion of the tar sands that followed the US invasion of Iraq: the price of a barrel of oil is high, and likely to stay that way as a general trend.

There have been some major non–tar sands oil strikes in the last few years, and a casual glance at the business sections of most newspapers would have alerted many people to the "boom" underway in the Bakken shale around North Dakota and in other locales around the world. Such extreme extraction has also come with considerable confusion, as there is a fundamental difference between fracking for "tight" oil and mining for oil shale, or kerogen. Fracking is a procedure that releases normal liquid crude and natural gas from formations of shale that were impossible to recover prior to new fracking technologies. In the case of fracked oil, the crude oil itself is not from shale, which is why "tight oil" is more accurate than shale oil, as it is sometimes referred to ("tight" oil should be read as code for fracking). Oil shale, on the other hand, describes rocks that are fused with kerogen and set in geological formations similar to tar sands bitumen. Much like bitumen, kerogen is a proto–crude oil, in that it is essentially a building block that can be processed into crude oil after being mined or extracted in situ using vast quantities of energy (for heating) and often tremendous amounts of water to separate the proto-oil from the bearing rock. Thus, when this chapter speaks of oil shale, it is in reference to kerogen shale and not fracking, or tight oil.

Oil shale has been known about for over a century in the US, and decades ago there were various mini-cycles of booms, then busts, in exploration and experimentation in Australia, Scotland, and the US. However, today, with the advent of high oil prices, giant energy corporations are learning from Alberta to carry out similar extreme extraction procedures, which are spreading across the planet's tar sands and oil shale deposits in countries such as Estonia, China, Russia, and Brazil. In terms of their greenhouse gas emissions per barrel, their climate impacts are even greater than tar sands extraction and processing.

Although the expansion of fracking for "tight" oil and natural gas is geologically and technologically very distinct from bitumen-based tar sands and kerogen-based oil shale, they are becoming heavily interrelated because the rapid influx of natural gas released by fracking is serving to reduce overhead energy costs into the tar sands and similar developments. Given the ways in which fracking supports tar sands projects, and given the serious environmental risks associated with fracking, it is extremely deceptive and egregious to call fracked gas a "transition fuel," as both industry and some environmental organizations do.[1]

The goal of this chapter is to give a series of snapshots that help to illustrate the rapid race into bitumen and kerogen extraction that is occurring around the world. A comprehensive list is impossible in a short chapter, and is likely to become quickly outdated given the pace of exploration. Instead, the primary goal here is to show that Canada's tar sands are not merely a disastrous teraproject unto themselves, as the rising investment and technological innovation in extreme extraction occurring around Alberta is helping to drive new prospecting efforts around the world.

Venezuela

The only location outside of Canada where tar sands extraction is occurring on a considerable scale is in the Orinoco River Basin in Venezuela. Although it was recently recognized as the largest single potential oil deposit on earth by the International Energy Association, with an estimated three hundred billion barrels recoverable, the Orinoco Basin currently has no large-scale mines comparable to those in the regions north of Fort McMurray, Alberta, and only 8 to 12 per cent of the total Orinoco is estimated to be suitable for strip mining.

The nature of tar sands development in the Orinoco has been influenced by political shifts over time, and it is now tied to the ongoing Bolivarian Revolution. The previous, pro-US, government in Venezuela listed bitumen as a resource that should be priced on all levels in a similar fashion to coal,[2] and an industry was created to liquefy bitumen deposits into a feed stock for power plant energy generation. This process, called Orimulsion, treated bitumen as if it were not a proto-oil, and priced bitumen at about one-fourth of what is fetched for crude.

In 2007, however, the government of Hugo Chávez redefined bitumen as "ultra-heavy oil" so as to include these resources in its effort to recover control over previously nationalized oil. These reclassified reserves are part of that massive estimate given by the International Energy Agency; having been redefined as oil meant that the nationalization of oil in the 1970s applied to bitumen.[3]

While Venezuela has lagged significantly behind Canada in terms of tar sands investment and extraction (partly due to capital flight after bitumen was nationalized), as conventional reserves decline, attention continues to be turned to increasing production in its tar sands. After establishing bitumen as a nationalized resource, many of the same transnational energy corporations involved in Canada's tar sands, including TOTAL, BP, and Statoil, remained in Venezuela as minority partners with Petróleos de Venezuela (PDVSA), alongside many other global energy companies based in countries such as China, India, Malaysia, Russia, and Italy.[4] These corporations are poised to bring the technological innovations from Canada's tar sands to Venezuela, amid plans to rapidly scale up production—which could soon make this one of the largest oil-producing sites in the world. In 2013, roughly six hundred thousand barrels of bitumen oil were produced from the tar sands in Venezuela, and there are contracts and plans to see that number go well over two million by 2016, if production targets are maintained (which seems unlikely).[5] It is significant to note that the refineries in Texas and Louisiana were constructed to process Venezuelan heavy deposits in the past. In fact, these refineries are pining for the construction of Keystone XL and other pipelines from Alberta because their refineries need few if any technological changes. Yet, due largely to the political tensions between the two countries, Venezuelan exports have dropped from 15 per cent of the daily consumption of oil in the US to around 10 per cent from the early 2000s to 2013.

Further information is not readily available, however. Gaining accurate numbers and other key details from PDVSA is extremely difficult. Venezuela has been the target of multiple sabotage efforts since the onset of the Bolivarian government in 1999, and officials seem to have responded with increased secrecy. Security considerations also have been part of the complete overhaul of the management of PDVSA, which had unsuccessfully attempted to bring down the government by locking out workers, who instead insisted on showing up to their jobs. PDVSA, nationalized in name only before the attempted sabotage, completely changed the management of the state company in the wake of the failure to use their control of oil as a weapon to topple the Bolivarian government. When PDVSA subsequently removed the corrupt managers who led the sabotage operation, the company was taken out of the hands of the old elite that had controlled and profited from it. To protect this change in the character of the industry, the new administration has become extremely guarded against releasing any information, or allowing outside research to be conducted on their territory.

Trinidad and Tobago

Located near the mouth of the Orinoco Delta, the twin island nation of Trinidad and Tobago has a long history of oil and gas drilling, based largely in the southern half of Trinidad. In recent years, the government of Trinidad and Tobago has made open calls for the country to follow the Canadian example and begin to develop its tar sands reserves. An estimated one and a half to two billion barrels of recoverable bitumen lie mostly in the southwest peninsula of Trinidad.[6]

To give a sense of scale, the whole country has a population of a little more than 1.2 million people, and multiple Trinidad and Tobagos could fit within the space of Canada's tar sands (while Alberta tar sands deposits lie under more than 140,000 square kilometres, Trinidad and Tobago's entire land mass is over 5,000 square kilometres).[7] The southwest of Trinidad, where the bitumen mixed with sand lies buried, is already heavily crisscrossed by pipelines and conventional oil infrastructure. It is, however, densely populated, with precarious housing sitting atop much of the largest bitumen deposits south of the "Pitch Lake" asphalt deposit in the town of La Brea and adjoining villages. The sites of much of the infrastructure that would be required for tar sands extraction—including a bitumen upgrader, larger industrial highways, a natural gas–fired power plant, a desalination plant for water, and an upgraded refinery—are all proximate to the Union Industrial Estate and surrounding areas.

The largest financial investor in the Canadian tar sands is the Royal Bank of Canada (RBC), and RBC recently acquired the Royal Bank of Trinidad and Tobago, the second-largest financial institution in the country. Following this acquisition, Sandra Odendahl—the RBC's public face of greenwashing the tar sands in Canada—was parachuted into Trinidad to present the "Capital Markets Policy," an ostensible stakeholder process that the RBC announced in Canada around their financing of the tar sands. Upon her arrival in Trinidad, Odendahl touted the "oil sands energy sector" in Canada as the industry where their stakeholder consultation policies were developed, as if this were a model of participation.[8]

Meanwhile, government leaders from both Canada and Trinidad and Tobago exchanged public declarations of enthusiasm over the proposed developments. As an April 2012 press release from the government of Trinidad and Tobago noted:

[Canadian prime minister] Harper indicated that he was anxious for Canadian companies to participate as they have much experience in the energy industry.... Minister Ramnarine noted that Trinidad and Tobago is estimated to have approximately 2 billion barrels of oil in "oil sands" ... whilst Canada holds the world's third-largest reserves of crude oil and has the world's largest reserves of oil sands.[9]

As of 2014, none of the proposals for tar sands extraction had gone ahead in Trinidad and Tobago, nor have the requisite foreign partners signed on publicly. Although there are many advocates within and outside the country, the population can still prevent a huge area of this small island from being made another tar sands sacrifice zone.

Madagascar

The plans for a future tar sands sacrifice zone are far more advanced in Madagascar than in Trinidad. France-based transnational corporation TOTAL, along with US-based Madagascar Oil, have outlined plans for strip mining at a rate of up to 180,000 barrels per day (bpd) of bitumen in Bemolanga and Tsimiroro. In a deeper part of the same bitumen deposit, Madagascar Oil is already extracting a few thousand bpd via an in situ/steam process, and has long-term plans to extract over one hundred thousand bpd of synthetic oil there.[10] The plant and proposed mine are in the western region of Melaky, where few people speak the former colonial language of French and instead speak a local dialect of Malagasy, though signs upon arrival at the gates of the Tsimiroro in situ operation are in English—the only such place I have been greeted by English in all of the country.

Melaky is a very arid region, and roughly one hundred thousand people use the land and rely heavily on the local waterways traversing Tsimiroro and Bemolanga for fish, animals, crops, and drinking water. This water is collected by hand in buckets and carried to the villages on foot. There is no real cash economy whatsoever; when sustenance cannot come from the land, people don't get it. Zebu (African cattle) are sometimes sold as meat to people in the larger cities, such as Antananarivo—if Zebu are contaminated by heavy metals and PAHs, so too is the food supply of the whole country. The proposed industrial operations, and their large water demands, threaten this supply. Further, two large protected areas—Tsingy de Bemaraha Strict

Nature Reserve & National Park, and the Ambohijanahary Reserve—are next to the operations, threatening the Manambolo and Manambolomaty waterways (both much smaller than Canada's Athabasca River). Tsingy is a world heritage site, and the reserves are home to threatened species of lemurs, fauna, and birds. The leases for both TOTAL and Madagascar Oil to extract bitumen only demand royalty payments of 4 per cent of revenues, and to make matters worse, there is no guarantee that these revenues will go to affected communities, as royalties are destined to be paid to the national government. Rumours abounded that the military coup d'état in 2009, which installed Andry Rajoelina, was motivated—at least in part—by the goal of shoring up TOTAL's investment in Bemolanga, as Rajoelina's father is a former head of TOTAL's Madagascar operations, and all other exploration blocks in the country except for Bemolanga were ordered to renegotiate terms (though this order was ultimately rescinded).[11]

As of 2013, TOTAL had shelved but not abandoned the strip mine plans for Bemolanga, which some speculate may relate to the uncertainty surrounding the EU Fuel Quality Directive, with the belief that TOTAL is waiting to see the projected final cost of exporting bitumen from Madagascar under the directive.

Israel/Palestine

In Israel, perhaps the single most energy-intensive form of hydrocarbon extraction yet devised is nearly underway. This project has the aim of enhancing Israeli "energy independence," and openly proclaims that it is guided by the values of Zionism. As key investor Israel Energy Initiatives (IEI) puts it: "Zionism ... lies in the heart of our vision. The realization of our vision will help build a stronger, wealthier and more independent Israel."[12] Such energy independence is seen as a means of reducing the success of international Boycott, Divestment and Sanctions that attempt to isolate Israel for its apartheid regime.

In the Shfela Basin, not far outside of Jerusalem, there is a pilot project in which IEI plans to extend massive heaters into the ground, powered by natural gas, in order to heat the kerogen-infused oil shale for up to a year, until kerogen "bleeds" out and can then be shipped for further refining into gasoline, jet fuels, and various petro-chemical by-products.[13] According to Effie Eitam, president of Genie Energy Limited (a US-based holding company with operations in Israel), their goal is "to release the free world from the dependence from Arab, I would say Islamic oil. I think that this company, this vision, will change the whole balance of forces in the region." IEI's CEO, Relik Shafir, explained it in blunt terms: "As a person who used up a lot of fuel during his military career, I am very sensitive to the threat of embargoes."[14] (Shafir was a pilot in the Israeli Air Forces, and flew during the bombing raids against the Osirak nuclear facility in Iraq in 1981.)

This is not the first location of shale development inside Israeli-controlled territory, as electrical power generation from oil shale mining and combustion took place in the Negev desert from 1978 until April 2011, prior to a fire that clouded the city of Dimona with black, putrid smoke. Initially after the accident, the plant was announced as closed by operator Israel Chemicals, only to be reopened until closure by 2015, again according to the operating company. Bedouin communities across the Negev desert have been threatened by the twin dispossession of industrial developments like oil shale mining and well-known tree-planting projects to "make the desert bloom," carried out by the Jewish National Fund (JNF), that have had the effect of ethnically cleansing the Palestinian inhabitants. According to Alice Gray, a permaculture practitioner who coordinates the "Green Intifada" campaign, which works with both displaced Bedouin and Palestinians in the region,

> The state has repeatedly destroyed Bedouin crops of all sorts—they used to spray them with Round-Up [a broad-spectrum herbicide] out of helicopters until too many were hospitalized with chemical poisoning and the [high court] forbade it ... Between that practice and frequent house demolitions, the Bedouin of the unrecognized villages are subjected to continuous harassment and abuse by the Israeli state. Their entire way of life is delegitimized while at the same time the JNF is able to move with impunity.[15]

At the same time, there is a tension between the Zionist-inspired oil shale developments planned by IEI and local Zionist residents who oppose the project in the Elah Valley. Members of the latter group have stated to me directly during a visit to the communities adjoining the proposed Genie shale project that they have made no attempt nor have any interest in making connections with Bedouin communities living on or near oil shale developments in the desert. Instead, they collaborate directly with the JNF, while stating their firm opposition to the oil shale development. The JNF applied for an injunction against the IEI permit from the highest court of Israel, a filing that was denied on December 24, 2012. As one resident put it to me in 2011, these opponents to oil shale extraction are "motivated by a Zionist love for the Jewish homeland—indeed, the very heartland of the ancient kingdoms of Israel and Judah," and are "determined to keep Dick Cheney's [Cheney is a board member of Genie] oil company from destroying the beloved land."[16]

Unfortunately for these residents, the oil shale project is led by some of the more powerful Zionist forces both in and outside Israel, including individuals such as Howard Jonas, Lord Jacob Rothschild, Michael Steinhardt, and Rupert Murdoch, who are all among Genie's and IEI's partners and advisors, along with former American vice-president Cheney. In fact, since 2013, Genie has been preparing to start fracking for oil and gas in illegally occupied Syrian territory of the Golan Heights.

The initial project is projected to produce thirty to forty thousand bpd of synthetic oil out of kerogen-based shale oil reserves, but estimates of potential development run as high as three hundred thousand bpd, which would have enormous atmospheric and geopolitical implications. The Harper government, ever intent on supporting the Zionist strand in Israeli politics from Canada,[17] recently pledged to use tar sands know-how to help support this oil shale venture. As Natural Resources Minister Joe Oliver stated in early 2013, "Israel's current state of oil shale resource development has similarities to the early days of Canada's oil sands and we are pleased to share Canada's experiences with respect to policy and regulation."[18]

Jordan

Across the Dead Sea, in Jordan, there are other plans for massive new oil shale extraction projects. The long-term impacts of this development may involve other environmentally destructive industrial engineering feats as well, perhaps by leading to the construction of the long-conceived Red Sea–Dead Sea Canal. This is because Jordan has one of the largest reserves of oil shale in the world, but a very small and precarious water supply, and since Israel controls much of the water supply into Jordan, it effectively controls the Jordanian development of oil shale. The "Red to Dead" canal is one potential means of responding to this water shortage, which has been discussed as far back as the 1970s. The revival of this plan, touted often by former Israeli PM Shimon Peres, has been discussed at international venues since circa 2007.

The Jordanian government has an important role in the expansion of extreme fossil energy extraction, through collaborations with a range of foreign partners. These include Royal Dutch Shell, which has plans to test and possibly operate one or more in situ extraction sites in Jordan,[19] and the UK-based Jordan Energy and Mines Limited, which is operating Karak International Oil.[20] This oil shale mining operation is projected to produce sixty thousand bpd, and will be reliant upon a range of globally sourced technologies, including the Alberta Taciuk Process (ATP), which the Thyssen Krupp Group of Germany has employed for an ATP processor constructed in China. (The company has previously constructed the same facilities for tar sands extraction in Canada.) ATP mining in Jordan would be the first large commercial application of tar sands extraction technologies to the mining of oil shale, though smaller plants do already exist in China and Australia.

Perhaps even more ominous is the projected oil shale–fired electrical power plant, designed by Estonia-based Eesti Energia, which is slated to be built near Attarat Um Ghudran, southeast of Amman. Estonia is home to the oldest successful oil shale industry, the largest oil shale electricity–generating power plant, and the largest oil shale mine on the planet. The proposed power plant near Attarat Um Ghudran would be the second-largest oil shale–fuelled power plant.[21] There is also a proposal for an open pit mine to extract kerogen-based oil at this same location, using Petrobras's kerogen extraction technology (known as "Petrosix," which is currently used in the south of Brazil) in concert with mining techniques used by TOTAL in the tar sands of Alberta.[22]

Foreign investment and technologies are crucial to the materialization of these various projects in Jordan, as Brazil, Estonia, and China are the only countries operating commercial plants converting kerogen to oil, gas, and jet fuel. In short, it appears that Jordan is carrying out an experiment by accident that could accelerate the expansion of oil shale extraction by fostering new technological innovations and alliances of transnational corporations. Again, the Canadian tar sands are connected, as key technologies there are expected to contribute to new oil shale extraction projects, and it is notable that Canadian start-up company Global Oil Shale Holdings entered into contracts with the government of Jordan in the fall of 2012.[23]

Conclusions

Such development prospects are at the stage where the tar sands and related oil shale projects would become hard-wired into the energy grid, at a time when we need the exact opposite. Projects for tar sands expansion—and possible resistance to such projects—have gone global. If we are to prevent runaway climate change, it will be, in part, because these projects never get off the ground. And that will require international solidarity. The reality of climate change, likewise, is a global one.

Nationalist sentiments have held back nation-states from making any real arrangements to tackle the issue before it tackles us. As social justice and climate activists, we simply must discard the same nationalist sentiments that have brought us the problem in the first place. We can meet and resist on an international level—the only space where climate change can even be thought to be addressed anyhow. Ultimately we have a world to lose, and a future to snatch from the jaws of planetary defeat.

II

Communities and Resistance

Awaiting Justice

The Ceaseless Struggle of the Lubicon Cree

MELINA LABOUCAN-MASSIMO

The traditional territory of the Lubicon Cree covers approximately ten thousand square kilometres of low-lying trees, rivers, plains, and wetlands—what we call muskeg—in northern Alberta. For three decades, this territory has undergone massive oil and gas development without the consent of the Lubicon people and without recognition of our Aboriginal rights, which are protected under Section 35 of the Canadian Constitution.

In the 1970s, before this encroachment on the land began, my father's generation and my grandparents' generation survived by hunting, fishing, and trapping throughout the region. Back then, and even into my own generation, people were still living off the land. I remember going out on the trapline on the horse and wagon, and I remember when the water from the land was still good to drink. But as oil and gas have come through the territory, that's changed.

Currently, there are more than twenty-six hundred oil and gas wells in our traditional territories. Over fourteen hundred square kilometres of leases have been granted for tar sands and fracking development in Lubicon territory, and almost 70 per cent of the remaining land has been leased for future development. Where there once was self-sufficiency, we are seeing increased dependency on social services, as families are no longer able to sustain themselves in what was once a healthy environment with clean air, clean water, medicines, berries, and plants from the boreal forest. Our way of life is being replaced by industrial landscapes, polluted and drained watersheds, and contaminated air. And it's very much a crisis situation.

In the North, we are seeing elevated rates of cancers and respiratory illnesses as a consequence of the toxic gases being released into the air and water. And while over $14 billion in oil and gas revenues have been taken from Lubicon territory, our community lives in extreme poverty and still lacks basic medical services and running water.

Canada's treatment of the Lubicon has been repeatedly condemned by the United Nations, and UN special rapporteur Miloon Kothari has called for a moratorium on oil and gas development in Lubicon territory. On March 26, 1990, the United Nations Human Rights Committee ruled that Canada's failure to recognize and protect Lubicon land rights violated the International Covenant on Civil and Political Rights. In 2006, the United Nations Human Rights Committee again called on Canada to address outstanding land claims in Lubicon territory before granting further licences for economic exploitation. Yet this resource extraction is still happening.

In 1899, when Treaty 8 was officially signed in northern Alberta, treaty commissioners overlooked the Lubicon Cree due to their remote and hard-to-reach territory. The Lubicon people therefore never ceded their traditional territory to the Crown. This has led to a precarious and unstable relationship with both the provincial and federal governments, as both have continuously undermined the sovereignty of the Lubicon people. For decades, the Lubicon have tried to settle these outstanding land disputes, but unfortunately, it serves the government's interests to keep the Lubicon land claim in limbo due to the territory's rich oil and gas deposits.

When the construction of an all-weather road began in the early 1970s, the Lubicon people started to contest the encroachment on their traditional territory by transnational corporations intent on exploiting the land. For the fourteen years that followed, the Lubicon attempted to assert their rights through various court proceedings at both the provincial and federal level.

By 1988, the Lubicon concluded that it was necessary to use other means of direct action so that their voices and message would be heard. On October 15, 1988, the Lubicon people erected a peaceful blockade, which was successful in stopping oil exploitation in the territory for six days. Only then did Alberta premier Don Getty meet with the Lubicon chief and agree to a 243-square-kilometre reserve under the Grimshaw Accord.

Despite this agreement, the Canadian government offered the Lubicon substandard conditions in their land settlement agreement. Even Getty described the offer as "deficient in the area of providing economic stability for the future."[1] Unfortunately, due to the take-it-or-leave-it approach of the federal government, the land claim negotiations continued from 1989 until 2003, when the talks broke down completely and both parties walked away from the table. To this day, the Lubicon Cree have been unable to settle a land claim, which has drastically hindered their ability to protect themselves and their traditional territory from further exploitation and destruction.

On April 29, 2011, a rupture in the Rainbow Pipeline resulted in a spill of about four and a half million litres of oil in our territory—one of the biggest oil spills in Alberta's history. When the pipeline broke, oil went down the corridor and into the forest, but the majority of it was soaked up into the muskeg, which is like peatland moss and takes thousands of years to be generated. The muskeg is not an isolated system. It's not "stagnant water," as the government claims. It's actually a living, breathing ecosystem that supports life and is connected to all the water in the region.

On the first day of the spill, the school was not notified. When students started to feel sick, they were evacuated from the school under the assumption that it was a propane leak. When they got outside into the field, they realized that the problem was extended throughout the community. During the first week of the spill, community members experienced physical symptoms: their eyes burned, they had headaches, and they felt nauseous. We were told that air quality was not a problem, even though Alberta Environment didn't actually come into the community until six days after the spill. This is problematic, since a government granting permits for this type of development, often without the consent of the people, has an obligation to take care of those whom they are directly putting at risk. A lot of people were left wondering what they should do, and whether pregnant women, elders, and small children should even be in the community. We did not learn of the immensity of the spill until the information was finally released to the community—one day after the re-election of the conservative Harper government.

This oil spill was from a multi-use pipeline, which carried tar sands oil and sweet light crude, as well as condensate. The Rainbow Pipeline is over forty-five years old. Due to the corrosive nature of tar sands oil, it is no surprise that this was not the first major spill from this pipeline. When it broke in 2006 and spilled one million litres of oil, the Alberta Energy and Utilities Board stated that stress and corrosion in the pipeline's infrastructure contributed to the spill. Five years later, four and a half million litres spilled in our traditional territory. We're also seeing pipeline breaks like this in other parts of North America, from Kalamazoo, Michigan, to the Kinder Morgan spill along the West Coast, as well as spills along the first phase of the Keystone XL pipeline in the US. Will it ever end?

How many more communities have to be put at risk for this type of development, and who is really benefiting? Not only are we experiencing impacts at ground zero in Alberta and along pipeline corridor routes, but this megaproject affects communities all around the world through the devastation caused by climate change. What are we leaving to future generations? We need to shift away from a fossil fuel–based system and push for renewable energy systems that enable us to be self-sufficient and self-sustaining.

The tar sands are the largest industrial project on the face of the planet, and this industry will not stop if we cannot reorient economies to transition away from dirty fossil fuels. What we are seeing in the communities around these projects are elevated rates of cancers and respiratory illnesses like emphysema and asthma because of air quality issues and water contamination, as well as the destruction and complete fragmentation of the boreal forest. This boreal forest is one of the last remaining ancient forests in the world—and is crucial to the lungs of Mother Earth. It is also an invaluable carbon sink, which actually helps us combat climate change. Tar sands expansion will eventually drive out much of the remaining wildlife in the area that has not already been affected by underground mining (i.e., in situ projects) or the massive open pit mines. In my lifetime, I can expect to witness animal species going extinct in the tar sands. The woodland caribou, a food source that First Nations have used for millennia, are projected to be extirpated by 2040. And not only is wildlife declining in population and being driven away, but what remains is becoming a contaminated food source for local communities.

People in the North are concerned because they are seeing the impacts already. Though estimates suggest that no more than 2 to 3 per cent of the tar sands has been extracted, the scale of the industry and its pollution are already staggering. There are mines the size of cities, with ever more trucks, pipelines, transmission lines, and other tar sands infrastructure.

Within Lubicon territory, fourteen hundred square kilometres of leases have been granted for in situ tar sands development. This underground mining looks a lot more benign on the surface, but it is not. Companies superheat steam to 240°C, and push it down to the level of tar sands/bitumen, which may be hundreds of metres underground. When they melt the earth there and suck it back up, they bury the toxic by-products in the earth's core. We have yet to determine what the long-term impacts will be, namely on the underground aquifers. These projects also bring threats of steam leaks and explosions. In 2006, an explosion created a three-hundred-metre crater of melted earth and melted bitumen. It is frightening when one of these operation plants is near a community. In addition, there is the potential for pipeline explosions, which is a growing threat because fracked gas is needed to produce and transport tar sands.

The tar sands are managed to maximize profits, and not to protect the environment of downstream or affected communities like the one where my family lives. We have endured decades of broken promises, which have taught us that corporate promises of new technologies that will repair this damage are simply empty words—greenwash—intended to reassure people that this time it will be different.

For over a century now, the rights of the Lubicon Cree have not been protected or respected. For decades, the Lubicon have led local, national, and international lobbying efforts to fight for what is inherently theirs and to protect their right to land, clean air, and good water. But despite years of raising awareness and increasing exposure, the Lubicon people still wait for justice.

11

ᑭᐦᒋ ᐱᑭᐢᑫᐧᐃᐧᐣ

Kihci Pikiskwewin—Speaking the Truth

CRYSTAL LAMEMAN

When we go about things in a good way, with good intentions, our Creator will never leave us vulnerable. Things do not happen by chance. Everything happens for a reason, and when we embark on this challenge with love and light in our hearts, we are exactly where we are meant to be. We are warriors—Mother Earth's Soldiers.

Lakota Chief and Holy Man Sitting Bull said this:

> For us, warriors are not what you think of as warriors. The warrior is not someone who fights, because no one has the right to take another's life. The warrior, for us, is one who sacrifices himself for the good of others. His task is to take care of the elderly, the defenseless, those who cannot provide for themselves and above all, the children, the future of humanity.[1]

Mother Earth's soldiers believe in a better world, a better human existence, and a better future for the generations to come. We believe in the life-giving abilities of our one true Mother. And we believe that, with our truth-telling abilities, we will move forward into a better way of knowing and being.

I am a warrior because I gave life. I am a mother, and when you bring life into this world, you become the protector of those little blessings on loan to you from the Creator. My obligation is to my children, first and foremost. Following that is my role as a Nehiyaw, an Indigenous woman of Turtle Island. I come from the four-bodied people. I was born from ancestors who endured for the future generations and the life-giving abilities of our one true Mother, and it is my obligation as a conduit to ensure that what they endured was not for nothing. We must follow through for the children and our future. With our boots on the ground, we will persist as we resist the colonial structures that have been forced upon us.

The Beaver Lake Cree are among the peoples who are challenged by the strong arm of industry and its wilful ignorance. I will start to discuss our struggles by offering a glimpse into the trials and tribulations that we face.

On May 20, 2013, two oil spills were reported around the Canadian Natural Resources Ltd. lease pads, located on the Cold Lake Air Weapons Range in northern Alberta. Additional reports soon followed—three more spills were found on land, and the fourth was found under a lake. As months passed, these spills killed over two hundred birds, small animals, and amphibians. To date, over one and a half million litres of bitumen emulsion has seeped to the surface and is contaminating groundwater that we all depend on.

Welcome to ground zero of steam-assisted gravity drainage (SAGD) tar sands destruction in Treaty 6 traditional territory, which includes the Beaver Lake Cree Nation. Eighty-four per cent of the Beaver Lake Cree Nation's traditional hunting territory has been leased out to Big Oil without appropriate consultation with Beaver Lake Cree Nation. The Canadian government has not followed Canadian and international legal requirements to consult our Nation. Moreover, Canada has not achieved the minimum international standard of free, prior, and informed consent (FPIC).[2] Consultation and, more importantly, FPIC must be defined by us. Such processes must not be prescribed by the brass hands who are making decisions with real-life consequences that they are deliberately ignoring.

A major complication within Treaty 6 lands and territories is how the traditional hunting territory of the Beaver Lake Cree falls between two of the three oil deposits in this province we call Alberta: the Athabasca and the Cold Lake deposit areas. This is the land to which the First Nations people have inherent rights as per the Treaty of 1876, an agreement between the British Crown and the First Nations people of Canada.

This Is Where I Grew Up

I am a member of the Beaver Lake Cree Nation, in Treaty 6 territory, where I live and work. I am a mother, a daughter, a granddaughter, an aunt, a niece, and a friend. I am someone who loves my roots and my place of birth, because this is my homeland. I was born and raised in the Beaver Lake Cree Nation, and I have spiritual and cultural ties through ceremony and my ancestors. But my home is under attack by an industry and by the Alberta and federal governments, which will stop at nothing to get the bitumen from the ground. This bitumen is hundreds of metres underground and cannot be extracted without SAGD, a lot of wasted energy, and a complete dismissal of legal and ethical duties to protect our waters, our one true Mother, and the ecosystems that life depends on.

In our area, animals like the Northern woodland caribou were abundant species that we traditionally hunted, but the caribou are declining from a population of thousands to between 175 and 275 caribou in 2011.[3] As the habitat for wildlife is under threat from tar sands operations, so are the ecosystems upon which the frontline communities rely. My children cannot safely drink water straight from the land in the way I did as a child, and in the way my aunts, uncles, parents, and grandparents did. No longer do children relate to stories of water so pure that one had only to skim the top of the water, take their dipper from their backpack, dip, and have a drink. They cannot fully appreciate how water has life-giving abilities.

It is the milk of our Mother, who provides us with everything a human being needs to survive. But as with any mother's milk, it needs a body that is free from chemicals and toxic solutions to nurture it. Instead, here we are with reports of deer with green meat and moose with pus bubbles under their skin. There are boil-water advisories, and babies are being airlifted to the urban medical centres for sickness resulting from drinking contaminated water.

Our elders talk about how Turtle Island was a paradise before our visitors came over. Mother Earth is a natural grocery store. Just as we give before we take from a grocery store, we do the same when taking from our Mother. Indigenous peoples have traditions of conservation, and we are the first environmentalists. Those teachings are reminders that we should never take more than we need. Every day, we should be mindful of balance in everything that we do. Thus, when we see medicinal plants that are natural to us disappearing because they rely on a healthy ecosystem, we know that something is terribly wrong.

At the same time, our oral histories, knowledge systems, and teachings are under attack. We must react. It should never be okay for a people's way of knowing and being to become a part of history, rather than the present and future. I have heard of a time when the medicinal plants were so pure and powerful that, when combined, they could cure cancer. The elderly could talk of these medicinal plants with ease, knowing where they could be found in abundance. We are losing these connections with the land.

As a member of the Beaver Lake Cree Nation, I have seen the devastating impacts of industrialization first-hand. I am not the only witness. But governments are not addressing the root causes.

The response to the rapid decline of the caribou is a case in point. A study and report written and issued by Dr. Boutin on the woodland caribou prompted a recovery strategy that was formulated further in the *Species at Risk Act* (SARA), the Act created to satisfy, in part, international legal obligations under the United Nations Convention on Biological Diversity. SARA is an approach to protecting and recovering species at risk, and the Northern woodland caribou is listed as a "Threatened" species on the Species at Risk Public Registry.[4] But it is from SARA that one of the most controversial recovery strategy resolutions arose.

Carolyn Campbell, Alberta Wilderness Association conservation specialist, has observed that "because of ongoing mismanagement of caribou habitat, Environment Canada's data shows Alberta's herds are by far the most vulnerable to being wiped out in all of Canada.... This proposal will allow 95% habitat loss and many decades of massive scale wolf kills, for most Alberta herds. This is an absurd and deeply unethical strategy that sacrifices both wolves and caribou to unmanaged energy industry growth." In the name of caribou recovery, hundreds of wolves have already been poisoned and shot from helicopters in northwestern Alberta. The federal government's draft caribou recovery strategy is now calling for a massive expansion of this approach.

"There is no reason to think that killing wolves will recover caribou," says Campbell. "Only protecting caribou habitat will achieve that."[5] This is one of many reasons further oil and gas expansion projects that do not follow due process and consultation defined by the First Nations people must be stopped.

To date, over nineteen thousand permits have been granted to every major oil company in the world within the traditional hunting territory of the Beaver Lake Cree. Out of 38,972 square kilometres of natural habitat, 34,773 comprise oil and gas well sites. One well site is equivalent to ten thousand square metres of habitat loss. The government is accepting this without abiding by its legal obligations to consult. And the government is clearly not seeking the free, prior, and informed consent of the First Nations peoples in areas where activities have the potential to affect their rights.[6] Article 32 of the United Nations Declaration on the Rights of Indigenous Peoples states that "Indigenous peoples have the right to determine and develop priorities and strategies for the development or use of their lands or territories and other resources."

Treaty Rights

I will return to the question of consent, because First Nations rights are arguably some of the most important rights in the Canadian legal landscape, and certainly the most powerful environmental rights in the country (see chapter 22). Aboriginal rights are enshrined in Section 35 of the *Constitution Act* of 1982.[7] So there are legal grounds to challenge megaprojects that are destroying First Nations' rights to hunt, trap, and fish—in direct violation of their Constitutional rights, which are the highest law in Canada.[8]

There are people who will say that there must not be any recognition and/or utilization of the law of this country we call Canada. As Indigenous people, we abide not by a written law, but by the law of our Creator—a Natural Law, which puts the collective rights of all living things above all else. But it is with Canadian law—as well as associated treaty obligations, and the collective rights of Indigenous peoples—that we are able to set precedent in Canada.

On May 14, 2008, the Beaver Lake Cree, under the leadership of former Chief Alphonse Lameman, made a declaration that we would assert our rights and protect the ecological area known to us as our traditional territory. When the litigation was filed in the Alberta Court of Queen's Bench, over seventeen thousand treaty rights violations and infringements were cited. Basically, the Canadian and Albertan governments granted seventeen thousand permits to Big Oil without following due process by acting on their duty to consult the Beaver Lake Cree. Currently, grassroots members of the Beaver Lake Cree are supporting the leadership, who are carrying out the litigation by doing their part to raise funds for the cumulative impacts studies necessary to mount a full legal challenge.

When our ancestors entered into treaty, they did not do so with the thought that they were ever agreeing to surrender the land. Collectively, the First Nations people of Canada are holders of historical treaties that cover the breadth of the land that has come to be known as Canada. When we entered into Treaties 1 to 11—which extend across Canada—we used our own legal orders and exercised our inherent rights as Nations.

When my ancestors entered into the nation-to-nation agreement that is called Treaty 6, they did so with the thought that it could never be broken. They believed that our rights would never be surrendered, and that this treaty would be upheld as a lasting agreement of peace and friendship. The words "for as long as the sun shines, the grass grows, and the rivers flow" express how we will always have an inherent right to the land, with the ability to sustain ourselves in a meaningful way. This would mean that we could go to the land freely, as if we had never entered into this agreement. The treaty did not speak of owning land, which nobody can own. The land is our one true Mother, and you cannot own your mother, who has life-giving abilities and the ability to nurture.

Treaty 6 outlines rights that we will exercise until the sun stops shining, the grass stops growing, and the rivers stop flowing. As keepers of the land and water, we still exist, and we have obligations. We have not gone anywhere—nor do we plan to.

Canadian citizens also are treaty rights holders. As such, it is the responsibility of all Canadians to say, "Enough is enough; we will no longer be bystanders and act as the vessels of disaster for future generations."

Our Collective Struggle

If you breathe air and you drink water, this is about you. These are challenges we face as human beings in a collective struggle that involves each and every one of us. This is no longer an "Indian problem." The tar sands are the largest industrial project in the world, and the largest emitter of greenhouse gas emissions in Canada.

Yet, if tar sands developments are recognized to be unconstitutional, existing and future tar sands projects will no longer be permitted to proceed without the consent of the Beaver Lake Cree. This would also set a precedent for other First Nations, who could issue similar court challenges and potentially stop further tar sands expansion on their lands.

It is crucial to raise the platform of the rights of Indigenous peoples under this state we call Canada, a government that has dismantled environmental protections. Omnibus Bill C-38 has shortened the time frame for environmental assessments with greater federal control. Bill C-38 was quickly followed by omnibus Bill C-45, amounting to a First Nations land grab[9] and the complete erasure of virtually all legal protections of our surface freshwater systems. Prior to December 2012, we had thirty-two thousand protected lakes, and two and a half million protected rivers. The day after the passing of Bill C-45, we were left with ninety-seven protected lakes and sixty-two protected rivers. This bill was followed by Bill S-8, which the federal government supposedly enacted to provide safe drinking water for First Nations. In reality, it will result in the privatization of our water, thereby taking the milk of our Mother and turning it into a commodity.

Our people would be forced to pay fees for clean water because of this government's attempt to sell what was never theirs in the first place. Who can afford this? The poor First Nations people living in Third World conditions in a First World country? The poor farmer who relies on his crops to feed his family, and the 99 per cent? No. It is industry that can afford it, and this government has made sure of that.

This government also has pulled out of the Kyoto Protocol, and has signed a Foreign Investment Promotion and Protection Agreement with China. These behind-the-scenes, closed-door decisions deliberately ignore the democratic process that would involve all the citizens of this state we call Canada. So here we sit, with a government refusing to accept responsibility and hiding from accountability and transparency.

Yet this same government, as a successor state to the British Crown, is therefore a treaty partner. These treaty obligations arise from agreements among sovereign nations.

Under Prime Minister Stephen Harper, the Conservative government has made a promise to First Nations leaders, a promise of transparency and open lines of communication. Supposedly, this relationship would be based on "mutual respect, friendship and support."[10] As such, words are uttered at press conferences, while permits that support the industry are granted in the legislatures and municipal council halls. Bills that gut our environmental laws are being passed and implemented while the Albertan and Canadian governments claim to work on the "reclamation" of land that once was pristine boreal forest, but now looks like the Sahara Desert.

Unless the industry can show me that they have replaced the vegetation and wildlife that was natural to that area in its purest form—an ecosystem returned as if it had never been touched—only then will I stop talking about their false facts and their false ideas of reclamation. For me, reclamation is not poisoned life and barren lands; reclamation, for me, is solidarity with the 99 per cent, and planting the seeds of knowledge and love.

In the meantime, while additional permits are granted, tar sands projects are taking billions of dollars out of the traditional territories of Treaties 6 and 8 every year. On these territories, First Nations people suffer from endemic poverty, high unemployment, and severe health problems. As Susan Smitten, executive director of the organization Respecting Aboriginal Values and Environmental Needs (RAVEN), has observed:

> It's not fair to rely on the poorest people in our nation to stand alone and be the voice of reason in this effort. They have the power of their treaties to protect the planet, and we have the power of a nation to support them. I just encourage people to get behind the line they've figuratively and literally drawn in the tar sand.[11]

As our Indigenous rights are violated and our natural resources are exploited, we face environmental degradation and destruction every single day. Some examples include: the Northern Gateway and Kinder Morgan pipelines in British Columbia; the tar sands and natural gas and coal extraction in Alberta; the uranium and pot ash developments and crude oil extraction in Saskatchewan; the destruction of treaty lands in Manitoba for hydraulic power generation; TransCanada's Energy East pipeline; the mining of diamonds in Attawapiskat; Enbridge's Line 9 pipeline through Aamjiwnaang, Ontario; the mining of diamonds in the Northwest Territories; and the fracking of natural gas in Elsipogtog, New Brunswick. These are but very few examples of the ongoing exploitation. Members of these communities are making every possible attempt to curb the environmental racism that they endure.

Many of us are collectively standing together and demanding environmental justice, with the aim of understanding the need to address and reduce the disproportionate harm from environmental degradation that affects Indigenous, low-income, and minority communities. People of colour in frontline communities face environmental burdens from extreme resource extraction and exploitation, so we must begin to participate in processes designed by us to improve environmental health and safety.

Indigenous peoples are exercising our rights. We are standing up to protect the land, the water, and our collective future, not only for ourselves but for the very existence of the human race. We are doing what we can to stop the exploitation and abuse of Mother Earth from one end of this country to the other, all over what we call Turtle Island, and on a global level.

It is time to recognize that we are all Indigenous peoples. We all come from somewhere; we all have a connection to what we call Mother Earth, and it is time to reclaim these roots. It is time that we stand up and say, "We will no longer allow our air and our water to be coveted. These basic human rights cannot come from disaster. We will no longer be players in this game of environmental roulette. No more will we be pacified with money that has been making us hostages of this economy."

Our greatest battle will be a fight for the rights of Mother Earth and the rights of nature. It is terrifying that so many of the human race believe they supersede Mother Earth—as though she is a subject with no rights. But, truth be told, she was here well before us, and if we do not collectively work together—beyond the confines of race, colour, and creed—she will shake us from her and she will continue to exist.

Every day, more people are hearing our truth and saying enough is enough. My truth is part of the mobilization of the grassroots people I come from, and I hope to support the mobilizations of grassroots people in every community, and on a global level. I have realized that this cannot be done alone. This is a collective fight to stop Big Oil.

12

The Tar Sands Healing Walk

JESSE CARDINAL

We all have the ability to be connected to the askiy (land).[1] When you go out into the forest, or into the country, it becomes a lot clearer where our food and water comes from. The nipiy (water) seems cleaner, the air fresher, and the sky bluer. The forests I know are full of ka nikamot piwayisis (songbirds) singing and dancing, and niskak (geese), sisip (ducks), mawk-kwa (loons), apisimosis (deer), moswa (moose), mahkesiw (fox), mescakan (coyotes), wapus (rabbits), wachask (muskrats), amisk (beavers), muskwa (bears), kamamak (butterflies), kwaskohtsis (grasshoppers), ayikis (frogs), kwekwekocis (fireflies), kinosew (fish), mikisew (eagles), and so much more. This is our family too. Other beings have their own families, have their own homes, and depend on the land for food and water. In the cycle of life, they offer themselves at times to help sustain us.

Small ponds and lakes also surround where I live, and every year in spring I anxiously await the arrival of the geese and ducks. Both traditional knowledge and scientific studies confirm that migratory birds tend to return to the same locations year after year. So when geese and ducks fly far south to warmer regions, they go back to the same places, and do the same when they come back home in the spring.

But things are changing fast in northern Alberta, which has been home to the Cree and Chipewyan people since before the Europeans set foot on this land, known to many as Canada and to Indigenous people as Turtle Island.

Every year, more birds are returning to find their homes destroyed by more industry-access roads and industrial plants, more cleared and fractured land, more drained lakes and mining pits, and more pipelines, tailings ponds, and oil spills. It breaks my heart to imagine these living beings, flying thousands and thousands of miles to come home, only to find an industrial wasteland in place of their homes. What do they feel?

I know I feel sadness, anger, hopelessness, despair, rage, and many more toxic emotions that if felt often and for long periods of time will make someone sick, much like being exposed to the industrial toxins in our air, water, and food also makes us sick. This is why we pray: we pray for ourselves, our families, the food, water, air, trees, other living beings, so that we can change this and make it better. We pray so that we can heal this land. Healing turns the greatest adversities into the warmest and highest hopes, which our children and grandchildren can carry to light their way. This is the spirit we have brought to the Tar Sands Healing Walk.

Blueberry and Medicine Country

Northeast Alberta is part of one of the largest boreal forests in the world, and it contains a vast array of medicines, berries, and other natural foods. The Conklin-Janvier-Cold Lake area is home to some of the best and largest blueberry patches, and there are people from my community and others from all over northeast Alberta and into Saskatchewan who have always travelled up to this region to harvest food and medicines. As with the long history of Indigenous people, the people of this land have always shared, and they still follow that same value of sharing today. Some of the first teachings we receive are that when someone visits your home, you feed them, and if someone is in need, you help them. Many First Nations and Métis communities have tried to work with the Alberta and Canadian governments and with private industry, only to realize that the relationship is only take and very little give. So many applications for tar sands expansion are filed, and almost none are rejected. Our treaty and Métis rights to the land are regularly under threat, and we must still continually assert them.

Our land is being destroyed at an unprecedented rate, along with our berry patches and medicines, and the homes of so many animals. Now, when we go up to the Conklin-Janvier-Cold Lake area, what used to be blueberry patches are gravel pits, access roads, camps housing thousands of people, industrial plants and massive equipment, heavy industrial traffic, and signs that say "no access." It is chaotic and dangerous, and if I were to imagine what a gold rush looked like, I would think this is how it was, with so many "strangers" coming from different parts of Canada, many coming to try and "strike it rich." To go out on the land is not the same, and we no longer feel safe. The newcomers filling this land have no connections to it, and no connections to the Indigenous people who have called this land their home since time immemorial.[2] Like during the gold rush, many "outsiders" are driven here by their own economic desperation, and work in toxic conditions.

It is expected that steam-assisted gravity drainage (SAGD) operations will soon surpass open pit mining as the main method of bitumen extraction, if they have not already. SAGD injects extremely high-pressure steam into the ground where dense bitumen is located, in order to heat the bitumen enough to move it to surface for extraction. While the tar sands industry claims that this method is less harmful to the land than open pit mining, local First Nations know that SAGD is equally or more damaging due to the combination of large freshwater diversions, energy demands, chemical

BEN POWLESS

Elders lead the fourth annual Healing Walk around twenty-five kilometres of toxic industry encroaching on First Nations' traditional territory, 2013.

additives, and toxic wastewater produced—problems that scientific research has confirmed.[3]

The tar sands industry has also insisted (in Environmental Impact Assessments) that mined land will be reclaimed in about thirty years. But the berries and medicines are part of a very fragile and intricate ecosystem, and living here, we know that people cannot simply return land that has been stripped of all its complex life-giving elements to what it once was. Wetlands cannot be "reclaimed" once they are drained for tar sands earth-movers and watersheds filled with toxic tailings.[4]

Apart from Wood Buffalo National Park, there are few truly protected lands in northeastern Alberta, and there are no protected areas in the Conklin-Janvier-Cold Lake area. What will be left in ten or twenty years? Our berry patches and medicines that help feed and take care of our families are already getting harder to find and more dangerous to get to.

What Is the Healing Walk?

The Tar Sands Healing Walk was born out of the need to heal from the destruction produced by the rapid rate of tar sands extraction in Alberta. Some of the founders of the Healing Walk included Eriel Deranger, Cleo Reece, Sheila Muxlow, and the late Roland Woodward.[5] Having been on the frontlines for years, organizing rallies, marches, and protests to speak out against the destruction and call upon the government to put environmental protections in place, they were starting to feel frustration and fatigue with the lack of response and the unrelenting expansion of the destruction of the tar sands industry.

The idea of a healing walk was born as something distinct from a rally, march, or protest. Instead, it was conceived of as a ceremonial walk of prayer, to be coordinated by First Nations in the area and their elders and ceremonial people. The first Healing Walk, in 2010, was a one-day event focused mainly on the ceremonial walk itself, a twelve-kilometre loop in the belly of the tar sands beast, north of the city of Fort McMurray. As it subsequently grew, we realized that one day was not enough, and that we wanted to take the time to meet each other, welcome visitors, and learn where people had travelled from and what issues they were facing in their territories. In 2013, we hosted roughly five hundred people over a two-day event. On the first day, there was a "meet and greet," where people from local First Nations spoke and visitors also were invited to speak. Locals hosted workshops on a range of issues, from "Tar Sands 101" to solar energy to First Nations culture. Many organizers who work on environmental protection in other parts of Canada attended the Healing Walk and have hosted workshops, including alliance building between First Nations and the growing non-Indigenous resistance to pipelines across the continent.

The organization also reflects the strong belief in sharing in our First Nations and Métis culture, and our desire to show our appreciation to visitors for coming. We understand the cost of living is very high in Fort McMurray and that many guests travel from far away, so we work with the First Nations in the area, who provide land so that our guests can camp for free, and we do our best to provide some free meals, including an honouring feast at the end of the Healing Walk. In 2013, we worked very hard with the local caterers to ensure that traditional foods, such as bison, moose, deer, fish, berries, and more, were made available to participants.

On the walk itself, participants see tailings ponds and desert-like areas of "reclaimed land" that was once the boreal forest and now grows almost nothing. In the distance, participants can hear mimicked gunshots ring out, a pathetic tactic now used to keep waterfowl out of the toxic tailings ponds following the deaths of sixteen hundred ducks that landed on tailings ponds at a Syncrude site in 2008 (since it is still very common for First Nations and Métis people to eat wildlife, the loss of so many ducks must also be under-stood to have damaged the food supply). The mimicked gunshots are a stark reminder of the toxic impacts of the industry upon wildlife. Participants on the Healing Walk also learn how many elders still eat animals such as ducks, wild birds, rabbits, moose, and more, and how that has always been central to their livelihood, even though they know it may no longer be safe to eat these animals. The tar sands are arguably the largest and most destructive industrial project on earth, and the Healing Walk conveys the sights, sounds, smells, and feelings it creates. People see first-hand—often in disbelief—the polluted environments that the First Nations and Métis communities sur-rounded by all of this must deal with on a daily basis, along with the workers. The walk allows participants to experience the landscape first-hand, and leaves them deeply educated.

Along with the power of this education, we believe in the power of prayer and the power of healing. Healing is a lifelong journey, and to pray for the land, air, water, and all living beings, we believe, helps. The ceremonies are led by people from the First Nations of the region, and the intentions are explained during the walk and the day before the walk. We try to ensure that our guests understand why and how we are praying, how they can participate, and any protocols that should be followed, so that when we start the walk, we can start *in a good way*—meaning to have good intentions and a better understanding of what prayer is and how prayer can help to heal the land, the people, the water, the air, and all living beings. We want to begin the walk in a unified way and with the knowledge of our elders and ceremonial people. But we also note that no one is forced to pray in any way with which they are not comfortable; we have had people of different faiths attend the Healing Walk in the past, and we invite them to come and pray in their own way. However, the walk is led by the First Nations of the region, and our ceremonies are in the forefront. We want participants to learn our ways, and how we honour the water, the air, the land, and all living beings. In doing this, we want to find similarities and common ground, and learn from each other.

Building Community in Healing

The Healing Walk creates a safe space to talk about tough issues we are facing concerning Mother Earth. It brings people together from Canada, the US, and now even farther away to learn and establish a dialogue about the problems of the tar sands and how they relate to them. For example, every year there are Indigenous people from British Columbia who attend the Healing Walk who are concerned with what is going on in northern Alberta and who fear how proposed pipelines through British Columbia also directly threaten their ways of life. The diversity of people who attend the Healing Walk is amazing, brought together by a shared desire to see the tar sands industry first-hand, to hear about impacts from the local people, and to share how the tar sands are affecting them. For those of us from the region, it has been really eye-opening to see how the tar sands industry is affecting more and more people beyond Alberta through various pipelines, such as Keystone XL.

We are learning not only about destruction, but also about what is still left to save here on Mother Earth, and the dedication and determination that people of all ages are willing to put forward to try and save what is left. Throughout the Healing Walk, the words "future generations" are repeatedly spoken—and it is so much more than words. If we don't change, what will be left for future generations? We are working for, praying for, and healing for them. We owe it to future generations to leave them what we had: a mother who took care of us, who gave us water, food, air, and shelter.

Thank you for taking the time to read about the Tar Sands Healing Walk, and we invite you to come walk with us, pray with us, feast with us, and learn from each other in the coming years. We always send our guests home with messages of hope, sharing stories of how we can help each other, and as everyone leaves, it is with enlightenment, friendship, determination, warm winds to dry the tears, knowledge of prayer, and some healing for the journeys ahead. We need more people to learn about the scale of destruction, and we also need to sustain the hope that we can turn this around and build a new future, where governments support solar and other forms of green energy on large scales, and where people become conscious energy users who value the quality of life and the health of Mother Earth over the quantity of things.

13

Petro-Chemical Legacies and Tar Sands Frontiers

Chemical Valley versus Environmental Justice

●

TOBAN BLACK

•

A conference titled "Bitumen—Adding Value: Canada's National Opportunity" brought together industry representatives, technical specialists, and government officials in May of 2013. This conference was held to discuss how additional tar sands projects could be brought to Ontario, and to the Eastern Seaboard from there. As the deputy chair of a bank's board of directors outlined a vision of industrial expansion in the keynote presentation, a protest march arrived outside the venue. The conference attendees generally tried to ignore the shouting, the banging on the windows, and a siren that simulated the emergency warning system for major pollution releases from the petrochemical companies operating nearby.

This conference and protest took place beside Sarnia, Ontario (across the river from Port Huron, Michigan), and the location of this confrontation was significant. The conference emphasized "the capacity of [the city and surrounding townships] to support oil sands development."[1] The local industrial district is a focal point for the tar sands industry's plans for growth in the form of pipelines, upgraders, refineries, and the manufacturing of megaload modules that would be used to construct facilities in Alberta. Such expansion plans are discussed and critiqued in this chapter.

The demonstration that May was dubbed Bitumen: Canada's National Disaster. This protest was a convergence against local tar sands threats, and the broader expansion of the industry. Regional allies organized the rally with members of Aamjiwnaang, the local Anishinaabe Indigenous community. Protestors arrived from multiple cities and Native reserves in southwestern Ontario. Inside the venue for the Bitumen—Adding Value conference, a local Indigenous activist also disrupted proceedings. Vanessa Gray from Aamjiwnaang unfurled a banner that read, "You are killing my generation." As authorities forced her to end this silent protest, she shouted, "The tar sands are environmental racism. I have a right to clean air and fresh water. If you think money is really more important then there is something really fucked up here."[2]

The Aamjiwnaang community is situated in a strategic hot spot in the Midwest. Approximately 40 per cent of Canada's chemical industry has been located in an area of Sarnia-Lambton known as "Chemical Valley." This industrial district also hosts rubber and plastics facilities, as well as a set of refineries. These petro-chemical plants were built around the Aamjiwnaang Native reserve, which now is smothered in their pollution. Extreme energy industries have been prolonging and worsening this situation by taking advantage of established petro-chemical facilities to bring shale energy[3] and tar sands into the area. Bitumen is already processed in Sarnia-Lambton, and the facilities there are a hub for tar sands infrastructure, which the industry seeks to further entrench in the region. The pipeline giant Enbridge has received federal permission to send heavy crude eastward from their Sarnia terminal. And there is more to the strategic importance of this area—as I will explain. For the tar sands industry, Sarnia-Lambton could serve as a launching pad to extend their reach eastward. In multiple respects, Sarnia and surrounding townships in Lambton County could prove to be significant as sites for further tar sands expansion, *or* as targets for interventions to reverse or overturn this industry. In the meantime, tar sands would add to the impacts from existing petro-chemical operations and pipeline networks in the region.

As is to be expected, there is already severe pollution around petro-chemical operations in Chemical Valley. For instance, local facilities release benzene, which causes cancer, bone marrow damage, and reduced red blood cell counts. Benzene is only one of many thousands of substances drifting in and around these facilities. The local air and water are contaminated with neurotoxins, carcinogens, hormone disruptors, and respiratory irritants. Every day and night, companies are spewing out metals (such as mercury and lead), particulate matter, and petro-chemical fumes (including toluene) into the surrounding environment. Given that people live around Chemical Valley, there are severe human tolls. Of course, toxins settle into the bodies of community members.[4] Dramatically elevated miscarriage rates and skewed birth ratios are among the disturbing patterns that have been found by Aamjiwnaang researchers: half as many males as females are born.[5] Many Sarnia residences are located near the petro-chemical facilities—if not immediately beside these—but the Aamjiwnaang reserve receives the brunt of the industrial pollution. A tally of the companies' self-reported emissions found that 60 per cent of these pollutants were released within five kilometres of the Aamjiwnaang reserve.[6] If facilities on the Michigan side of the river are taken into account as well, there are approximately sixty industrial facilities within twenty-five kilometres of Aamjiwnaang and south Sarnia.

Industry Plans and Impacts

Although Chemical Valley is concentrated in south Sarnia, this industrial district ultimately stretches across twenty kilometres. For the tar sands industry, Sarnia-Lambton has numerous attractive features. These include: a network of petroleum pipelines; workers with technical skills and expertise; a major railway yard; cross-border shipping by land and water; a river that can be used for industrial purposes; underground caverns, which have been receptacles for petro-chemical products; a local facility that incinerates and buries toxic wastes; and an established industry lobbying and PR organization (which proclaims itself an "Environmental Association").[7] The local college has specialized in petro-chemical training for decades, and the industry has much deeper roots in the area. Sarnia-Lambton may continue to attract fossil fuel and chemical industries because the overall economic, political, and cultural situation has been very favourable to these petro-chemical companies.

Yet, there are already various links between the tar sands and Chemical Valley. Local refineries are processing blends of oil and tar sands. Bitumen is pumped there through Enbridge's Michigan pipelines, and this company plans to use its regional pipeline network to bring tar sands from Sarnia to the East Coast. Hence, local residents and the local environment are pulled in two directions: even as the fossil fuel industry seeks to process additional bitumen there, companies are attempting to pump unprocessed bitumen through the local area to bring it farther east. At the same time, fabrication companies operating in Sarnia-Lambton have begun to secure deals to produce modules that are used to build tar sands facilities in Alberta. Municipal officials have been preparing the way for these regular shipments of petro-chemical modules via a downtown Sarnia harbour. This section of the chapter addresses the threats and impacts from these three strands of the tar sands industry—that is, pipelines, refining, and modules.

Pipelines

As with tar sands pipelines elsewhere, any flows of bitumen in and out of Sarnia-Lambton come with increased spill risks. The stakes include the likelihood that the Great Lakes would be contaminated by a spill in the area. Enbridge's Line 5 and 6B pipelines have brought bitumen into Ontario underneath the St. Clair River, which flows into Lake Erie. To make matters worse, Enbridge's plans for their Line 9 pipeline involve bringing heavy crude through a terminal located beside a drain that flows into the Great Lakes via the St. Clair River.

Enbridge is responsible for piping Athabasca tar sands into Chemical Valley. The company's Line 5 and 6B pipelines bring bitumen from Alberta to Sarnia, via Michigan. When Line 6B ruptured in 2010, 3.8 million litres of diluted bitumen spilled into a river around Kalamazoo, Michigan (see chapter 18). Even so, the company is more than doubling the flow through this pipeline—from 240,000 to 500,000 barrels per day—to send more petroleum to Sarnia, Detroit, and Toledo. This Line 6B expansion is part of Enbridge's multibillion-dollar "Eastern Access" plan. Enbridge has also begun to pump an additional fifty thousand barrels per day through its Line 5 pipeline, which runs through northern Michigan on its way to Sarnia. Moreover, in Ontario, the company is increasing the eastward flow through its Line 7 pipeline.[8] Given that there are at least seven Enbridge pipelines in southern Ontario, there is considerable potential for this company to expand its capacity to pump Alberta oil and tar sands eastwards.

In Ontario and Quebec, Enbridge has been focusing on plans for the Line 9. After denying that it would pump bitumen through Line 9, the company

successfully applied to send heavy crude through this pipeline. Line 9 was
built in 1975 with the same materials that were used to construct Line 6B in
Michigan. Enbridge plans to add bitumen to Line 9, while increasing the flow
through this pipeline by sixty thousand barrels per day—to a total of three
hundred thousand barrels per day. In recent years, Line 9 had brought conventional oil into Chemical Valley from the East Coast of the US, but Enbridge
and Imperial Oil are reversing the flow to transport fossil fuels from Alberta
eastward, with shale oil from the Bakken formation.[9] However, an estimated
9.1 million people—including eighteen Indigenous communities—live within
fifty kilometres of Line 9. The pipeline runs between Sarnia and Montreal,
and it is evident that there are plans to use it to pump petroleum towards the
East Coast.

In previous years, Enbridge was upfront about its intentions to pump
bitumen from Montreal to the ports in Maine to ship petroleum to existing
refineries (as outlined in their "Trailbreaker" plan). There have been indications that this plan continues to be the ultimate intention behind the Line 9
reversal—in accordance with commercial motives to send tar sands eastward.
The Line 9 reversal is one of many schemes to reduce the industry's reliance
on Midwestern refineries, such as those in Chemical Valley. The industry-
friendly mayor of Sarnia has offered vocal support in favour of the Line 9
reversal. Provincial governments have remained closer to the sidelines, while
the ruling federal party has enthusiastically supported this project. Yet, the
Line 9 project falls in the jurisdiction of Indigenous peoples, in accord with
treaties along the route.

In Sarnia, the Enbridge terminal is located beside the current
Aamjiwnaang reserve, on a section of the original reservation that was never
ceded. Under Canadian law, this land was not surrendered by Aamjiwnaang,
and two provincial courts have recognized this fact.[10] But these courts simultaneously suggested that the ongoing theft of this land should be accepted,
and they blamed Aamjiwnaang by suggesting that community members
"accepted" the sale. These judges did not take into account how the *Indian
Act* had prevented members of Aamjiwnaang from challenging this theft in
previous decades. After a more extensive history of colonization, thousands
of businesses and individuals now claim ownership over portions of the
1,028-hectare tract of land upon which the Enbridge terminal is located. In
1840, this land was seemingly transferred to private owners, but without

Aamjiwnaang community consent. One of the individuals involved in this land deal was Joshua Wawanosh—who would be deposed as a chief five years later. An Ontario court has recognized how "the many complaints against Wawanosh included allegations that he abused his authority as chief, misappropriated band assets, and showed gross favouritism towards friends and allies. There were also allegations that Wawanosh sold, or at least tried to sell, Chippewa land without authority."[11]

Such treaty violations are not addressed in the federal government's pipeline review process, however. The National Energy Board's (NEB) assessments for pipeline applications barely note the locations of official reserves, and earlier treaties are not considered. Accordingly, the NEB does not seek the free, prior, and informed consent of *anyone* along a pipeline route. At 2012 and 2013 Line 9 hearings, the Aamjiwnaang band council voiced concerns about the reversal and expansion, and objected to a lack of meaningful consultation. The NEB approved each of Enbridge's Line 9 applications anyway.

Refineries

In 2013, tar sands had not yet been pumped east of Chemical Valley, but there was already bitumen in the mix of Alberta fossil fuels that had been fed into Sarnia-Lambton facilities. Suncor has invested $1 billion for upgrades to its refineries, which largely consist of "strengthen[ing] integration with oil sands operation[s]" in Alberta.[12] In part, these resources were spent to increase the capacity to process tar sands at their Sarnia refinery. Bitumen is fed into Shell and Imperial Oil refineries in the area as well, and tar sands could be a feedstock for nearby petro-chemical operations. What is clear is that Enbridge was pumping bitumen there before the company had applied for federal approval to send heavy crude farther east. Public pressure could bring to light information about bitumen in Chemical Valley, and companies' plans to expand their tar sands processing in the area.

For years, there has been some industry interest in building an upgrader in Sarnia-Lambton so that raw tar sands can be processed there. These objectives are apparent in a two-volume document entitled "Canada: Winning as a Sustainable [sic] Energy Superpower," which was associated with the May 2013 tar sands conference in Sarnia (noted earlier). The authors of this "Superpower" document name Sarnia as a possible location for "an integrated complex of value-added investments" for tar sands processing,[13] and this agenda has subsequently been promoted through other media and meetings. For the time being, bitumen is only a percentage of the petroleum feedstocks that are pumped into the refineries and petro-chemical facilities in Chemical Valley.

So far, these companies have succeeded in maintaining a low profile for any tar sands processing, even as it is worsening the impacts around their facilities. For instance, additional sulphur dioxide is emitted as more bitumen is pumped into refineries as a portion of their total feedstocks.[14] We are only beginning to understand how much worse the pollution is around refineries that process tar sands.

Any further pollution from extreme energy in these facilities must be viewed as an extension of decades of petro-chemical industry impacts. At the Aamjiwnaang reserve, community members report a life expectancy of fifty-five years of age, and intense health impacts are experienced throughout these years. Forty per cent of the individuals approached for a community survey reported that they required an inhaler.[15] A summary of this survey notes how "members of the reserve identified releases of chemicals and incidents such as spills as their primary concerns. In addition, these chemicals and related incidents have significant impacts on their cultural life, including hunting, fishing, medicine gathering and ceremonial activities."[16] For instance, cedar in their territory is contaminated with cadmium, a metal that is associated with cancer and learning disabilities. Cedar is sacred to people of Aamjiwnaang, for whom it is a medicine. As the petro-chemical industry has taken over the area, numerous traditional herbal medicines have been made toxic. Aamjiwnaang spirituality has been assaulted as it has become more difficult for community members to relate to such a contaminated landscape, and much of the traditional hunting and gathering practices have been lost.

Treaty violations only magnify these injustices, as the community has lost much of its former autonomy. I have noted how companies such as Enbridge have claimed the unceded section of the reserve. Neighbouring petro-chemical facilities are located on land that had only been surrendered after federal officials threatened to take Aamjiwnaang territory by force.[17]

The industry is a very intrusive and devastating presence on the remaining reserve land. Suncor's facility is located directly beside Aamjiwnaang residences, as well as the community cemetery. The company intrudes on the reserve further by using an Aamjiwnaang road as if it were company property. Examples like these are important, but ultimately it is very difficult to convey the industry's impacts on residents and workers. I can only offer selected indications here. Pollution may be the worst of these impacts, but there is far more to the local presence of the petro-chemical industry.

In addition to the everyday clouds of toxins, there are recurring surges in industry releases—and without an adequate warning system, or reliable journalism. To mention one of a seemingly endless list of examples: In May of 2011, a mile-long cloud of bluish-grey vapour was released from an Imperial Oil facility. No emergency siren was sounded, and the company initially did not take responsibility for the release. When Imperial Oil did acknowledge that a cloud of sulphur dioxide had come from its facility, it suggested that the cloud was not toxic—an absurd claim that was repeated by the press. This case demonstrates the severity of local pollution, as well as the laxness of government oversight and public health monitoring. In Sarnia-Lambton, the local warning sirens are unreliable, and information about major pollution releases is generally minimal—and often difficult to obtain. In these conditions, many residents experience anxieties about safety and health. Interviews with members of Aamjiwnaang have found that "the most common reported impact was fear. People on the reserve feared the outdoors, the warning sirens, and unreported incidences [sic]."[18]

Officials typically have tolerated and enabled the many impacts of Chemical Valley. In rare instances, fines[19] and stern words have been issued in response to extreme releases, but the vast majority of the pollution has been sanctioned by the state. The government provides permits for toxic releases, and their pollution standards usually amount to suggested guidelines. To make matters worse, these standards are calculated as though none of the sixty industrial facilities in the area have any offsite impacts. Background pollution levels around each facility are assumed to be zero, and there is a complete failure to take into account synergistic combinations of toxic substances. Even so, there has been a pattern of granting exemptions to these weak regulations.[20]

Officials have also failed to provide basic information regarding health impacts. Local requests for funding to study health impacts have basically gone unanswered. There is currently no independent and officially recognized study of any of the impacts from the thousands of dangerous substances in and around the Sarnia-Lambton petro-chemical facilities. Nevertheless, certain officials have blamed these health impacts on individual lifestyle choices (such as smoking).[21] In the meantime, the vast majority of local pollution monitoring is conducted by the petro-chemical industry. Ten of fourteen of the local monitoring stations are maintained by these companies, and it seems that very little is done with the measurements collected by government agencies.

Modules

If current plans unfold, Sarnia-Lambton will be manufacturing large components for tar sands operations in Alberta, where new facilities would be assembled with these modules. One company plans to produce modules for steam-assisted gravity drainage, a bitumen extraction technique. At least twelve of these modules would be built, and each of these would be twenty metres long and more than four metres wide. Sarnia-Lambton hosts a long list of machine shops and engineering firms, so there is far more potential to further integrate their operations into building up the Alberta tar sands industry. While other locations in Ontario also have manufacturing histories that could serve the tar sands industry in the same way, Chemical Valley is at the forefront of what might prove to be much more extensive expansion through southern Ontario. Again, the existing facilities that are already integrated into the petro-chemical industry would allow the tar sands industry to grow more quickly, with fewer economic costs.

Sending modules across thousands of kilometres also entails transportation corridors. Petro-chemical modules have previously been shipped out of a downtown harbour in Sarnia, and companies have sought more regular access. By 2012, municipal officials were offering considerable support for these plans. Government subsidies will evidently be among the millions of dollars invested in a module transportation corridor that will make further use of downtown Sarnia streets. Roads would be blocked as modules are sent through them with a police escort—at taxpayers' expense. The module corridor also cuts through residential areas, where locals may be disturbed by low-frequency sound waves. A dedicated corridor for these modules ultimately would entail a list of costs and risks. However, most of the impacts would be far from Sarnia, in northern Alberta, after the modules are put into operation there. Along the way, the shipments would be transported along two Great Lakes, and through three provinces.

Although producing and shipping these modules could prove to be a very important tie between Sarnia-Lambton and the tar sands, I am focusing on industry plans for which there is much more potential to mobilize around. Pollution from refineries can be expected to be far more of a concern for locals, and—hopefully—for regional supporters. So far, petro-chemical paycheques have pre-empted most of the potential opposition towards such refining, however, and we can expect this dynamic to be much more pronounced in regards to module production.

Resistance: Only the Beginning?

In 2013, the connections between Chemical Valley and the tar sands were primarily being addressed by campaigners challenging Enbridge's plans for their Line 9 pipeline. At times, these campaigners have looked beyond the pipeline to oppose any industry plans to bring additional tar sands into Ontario. When they have confronted Chemical Valley, activists have objected to plans to process tar sands there. Concerns about Line 9 and tar sands have been central to a set of regional marches that were called by the community group Aamjiwnaang and Sarnia Against Pipelines (ASAP). The first of these was a ten-kilometre march through a section of Chemical Valley in the winter of 2013. This march included a round dance at an intersection, a mobile drumming circle, a picnic on the road in front of a Suncor facility, a water ceremony, and a driveway die-in outside of a Shell plant. Months earlier, ASAP had organized a small protest against Line 9 at the Enbridge terminal in Sarnia. The following May, the protest at the Bitumen—Adding Value conference was more of a regional collaboration, with links to the community mobilizing in previous months. There are many other tales of resistance around Chemical Valley, and I can only mention some of these in passing.

Much of this resistance has come from Aamjiwnaang. A case in point was a six-week blockade in 2004, on a road that Suncor normally claims for their day-to-day operations. By blockading land that is part of the reserve, Aamjiwnaang community members pressured the company to locate their new ethanol plant. A series of community research and lobbying initiatives began around this time. In previous decades, members of Aamjiwnaang had challenged industry land claims in court, but without regaining traditional territory, or even monetary compensation. In recent years, two members of the community have taken a different approach by filing a lawsuit against Suncor and the Ministry of the Environment. In late 2010, Ada Lockridge, Ron Plain, and the organization EcoJustice launched this ongoing lawsuit to challenge the cumulative effects of industry pollution, and to seek government protection for their right to clean air.

Around the end of 2012, local organizing took another turn, as part of a wave of activity sparked by cross-Canada Idle No More mobilizations for Native sovereignty. Members of the community organized and joined a set of actions and rallies. Beginning in December of 2012, there was a twelve-day Aamjiwnaang blockade on a rail spur line that serves local petro-chemical facilities. Regional allies joined and supported the blockade. A local highway that leads to the US border was also blocked by regional Idle No More rallies on two separate occasions. And after there was a major pollution release from a Shell facility that January, an Idle No More protest brought together children, parents, and daycare staff, among other community members. Thirty-seven individuals have since filed papers regarding the impacts they have experienced.

There has been further opposition from Sarnia-Lambton residents who are not from Aamjiwnaang. In 1999, a network of mostly non-Native residents, health clinic workers, and labour organizers began to confront a deadly legacy of asbestos exposure in local workplaces. They sought justice by holding memorial events, and pursuing monetary compensation. A community group called Victims of Chemical Valley succeeded in establishing a memorial site in a downtown park, along a waterfront. Yet, the legacy of contamination overshadowed this memorial when asbestos was discovered in the surrounding park, which was fenced off in 2013. In recent years, such environmental pollution from Sarnia-Lambton petro-chemical companies has been highlighted and challenged by SHAME: Sarnia Hometown Activist Movement Emerging, a separate organizing network led by Zak Nicholls. The year after this network began to form in 2009, SHAME organized protests and a campaign against Enbridge and BP. SHAME has encouraged locals to contact the government to raise their concerns about major industry releases, and the individuals involved in SHAME also conducted a door-to-door survey to gain insights into the experiences of Sarnia residents. From a neighbouring city, I helped with the various efforts of this network, and our collaborations included the organizing of a 2011 protest outside a shale gas conference in Sarnia. That year, a SHAME organizer also attempted to support Sarnia-Lambton residents voicing their objections to industry fumes from a "Clean Harbors" waste facility near their homes.

In recent decades, some of the opposition towards Chemical Valley has also come from downstream residents. Resistance towards industrial pollution has come from those who live to the south along the St. Clair River—at the Walpole Island Native reserve,[22] and in the town of Wallaceburg. In 2008, the resistance of Walpole water protectors factored into Shell's decision to abandon their multibillion-dollar plans for a new tar sands upgrader in Sarnia-Lambton. A few years later, Michigan "Wipe Out Wilms" events raised concerns about tumours in children living downstream in Marine City. A network of concerned residents in the area has continued to scrutinize Chemical Valley.

In the mid-1980s, there was symbolic support for residents along the St. Clair River when a "blob" of chemical pollution in these waters was a national news story. Greenpeace even visited to carry out protest actions in Sarnia. Yet, since the 1990s, the concerns about these waters have been much more localized.

These preceding points certainly do not amount to an exhaustive list; I am only offering brief indications of previous opposition that could be extended. So far, this resistance has amounted to the beginnings of what might prove to be much more intense and sustained mobilizing around the petro-chemical facilities in Sarnia-Lambton. There has also been a series of speaking events about Aamjiwnaang and Chemical Valley, and a host of documentaries have highlighted the situation there, but active solidarity has been far from adequate. Hence, the opposition and community research have often been taken up by dedicated locals, who have had little support. Petro-chemical companies remain well entrenched in Sarnia-Lambton, and campaigners have not yet succeeded in building up the capacity to contend with their power. Further tar sands industry expansion in Ontario can only be prevented if there is much more of a base of opposition. Chemical Valley and pipeline campaigning may be limited focuses in themselves, but these struggles would be enough for many people to take up—to do their part to confront the tar sands industry.

There are many parallels with other places where petro-chemical facilities are located, and where much the same mobilizations should occur. As in Chemical Valley, we can expect comparable impacts, as well as similar prospects for constructive change. Everyone has a stake in these struggles, given how pervasive petro-chemicals are in modern societies.

14

Beyond Token Recognition

The Growing Movement against the Enbridge Northern Gateway Project

●

TYLER McCREARY

•

Introduction

In 2002, Enbridge, a Calgary-based energy transportation company, began exploring the feasibility of constructing a pipeline system that would connect bitumen extracted from the Alberta tar sands to the Pacific Coast of British Columbia.[1] In its proposed development, the Enbridge corporation has sought to construct two approximately 1,170-kilometre pipelines: one that would deliver an average of 193,000 barrels per day of condensate east to thin bitumen for transport, and a second to transport 525,000 barrels of diluted bitumen per day to a Pacific port in Kitimat, British Columbia.[2] The project, if built, would connect the vast bitumen reserves of the tar sands to be marketed globally without first passing through the United States. The Northern Gateway Project, as the proposal would become known, would permit both the expansion and diversification of tar sands exports to new markets, particularly in Asia.[3] It would also be a basis for the introduction of new environmental concerns. Developing this transportation corridor would introduce risks of pipeline and tanker spills to watersheds and coastal ecosystems, and, as part of an expansion of the production and consumption of petroleum resources from the tar sands, it would contribute to cataclysmic growth in greenhouse gas emissions that would threaten to press climate change beyond the point at which carbon reduction strategies could be effective.[4] Connected to both political economies of resource exports and the political ecologies of petroleum development, the proposal to build a pipeline to the Pacific Coast has come to represent a synecdoche for both the dream of a new frontier for expanding Canadian bitumen trade, and the nightmare of an unmitigated environmental catastrophe.

As other contributors in this book make clear, expanding Canadian pipeline capacity to enable further export of bitumen from the Alberta tar sands rests at the centre of the current Canadian government strategy for economic development. But this expansion also threatens to disrupt ecologies and inhibit Indigenous peoples' ability to maintain traditional sustenance economies. The federally appointed panel reviewing the Northern Gateway proposal recognized significant environmental effects associated with the project, but ultimately prioritized the economic interests linked to pipeline construction. After months of hearings, the panel determined that the benefits of a pipeline connecting the tar sands to the Pacific Coast outweighed the risks. In a two-volume report released on December 19, 2013, the review panel suggested that imposing 209 conditions on the proposed development would be sufficient to protect the environment. "After mitigation, the likelihood of significant adverse environmental effects resulting from project malfunctions or accidents is very low," the panellists concluded.[5]

In this chapter, I focus critical attention on the contested process governing the proposed Enbridge Northern Gateway project. I explore the ebb of regulatory consideration for environmental and Indigenous concerns, while examining the rising tide of voices against the project. I begin by outlining the early incarnation of the Northern Gateway project as the Gateway Pipeline, and how the contours of the struggle were first defined in initial debates over its governance. Then I shift to the current incarnation of the Enbridge proposal, examining how the review process has constrained possibilities for asserting environmental concerns, and how recent legislative changes have introduced further limits on the consideration of environmental impacts. I then turn to how the review process addresses Indigenous peoples. The review process incorporates Indigenous peoples as interveners arguing before the panel, and also includes consideration of evidence on traditional knowledge. However, I argue that the panel structure denies Indigenous peoples the possibility of participating in formal decision-making. This constrained politics of recognition has seeded a growing movement of resistance, challenging not only the wisdom of pipeline development but also the legitimacy of the processes governing it. I thus conclude the chapter with a discussion of the voices denouncing this review process and its exclusionary calculus of balancing interests. Through a vibrant and inventive movement in the streets, on social media, and before the panel, people have sought to reclaim politics from nullifying governmental calculations, and with it the basic ability to debate, question, and challenge a given social order to fight for a new and better one.

Opening Salvos in the Struggle over Northern Gateway

From its inception, the governance of the Northern Gateway project has been contested, with corporate interests lobbying to streamline the approvals process while Indigenous and environmental groups struggled to assert competing interests to those of industry. In 2005, Enbridge released a preliminary information package and requested that the government establish a joint review panel (JRP) to streamline the regulatory process for what it then referred to simply as the Gateway Pipeline. Particularly, the company wanted to combine the environmental assessment of the project with its application for certification by the National Energy Board.[6] As the project resonated with the economic development strategies of the federal government, regulators appeared keen to support the development of this pipeline infrastructure by easing the regulatory burden. However, Gateway encountered stiff resistance from environmentalists and Indigenous organizations. When the Minister of the Environment and the National Energy Board drafted a Joint Review Panel Agreement in 2006, the Carrier Sekani Tribal Council initiated legal action, filing a suit in federal court against the exclusion of affected Indigenous peoples from the Gateway regulatory decision-making process.[7] The company delayed the project, and the claim was dropped; however, the contours of the conflict had been clearly established.

When Enbridge restarted the review process in 2008 for the Northern Gateway project, the struggle began again in earnest. In late 2009, a Joint Review Panel Agreement was released, and in early 2010, the three members of the panel were announced. They were: Sheila Leggett, a biologist with extensive regulatory experience; Kenneth Bateman, a Canadian energy lawyer and former senior executive in the Canadian energy sector; and Hans Matthews, an Indigenous geologist with extensive experience in industrial development and liaising between industry and Indigenous communities. Many remained suspicious of the panel and its perceived industry bias. Environmental organizations and community groups responded with a campaign that helped approximately four thousand people register to speak against the pipeline in the panel hearings. They also launched a public campaign attacking the project and challenging the legitimacy of the review process. Indigenous people have become leaders in this protest movement, raising concerns about the potential impacts on their traditional territories and asserting the necessity of engaging with their communities regarding developments on their traditional territories.

Development Unbound

To ensure a secure supply of bitumen exports, the government has sought to streamline regulatory processes and lift environmental protections that impede development. The formation of the JRP reduced regulatory duplications, but it also allowed the government to privilege economic frames over environmental or Indigenous concerns. In July 2006, newly elected Conservative prime minister Stephen Harper used his first international speaking engagement to boldly declare Canada's status as an "energy superpower," and laud the country as "a stable, reliable producer in a volatile, unpredictable world."[8] While the Canadian state has long supported Canadian petroleum production, the Harper government employed particular vigour in their dedication to the task. In particular, the state has committed to facilitating the expansion of the Alberta tar sands and its related export infrastructure, including the construction of the Enbridge Northern Gateway and the TransCanada Keystone XL pipelines, and the retrofitting of older infrastructure, such as the Kinder Morgan Trans Mountain pipeline. Government support has helped smooth the regulatory hurdles that energy transportation projects must overcome.

With relation to the Enbridge Northern Gateway project, the JRP agreement constituted the panel to consider the environmental impacts of the proposed pipeline, public and Indigenous concerns, possible measures to mitigate adverse impacts, and the broader national interest served by the project. Interpreting its mandate, the panel has narrowly framed the environmental impacts to be reviewed. Moreover, the government has enacted legislative changes subsequent to the initiation of the review process, further delimiting the breadth of issues under consideration and ensuring that the federal cabinet has final decision-making authority. Thus, there has been a consistent pattern in regulatory and government action that has constrained the recognition of environmental concerns to the benefit of the economic interests involved in the development of the tar sands and related pipeline infrastructure.

Throughout the formation and implementation of the review process, there has been a steady elision of crucial environmental issues involved in the Northern Gateway project. In a 2009 scoping document produced by the Canadian Environmental Assessment Agency prior to the formation of the JRP, climatic issues associated with the pipeline were narrowly bound to the "project-related emissions of greenhouse gas that could result from the construction and operation of the marine project components and from accidents or malfunctions."[9] Similarly, in focusing cumulative effects analyses on the socio-environmental issues associated with pipelines and shipping in isolation, the scoping document neglects the cumulative impacts of tar sands development. This frame was repeated in the JRP agreement, and when the JRP determined the issues it would be considering. This means the greenhouse gases associated with the upstream tar sands development and the downstream consumption of the bitumen shipped through the pipeline are beyond the pale of consideration for review. Similarly, the environmental impacts of continued tar sands development remained beyond the scope of the review.

Further, after vast numbers of people registered to speak before the panel and continued to raise concerns about the project despite the narrowed scope of the review, the government signalled its staunch commitment to industry over democracy. In a January 2012 open letter, Joe Oliver, the minister of natural resources, argued that the Canadian regulatory system was "broken," and thus reforms are "an urgent matter of Canada's national interest."[10] In particular, he criticized "the slow, complex and cumbersome federal Government approval process," and railed against how "environmental and other radical groups" stack "public hearings with bodies to ensure that delays kill good projects."[11] To ease the regulatory burden on development, the government proceeded to rewrite Canadian environmental protections under the auspices of omnibus budget bills. Legislative changes established time limits on the review processes (including the Enbridge review already underway) and further restricted the issues under consideration.

In Bill C-38, the *Jobs, Growth and Long-term Prosperity Act*, the Conservative government forwarded an omnibus budget implementation bill radically rewriting environmental assessment and energy-permitting processes in Canada. The omnibus budget bill institutionalizes federal cabinet authority over environmental and energy governance processes. Changes to the *Canadian Environmental Assessment Act* grant the minister of the environment sweeping decision-making authority. The government introduced new language to the *National Energy Board Act*, providing the federal cabinet with the authority to order the National Energy Board to certify a pipeline even if the review panel recommends against certification. Under the previous regime, the cabinet could deny an application for certification under the National Energy Board that the board had approved, but could not approve an application that the board had denied. The National Energy Board, formerly in possession of regulatory authority, now serves to conduct the environmental assessment and regulatory review process, and simply recommends terms and conditions to the government. Cabinet will make the final decision, and direct the National Energy Board to deny or issue the certification for the project.

Within review and assessment processes, the omnibus bill has also made sweeping changes restricting the consideration of environmental effects. The bill repealed the *Canadian Environmental Assessment Act*, replacing it with a new law that significantly altered the rules about how, and if, federal environmental assessment of projects occurs. Review panels are now subject to strict timelines. For joint review processes already underway, the minister of the environment and the National Energy Board must jointly establish a time limit for a "decision statement" to be issued, although the National Energy Board is designated the sole authority regulating the environmental impacts of pipelines for future projects. Further amendments reduce protections under the *Fisheries Act* so that only species related to human use—members of "commercial, recreational or Aboriginal fisheries, or [fish] that support such a fishery"—are protected. The revisions also introduce a new doctrine prohibiting serious harm to fish.[12] This is in contrast to the prior version of the *Fisheries Act*, which prevented all harmful alteration of fish habitat. Under the doctrine of serious harm, industrial activities could reduce the quality of fish habitat for years, stunting the growth of fish and decreasing their numbers, so long as the impact of these activities does not beyond a reasonable doubt actually kill the fish or prevent the fish habitat from ever recovering. Changes to the *Species at Risk Act* exempt energy development regulated by the National Energy Board from the requirement to minimize impacts on the habitats of species at risk.

This trajectory of governmental deregulation, streamlining environmental hurdles to development, continued with further omnibus legislation: Bill C-45. This bill replaced the *Navigable Waters Protection Act* with the *Navigable Protection Act,* largely dropping consideration of marine environments and focusing on ensuring easier transport of goods, such as bitumen. The new act delimits protection to a proposed schedule of three oceans, ninety-seven lakes, and portions of sixty-two rivers. Absent are the vast majority of the nearly thirty-two thousand major lakes and more than 2.25 million rivers in Canada from protection, notably including many of the watercourses in British Columbia along the route of the proposed Northern Gateway pipeline.

In addition to limiting the consideration of environmental issues, the government has sought to constrict the funding available to environmental organizations, and has restricted the ability of environmental organizations to participate in public reviews. It has also heightened the financial reporting requirements of environmental charities, and devoted funds to investigate whether environmental charities were engaging in political activities deemed to be incompatible with their status. Further, documents released through freedom of information requests highlight the increased dedication of government resources to surveying pipeline opponents, particularly those expected to participate in civil disobedience.[13] Thus, the government has turned its attention away from monitoring environmental issues and towards monitoring environmentalists and Indigenous activists. This shift fits within a long-term strategy not only to secure pipeline access to exports, but also to inhibit the political contestation of tar sands development.

Indigeneity Contained

Indigenous politics have also been subject to a similar, although distinct, systematic elision. While legislative changes disappear environmental concerns from review processes, the constitutionalization of Indigenous rights in Canada provides Indigenous concerns greater resilience within formal processes. Thus, Indigenous interests continue to be selectively included, considered, and accommodated within government review processes. The JRP recognizes its obligation to consider Indigenous traditional knowledge and consult with Indigenous peoples regarding the impact of the pipeline; however, these duties are interpreted in only the most limited frames. Despite vociferous protests, numerous letters, and testimony that clearly rebukes the creation of the JRP without adequate consultation with affected Indigenous communities, the panel disregards Indigenous claims to unceded jurisdiction in their territories. Rather, much as Nadasdy has described in the Kluane territories of the Yukon, the discussion of Aboriginal traditional knowledge works to situate the "place at the table" of local Indigenous peoples, "preventing rather than fostering meaningful change by ensnaring participants in a tangle of bureaucracy."[14] Thus, rather than empowering Indigenous peoples and respecting their traditional knowledge, the limited politics of inclusion within formal review proceedings forecloses on real possibilities of addressing power relations in the colonial present.

Aboriginal rights are recognized and affirmed in the Canadian Constitution.[15] Yet, in recognizing and affirming these rights, the Constitution does not create them. Rather, Aboriginal rights are a doctrine developed within Canadian jurisprudence to account for its encounter with Indigenous legal orders that preceded the existence of Canadian law, and continue to remain other to it. Indigenous peoples existed on this land as organized societies governed by their own laws prior to the Canadian Constitution, prior to the formation of the Canadian government. Further, in British Columbia, the majority of Indigenous peoples have never ceded their lands or their systems of governing them. The Supreme Court of Canada has established that the government holds a responsibility to reconcile the settlement and development of the land with Aboriginal rights and title.[16] It is on this basis that the Canadian government retains distinct obligations with regards to Indigenous peoples.

However, the current Conservative government has sought to recognize these obligations in a minimal form. The process through which the government is rewriting environmental law disrespects the aforementioned relationship between Indigenous peoples and the Canadian state. The omnibus bills not only truncate parliamentary debate and further denude the already limited democratic process in Canada, but they also fail to consider and consult with Indigenous communities affected by the changes. In contrast to the majority of the Canadian population, which is concentrated along the American border, Indigenous peoples maintain significant populations in remote regions affected by industrial developments. While the benefits of industrial developments often enrich investors, environmental degradation regularly has the most pronounced impacts on Indigenous communities.

With regard to the Enbridge Northern Gateway project, the government has suggested that the review process will address the majority of state obligations regarding the consultation of Aboriginal peoples. However, the JRP was unilaterally imposed on Indigenous peoples without their consent. The terms of reference and the list of issues were not developed through meaningful consultation. Furthermore, in practice, much of the consultation has been left to Enbridge, which routinely misunderstood local Indigenous protocols—for instance, showing disrespect by leaving a feast early in Gitxaala. Indigenous communities raised substantial concerns about consultation, including inadequate time or funding to participate, lack of discussion around specific mitigation strategies, insufficient respect for Aboriginal title, and failure to incorporate culturally relevant concepts into project planning.

Indigenous concerns are only selectively included in the review process for the Enbridge pipeline. As Richard Milligan and I have detailed elsewhere, the containment of Indigenous concerns, the studied neglect of Indigenous jurisdiction, and the normalization of colonial structures of authority are evident in the selective inclusion of Carrier Sekani concerns.[17] The Carrier Sekani Tribal Council used Enbridge funding to conduct an independent Aboriginal Interests and Use Study on the impacts of the pipeline.[18] This study highlighted their concerns that the JRP process did not respect their Indigenous jurisdiction over their lands.[19] On this basis, the Carrier Sekani decided not to participate in a review process. Nonetheless, Enbridge putatively included its concerns by summarizing the study in one of the volumes of its application.[20] However, the original research has not been submitted—only the Enbridge summary, which crucially neglected the jurisdictional concerns of the Carrier Sekani. Thus, while the Enbridge application gestures to a consideration of their traditions and interests, the key findings delegitimizing the JRP are excluded from the review process.

The bounded recognition of Indigenous difference is also inscribed on the JRP record in its approach to what the record refers to as "native words." While numerous Indigenous witnesses insisted on presenting their evidence in their own language, or employed Indigenous concepts as part of their presentations on their traditional knowledge, this information only irregularly entered the record. The transcriber never asked speakers to clarify or spell terms in their own language, and instead regularly dropped terms from the record, simply inserting the phrase "native word" in bracketed text, or occasionally interjecting haphazard phonetic attempts to capture concepts. For instance, in Fort St. James, when Jim Munroe was presenting on the traditional system of *keyoh* (territory or trapline) holdings, a series of Dakelh terms were rendered illegible in the published transcript: "There are laws around that. There's terms in our language it's called (native word) and (native word) and it means they did—people disappear if they don't respect the land and they don't ask."[21] This silencing of Indigenous terms from the official record reflects an underlying disregard for Indigenous conceptual frameworks, despite the putative inclusions of Aboriginal traditional knowledge in the hearings. These exclusions are rationalized on the basis that the hearings process is recorded in "either of the official languages [French and English], depending on the languages spoken by the participant at the public hearing."[22] The fact that Indigenous languages are unrecognized as "official" languages underlines how, despite the ostensible inclusion of Indigeneity, the underlying framework of regulation remains an imposed and colonial one.

Further, in calling forth Indigenous testimony in oral evidentiary hearings, the panel sought to foreclose Indigenous traditions to remembrances of hunting and gathering. While the panel listened disinterestedly to testimony of Indigenous governance traditions, they rebuked Indigenous presenters who dared challenge the legitimacy of the JRP process. For instance, Haisla Hereditary Chief Gupsalupus, Henry Amos, in his testimony before the panel, questioned how people could trust the JRP, noting the panel had no Haisla representation. Instead, the panel was solely "appointed by the Federal Government ... the same government that is telling the world that this project should go ahead."[23] Chief Amos challenged how the review process had from its outset systematically disadvantaged Haisla people. The process was designed by and ultimately accountable to a federal government that felt the need to articulate its "commitment to diversify our energy markets" on the eve of hearings on an export pipeline.[24] Joint Review Panel chair Sheila Leggett chastised Chief Amos, informing him that their purpose was "to listen to your oral evidence that wouldn't be able to be put in writing."[25] She elaborated that the hearing order and published JRP information indicated that the panel was looking for Aboriginal people to present "traditional knowledge."[26]

Sadly, Haisla traditional knowledge provides not simply a record of how their people used their lands, but also how government indifference to Haisla concerns has continually supported industrial development to the detriment of Haisla territories and self-determination. Ellis Ross, elected chief councillor of the Haisla Nation Council, relayed how his father had been unable to continue generations of traditional harvesting on the Kitimat River due to pollution from the mill. "That is my traditional knowledge," Ross stated.[27] Where the Haisla once taught their children to use their traditional resources, now the elders can only remember how they once used their lands and waters. These stories of environmental degradation and government neglect are now the traditional knowledge of the Haisla people. Speaking of his traditional knowledge and responsibilities, Ross described the need to continue to listen to and learn from these horrible stories of the destruction of their lands and impositions on their self-determination. This, according to Ross, was necessary so people would "make sure that doesn't happen again."[28] Permitting the Enbridge pipeline would violate these responsibilities to Haisla tradition, although considering this breadth of tradition as a framework that included contemporary politics remained beyond the scope of the JRP process.

Resistance Unfurled

Government servitude to oil and gas interests has spurred further resistance. In the review hearings, Indigenous people and settlers have spoken poignantly about their frustration and feelings of government disregard. There has been eloquence, but also anger. Throughout their travels, the panel has been accompanied by protests. Indigenous peoples have been at the centre of this

BEN POWLESS

Members of the Wet'suwet'en Nation protesting all proposed pipelines that would cross unceded Wet'suwet'en lands, as part of the first annual Unist'ot'en Action Camp, 2010.

movement against the pipeline since its earliest inception. They remain on the frontlines of environmental struggles as the first affected, living in remote communities and often continuing to rely on traditional foods as a key source of nutritional and cultural sustenance. But more than this, Indigenous peoples are becoming the last defence against the Conservative agenda, as Indigenous rights derive from their inherent status as distinct peoples rather than from statutes that can be amended at any time. In the wake of the recent omnibus amendments, the prominence of Indigenous peoples in the movement against government toadying to industry has only grown. The movement against Enbridge has not only fought unsustainable tar sands development; it has reclaimed democracy and reasserted Indigenous space with flash mobs of round dancers in crowded malls, marches through city streets, and blockades on rail lines and highways.

Struggling to uphold traditional responsibilities to govern the land, Indigenous peoples have banded together in opposition to the pipeline and allied with concerned settlers across the country. In December 2010, sixty-one First Nations issued the *Save the Fraser Declaration*, asserting a collective commitment to prevent "the proposed Enbridge Northern Gateway Pipelines, or similar Tar Sands projects, to cross our lands, territories and watersheds, or the ocean migration routes of Fraser River salmon."[29] By December 2012, the declaration had garnered more than 130 signatories. In 2013, a Solidarity Accord was added to the declaration, adding the voices of municipal governments and leaders from the tourism industry, health and environmental organizations, and prominent unions.[30]

A series of lawsuits have sought judicial review of the JRP. These include applications by the Haisla and the Gitxaala, as well as environmental groups. The lawsuits assert that the JRP erred in privileging consideration of the economic benefits of the Enbridge Northern Gateway project over the adverse effects of the development on Indigenous peoples and the environment. But activists are not simply relying on state law.

In building these networks of solidarity, Indigenous people have mobilized their traditional connection to their lands and asserted the necessity of recognizing new geographies of responsibility that follow the contours of global financial networks and supply chains. Carrier Sekani communities have erected signs on their territories warning Enbridge and its contractors against trespassing, and threatening to prosecute violators on the basis of Indigenous law. Indigenous activists also brought their claims to Enbridge's 2011 and 2012 annual general meetings in Calgary and Toronto, respectively. Wearing traditional regalia bearing symbolic connections to their territories, Indigenous peoples extended Indigenous legal orders to engage companies as subject to this body of law, thereby reterritorializing the geographies of resource development and environmental governance.[31]

Further materializing Indigenous jurisdiction on the landscape, particular Indigenous groups have begun to establish blockades. The Unist'ot'en, associated with the C'ihlts'ehkhyu or Big Frog Clan of the Wet'suwet'en people, have established a camp along the Enbridge Northern Gateway route at the junction of Gosnell Creek and Wedzin Kwah (Morice River). Blocking the development of pipelines, activists such as the Unist'ot'en invert the geographies of resource extraction. Where Canadian regimes governing industrial development contain Indigenous politics to mobilize processes of resource extraction, blockades mobilize Indigenous politics to stop the movement of resources through Indigenous territories. The Unist'ot'en resurgence has further sought not only to politicize the Enbridge Northern Gateway, but also to highlight the proliferation of pipeline projects in association with natural gas fracking in northeastern British Columbia. The route of Northern

Gateway across Unist'ot'en territories overlaps with that of the proposed Pacific Trail Pipeline for liquefied natural gas. Linking the issues involved in unconventional natural gas and tar sands development, the Unist'ot'en have helped raise the profile of the many proposed liquefied natural gas pipelines in northwestern British Columbia.

The Canadian government has sought to recognize only a delimited sense of its obligations to Indigenous peoples, who have issued vital challenges on the basis of their own dynamic traditions. The content and meaning of Indigenous law cannot be restricted to government frames. Indigenous traditions, contrary to the constrained frames of the review process, are not only about how Indigenous peoples traditionally used their resources. Their traditions are also about how they governed, and the legal responsibilities of stewardship that framed their governance activities. As the government seeks to systematically abandon its environmental responsibilities, increasingly, Indigenous law has become a crucial framework to articulate both the possibility and the necessity of an alternative.

15

Culture Works

●

CHRISTINE LECLERC AND REX WEYLER

•

Until the army of my sorrow lays waste to the kingdom of my heart
I will send my dear life to you as a train of provisions.
　—Hafiz

Can poetry stop the ecocide sponsored by banksters and corporados—Goldman Sachs, Syncrude, Enbridge, Kinder Morgan, Shell Oil, and PetroChina? It may seem like a mismatch. The corporados have all the money, own their media, bribe governments, and con the public. Poetry has only itself, its soul, and its agony for a truth deeper than oil wells. But keep in mind: historically, poetry always wins. Bashō lives long after the warlords are vanquished. Rumi and Hafiz survive the Persian empires. Harriet Beecher Stowe outlives American slavery.

There is a simple reason for this: truth is eternal. Truth endures, even if only half glimpsed as a passing apparition in struggling verse. Truth endures when corporate lies, imperial deceits, armed troops, and treasure hoards all fade to dust. Truth resonates across time and cultures in poetry. These cultural truths live on and inspire beyond the bounds of long-gone empires and regimes of oppression. Today, an empire of greed and treachery appears to have risen to new heights, but this is an ancient story. Arrogant civilizations always fall.

This chapter highlights one effort to speak truth to the power and devastation of the tar sands in a project called *The Enpipe Line: 70,000+ kilometres of poetry written in resistance to the Enbridge Northern Gateway Pipelines proposal*. This book grew as a community-based art project that mobilized poems from around the world to counter Enbridge's tar sands pipeline proposal.

Since *A Line in the Tar Sands* will likely be read by those busy with the work of achieving an energy revolution, we would like to highlight a key feature of *The Enpipe Line*'s poetry: its communal process. The project has involved hundreds, who remain in touch and continue to collaborate on writing projects, cultural events, education, and civic engagements—in short, it has grown from a project into a community.

How this was accomplished need not be explained in detail, but the essence was simple: people came to know each other through common cause and cared for one another through an appreciation of each other's work. The supportive environment that creative projects require to flourish is one that sustains friendships, and this sustaining quality is essential to any long-term social work.

But community building is not unique to *The Enpipe Line*. If it were, it might be an interesting fluke, but nothing for the pages of this book. What is fascinating is how people across diverse cultural and geographical spaces are driven to creative, community-based engagements opposing unconventional oil extraction.

In British Columbia, and in the many unceded territories that make up Canada, we have seen a wide range of acts of creative resistance, including massive murals, Rogue Ram puppet shows, burlesque, illustration, quilting, documentary, stop-motion animation, landscape painting, songwriting, photography, chapbooks, sculpture, choral arrangement, political comics, and performance-protest. There are too many projects to name, and more keep appearing all the time.[1] We obviously cannot speak to how every one of these projects sustains community around visions of cultural diversity and ecological integrity, but we can note our conversations with artists who have consistently spoken to us about the collaborative spirit involved in their efforts.

We believe that the transition to a fossil fuel–free future is as much about building friendship and community as it is about understanding the potentially devastating social and environmental stakes of continued dependence on fossil fuels. Thus, while we start here with a few words about the frightening prospects, the focus of this chapter is on creativity in resistance, and the importance of nourishing the bonds that can help to sustain the long efforts of action that lie ahead.

Pipelines to Mordor

The Enbridge pipelines, the subject of *The Enpipe Line* poetry collection, represent more than just the prospect of tar sands bitumen being shipped overland to the BC coast. Enbridge represents collective insanity, the globalized, industrial ruin of the world—something akin to the dark fires of Mordor, the hell in Middle Earth depicted in Tolkien's epic *Lord of the Rings* series.

The insanity may engulf northern British Columbia, where energy companies want to build a new dam on the Peace River to send electricity to shale gas fields. This gas would be piped to Alberta to melt and dilute the tar sands bitumen torn from the earth. As other chapters in this collection indicate, tar sands extraction represents the biggest, most destructive industrial project in the history of the world. The bitumen is already sent down pipelines to the West Coast, where fossil fuel companies want to turn BC into the tar sands shipping port that connects it to world energy markets.

In British Columbia, a number of proposed pipelines lead back to the tar sands: the Keystone XL route through the central US to Port Arthur, Texas; the Kinder Morgan Trans Mountain pipeline over the Rocky Mountains to the port of Vancouver; and the proposed Enbridge Northern Gateway line, which would run from Bruderheim, Alberta, to a marine port near Kitimat over the Rocky Mountains, crossing boreal forests, wild watersheds, and Indigenous territory. The proposed pipelines would intersect over seven hundred rivers and streams, including salmon-spawning habitat in the upper Fraser, Skeena, and Kitimat watersheds. Once received on British Columbia's coast, oil tankers larger than the Exxon Valdez would have to navigate the treacherous waters of the Inside Passage.

The pipeline would end at Kitimat, where oil tankers would travel through Haisla territory 150 kilometres down the narrow Douglas Channel, past the Gitga'at Nation at Hartley Bay and through Squally Channel into Hecate Strait, and on to the North Pacific. These are treacherous marine passages, with severe tidal currents and extreme weather. Over time, oil spills are inevitable.

At every stage, Enbridge's proposal risks ecological devastation—to the health of British Columbia's land, river valleys, lakes, water tables, coastline, and marine ecosystems, and to the people and other species that depend on them. And the impacts do not stop in British Columbia, as releasing the "carbon bomb" from the tar sands into the atmosphere threatens to wreak havoc on all of the earth's inhabitants. Such a perilous course with such a simple motive: money.

Enbridge represents nothing less than a crime against the earth, our children, and future generations, for the sake of a short-term boom in profits. As Chief Larry Nooski of the Nadleh Whut'en put it: "The Enbridge pipeline would risk an oil spill into our rivers and lands that would destroy our food supply, our livelihoods, and our cultures. There is not any amount of money that compares to the possible damage."[2]

Enpipe, *verb*: To block up and/or fill a pipe to bursting

In July 2010, Leclerc chained herself to a door in the Enbridge Northern Gateway Pipelines office in Vancouver, along with several other activists, while many more were outside in support. The occupation was undertaken by Greenpeace Canada to protest the proposed Enbridge pipelines, and in solidarity with First Nations, through whose unceded territories Enbridge proposed to run the pipelines. We were well aware of the widespread opposition to the project among First Nations and the non-Indigenous population of British Columbia.

In the hours Leclerc spent in the Enbridge Northern Gateway Pipelines office waiting room, Enbridge CEO John Carruthers observed our group from time to time. After fourteen hours, the police cut through the chains of the occupation and carried the occupier's limp bodies to an oddly vacant office. In the midst of this removal, the image of a poetry-jammed pipeline suddenly struck. Soon after, Leclerc was afforded an artist's residency, which gave her the time and space to develop and workshop *The Enpipe Line* concept—a 1,173-kilometre-long poetry collaboration that was meant to go dream versus dream against Enbridge's 1,173-kilometre-long Northern Gateway pipeline proposal (which Enbridge later updated to 1,177 kilometres).

On November 1, 2010, *The Enpipe Line* project was launched in Prince George, British Columbia, a city close to the proposed pipeline route. Poet and professor Rob Budde read about the Enbridge office occupation in July, and invited Leclerc and poet Reg Johanson to read at the University of Northern

British Columbia. A call for submissions went out over the Internet, and contributions started to arrive from poets across many parts of the world. Leclerc began to measure the poems, and post on a website. The long poem found in the book is comprised of the poems submitted to *The Enpipe Line* website in resistance to the proposed pipelines, and acts in solidarity with similar projects that resist social or environmental destruction. While the initial goal was to collect 1,173 kilometres over a two-year period, *The Enpipe Line* grew to over 50,000 kilometres in less than one year, and as of 2014 measures over 70,000 kilometres.[3]

The Enpipe Line's poems come from people who fight Enbridge in their communities. They come from people who are ready to move towards renewable energy and away from fossil fuels. They come from some of the world's finest poets. They come from people who have never written poetry in their lives. *The Enpipe Line*'s contributors are of all ages and from all walks of life, and come from sister struggles against a range of related social and ecological disasters.

As the months wore on, *The Enpipe Line* became part of several protests in Vancouver. The Anonymous Collective generated text in resistance to Vancouver-based Goldcorp's socially and environmentally destructive mining practices in Guatemala. Simon Fraser University (SFU) had accepted a $10-million donation from Goldcorp, which entailed renaming the SFU Centre for the Arts the Goldcorp Centre for the Arts. The community at SFU rallied to get Goldcorp on the agenda at the school's Board of Governors meeting, as the university had accepted the donation prior to making it known to the SFU community. The Anonymous Collective staged a "mutterance," a performance in which a group of people mutter a text together, though not necessarily in unison (the text of which is contained in the collection).

On April 20, 2011—the one-year anniversary of the five-month-long BP oil spill in the Gulf of Mexico—poet-activists took to the same site of the Enbridge occupation in order to perform a piece of poets' theatre called "Irresponsible Extraction, We're Through with You." This play was created for the Rising Tide Day of Action Against Extraction, in which a number of *Enpipe Line* contributors took part, including Ta'Kaiya Blaney, Stephen Collis, and Ben West.

In the spring of 2011, Creekstone Press expressed an interest in publishing the project as a book. Creekstone's location in Smithers, BC—just downstream of the proposed pipeline route—made it an obvious fit.[4] In the fall of 2011, *The Enpipe Line* was part of a global event known as 100 Thousand Poets for Change. A number of contributors participated in a shoreline cleanup in the morning, a reading hosted by Vancouver's Carnegie Centre, and The Word on the Street Festival in the afternoon.

Just as the book's contributors and publisher were self-selected, so was the editorial collective, producing a truly grassroots effort whose discussions broadened our understanding of what it is to work collectively.[5] Proceeds from the sale of the book were then deposited into a Northern Gateway Pipelines resistance legal defence fund, in order to support the physical processes of resistance that inspired the book in the first place.

As the poetry collection was coming together, we found inspiration in other forms of collaborative resistance unfolding, including the struggle to oppose the Keystone XL pipeline in the US, the resistance to oil tankers in BC, the strength of the Yinka Dene Alliance (which includes Nadleh Whut'en, Takla Lake, Wet'suwet'en, Saik'uz, and Nak'azdli Nations), and the historic Fraser River Declaration, signed by sixty-one First Nations in 2010 (and subsequently expanded to more than one hundred), which promised to stop the Northern Gateway pipeline. As Chief Jackie Thomas of Saik'uz Nation put it, "Enbridge has spills all over North America ... We refuse to be next."[6]

In short, we see *The Enpipe Line* as part of a much wider public resistance. We believe that its contribution reflects the inspiring union of art and social politics, and the role it can play in building strong connections between people in struggle. The voices and dreams of contributing poets are arrows in the public's nonviolent arsenal, to resist the machinations of the greedy and powerful forces, like Enbridge, bent on destroying the earth. It is our visions and dreams that will still be alive when these destructive forces have been overcome.

16

Lessons from Direct Action at the White House to Stop the Keystone XL Pipeline

●

JOSHUA KAHN RUSSELL, LINDA CAPATO, MATT
LEONARD, AND RAE BREAUX

●

Introduction

There were a few hundred of us gathered in St. Stephen's Church in Washington, DC, the night before our first wave of sit-ins at the White House. "Make some noise if you are in your teens! Okay, who is in their twenties? Thirties? Forties? Fifties? Who here is older than sixty?" The most thunderous applause came at the end, from all the elders in the room. The next day, after hundreds participated in a sit-in in front of the White House to stop the Keystone XL pipeline, we greeted people with hugs and water as they got out of jail. A woman in her eighties approached one of us. "When I saw you young people leading the trainings for this, I thought, 'Yes, the youth are going to save us!' ... But as I sat in with people in their seventies and eighties, I thought, '*No, we have to do this together!*'" We embraced, moved by the intergenerational collaboration of a series of actions designed to be a gateway into the movement for people who had never taken action before.

It was just one moment in one series of actions to stop Keystone XL, but for us it indicated the potential of these protests—that they could serve as a catalyst to reinvigorate the US climate movement. Keystone XL (or KXL) is a pipeline project undertaken by the energy firm TransCanada. It is designed to carry tar sands bitumen through roughly 1,500 miles (about 2,400 kilometres) of pipeline from the tar sands in Alberta to the US Gulf Coast for refinement and export. In the time since the White House sit-ins, campaigns to stop KXL have been diverse in strategies, tactics, actors, and approaches. The campaigns are complex, marked by both losses and hope.

While we do not have space (nor are we necessarily the right people) to offer a reflection of the full campaign, in this chapter we aim to highlight some lessons we've learned from one style of direct action that helped propel the campaign in the United States in 2011: the fourteen days of White House sit-ins called the Tar Sands Action.

In the mid- to late 2000s, the US climate movement was flailing and fractured, and had not unified around common opponents. With the lead-up to the United Nations ministerial negotiations of 2009 in Copenhagen, and with a climate bill in the US Congress, many large environmental NGOs were pouring resources into the Washington, DC, "beltway" and striving for legislative action on such efforts as emissions standards, carbon markets, and other provisions in the climate bill. However, many environmental justice groups were positioned on the other side of the fence, opposing those same policy proposals relating to offsets and polluter giveaways. The dividing lines tended to hinge around differing theories of change and analyses of impacts, and the role that "green capitalist" markets should play in reducing greenhouse gas emissions, which mattered a lot when there were concrete policy proposals on the table that had real consequences for communities on the frontlines of fossil fuel extraction. Environmental justice groups argued that such bills threw communities of colour, Indigenous communities, and low-income communities under the bus, and that national NGOs were pursuing goals that actively hurt the communities they served.

That landscape shifted dramatically in 2010. Copenhagen was a dismal failure from a policy perspective, after weak, non-binding agreements were settled on—with the United States and Canada both central forces working to water down any substantive commitments. From a movement-building perspective, however, the international demonstrations in Copenhagen engaged a wide diversity of Southern peoples' movements and grassroots forces, and pointed the way to a deepening consensus about the urgency of fighting climate change. Later that year, the US climate bill was also killed, and some US NGOs found themselves re-evaluating their tunnel-vision "inside-the-beltway" strategy. Between 2007 and 2010, climate justice groups, such as grassroots activists in the Navajo Nation, community groups in Appalachia, Western Mining Action Network, Global Alliance for Incinerator Alternatives, Resisting Environmental Destruction on Indigenous Lands (REDOIL), community groups in Richmond, CA, Klamath River Native organizing, and Southwest Workers Union (and many more),[1] seemed more capable of keeping carbon in the ground than the lobbying efforts in Washington; the political frameworks of grassroots movements gained much greater legitimacy among younger demographics. For many years, some of the Big Greens had acknowledged the need to deepen their relationships with and accountability to the environmental justice community, but often struggled around *how*. This new moment opened up new possibilities. One lesson seemed clear: *people must organize where they have power*, and at that moment, peoples' power was certainly not in the halls of Congress.

Across the political spectrum of US environmentalism, a focus on fighting the fossil fuel industry was intensifying and becoming entwined with renewed interest in grassroots organizing. This led many campaigners to seek opportunities to create a so-called "big tent" that could pull a range of groups into alignment over a common struggle.

Strategy Lessons from the Tar Sands Action to Stop Keystone XL

In the autumn and winter of 2010, a number of experienced direct action organizers had been circulating ideas and proposals with various people in the climate movement, aimed principally at the hope of building bridges through escalated climate-centred direct actions. Many of us had worked professionally at organizations such as Rainforest Action Network and Greenpeace, had roles as trainers and action coordinators with the Ruckus Society, and had been part of grassroots efforts like Direct Action Network, Earth First!, Mobilization for Climate Justice, Direct Action to Stop the War, Rising Tide North America, and others. We were inspired by the impressive mass actions of the Climate Camps in the UK and Europe, which drew thousands of people; the growth of the anti-globalization movement in the US in the late 1990s and early 2000s; and the powerful organizing of the anti-nuclear movement in previous decades.

By contrast, the climate movement in North America was mainly active at a relatively small scale. Some grassroots groups were effectively using actions to win local campaigns and build power, such as in forcing the cancellation of the Life of Mine permit in Black Mesa, Arizona, resisting the construction of the Desert Rock coal plant, and halting refinery expansion in Richmond, California; and some NGOs were successfully using targeted, campaign-specific direct actions (often involving highly trained people taking a very technical action), such as banner drops off of Bank of America skyscrapers and other funders of fossil fuels. But outside of a few experiences in the US (such as the 2009 Capitol Climate Action that many of us organized), we were lacking "movement moments"[2] that escalated into bigger and broader connections and could open up political space in a way that nuanced campaigning on short-term struggles often cannot do.

That winter, 350.org invited some of us in the San Francisco Bay Area into a more concerted conversation on this topic. During the brainstorm, Bill McKibben and others at 350.org highlighted the upcoming proposal for the Keystone XL pipeline as a key objective for climate organizing in the US. Tribal communities had been fighting the tar sands across the continent for years, with little support or attention from national groups. Some of us had already worked for a few years on solidarity campaigns focused on fighting the tar sands in Canada, but this issue had yet to gain much traction among broader movements in the US. Many US climate activists had never even heard of the tar sands. While there was already organized resistance to the tar sands, which had primarily been led by Indigenous groups north of our border, US environmental organizations saw it largely as a "Canadian issue" and, with a few exceptions (such as reports, basic press support, and online campaigns), were unsure of how to engage inside our own country. It was an uphill battle to show the relevance of the tar sands fight for people in the United States. On top of this, some Washington insiders told us that the approval of Keystone XL was a "done deal," essentially already rubber-stamped, and encouraged us to focus our attention elsewhere. We were also warned that many liberals were not ready to embrace full-on campaigning against the Obama administration—that we would only be able to mobilize radicals from the margins.

While we appreciated the advice, we came to a wholly different conclusion with some of our other allies. Far from wasting energy on a lost cause, we hoped that this project could be the catalyst that the climate movement was looking for to grow into something bigger, and demonstrate that *we need not be held hostage to the politics of what is considered "reasonable" in DC.* We thought we could thread a needle that would mobilize Obama's own base to confront him on the pipeline as a campaign target. We were excited and hopeful, but we did not really know what we were doing.

It would be impossible to chronicle the entire span of the multiple campaigns confronting KXL over the last three years, but we are convinced of the importance of seven basic lessons that we have learned from this initial set of Washington sit-ins, and its direct consequences.

Lesson 1: Collaboration Requires Flexibility and Leading with Action

We came to 350.org as unaffiliated activists, but relied on consultation with a lot of groups that had been opposing the tar sands, such as the Indigenous Environmental Network. We worked with 350 to set up an independent campaigning group called Tar Sands Action, which was connected to 350.org via shared resources, organizers, and spokespeople, but which had autonomy. We did not call a huge coalition meeting of groups who disagreed with each other, only to slog through the "lowest-common-denominator politics" that are commonplace when trying to get different actors to agree on an overarching strategy. Instead, we put out a call to action to see who would join with us, while continuing to do our best to take direction from frontline stakeholders. To use an analogy, we thought *it would be easier to balance a bicycle once it was already in motion.* By combining some elbow grease with the vision of 350.org board members like Naomi Klein and Bill McKibben, we were able to garner support from some big-name public intellectuals, celebrity advocates, movement leaders, and scientists, like Maude Barlow, Wendell Berry, Tom Goldtooth, Danny Glover, James Hansen, George Poitras, David Suzuki, and Gus Speth, among others, which helped add public legitimacy to Tar Sands Action. Calls to action were one thing, but it took the rolling momentum of fourteen days of consecutive sit-ins, "pedalling our bicycle," to build a level of mass engagement and media interest.

Though this sort of action was not original, we approached our organizing differently than we had in the past. Here, our goal was not to simply mobilize *existing* activists or action affinity groups, but rather to create a gateway into the movement for thousands of people who may never have participated in a protest before, let alone risked arrest in civil disobedience. Similar actions had happened regularly in preceding years, but without much recognition or support from larger, mainstream groups. Our hope was to demystify direct action for mainstream environmentalists, and invite influential groups (sometimes referred to as "grasstops") to join in whatever way they were comfortable with. This approach was an effort to pierce some of the divisions that had hardened in the lead-up to the UN Copenhagen Ministerial, *and shift mainstream groups a little bit to the left.*

It worked. Over two weeks, 1,250 people—engaging a wide range of constituents, including farmers, faith leaders, ranchers, students, Indigenous elders and community members, students, scientists, grandparents, celebrities, and more—were arrested in front of the White House. They represented a committed core who inspired thousands of others to come off the sidelines. On the first day of sit-ins, there was little media interest, and we had to create our own. But each day saw more and more people coming to Washington. Skeptical groups that were on the fence joined in once they saw our credibility and others coming on board. By the end, the steady drumbeat yielded attention in nearly every major media outlet in the country, and a wide breadth of participating organizations. This affirmed our approach to navigating coalition politics: *leading with action*, rather than trying to get a wide variety of groups to agree on a unifying theory of change and a single strategy. Such a diversity of groups may not agree on everything, but they could at least recognize that this action was worthwhile. Almost overnight, people could feel a sense of being part of a nationwide campaign to stop the pipeline, propelled by a wide variety of autonomous, grassroots groups demanding action on climate change. The ability of multiple groups to maintain differing theories of change in the wake of the tar sands action was an affirmation that "movement moments" can open up space for a diversity of campaign approaches.

Lesson 2: Sometimes Making a *Big* "Ask" Is Vital to Getting People to Respond

Our recruitment strategy relied on making strong appeals to people and being open to their responses. One common message that we've heard consistently throughout our experience as organizers is to "meet folks where they are at." This often means finding "soft" ways of bringing people into the fold. For instance, someone might initially sign your online petition; then they might attend a meeting or an event; then they might become regular members and facilitate meetings; and then they may join a protest, and then organize their own actions. This is what organizers call a "ladder of engagement." We took a different tack—by finding ways to support people leapfrogging the ladder entirely.

One pitfall of using "soft" approaches, with more limited engagement from people, is that these can lead to the continuing use of tactics that are outdated, and might not match the severity of the problem you are trying to solve. Many of us can be overwhelmed by the scale and urgency of the climate crisis and the power of the industry propelling tar sands expansion. We are regularly confronted with doomsday climate scenarios, and people who are aware of the tar sands recognize their devastating health impacts. In the face of these problems, asking people to sign a petition or come to a rally is not likely to psychologically fit the scale of the crisis. People want to take action only when they believe it will have a meaningful impact. Thus, we wagered against a soft approach to engagement, with the assumption that more people would be mobilized by a big and bold ask, rather than a small and shallow one, and this seemed to work.

We also recognized that asking anyone to risk arrest for any reason is a big deal. For seasoned activists, the White House sit-ins seemed "low risk," but for people who had no experience with direct action, such an ask can appear as a major life decision to risk one's physical well-being and face possible legal consequences, as well as social stigma. We knew we had to be honest about these risks.

Lesson 3: Organize Openly and Transparently for Mass Actions

It may seem obvious that being *transparent* should be one of the first things we do as organizers. After all, "transparency is the first rule of accountability."[3] Often, however, transparency in public actions can be muddled by distrust, busy-ness, negligence, or "security culture" (that is, withholding information for fear of the police, industry, or opposition learning our plans). Intentionally or not, it is not always easy for organizers to share everything they are thinking with volunteers, or with prospective recruits. Sometimes it is necessary to be clandestine, especially with intentionally small or covert

actions. *But not in mass actions that are providing doorways.* When working on Tar Sands Action, we realized that if our participants knew everything,
we could make our movement more accessible. But transparency requires a
lot of active *work*.

Our first step in making things transparent was explaining our process
to potential action participants. We sent folks regular emails, mapping out
every detail of the action we could communicate. As soon as someone signed
up, they would receive a message confirming that they understood the action
they had signed up for. We prided ourselves on a comprehensive Frequently
Asked Questions backgrounder, and one-on-one communication with literally thousands of people. We had lawyers available to help offer guidance,
and posted their legal assessment so that anyone who went to our website
could see what the risks were. Some of us fielded emails full of questions for
almost fifteen hours a day. We had regular public web video chats to give
updates about how the action planning was coming along. We held public
strategy sessions to get feedback from thousands of people and be guided by
the work people were already doing in their own communities. We did our
best to model the principle that organizers should take direction from the
communities they serve.

Our hope was that given a sense of urgency, with all of the information
on the table, and the media interest towards our spokespeople like Bill
McKibben and Naomi Klein, participants could be fully engaged and prepared for the action. They knew they may need an extra day off work, in case
they were held overnight if they were arrested. They knew what they should
wear, what they should bring, and what time to be at the trainings.

When organizing for such actions, we often assume that if people hear
the worst-case scenario (the possible legal charges, days in jail, and so on),
they will get too nervous, and take a step back. There were some who did;
however, it was clear that many more people joined because we demystified
this particular style of public nonviolent direct action (NVDA) and made it
accessible. We knew that if we created an open framework for folks, they
would be more willing to trust us.

The action framework we created for folks was a *first step*. It was a
somewhat-controlled situation that had relatively low legal consequences,
and allowed participants to access NVDA as a tactic. Like all messy, real-
world organizing, *the effort was not without its contradictions.* "Big tents"

can quickly fill up with groups whose structures are at odds with one another, and groups with power can cluelessly misuse it at the expense of those who don't. Openly facing these challenges head-on is part of the task of building mass movements.

Some critics correctly pointed out that by negotiating with the police in advance, with a lot of directive handholding, we were sacrificing a degree of organic energy and spontaneity in service of a flashy media action. We did not encourage people to refuse fines and cite-and-release procedure to jam up the jail system until their trial. The sit-ins did not cause an economic disruption to our target, and we did not follow a common "affinity group" style, with the small collectives and personal relationships that are common in the environmental movement. Such criticisms, we replied, were missing the point in this circumstance. The participants who took their very first step wearing zip ties have put NVDA in their toolboxes as organizers. The doorway that this carefully designed action created had the effect of ushering in a much broader group of people, who then went and initiated their own actions across the country, and have been doing so consistently in the years since. One woman approached us upon her release from jail, saying, "I feel like this action was training wheels—and I needed that—but now I'm ready to ride a bike!"

Our entire model relied on trusting the ability of people to make use of a transformational flashpoint and go back home to organize in ways that serve their own communities' needs, as well as link up in solidarity with those facing the worst impacts of the pipeline.

Suddenly, our Tar Sands Action organizing team was sprinting to catch up with and support the organic energy springing up against the Keystone XL pipeline around the country. Within weeks of the action, Obama could not make a fundraising or campaign stop without being confronted by protesters. Obama for America offices were regularly stormed by community activists around the nation. The first time Obama spoke directly about the pipeline was in response to pointed questions from Tom Poorbear, Oglala Sioux vice-president. In the months following the sit-ins, we sought to help highlight and connect all these efforts.

Lesson 4: Campaigns Are Complex and Involve a Variety of Styles of Action

... And actions that include influential voices and scripted elements need not be mutually exclusive from bottom-up grassroots initiatives. Sometimes the former can help open up space for the latter, and support spontaneity and long-term grassroots empowerment.

Our organizing model for the campaign following the sit-ins depended on organizers letting go of most of our control. Our movement has rightly inherited a lot of distrust. National organizations have a checkered history of supporting (and undermining) grassroots organizing, and the severity and seriousness of the issues often leave little room for compromise between conflicting strategies and theories of change. This can lead to paid "professional" organizers and campaigners micromanaging protests or community meetings. We thought we could help build trust between groups by modelling being trusting: pushing bigger organizations to get more comfortable not being in the driver's seat. We highlighted a diversity of messages coming from communities, regardless of whether or not they were the perfectly polished talking points that make NGOs feel secure. Similarly, we worked with bigger organizations and trusted them to do what they were good at doing. For example, the Natural Resources Defense Council does not have the capacity or skill for direct action or community organizing, so it is not appropriate for them to have a community meeting in Nebraska, but we trusted their media savvy, technical analysis, insider perspective on Capitol Hill, and celebrity outreach. Each organization acted as its own piece of the puzzle, without attempting to do things they were not built to do.

Lesson 5: Know the Landscape of Your Organizational Partners— and the Difference between Your Target and Your Enemy

We sought to trust our partners in what they are good at doing, and draw clear boundaries so groups didn't inadvertently step on each other's toes. One way we tried to build alignment was by identifying a clear target. Most campaign strategy processes would have placed Secretary of State Hillary Clinton in the centre of the bull's eye. She was in charge of the State Department, which was in charge of the review and approval process. We decided to roll the dice and go bigger. In theory, Barack Obama is in charge of most federal processes. In practice, decisions are made at a variety of levels, covered in red tape, and Obama's office simply rubber-stamps decisions at the end of the line. Some of our allies said that choosing Obama was sloppy, since Clinton is the actual decision-maker. We hoped that if we hung the decision on Obama's head and generated sufficient public controversy, it would *force* the decision into his court. This would be ideal, because it's difficult to pressure Clinton outside of DC—but Obama has offices in every city, had to raise money around the country, and had a track record of nice words on climate change that we could confront him with.[4] We often held signs with his own rhetoric that we must "be the generation that frees America from the tyranny of oil,"[5] and that his presidency would see the time when the "when the rise of the oceans began to slow and our planet began to heal."[6] We took a gamble by attempting to mobilize Obama's own disaffected base to force him to live up to his rhetoric and promise. We trusted that people could handle complexity and understand that while Obama was our *target*, TransCanada was our *enemy*.

This choice included another risk: while we believe Obama was a proper target for this specific *campaign*, we did not want the larger *movement* to lose sight of its own power by *simply trying to persuade decision-makers*. Our movement goals are about exercising our own power directly, regardless of the political whims of elected officials. Our campaign choice to target Obama was taken within that larger context—and in our public training sessions and strategy conversations, we did our best to consistently emphasize that we were doing more than *asking* power holders for change; whether or not

Members of the Indigenous Environmental Network at the front of a White House sit-in during the fourteen days of the Tar Sands Action, shortly before arrests, 2011.

Obama approves the pipeline, we need to build the energy of the movement and escalate our demands and actions. We hoped we could foster a direct-action theory of change that built bottom-up power in the big picture, while still having space for specific campaigns that achieve policy gains. Despite our clarity on this in our trainings, and finding some success in shifting mainstream concepts of how change happens, our campaign choices still had the cost of this concept getting muddled and confused in the following years.

Lesson 6: Create Your Own Battlefield

By hanging the decision on Obama's head, we created our own battlefield. Had we focused on Clinton, our main opportunities for intervention would have been limited to State Department hearings and Clinton's own state-ments. By reshaping our landscape, we were able to go on offence, and prevent our campaign from being caught in a cycle of simply reacting to our opposition's timeline. We were successful in this for the first several months, and this streak culminated in our first partial "victory." Obama sent Keystone XL back into another two-year review process. We were not as prepared for the next stage of the fight, however, when Republicans and oil-backed Democrats made several attempts to override the decision in Congress. Our playing field shifted. Suddenly we were faced with organizing where we did not have as much power—in the DC beltway. We engaged in mass petitions that got over 800,000 signatures with dramatic public deliv-eries, and media events that were meant to shame and stiffen the spines of wavering Democrats. The movement defeated their attempts to override the Congressional decision and helped broaden our base of support, but we were stuck putting one foot in front of the other, and needed multiple approaches to keep our opponents at bay. In response, we organized another major DC event in which ten thousand people surrounded the White House, acting as another tipping point and movement moment.

Lesson 7: Don't Fetishize "Winning"; Do Keep Your Eyes on the Prize

Much of the following three years were like a roller-coaster ride, with short-term victories tempered by losses—which sometimes were big ones. One step forward; three steps back; two steps forward again. When Obama did a photo-op approving the southern leg of the pipeline, our hearts sank. One consequence of the DC-centric national narrative carried by louder groups around Keystone XL was a general lack of attention to communities in the South, for whom legislative goals had failed. While there were many factors leading up to this, we wondered if the tone set by our initial fourteen-day action had cluelessly planted a seed for this dynamic. Furthermore, it seemed inevitable that if the southern leg were approved, the northern leg would follow. Bolder, more confrontational direct action emerged. Alliances were forged between Texas landowners concerned with property rights and eminent domain (the seizure of land by the government) and radical tree sitters. Alongside a wide variety of community organizations, the direct action group Tar Sands Blockade took serious risks by physically blocking the construction of the pipeline, and had to face violent responses from the police in Texas (for more on this, see chapter 17).

For conditions in communities along the southern route of the pipeline, there was no "victory" with federal KXL campaigning to be had, regardless of the outcome for the northern leg. But there was still much to fight for in stopping the project writ large, and much that could be done to support groups diversifying their tactics in the South.

In this context, it was often difficult to know when to celebrate short-term victories, especially when the long-term fight sometimes seemed bleak. We knew that movements are fuelled by a sense of momentum and the hope that winning is possible, and that it is important to cherish every step forward, but with land being seized and people suffering because of the pipeline, it is difficult to celebrate. Often, celebrating small steps forward in the national arena can be a slap in the face for frontline communities dealing with ongoing local impacts and not experiencing improvement in their conditions. We learned that there are ways to talk about and celebrate victories that offer support and momentum to groups on the ground—and there are ways to talk about victory that undermine them. In the time since the Tar Sands Action, many national groups did not understand this difference, and this exacerbated movement fractures that continue to this day.

Nebraska ranchers with an organization known as Bold Nebraska organized along the Midwest; residents fought infrastructure across the Gulf Coast; Lakota tribal members blockaded megaload trucks going up north; and many, many more groups vigorously organized around North America. At the same time, the right wing hardened, which included Mitt Romney's campaign ads for the 2012 presidential election stating that approving the

Keystone XL pipeline would be his first act in office.[7] Each time Keystone entered the media, there was an opportunity to get our message across—but also a lot of internal peril, since so many groups had different perspectives on what it all meant. Responding to the twists and turns of the political cir- · cumstances was easier said than done. It was often challenging to overcome distrust when some actors in the movement were celebrating any positive words that came out of Obama's mouth, while others were decrying them as nefarious pandering.

Our opponents are not monolithic or static. They are re-strategizing with every step. It's possible that even if we defeat the northern leg, they will find a way to transport tar sands bitumen across the US for refinement in the Gulf through the southern leg. Oil company plans for new pipelines and transporting crude by rail have sprung up in the campaigns' wake. When we stop one part of their strategy, we need to remain vigilant enough to adapt to TransCanada's plan B (and plans C, D, etc.).

Defining victory becomes even more complex when one considers the distinction between the impacts of *climate change* versus the impacts of *fossil fuel extraction*. If the northern leg is defeated, and that translates to a meaningful amount of carbon being left in the ground, it is a genuine "win" for the climate. And if that same "win" also carries with it the devastating impacts of fossil fuel extraction, transport, and refinement from the southern leg or crude-by-rail, it is a material "loss" for many communities. Sometimes the specific frontlines of extreme weather are the same specific frontlines as extraction; sometimes they are different. Often these efforts share the same targets, but disagreements proliferate depending on which lens people are using to measure victory, and climate justice movements have to grow to develop clarity about the difference. The intersections and the distinctions matter. Whether using a *climate* lens, an *extraction* lens, or both, another question is who "gets" to declare victory. In our experience, the most honest answer is that communities most affected are the ones best equipped to determine whether or not "big tent" efforts have been successful.

In some ways, any language about "winning" environmental fights inherently whitewashes complexity.[8] We need a new language with which to celebrate steps forward that doesn't default to the zero-sum thinking of winning and losing. We're inheriting a broken world of increasing insecurity and crisis, and true solidarity means encouraging each other to be honest about

our limitations while thinking optimistically about our future and prefigur-
ing our vision of a just world, without rendering invisible the plight of those
left out of particular "wins." And yet, amid all this, we need to always keep
our eyes on the prize of the real "win"—a new society driven by interdependence, locally controlled economies, self-determination, social justice, and
ecological balance.

Conclusions

We should be clear that *all environmental victories are temporary* as long as
the underlying system of exploitation of both people and the planet persists.
If we defeat one project, like Keystone XL North, another company will try
another one, as we can see with the various efforts to push tar sands pipelines
east and west. It was humbling to learn that in the cases where some activists attempted to celebrate progress, those dealing with the worst impacts
of the tar sands sometimes felt like their struggles were being made invisible. Navigating this complexity will be a constant feature of any movement
struggle. We are not sure we always made the right decisions, but we are
clear on our intention to keep momentum rising and apply our lessons. We
see the creation of a "movement moment" around this fight as successful—
though we have yet to see if the movement energy in its wake will ultimately
be enough to beat the northern leg and translate to other victories. Our hope
is that the focus on Keystone XL has grown the movement writ large, which
can continue the fight against *all tar sands extraction and pipeline projects*.

    We don't know what the future holds for the northern leg of Keystone XL,
but we do know that "win or lose," this project is just one piece on a massive chessboard. If the project is defeated, we will still have an astronomical
amount of work to do. The step forward for the movement, nevertheless,
would be tremendously significant, both in reducing on-the-ground impacts
of extraction and carbon emissions, and also as a symbol: it would be a declaration that people power is stronger than the people in power. Onward.

17

Gulf Coast Resistance and the Southern Leg of the Keystone XL Pipeline

●

CHERRI FOYTLIN, YUDITH NIETO,
KERRY LEMON, AND WILL WOOTEN

●

It has been almost a decade since former president George W. Bush famously proclaimed that the United States was addicted to oil. Yet that addiction has gone untreated, while communities and ecosystems are forced to bear the costs of extraction industry profits. Much like the sores of a methamphetamine user, there are symptoms of addiction to the production of oil and tar sands, such as pipelines, spills, and refinery fumes. Those of us living along the Gulf of Mexico know well how the oil industry holds the needle to our arms. We are a prime illustration of the battered-spouse paradigm that can be found in so many "trade-off" communities. For us, the "damage done" often includes industry bought-and-paid-for politicians, toothless and underfunded regulatory agencies, polluted air and water, and sickened populations. Sadly, Gulf Coast communities often find themselves shackled to their dealer.

Commonly identified as one of America's "sacrifice zones," our region is home to numerous environmental and social atrocities, including the BP deepwater drilling disaster (marked as the largest environmental catas-trophe in oil industry history thus far); an industry-induced sinkhole in Bayou Corner, Louisiana, currently spanning twenty-five acres (and grow-ing) along the infamous chemical corridor, or "Cancer Alley," as it has been tagged; a wide array of communities living with environmental injustice for decades; and more. Add to these the occurrence of five major hurricanes in less than a decade, all super-charged by climate change. The Gulf Coast is surely an example of the human endurance of spirit. The stories of our resistance towards the industries that are killing us offer a sense of what we are up against. With the delivering of tar sands to our region, our commun-ities are bonding together in an attempt "kick the habit" of oil dependency before it is too late.

Communities like Houston's Manchester have suffered for years from chronic health problems, many of which mirror those of communities living near tar sands extraction in Canada. With the completion of the southern leg of the Keystone XL pipeline, the effects of this highly toxic product further burden this community.

The Chevron refinery in Pascagoula, Mississippi, also currently receiving tar sands bitumen, has been ranked as one of the highest-polluting facilities in the nation. In the same year that Hurricane Katrina flooded 95 per cent of that refinery, health statistics for the area included 622 incidents of cancer, including 245 cancer-related deaths. In 2007 alone, the refinery released over one million pounds of forty-seven different toxic chemicals, including 50,000 pounds of benzene and 150,000 pounds of ammonia. With the new intake of Canadian tar sands, high levels of life-stealing sulphur dioxide have been added to these toxic fumes.

The impacts of tar sands refining emissions on our communities are dwarfed only by the overall effects of tar sands to our planet. As the ferocity of hurricanes increases, so does the vulnerability of Gulf Coast families. Coastal erosion, skyrocketing insurance premiums, and a loss of cultural identities caused by gentrification and rising water-induced relocation are examples of how the effects of climate change are already ravaging our communities.

Added to this, and a source of great concern, is the extreme danger of transporting fossil fuels. Recent rail disasters, such as those in Lac-Mégantic, Quebec, and in Aliceville, Alabama, as well as bitumen leaks in the Kalamazoo River in Michigan and Mayflower, Arkansas, demonstrate that any transport method has a potential for environmental destruction, serious health impacts, and loss of life.

This is completely unsettling when coupled with the fact that these disasters have also uncovered a general lack of preparation and research regarding safe, effective cleanup practices after a potential bitumen release. Beyond the possible use of toxic chemical dispersants and the archaic paper-towel wiping technique,[1] little progress has been made in the last few decades regarding recovery and restoration from a catastrophic spill or explosion.

This is most concerning, since Canadian National is presently carrying diluted bitumen by rail, travelling south from Canada through Memphis, Tennessee, and Mississippi, to Mobile, Alabama. From there, it is trucked across the Mobile River to the Arc Terminal, where it is loaded on a barge for transport back to the Chevron Refinery in Pascagoula. A disaster in these areas would likely cause significant loss of life, and long-term environmental damages.

As if these anxieties were not enough, plans are in the works to complete rail facilities that would move even more bitumen to the Gulf Coast, with operations either planned or under construction in Louisiana (in Manchac, St. Rose, Norco, Geismar, St. Gabriel, and Baton Rouge) and Mississippi (in Natchez). All of this while Alabama governor Robert Bentley and Mississippi governor Phil Bryant ponder the commercial development of the Hartselle Sandstone area, in the northern portion of both states, for tar sands development. Meanwhile, the Enbridge Eastern Gulf Pipeline from Patoka, Illinois, to St. James, Louisiana, is preparing to force tar sands through their mostly repurposed natural gas line. This line will bring 660,000 additional barrels of tar sands crude per day to the Gulf Coast by 2015.

Together, all of these projects might seem overwhelming, were it not for the encouraging and motivational work of organizations like Texas Environmental Justice Advocacy Services, Tar Sands Blockade,[2] Great Plains Tar Sands Resistance, Mobile Environmental Justice Action Coalition, BridgetheGulfProject.org, NacSTOP, and individual landowners. Even with the sometimes debilitating problems of disparity of resources and an overall lack of national attention, the Gulf Coast struggle to end this destruction and the selfish practices behind it is alive and growing. This chapter will cover some of the scope and breadth of resistance across our region by following the efforts of a few of these groups.

• •

Impacts in the Manchester Community in Houston, Texas

By Yudith Nieto, who was born in the small city of Reynosa,
Tamaulipas, Mexico, and grew up in Manchester, Texas

My family immigrated towards the city of Houston, Texas, after leaving the beautiful mountains of San Luis Potosi, Mexico. They could no longer sustain their land-based way of life due to droughts and loss of crops. The dream of reaching a better life to give to the younger generation seemed very possible at the time. Yet they did not anticipate that the community they chose to settle in was one of the most polluted in the country. The Latino and Mexican-American community of Manchester is completely surrounded by industry, sitting next to the Houston Ship Channel. To the northeast is the Valero refinery, with the LyondellBasell refinery to the southeast, the Texas Petrochemicals plant to the south, a Rhodia (now Solvay) fertilizer plant and a metal shredding facility to the west, a wastewater treatment facility to the east, a Goodyear Tire plant along with the Interstate 610 overpass bisecting the community to the southeast, and an industrial rail yard forming the community's southern perimeter. On a daily basis, there are at least eight identified known human carcinogens in the air. Acrolein, chromium V1, diesel particulates, formaldehyde, benzene, chlorine, 1,3-butadiene, hexamethylene, diisocyanate, and now the toxins found in tar sands are just a few of the dangerous chemicals entering people's lungs every day.[3] Manchester is clearly a case of environmental racism, as you would never see this in Houston's most affluent communities.

The environmental justice movement began with oppression: the poisoning of peoples who knew how to be in harmony with the lands that they worked and lived on. The battle has been ongoing. Sharing my perspective has granted me the opportunity to reach many more people than I intended. All I really wanted to do was help my family understand what was happening in their own backyards, not realizing that they were not alone.

Millions of dollars have gone into conducting air-quality tests and monitoring in Manchester, along with the neighbouring communities that are also imprisoned by these deadly emissions. Yet there is still no law with enough teeth to protect our communities, and the city of Houston's elected officials claim the state cannot use its screening levels for enforcement. The University of Texas's School of Public Health conducted a study[4] in which they found that children who live within two miles of the Houston Ship Channel have a 56 per cent greater chance of contracting leukemia than children living elsewhere. Even with that information, the city has failed to create buffer zones, which would keep people from moving next to the refineries. Part of that is also due to misinformation about air quality in the area. The city of Houston allows monitors to be placed in Manchester by the same industry that is responsible for the pollution (Valero). Along with other organizers and science students, we revealed that the monitor is not always running, and the information collected is ambient and not used to reinforce any laws. The grassroots organization Texas Environmental Justice Advocacy Services (TEJAS) and the Environmental Integrity Project (EIP) partnered up to conduct our own air monitoring, and found that there is in fact particle pollution in the air that exceeds the amount allowed by federal agencies. Some of those regulations are not as high in Texas as in other states. However, we are hopeful that the efforts of groups like TEJAS will play a key role in bringing about change in our affected communities and the way the nation regulates these capitalistic corporations that only destroy the gifts our Mother Earth has honoured us all with.

Growing up in a heavily polluted community has been an ongoing paradigm shift throughout my life, from when we first moved into the community and experienced first-hand the horrible smells, the sound of machinery, the screeching of trains, and the constant alarms; to realizing my environment was affecting my health, leaving me suffering from respiratory issues like bronchitis and asthma; and lastly, to learning about tar sands and the implications they would bring to my community. Over time, my experiences led me to recognize that people all over the country and the world were being affected by the same struggles. I had the honour of meeting other determined warriors from all walks of life, from the First Nations of Canada to Indigenous leaders of Central and South America, Tar Sands Blockade organizers, and other Gulf Coast community leaders. We were all connected through struggle, and our shared fighting spirit brought us together. In late 2011, I discovered that the Keystone XL pipeline would be transporting tar sands from Alberta, and I became an advocate to oppose it, along with TEJAS and later Tar Sands Blockade.

Today I work with Juan and Bryan Parras, founders of TEJAS, and other talented organizers. Together we help families learn more about the impact these industries have on our health and understand the violations of our basic human rights to clean air, water, and soil. Having this amazing team of justice warriors to mentor me and give me the tools I need to fight environmental injustice has continued to help not only my family, but my community as well. Linking with other communities only strengthens our voice, not just for our present communities, but also for our future generations.

● ●

Direct Action against Keystone XL South in Texas

Tar Sands Blockade (TSB) formed in March of 2012, after President Obama approved and expedited KXL South by executive order. There were calls for direct action from East Texas after the failure of courts, elected representatives, and government regulators to address any of the grievances of landowners left residents frustrated with the process. Filling the space left open by the NGOs allocating resources elsewhere and unresponsive government representation, climate activists with Rising Tide North Texas joined forces with residents to hold trainings on nonviolent civil disobedience and to prepare for the start of construction. TSB organizers travelled across the region, giving talks about the tar sands, building awareness, and connecting with activists interested in taking action. By the time construction began in August 2012, hundreds of Texans were ready to use and support a variety of direct action tactics to delay pipeline construction.

TransCanada discovered the Winnsboro Tree Blockade near the end of September 2012. Built on the property of East Texas landowner David Daniel by local community members and TSB, the blockade spanned the entire width of the pipeline easement[5] with a 30-foot-tall-by-110-foot-long wall made of tree scaffolding. The blockade also included an elaborate web of tree-sits behind the wall—some as high as 80 feet above the forest floor. Activists maintained an occupation for eighty-five days. TransCanada eventually built the pipeline outside of the original easement, avoiding a confrontational extraction. This proved that the route of the pipeline could be adjusted at will, despite what landowners were routinely told.

With the launch of the Winnsboro Tree Blockade came a large amount of media exposure, not only from alternative media and popular progressive blogs, but also from mainstream media outlets like *The New York Times*,

TAR SANDS BLOCKADE

Tar Sands Blockade activists at the launch of the
Winnsboro Tree Blockade, 2012.

broadcast television, and major Texas newspapers, such as the *Houston Chronicle* and *The Dallas Morning News*. This significant exposure led to even more tangible national support from different activist communities, as well as an open letter in support of TSB signed by over fifty organizations, including 350.org, Sierra Club, Greenpeace, Rainforest Action Network, active Occupy Wall Street working groups, Indigenous Environmental Network, and many more, large and small. Over eighty thousand people signed a petition in support of the blockade when two protesters were pepper-sprayed, tasered, and choked by police under direct orders from a TransCanada employee—forcing the activists to unlock from construction equipment.

Hundreds of activists from around the country came to Texas for training camps and mass actions to learn new skills to take home to their own campaigns against not only tar sands, but also fracking and other extreme energy projects. The first mass action occurred in October 2012 after a four-day-long training, when over sixty people shut down a construction site and resupplied the Winnsboro Tree Blockade, by then guarded 24/7 by local police being paid privately by TransCanada to keep everyone away from the easement. Anyone who approached the easement was detained and questioned, including a reporter for *The New York Times*. The next mass action and training camp occurred a month later, this time farther south, near Nacogdoches. Activists tied tree platforms to construction equipment and locked themselves to other machines a few miles away, while over one hundred residents rallied in support. Sheriffs pepper-sprayed a line of protesters, including a local seventy-five-year-old grandmother who was standing in the way of the cherry picker sent to extract the tree-sitters. That grandmother was Jeanette Singleton, one of the many residents of Nacogdoches who helped TSB as the campaign moved south to keep pace with pipeline construction.

TSB found a safe haven in Nacogdoches at the Austin Heights Baptist Church, a congregation with a rich history of progressive social politics. The church community supported activists with food, basic necessities, and guidance, which helped forge a deeper connection between local landowners and community groups like NacSTOP, while keeping the low-budget, all-volunteer TSB campaign going through the fall. During this time, dozens of activists lived communally in a nomadic tent village and moved frequently to keep pace with pipeline construction. Everything from dish duty to direct action strategy was discussed through long consensus meetings and spokes-councils of affinity groups. Important internal work included ongoing anti-oppression[6] discussions and several identity caucuses, like People of Color and the Trans, Women and Queer caucus.

Around seventy people were arrested in eleven counties across Texas before TSB was taken to court by TransCanada with a Strategic Lawsuit Against Public Participation (SLAPP) in January 2013. The SLAPP suit was filed against Tar Sands Blockade, Rising Tide North Texas, Rising Tide North America, and individuals arrested in early blockade actions, almost entirely born-and-raised Texans. In the filing, TransCanada claimed that TSB actions caused $5 million in financial damages due to construction delays and demanded a gag order on all TSB speech activity, including associated websites, social media, and public interviews. After being chased around Texas by process servers, the entire organization was served due to bad legal representation, and a decision was made to sign a deal. Under threat of personal financial ruin to those named in the lawsuit, TSB agreed not to trespass on the pipeline easement or TransCanada property.

Bound by potentially severe legal and financial penalties for certain actions, TSB adapted, and began a series of actions aimed at other tar sands–related events and companies. Activists disrupted two separate industry conferences by locking themselves to loudspeakers and projector screens while TransCanada executives were speaking. An activist climbed a flagpole outside LyondellBasell's headquarters in Houston and dropped a banner to draw attention to the tar sands refining company. Another activist became an official caddy at the Valero Open PGA golf tournament in San Antonio. He waited until the eighteenth hole green before unveiling a TSB T-shirt and a score sign asking Valero to respond to the demands of the Manchester community. Great Plains Tar Sands Resistance, a new group organizing in Oklahoma, continued direct actions delaying pipeline construction as work moved north during the spring.

Another way in which Tar Sands Blockade responded to the SLAPP suit was by creating a campaign centred around TD Bank and other major investors in Keystone XL and tar sands. This move coincided with TSB's call, in March 2013, for a nationwide "Week of Action to Stop Tar Sands Profiteers." Over fifty-five actions were held by allies across the continent, including actions at TD Bank branches in Washington, DC, New York City, and Asheville, North Carolina; mass bike rides occupying gas stations in Portland, Oregon; and blockades of a tar sands refinery in Utah and a fracking facility in New York. During the spring, many TSB organizers also took their experience on the road to help train more activists and meet with communities resisting tar sands and other extreme energy extraction. Owe Aku (Bring Back the Way), a community organization based out of the Pine Ridge Reservation, invited organizers with TSB and Great Plains Tar Sands Resistance to help with their series of Moccasins on the Ground nonviolent direct action trainings, to help generate a cross-cultural dialogue about tar sands resistance and forge a collaboration that could prove important in future tar sands resistance, or in the event that KXL North is ever approved.

Critically, the SLAPP suit did not remove the media infrastructure TSB built, including TarSandsBlockade.org and associated social media pages. When the Exxon Pegasus pipeline burst in Mayflower, Arkansas, in late March 2013, activists with TSB went to investigate and document the true extent of the tar sands spill. When journalists reached Mayflower, they were banned from certain areas and could not investigate under threat of arrest. But activists went into the off-limits areas with cameras anyway, and found a massive portion of the spill diverted to a wetland. Pictures, videos, and associated blog posts on TSB's website reached millions of people because of the unique and shocking documentation of the spill. TSB's video of the spill was used on *The Rachel Maddow Show* and Comedy Central's *The Colbert Report*.

One direct action that proved to be a prophetic moment was when blockaders locked themselves to two six-hundred-pound concrete barrels inside the Keystone XL pipeline just before it was buried in December 2012. While inside the pipeline, activists took pictures of shoddy welding, with sunlight shining through from the outside. The three people arrested at this action spent almost a month in jail each, while the pictures remained in police custody. When the campaign finally saw the pictures, a TSB spokesperson disrupted an industry speech about pipeline safety by TransCanada and released the photos. More documentation and evidence collected by activists shows that 125 anomalies, such as dents and bad welds, were discovered in 250 miles of KXL South. While watching pipeline repairs continue uninspected, TSB organizers began interacting with the Pipeline Hazardous Materials and Safety Administration, the federal regulatory agency for pipelines, in conjunction with rural community groups and environmental justice groups who are attempting to discover the full extent of construction problems.

Throughout the entire campaign, particular attention is being given to the participation and leading role of those affected most directly by tar sands. Landowners and rural communities, Indigenous communities along the pipeline route and those living near the point of extraction in Alberta, and refinery communities along the Gulf Coast all live with the impacts of tar sands on a daily basis. They are taking the lead to defend their own communities. Direct action in Texas has played a role in empowering those who are taking action in the face of the failure of our political and economic system to react to their demands. TransCanada and Keystone XL have a tough, unexpected fight in Texas that is still growing stronger.

Connecting through Stories and Grassroots Organizing in East Texas

The southern segment of Keystone XL cuts through East Texas. During construction the red clay was ripped open by bulldozers, and on rainy days water and soil ran red like blood off the winding, wide path of this toxic and dangerous pipeline. Schools, families, and rivers are all at risk. TransCanada, the company building and operating KXL, used the common carrier eminent domain status[7] granted by the state of Texas to take Texan land. Throughout the planning, construction, and now operation of this pipeline, we have raised our voices to speak for the things that we love and wish to protect. At times, we have felt invisible. The spin of the national Keystone XL story has often ignored the existence of the southern portion. This multinational corporation's pipeline officially went into operation in January of 2014. Despite the efforts of many, the pipe was put in the ground, covered with dirt, and now pumps tar sands through our communities.

The story of our community resistance, centred in the town of Nacogdoches, must be understood within a place-based context. Located in the Pineywoods of East Texas, Nacogdoches County is a unique ecosystem of upland pines and hardwood bottomlands nestled in the Angelina and Neches River floodplains. This region has been immersed in the petroleum industry for over eighty years. In contrast, the county is also littered with oil and gas wells and crisscrossed with pipelines. Many of the people most deeply committed to stopping Keystone XL South have personal experiences with oil and gas production on or near their homes, frequently related to extreme extraction practices, such as fracking. We are a community of people who carry the lived experience and stories of the intrusion of extraction industries affecting our families, relationships, bodies, and beloved natural spaces.

When the local Sierra Club chapter began receiving information regarding a proposed pipeline that would transport tar sands from Canada, we were immediately concerned about this dangerous and toxic product. With a greater potential loss of land resources, this pipeline would be more of an affront to landowners' rights than had been previously experienced. The first important catalyst to our direct opposition to Keystone XL South was the arrival of national Sierra Club organizers in 2010, sent to support community outreach about the pipeline. Through their connections we met David Daniel, a landowner from northeast Texas. Daniel had started STOP (Stop Tar Sands Oil Pipelines) out of frustration with TransCanada's plan to lay pipeline across beautiful and ecologically sensitive parts of his property. Moved by the ways his story resonated with our own, we began our formal opposition to KXL South with the formation of our spin-off group, NacSTOP (Nacogdoches County Stop Tarsands Oil Permanently).

Initially focused on the presidential permit for Keystone XL, we expected a short-term organizational campaign that would last a few months. Yet for the past three years, our group of unpaid volunteers has spent endless hours holding meetings, talking to public officials, and writing letters. We have given our time and energy in an attempt to educate our community about this pipeline and convey our perspective about its impact in our county. Through our work, we have met many heroic landowners, like Julia Trigg Crawford, Mike Bishop, Eleanor Fairchild, Jerry Hightower, Susan Scott, David Whitley, Mike Hathorn, and others who stand bravely before this mammoth corporation, demanding to have their rights respected.

In March of 2012, President Obama announced the postponement of his decision on the northern segment of Keystone XL, while fast-tracking the southern leg of Keystone XL through Texas and Oklahoma. When this speech was delivered in Cushing, Oklahoma, it was a devastating blow to those of us working on this critical issue. Landowners were knocked to their knees by this news, and those of us living on the frontline felt betrayed and frightened. While seen as a temporary victory for the larger movement, Obama's actions treated those along the southern route as an expendable loss. However, instead of draining energy from our cause, this political slap in the face brought renewed passion and clarity to the movement.

The underbelly of southern rural Texas contains the shadow of closed-minded ideas and a history of oppression in varying forms. The other side of this dichotomy is a warm, caring people with grit and determination, such as can be observed in the small congregation of Austin Heights Baptist Church. The interface between Austin Heights, Tar Sands Blockade, and NacSTOP demonstrates the importance of spiritual grounding in grassroots movements. A special kind of connection occurred when this small church opened their doors and hearts to this group of activists. On Sunday mornings, church pews were filled with church members and activists sitting side by side. On Sunday afternoons, food was shared and lasting relationships formed. What began as an alliance became caring friendships, and grew into a true sense of family that persists today.

Women have been the backbone of many grassroots movements, and the dedication of strong women has been essential to the work done in East Texas as well. Organizing for the safety of our homes and families, a strong alliance of female leaders has emerged. In February of 2013, a group of nine women from East Texas travelled to Washington, DC, to participate in the Forward on Climate rally. In DC, we heard first-hand the stories of First Nations women affected by tar sands. We felt solidarity with their struggle, understood their resolve to protect their children, shared their grief, and were uplifted by their strength. As women, we form enduring bonds with each other and with our work; this makes our involvement in grassroots organizing essential. Women like us, and the First Nations women we encountered in DC, understand that resistance to tar sands oil is essential, because families should not have their homelands destroyed and threatened.

In frontline communities, our work requires perseverance. Although Keystone XL South has started up, our resolve to protect the safety of our homes persists. One of the ways we are continuing to organize is by coordinating with local officials in East Texas to ensure our first responders are prepared to respond safely to a tar sands–related emergency. We know that the stories that connect us are the foundation of our work. We will continue to create relationships in our community that focus on key values that we share. We know that now is not the time to be quiet, but instead we must speak for our community, in solidarity with all peoples who carry the burden of tar sands extraction, transportation, and refining.

Grassroots Liberation

As we see it, the fight against tar sands production is one of liberation. *Addicted* is another word for *imprisoned*, and is a destiny we must refuse for our children and grandchildren. Those who stand in protection of these future generations are no less than freedom fighters. We draw inspiration and courage from their examples.

Regardless of the operation of Keystone XL South or the ultimate decision on Keystone XL North, those of us living in Gulf Coast communities must continue resisting the destructive impacts of energy industries and work for the safety and well-being of all communities. We must empower ourselves to stand up for the people and places we care about that are threatened by these multinational corporations. We resist by speaking out against things that are unjust, even though they may not be easily stopped or changed. Many lessons have been learned over the course of our resistance movement. Some are the inevitable results of being local grassroots organizers living and working in affected communities who have obligations, family commitments, jobs, civic responsibilities, dedication to our church families, personal struggles that include health impacts from our living conditions, and the need and desire for time to enjoy our lives. Many times, the results of our actions are not easily measurable. By voicing our concerns repeatedly to our local officials and community members, as well as to national politicians and corporations, there are opinion and policy changes occurring that cannot be compared to what would have been had we not spoken out. The good that we do for our world is measured by our willingness to devote ourselves to create a better world for all.

We are nose-to-nose with giant beasts. The petroleum industry and the political systems that support it will not let go of their power easily. Yet, through this grassroots movement, a new kind of giant has awakened. It is HUGE. This giant is the voice of the disenfranchised and neglected coming together in a collective roar that will not be put to sleep again. Our story is one of connection and relationships. We come from a long history of grassroots organizers and draw from their wisdom in our work. We have a long future ahead of us, and the momentum and commitment to our community is growing. We are here for the long haul—we will not be ignored, silenced, or stopped.

18

The Enbridge Pipeline Disaster and Accidental Activism along the Kalamazoo River

●

SONIA GRANT

●

Introduction

The Kalamazoo River weaves through southwestern Michigan, passing through the town of Marshall, the city of Battle Creek, and a number of small communities in between before eventually discharging into Lake Michigan.[1] Nicknamed "Cereal City," Battle Creek is home to the world headquarters of the Kellogg Company and other cereal manufacturing facilities, and on most mornings a faint smell of sugary breakfast foods hangs in the air. However, on July 26, 2010, residents awoke to a thick, oil-like stench. Some had noticed noxious odours the night before, but local fire departments that initially responded could not identify the origin of the smell. It was not until the next afternoon that Enbridge officially reported to the US National Response Center that its Line 6B pipeline had ruptured into Talmadge Creek, a small stream just outside of Marshall that flows into the Kalamazoo River. Weeks later, residents discovered that it was diluted bitumen piped from the Alberta tar sands that was pouring into these waterways.

The story of the Kalamazoo River disaster can be told in many ways. On one hand, it is a tale of corporate greed and negligence, and of a profound lack of regulatory oversight. On the other hand, for local officials, the spill is a story of multiple agencies working together to manage a situation that they had never received training for, involving thousands of contracted response workers suddenly pouring into a small town, with lawsuits later flooding a county court. The spill also revealed the many environmental health problems that ensue when diluted bitumen spills into a freshwater ecosystem and people are exposed to contaminated air and water. The story is often told in numbers: over 1.1 million gallons of diluted bitumen spilled; thousands of animals affected; roughly 2,500 cleanup workers employed; and ongoing cleanup costs exceeding $1 billion US as of 2014. But such numbers fail to capture the full and ongoing impacts of this disaster, especially when corporate and government bodies decide what counts, what does not, and when to stop counting.

This chapter begins with an overview of the spill itself and the controversies that surrounded cleanup efforts before examining the uncertainties about the long-term health impacts associated with exposure to diluted bitumen and what this means for residents. I argue that gaps in knowledge about these health impacts and gaps in environmental and public health policies reinforced each other in significant ways in Michigan. These gaps have important implications for environmental justice in other areas through which the tar sands industry is trying to push new pipelines, as well as for toxic developments more broadly. I conclude by briefly examining how a crop of "accidental activists" has emerged along the Kalamazoo River, forming unexpected alliances with neighbours and standing up for their communities and the environment—part of the growing resistance to tar sands pipeline expansion occurring throughout North America.

The research for this chapter was conducted in Michigan in the summer of 2013 and included seventy-five interviews with key informants, such as affected residents, government officials, industry representatives, scientists, lawyers, environmental activists, and journalists, as well as numerous informal conversations. A major challenge in telling this story is that it is replete with uncertainties, some of which may only come to be understood over very long periods of time. Moreover, because affected communities have been unable to substantiate many visceral experiences of injustice with the kind of evidence that could lead to political and legal victories—as this evidence is often very costly and time consuming to produce—important questions about the impacts of the spill and response efforts to it remain unanswered. In the face of these kinds of uncertainties, this chapter poses questions about *where* the burden of proof should be located and *what kinds* of proof should be required. Thus, the Kalamazoo River spill illustrates how weak regulatory regimes coupled with limited community resources and scientific uncertainty can serve to insulate polluters after disasters.

The Spill

Enbridge's Line 6B runs from Griffith, Indiana, to Sarnia, Ontario. It was installed in 1969 to service the company's Lakehead System, which is a network of pipelines that begins in Alberta and passes through the midwestern United States to eventually reconnect to Enbridge's Canadian network. Together, these pipelines have been transporting roughly two and a half million barrels per day (bpd) of various types of oil, with Line 6B having begun to carry tar sands bitumen in 1999.[2]

At the time of the spill, very few residents even knew Line 6B existed, much less that the diluted bitumen it carried was markedly different and more hazardous than conventional crude (as it contained 30 per cent condensate with numerous toxic chemicals, including benzene).[3] In the days after the spill, Enbridge withheld this crucial detail and instead presented the agencies in charge of response with a Material Safety Data Sheet (MSDS) for generic crude oil,[4] thereby implying this is what had spilled. This misperception lasted for weeks, until investigative reporting prompted Enbridge to provide the agencies leading the cleanup with the proper MSDS and Hazmat guidelines for the known safety hazards of exposure to the chemicals contained in diluted bitumen. If Enbridge had been candid from the outset, people living within one thousand feet of the river would likely have been immediately evacuated.[5] But since public health officials based their decisions on the chemical properties of crude oil, they only suggested a voluntary evacuation four days after the spill for about fifty homes in certain areas where dangerous levels of benzene were detected.[6]

In the hot summer months following the spill, thousands of people were exposed to airborne toxins. Many of those living outside of the suggested evacuation zone chose to self-evacuate, and Enbridge reimbursed hotel bills for most evacuees who were persistent enough to demand it. However, for low-income inhabitants of Baker Estates, a riverside trailer park, retroactive compensation was simply not an option because they could not afford the expense of relocation out of their own pockets, and it took several days of lobbying before Enbridge agreed to pay upfront for hotel rooms for evacuees. Because of this, as a woman from Baker Estates explained it, "we ended up getting evacuated 10–13 days later. A lot of people didn't get evacuated at all, even upriver. It took bringing the press in; it took making signs [that read] *sick children, sick dogs, sick people.*"[7]

The Kalamazoo River spill was the first time the US Environmental Protection Agency (EPA)—the organization leading the cleanup efforts—had ever had to deal with a spill of diluted bitumen, and cleanup workers quickly discovered that removing diluted bitumen from freshwater is extremely difficult. "We all had this naïve assumption that this oil was going to float," explained one official overseeing the cleanup.[8] Instead, the condensate mostly evaporated into the air or dissolved into the water, while the bitumen slowly sank to the riverbed and mixed with moving sediments. As a result, the EPA and Enbridge had to develop new cleanup techniques to deal with submerged bitumen, which affected approximately sixty kilometres of the river.

In 2013, the EPA estimated that about 180,000 of the 1.1 million gallons of diluted bitumen spilled into the Kalamazoo River in 2010 remained in the aquatic ecosystem. The EPA ordered Enbridge to collect an additional 12,000 to 18,000 gallons by dredging parts of the river in late 2013, leaving an estimated 162,000 to 168,000 gallons of bitumen clinging to river sediment. This remaining bitumen is deemed "unrecoverable" in the short term, and it may only be collected over a period of many years with the use of sediment traps that will slowly catch it in the river's natural depositional areas. The EPA cannot say with certainty when or if all of the bitumen will ever be removed from the river.[9]

Investigations conducted by the US Pipeline and Hazardous Materials Safety Administration (PHMSA) and the US National Transportation Safety Board (NTSB) later revealed multiple organizational failures involving Enbridge and various federal regulators.[10] For instance, internal Enbridge inspections disclosed 140 corrosion-related defects in Line 6B in 2008, and an additional 250 defects in 2009. Some defects were detected as early as 2004, yet most remained unaddressed at the time of the spill. Weak safety regulations at PHMSA meant that these necessary repairs in Line 6B went unenforced.

On the evening of July 25, 2010, multiple alarms about abnormal pressure in Line 6B were triggered in Enbridge's control centre in Edmonton, though the company did not discover or report the spill for another seventeen hours. Instead, Line 6B was restarted twice, and it was during these attempts to restart the flow of the pipeline that 81 per cent of the diluted bitumen spilling into the river was released. Although the PHMSA cited Enbridge for twenty-four violations of US pipeline safety regulations, the fine levied was a mere $3.7 million.[11] The NTSB's thorough inquiry ultimately placed blame for the Kalamazoo River spill on a combination of Enbridge's inadequate pipeline integrity management procedures, lack of public awareness programs, and deficient training of control centre staff, concluding that these problems together led to unchecked corrosion fatigue in Line 6B.[12]

Health, Science, and the Burdens of Proof

It is especially haunting to explore the Kalamazoo River with those who are familiar with its ecology, as they regularly point out patches of sky where there used to be a canopy of trees, or speak about particular species of flora and fauna that are nowhere to be seen. The extent of the ecological impacts of the spill is still unknown, although a team of federal, state, and tribal agencies are collaborating on a Natural Resources Damage Assessment (NRDA) and river restoration plans following regulations under the US *Oil Protection Act*. A number of people involved in the NRDA expressed dismay about a lack of cooperation from Enbridge.[13]

During my field trips with residents, it rarely took long to identify oil-saturated logs on the riverbanks or rings of oil that linger on tree trunks, and our attempts to wade into the water brought oil sheen to the surface and a toxic smell to the air. Nonetheless, at a quick glance, parts of the river still look quite beautiful. This is precisely what bothers many residents: it is as if a life-changing disaster has simply been swept under the rug, and forgotten.

Allegations of a cover-up have been circulating since August 2010, when a former employee of a company subcontracted by Enbridge to work on the spill alleged that cleanup workers had been ordered to bury bitumen rather than remove it. This worker and other observers have publicly released photo and video documentation that shows the extent of what they call a major cover-up. Residents and journalists I spoke with confirmed hearing that cleanup workers had received orders to hide rather than remove the bitumen.[14] Others recounted seeing cleanup workers who "brought dirt in and mixed it up [with the bitumen] and just left it there,"[15] though Enbridge and the EPA have dismissed these allegations.

The Kalamazoo River was reopened for public use in June of 2012, nearly two years after the spill,[16] when the Michigan Department of Community Health concluded that contact with residual bitumen posed no significant health risks. This assessment has not gone uncontested, however, as many residents are suffering from new or aggravated medical problems. In the course of my research, I heard countless stories about health problems that residents experienced in the aftermath of the spill. Acute symptoms in the ensuing months included headaches, nausea, respiratory difficulties, and skin lesions. Worse, some residents (especially those with already weakened immune systems or underlying conditions) described the onset of more serious and long-lasting problems in the wake of the disaster, such as heart attacks, seizures, asthma, chronic colds, lung problems, kidney failure, and worsened cancers. These concerns were amplified after a petition for the federal Agency for Toxic Substances and Disease Registry to fund a long-term health study was denied on the grounds that it would not provide useful information.[17]

In Baker Estates, the riverside trailer park noted earlier, at least fourteen people have died since the spill from illnesses that other residents confidently attribute to their exposures. Seven others living nearby have died from health problems that could be related to the ensuing toxicity. Many residents have also witnessed pets die from conditions that developed after the spill. One former resident of Baker Estates, who recently lost her husband and is herself very ill and undergoing chemotherapy, explained that she has "a quarter million dollars in hospital bills." Yet, like many sick and disadvantaged park residents, she has endured a range of dismissive responses from both local government officials and more affluent members of society, who have assumed that her health conditions are unrelated to the spill and are instead a result of "poor lifestyle choices."[18]

In low-income riverside communities like Baker Estates, the confluence of poverty, higher rates of existing health conditions before the spill, and an initial belief that Enbridge would do right by those adversely affected left residents simultaneously vulnerable to exposure and susceptible to manipulation. In the days after the spill, Enbridge employees offered some residents of Baker Estates air purifiers and a few hundred dollars in exchange for a signature on a form—which they later learned was a release waiver ensuring they would not take legal action against Enbridge in the future.[19] Many of those who did not sign these waivers went on to join a mass action lawsuit against Enbridge in September 2010, hoping it would yield enough money to relocate and pay for medical bills.

However, most had no choice but to prematurely settle with Enbridge for a very small sum. As one resident who settled put it, "I was stuck in-between a rock and a hard place, and had nowhere else to go."[20] By the spring of 2013, a handful of residents had yet to receive their payment, but only a few members of the park were continuing to fight Enbridge in court. One woman who had undergone two surgeries since the spill and was persevering with the suit noted how wealthier communities upriver had generally had more success in court with Enbridge, asking simply, "Why is my life worth any less than theirs?"[21]

At the crux of the legal challenge for some residents is that, unlike cases of property damage and devaluation, it is extremely difficult to prove that newly diagnosed health problems or the aggravation of existing conditions are direct results of the spill. Survivors of the spill are thus left without recourse for obtaining compensation from Enbridge for medical or vet bills. While Enbridge purchased about 150 houses along the stretch of affected river, many of those who did not own property at the time of the spill have only been successful in obtaining a small amount of financial compensation from Enbridge, if any. Yet even for those who were compensated, there is no closure. Rather, a sense of uncertainty about future health problems and associated costs weighs on residents, who are now keenly aware that illnesses from toxic exposure can take years to appear. Moreover, they fear that the lack of knowledge about the links between oil spills and health means that lawsuits on the basis of speculative injury are unlikely to succeed. As in all too many cases of environmental injustice, the burden of proof has fallen on affected communities.

Gaps in Knowledge and Policy

At the congressional hearing on the Kalamazoo River spill in September 2010, Scott Masten, a toxicologist with the US National Institute of Environmental Health Sciences, testified that "there are hundreds, if not thousands of chemicals present in crude oil, and we have incomplete knowledge of the toxicity of many of them."[22] There have been very few studies into the human health impacts of oil spills, and most existing studies have focused on acute and psychological impacts. Recent assessments have called for further bio-monitoring of communities exposed to oil spills because of the known potential for DNA damage and endocrine effects.[23] Further, there have been no studies about the particular impacts of spills of diluted bitumen, which is yet another reason many residents are astounded that no government agencies are investigating the long-term health impacts of the Kalamazoo River spill—the first major accident involving diluted bitumen in the US.

Along with the limited knowledge about the chronic health impacts from exposure to spilled oil, there is an absence of clear national guidelines for assessing whether evacuation is mandated after an oil spill. For instance, the US federal government provides dozens of different recommendations for maximum safe exposure to benzene—a chemical found in oil that is known to cause cancer and neurological problems at high exposure rates—but none of these are specific to oil spills in residential areas.[24] Despite these gaps in knowledge and policy, it is important to recognize that similar symptoms have been observed in many communities affected by oil spills, according to Dr. Riki Ott, a marine toxicologist, author, and activist who has been studying the subject since the 1989 Exxon Valdez spill in Alaska. Ott first visited Michigan in 2011 at the request of affected residents, and noted how she "was shocked at the similarity of the illnesses that were reported and documented by people" in Michigan to what she had seen in Alaska.[25]

After the Kalamazoo River spill, public health officials scrambled to grasp the extent of the potential health risks and respond accordingly. Appropriate resources were not always at hand. "All my detection equipment was in the Gulf shores," explained Jim Rutherford, the director of the Calhoun County Health Department.[26] The massive spill caused by the explosion of a British Petroleum (BP) oil rig in the Gulf of Mexico had occurred in April 2010, just a few months prior to the Kalamazoo River spill. The fact that cleanup efforts were still underway in the Gulf at the time of the disaster in Michigan proved significant. In addition to the BP disaster overshadowing the Kalamazoo River spill in the national press, this timing also meant that the majority of the country's oil spill response capacity (e.g., workers, equipment, and air-monitoring tools) was concentrated in the Gulf and took days to arrive in Michigan.

"I had to base my decisions on *science*—not on emotion or just reaction,"[27] Rutherford explained, as he recalled struggling for days to decide whether or not to issue a voluntary evacuation order of some areas affected by the spill. This is where undone science encounters public health decisions—and by extension people's lives—in very damaging ways. I borrow the concept of "undone science" from Scott Frickel and colleagues to refer to "areas of research identified by social movements and other civil society organizations as having potentially broad social benefit that are left unfunded, incomplete, or generally ignored."[28] In the case of the Kalamazoo River spill, incomplete knowledge about the effects of exposure to toxins in oil was used by certain government and corporate parties—those same agencies that are called upon but decline to fund further research—as justification for inaction. Genuinely concerned public officials like Rutherford are thus constrained by their institutional surroundings when it comes to making crucial decisions, such as whether or not—and whom—to evacuate after a major spill.

Accidental Activists

What happens when communities no longer trust the information provided to them by agencies that claim to be looking out for their best interests, such as a state health department or the EPA? For some, including one resident I spoke with, there is a sense of hopelessness: "What are we going to do? We're just the little people. That's big business, right there. We can't compete with them."[29] As one lawyer told me, Enbridge "fought tooth and nail" against residents' requests for compensation and transparency.[30] Struggling against Enbridge, especially when ill, has been extremely time consuming and exhausting for those residents who have not settled. For them, it has been immensely politicizing to realize that, as one resident put it, "the county failed us, the city failed us, the state failed us, the federal government failed us."[31]

The Kalamazoo River spill and the ensuing corporate and government response has transformed many residents into self-described "accidental activists." One man whose family was adversely affected by the spill and dismayed at the lack of support available explained: "I've never been considered what you call the proverbial 'tree hugger.' Never really fought for the environment. I mean [the spill] kind of opened my eyes a bit, and I thought, you know what, this is wrong."[32] Prompted by the injustices they experienced, some residents began organizing community meetings, speaking to local politicians, doing research, filing freedom of information requests, sharing their stories with news outlets and on social media, and conducting their own health and water column studies in disbelief of the results of those performed by the state.[33]

These accidental activists also began to connect with other oppositional struggles against the tar sands industry. For instance, some travelled to Washington, DC, to participate in the large national demonstrations against the Keystone XL pipeline, and others have begun building relationships with members of Indigenous communities in northern Alberta and in British Columbia, where many are fighting Enbridge's Northern Gateway project. Some have also begun to educate themselves and others about a range of interlocking dynamics, such as: tar sands extraction, fracking, and other forms of dirty energy production; capitalism and the entanglements of governments and corporations; and the quest for sustainable energy options and alternative models of social organization. These growing connections between different communities and grassroots resistance to the expansion of tar sands infrastructure seems crucial to any prospects for environmental justice, in Michigan and elsewhere.

Line 6B Expansion and the Future of Tar Sands Resistance in Michigan

The impacts of the Kalamazoo River spill are still unfolding, and will be for years to come. In addition to a pervading sense of apprehension about the long-term human and ecological health impacts of the spill, there is also an air of mystery that hovers around riverside communities. For how long will toxic contamination persist? Has money changed hands, as many residents suspect, between Enbridge and local government officials, news reporters, doctors, or lawyers? Were threats made, either implicitly or explicitly? Have

Enbridge's generous donations to local organizations bought silence, or were these honest attempts to improve a dire situation? These questions, which preoccupy many residents, may never be definitively answered. But one thing these "accidental activists" are sure of is that they are in this fight for the long run.

In late September 2010—just a few months after the spill—PHMSA authorized Enbridge to restart the flow of the repaired Line 6B,[34] and by 2013 Enbridge was granted permission from the Michigan Public Service Commission to replace the pipeline entirely and increase its capacity from 240,000 to 500,000 bpd by 2014.[35] But some aggrieved landowners along the new Line 6B pipeline have resisted, and a flurry of direct actions by the Michigan Coalition Against Tar Sands successfully halted construction on the new Enbridge Line 6B on four different days in the summer of 2013.[36] In addition, some concerned landowners have organized events to educate communities along the pipeline route about their legal rights in dealing with Enbridge and the heightened risks associated with bitumen spills. As with the Kalamazoo River disaster, new solidarity is being forged in opposition to the new pipeline.

Enbridge's plans for accessing US markets do not end with Line 6B. Between proposals for four new pipelines and expansions to eight existing pipelines underway, Enbridge is assembling a five-thousand-mile network throughout the US. The backbone of this network is the Alberta Clipper (Line 67) running from Alberta to Wisconsin, and if its expansion is approved, this alone could carry up to 880,000 bpd of diluted bitumen and other Canadian oil—even more than the proposed capacity of the notorious Keystone XL (830,000 bpd).[37]

There are, of course, many reasons to resist tar sands production long before this dirty oil is diluted and shipped through poorly maintained pipelines, and there are limitations to using case studies like the Kalamazoo River spill as tools for mobilizing against future pipelines. In particular, episodic disasters should not overshadow the ongoing devastation in those places where tar sands and other fossil fuels are produced and refined, and the damage this inflicts on the entire planet. Nevertheless, this spill does shed light on how the impacts of environmental disasters map onto patterns of social inequality, and can teach us something about how struggles over proof and reasonable doubt, situated knowledge and scientific expertise, and corporate accountability play out on the ground. Most of all, the Kalamazoo River spill illustrates that bitumen should never be pumped over rivers, forests, farms, or anywhere. Instead, it should be left in the ground.

19

Getting Europe Out
of the Tar Sands
The Rise of the UK Tar Sands Network

●

JESS WORTH

•

The UK Tar Sands Network (UKTSN) appeared in 2009 and very quickly put the tar sands on the political map in the UK. Working in solidarity with First Nations in Canada, it grew out of Britain's lively climate activist movement. This broad campaign has focused on: targeting UK companies and banks involved in the industry (most notably BP, Shell, and the Royal Bank of Scotland); exposing Canadian lobbying of the British and European Union (EU) governments; pushing for the EU to legislate against tar sands imports; and rolling out public education and network-building across the UK and beyond. As a result of the activities of the UKTSN and its partners, the negative impacts of the tar sands have received widespread media coverage in the UK and increasingly across Europe, which has helped to catapult these issues into boardrooms, debating chambers, and policy circles.

This chapter provides an overview of this initial campaigning success while exploring how the wider UK campaign can move from raising awareness to provoking real-world policy change, and highlighting some key aspects of organizing that may be useful to other groups.

Origins: Climate Camp and Solidarity

On a sunny September morning in 2009, a huge crowd builds outside Canada House in London's iconic Trafalgar Square, raucously singing a rewritten version of *South Park: Bigger, Longer & Uncut*'s "Blame Canada"—giving the spoof a serious twist; now Canada really is to blame "since the tar sands came along." CBC TV cameras scramble to get a good shot among the flurry of activity. Next, the crowd marches purposefully around the corner to BP's headquarters, where George Poitras of the Mikisew Cree First Nation speaks movingly of watching a young man die from a rare form of cancer in his community of Fort Chipewyan, and his fears that their health is being jeopardized by living downstream from the Alberta tar sands. BP, the crowd learns, is poised to invest in its first major tar sands extraction project—something the hundreds gathered vow to oppose. The protest outside BP airs live on BBC London's lunchtime news, and a few days later a leading Canadian newspaper explains the significant new development this reflects: tar sands protests have spread to the UK, with First Nations voices at their heart.[1]

The protest was part of the Blackheath Camp for Climate Action—the fourth of its kind—where thousands of climate activists gathered from all over the UK for workshops and action skills training, which catalyzed a series of direct actions and protests during and after the event. In conjunction with Clayton Thomas-Muller, I had helped to bring a First Nations delegation over from Canada to the Climate Camp, in order to start raising popular awareness about the devastating impacts of the tar sands. At the time, this awareness was almost nonexistent.

Our basic plan was to run a couple of workshops led by the delegation of George, Clayton, Lionel Lepine (a resident of Fort Chipewyan and a member of the Athabasca Chipewyan First Nation [ACFN]), and Heather Milton-Lightening (from the Indigenous Environmental Network), in the hope of sparking enough interest for a small action. We did not anticipate what transpired: our First Nations visitors became the "rock stars" of the camp, rendering the crowd dumbstruck with their accounts of almost unimaginable environmental destruction, and the terrifying climate implications of the industry's expansion plans. Further, they educated an already well-informed audience about the oft-ignored links between climate issues and Indigenous rights, and invited UK activists to rise to the multiple challenges of becoming allies and working in solidarity with frontline communities who are fighting the tar sands on their doorsteps. The workshops and action-planning meetings were packed, to the extent that we filled an entire train platform with our impromptu posse when we set off for the Canada House/BP action. The energy was immediate, and the commitments inspired were enduring.

Speaker Tours, Shareholders, and Superglue

In short, the UKTSN arose organically, spontaneously, and somewhat chaotically. The need to confront the tar sands was a struggle whose time had come in the UK. Grassroots interest, awareness, and activism soon spiralled out from the Climate Camp into a variety of activities. These were underpinned by a core group of organizers, particularly Suzanne Dhaliwal and myself, and we began to take on fundraising and coordinating efforts with support from London Rising Tide.

The budding movement was strengthened over the next few months by an Indigenous women's speaker tour around the UK, which featured Heather, Eriel Deranger from ACFN, and Melina Laboucan-Massimo from the Lubicon Cree.[2] This tour included a parliamentary event hosted by Simon Hughes, MP, a senior Liberal Democrat who (while in opposition, at least) was most supportive, and issued a call for the government to intervene to ensure that the Royal Bank of Scotland—83 per cent taxpayer owned—stopped financing tar sands companies.[3] In December 2009, at the UN climate change negotiations in Copenhagen, I joined an Indigenous-led protest outside the Canadian embassy in Denmark. Simultaneously, there was a dramatic action in London, as three activists scaled Canada House, dipped the Canadian flag in an oil-like substance, and then superglued themselves to the windows so that security could not remove them.[4] In April 2010, Clayton and George returned to London to speak in support of a shareholder resolution raising concerns about the risks involved in investing in tar sands at BP's annual general meeting (AGM), working with FairPensions, Greenpeace, Platform, and Co-operative Asset Management, who were all behind the resolution.[5]

In the ensuing years, the UKTSN has grown into a full-fledged organization, with a few paid staff, a website, several thousand followers on Facebook and Twitter, and (sometimes only just enough) funding from a range of sources to keep us going. Alongside our partners, we have run a variety of educational and political campaigns, targeting various aspects of UK involvement in the tar sands industry. These include:

- a massive anti-BP brand damage push around the company's Orwellian role as a "Sustainability Partner" of the London 2012 Olympics, and its sponsorship of the associated World Shakespeare Festival, which has included "guerrilla Shakespeare" theatrical stage invasions in iambic pentameter;[6]
- efforts to expose and resist Valero's plans to be the first company to import large quantities of tar sands oil to the UK if eastern-bound pipelines are successful;[7]
- interventions in the ongoing battle over the EU Fuel Quality Directive, which aims to label tar sands oil as more polluting than conventional oil;[8]
- helping to bring First Nations delegates to the BP, Shell, and Royal Bank of Scotland AGMs to challenge the board and shareholders directly over their tar sands investments;[9] and
- confronting, disrupting, and exposing Canadian officials and tar sands lobbyists wherever they meet—as with the headline-grabbing protests in June 2013, when Canadian prime minister Stephen Harper was invited to address the British Parliament.[10]

Taken together, these activities have generated considerable national media coverage in both the UK and Canada, such that awareness about the impacts of the tar sands within the UK has vastly improved, particularly among policy-makers and the environmental community.

Measuring Success

As much as we have grown, we are still a relatively small and young grass-roots organization, and, as with most long-term campaigns, it is difficult to measure success. Certainly, our first few actions were significant in that they helped to break through the pervasive media silence in Canada on these issues, with First Nations communities now able to voice concerns via mainstream media on an international scale. Sometimes we have been lucky enough to get a clear "win"—such as the Royal Bank of Scotland ending its sponsorship of "Climate Week" after being met with vociferous cries of "greenwash!"[11] Sometimes the media coverage has demonstrated our success in shaping a particular debate, such as in the consistently negative coverage that hovered over BP around their April 2011 and 2012 AGMs. No less than the *Financial Times* branded tar sands campaigners as the "winners" of the 2011 meeting, praising the combination of eloquent, pointed, and informed questioning by First Nations representatives and gutsy direct action by ten activists who attempted to spell out "NO TAR SANDS" with their T-shirts at the front of the hall, before they were dragged out by security.[12]

Still, however much we raised awareness, our efforts have not yet prevented either Shell or BP from going ahead with any new tar sands extraction plans. We continue to work with ACFN to support their legal challenge and opposition to Shell's massive proposed Jackpine Mine Expansion and Pierre River Mine.[13] We also played a role—in alliance with many others, particularly the Co-operative Bank—in shifting the British government from an "anti" to a "neutral" position in the EU's vote on the Fuel Quality Directive in

Fifty protesters at the UK Parliament respond to Canadian prime minister Stephen Harper's visit to lobby for tar sands imports into Europe, 2011.

2012, which revolved around whether to label tar sands oil as more polluting than conventional oil and thus discourage its future import into Europe. The oil industry was furious at the UK's last-minute decision to move onto the fence, though their virulent lobbying hand-in-hand with the Canadian government (see chapter 4) had done enough to stall the negotiations for over a year. While that battle continues, evidence of our impact can be seen in Canada's intensive lobbying offensive, the Pan-European Oil Sands Advocacy Strategy, which references our actions as one of the reasons they have had to deploy countermeasures.[14]

Elements of Effectiveness

In spite of our small size, especially in relation to the enormous industry we are confronting, we have always aimed big. It is my belief that our success in putting the problem of the tar sands on the UK map derives from four key aspects of how we organize, which might provide some ideas and inspiration for other grassroots groups seeking to lead campaigns against the tar sands.

First, the UKTSN has, from the outset, been rooted in a relationship of solidarity and partnership with frontline Indigenous communities in Canada. This relationship, which was initially facilitated by the Indigenous Environmental Network and more recently the Canadian Indigenous Tar Sands Campaign, informs the way we approach many of our activities. We develop our strategies jointly and make relevant decisions in consultation with our First Nations partners. Our aim has always been to create a platform to elevate First Nations voices, rather than attempting to speak on their behalf. After all, they are the experts, and we believe that their perspectives, experiences, and treaty rights provide a vital foundation for ultimately shutting down the tar sands. This is why we have put a lot of energy into organizing and supporting speaker tours and trips by First Nations representatives to speak to policy-makers and at AGMs. We recognize that they are the most powerful and effective public advocates.

This recognition also means we need to approach actions in a different way than UK-based activists would typically consider. Rather than being fully autonomous, when we work with Indigenous peoples, we take our lead from them on the tone, style, and messaging of a particular action, as we must be conscious of how our tactics could potentially have negative implications for their struggles and livelihoods back in Canada. Even so, there is at least one example of how our effort to elevate First Nations advocates has had serious consequences back in Alberta. George Poitras was forced out of his job with his First Nation by an oil company, following the increasing attention he received on multiple speaking trips—though he has been brave enough to speak openly about this, and to continue undeterred with his vital work.[15] It is essential to bear in mind how much higher the stakes are for the communities we work in solidarity with, and to ensure they have free, prior, and informed consent over their allies' activities, just as we demand it of the oil industry we oppose.

This solidarity relationship has also involved Suzanne from UKTSN travelling to the tar sands to bear witness to the destruction, to learn first-hand about the impacts on First Nations in Alberta, to connect with communities affected by the associated infrastructure of refineries and pipelines, and to participate in the October 2012 tour She Speaks: Indigenous Women Speak Out Against Tar Sands. These events in western and central Canada emphasized the fact that women are at the forefront of the struggles to oppose the tar sands in both Canada and the UK, while deepening our relationships with frontline communities and spreading awareness about the growing support coming from Britain.

Second, UKTSN works primarily through partnerships with a wide range of different actors, from activist networks to large NGOs to policy-makers. From our inception, there was no desire to set up a big new NGO or campaigning network that would compete with existing organizations for supporters, funding, and attention. Instead, the goal was to provide established organizations and networks that stood in opposition to the tar sands with support, information, and assistance in building relationships with First Nations. This approach has led to a range of effective partnerships between different groupings of UK-, EU-, and Canadian-based organizations. It has also broadened the scope of our movement-building mission, as the struggle against the tar sands ties into a range of other connected struggles. This includes deepening relationships with US Gulf Coast communities devastated by the BP Deepwater Horizon drilling disaster in 2010, and with community members resisting Shell operations in both the Arctic and Nigeria—including joint events and shared strategizing around AGMs. Our hope is that by bringing these geographically separate struggles together, we can find common ground with those working on related issues and present a united front, which we suspect could be one of the oil industry's worst nightmares.

A third key element of our organizing is our willingness to employ a wide spectrum of tactics. Like other NGOs, we conduct in-depth research, produce reports, and lobby politicians to support the Fuel Quality Directive. But we are also not afraid to engage in direct action, such as invading a stage, interrupting a Canadian minister's speech, or blockading an energy summit—if that is the best way to get our point across. Indeed, we did all these things just in the last three months of 2012![16] In short, our tactical toolbox is large and creative: a well-rehearsed, daring, and original intervention by a small number of people can sometimes have a greater impact than the mobilization of many more people for events that are less targeted and noteworthy to the mainstream media, such as a march or rally.

Finally, because we are small, we are light on our feet; this enables us to respond quickly to unfolding events, such as the sudden emergence of the Idle No More movement in Canada, or an announcement that Stephen Harper is coming to London on short notice. Our small size and lack of budget is less of a constraint than one might expect, because we make substantial use of social media and self-generated press to mobilize people, share information about our activities, and communicate our messages. We have also been privileged to work with several talented filmmakers who have documented many of our direct actions, such as:

- suddenly popping up in a meeting chaired by Canadian High Commissioner Gordon Campbell, stripping down to Maple Leaf and Union Jack underwear, and having an "oil orgy" to demonstrate the intimate relationship between Canada, the oil industry, and the UK government;[17]

- exorcising the evil spirit of BP from the Tate Modern, one of the UK's biggest art galleries, with performance activist Reverend Billy;[18] and

- holding an unannounced and somewhat noisy "teach-in" inside the foyer of the UK Department for Business, Innovation and Skills about the dangers of the Comprehensive Economic Trade Agreement (CETA) being negotiated between Canada and the EU.[19]

These three films were made by Felix Gonzales (of You and I Films), and each took on a life of their own online and helped to widen awareness about struggles to resist the tar sands.

The Continuing Battle

Although we take pride in our various actions and achievements, we are under no illusion as to the scale of the battle that is necessary to keep the tar sands in the ground and help avert the worst nightmares of climate change. Yet, we continue to be motivated by our recognition that we have an important strategic role to play on the other side of the Atlantic. After all, Shell and BP are based in the UK, and much of the finance that flows into the tar sands comes from the City of London, the world's biggest oil and gas financial hub. It was no accident that the Canadian government, aghast at the political opposition to its dirty exports bubbling up all over the EU, chose oil-friendly London as the headquarters for its multimillion-dollar Pan-European Oil Sands Advocacy lobbying offensive to kill the Fuel Quality Directive. The right-wing prime ministers of the UK and Canada get on like a house on fire, and perhaps owing to the historic bonds of the Commonwealth, the Canadian government seems to be very concerned about what the UK thinks of it. It is telling that the Canadian media has regularly covered opposition to the tar sands in Europe, when it has been ignoring it at home for years.

Although awareness and opposition to the tar sands industry in the UK may have grown as a result of our activities, the links between the EU and Canada were strengthened considerably with the official signing of the Canada-EU free trade agreement (CETA) in October 2013. The details of CETA have long been hidden (and remain unclear at the time of writing), but it seems certain that these negotiations and the ultimate agreement delayed the implementation of the EU Fuel Quality Directive. It also seems certain that the implementation of CETA will pave the way for deeper involvement by European companies in the tar sands industry, and it is probable that the investor-state dispute settlement mechanism will give the likes of BP, Shell, TOTAL, and Statoil a corporate-friendly mechanism to appeal against existing and future environmental regulations.

We know we are part of an epic battle with one of the most powerful industries in the world, and that as a movement, we need to up our game and grow our numbers. In this, we can take heart from the words of Canadian High Commissioner Gordon Campbell during a recent high-level meeting with British diplomats, in which he complained that the tar sands have become "a totemic issue, hitting directly on Brand Canada."[20] This is testament to the hard work, passion, and commitment of all those who are part of the global anti–tar sands movement. We will continue to play our part, working in solidarity and partnership with First Nations and others, in what history will undoubtedly look back on as an iconic and pivotal struggle for climate justice.

20

Labour Faces Keystone XL and Climate Change

●

JEREMY BRECHER AND THE LABOR NETWORK
FOR SUSTAINABILITY

●

The coming of climate change represents an existential threat unlike any-thing our society, or even our species, has faced. Organized labour, like every other segment of American society, is having a tough time coming to terms with climate change and the witches' brew of environmental and other issues that interact with it. Can organized labour rise to the challenge?

The greenhouse gases humanity has already put in the atmosphere will raise global temperatures by 2°C (almost 4°F, and the level the nations of the world agreed to avoid) from pre-industrial levels even if we stop putting car-bon in the atmosphere today. After a quarter-century of delay, we will have to cut greenhouse gas emissions radically and rapidly to prevent 4°C (7°F) of warming, which would almost certainly lead to global ecosystem collapse. This year's floods, fires, storms, and other extreme weather events provide our gentle reminder.

While organized labour has perhaps changed less than any other major institution in American society over the past two-thirds of a century, labour does change. A movement that once pursued racial exclusion became a bas-tion of ethnic diversity; a movement that once supported discrimination against immigrants became a beacon for immigrant rights; a movement that never met a war it didn't like, even Vietnam, became an opponent of the Iraq and Afghanistan wars. Organized labour is also changing its approach to global warming. But that change—like these previous ones—involves tension, and sometimes conflict.

The American Federation of Labor and Congress of Industrial Organizations (AFL-CIO) (in contrast to most of the world's labour movements) opposed the 1997 Kyoto Protocol agreeing to cuts in greenhouse gas emissions. In 2006, it created an Energy Task Force, whose statement "Jobs and Energy for the 21st Century"[1] acknowledged the scientific evidence that fossil fuels are contributing to global warming, but opposed "extreme measures" that would "undermine economic growth," "harm particular sectors," or place the US "at a disadvantage to other nations." It held that any program for tradable emission permits (e.g., cap-and-trade) should initially seek only to "gradually slow the growth in greenhouse gas emissions"—in other words, allow emissions to continue to grow. Measures to actually reduce fossil fuel use should wait until nuclear, clean coal, and other alternatives assured abundant energy. This approach has guided the AFL-CIO's lobbying around climate protection legislation.

Like the rest of American society, organized labour's approach to climate change has continued to evolve. For example, when he was head of the United Mine Workers of America (UMW), Richard Trumka led the charge against the Kyoto Protocol and for expanded use of coal and other fossil fuels. But in his current role as president of the AFL-CIO, Trumka recently said, "Scientists tell us we are headed ever more swiftly toward irreversible climate change—with catastrophic consequences for human civilization." Far from being a threat only in a distant future, "climate change is happening now." And that demands action: "The carbon emissions from that coal, and from oil and natural gas, and agriculture and so much other human activity—causes global warming, and we have to act to cut those emissions, and act now."[2]

However, the AFL-CIO still has not endorsed even the minimal targets for carbon reduction proposed by the world's leading body of climate scientists, the Intergovernmental Panel on Climate Change (IPCC), let alone the reduction of carbon in the atmosphere to 350 parts per million, which America's leading climate scientist, James Hansen, and many other experts say is necessary to prevent those "catastrophic consequences for human civilization."

Meanwhile, organized labour has become an enthusiastic proponent of "green jobs." The AFL-CIO established a Center for Green Jobs to promote green jobs, establish appropriate job standards, and help train workers to fill them. The Steelworkers co-founded the Blue-Green Alliance (BGA) with the Sierra Club to expand the "clean economy." Many unions established green jobs programs. Labour and environmental groups helped make green jobs a key part of Obama's 2008 campaign message. But by and large, unions also continue to support jobs that accelerate climate catastrophe.

In part, this reflects underlying structural problems in organized labour that make it difficult to confront broad social issues like global warming. On the one hand, US unions represent particular groups of workers. On the other hand, union federations like the AFL-CIO and Change to Win have in principle represented the interests of workers as a whole. However, since the days of Samuel Gompers's "craft autonomy," the interests of individual unions have almost always trumped those of workers as a whole. Within the Federations, by tradition the unions perceived as most affected by an issue call the shots. As a leader of the Laborers' union put it, "If there's legislation or a project that's good for another union, and my members don't have equity in the work, I'm going to be supportive or I'm going to say nothing."[3] Following the same principle, the AFL-CIO's energy task force is composed primarily of the miners, industrial unions, and construction trades. The existential interest of all workers in halting climate change, and the interest of all the unions that stand to gain from effective climate protection, play only a marginal role.

The Keystone XL Pipeline

These contradictions came to the surface in September 2010, when TransCanada, a Canadian pipeline company, signed a project labour agreement with the Teamsters, Plumbers, Operating Engineers, and Laborers for work on the Keystone XL (KXL) pipeline, which would carry oil produced from tar sands in Alberta, Canada, nearly two thousand miles to Nederland, Texas. The union presidents issued a statement saying that the project would "pave a path to better days and raise the standard of living for working men and women in the construction, manufacturing, and transportation industries." It would allow American workers to "get back to the task of strengthening their families and the communities they live in."[4]

The KXL issue didn't come to a head, however, until June 2011, when 350.org leader Bill McKibben and a group of other movement leaders called for a month of unprecedented civil disobedience actions against the pipeline.[5] He pointed out that burning the recoverable oil in the Alberta tar sands by itself would raise the carbon in the atmosphere by 200 parts per million (ppm). It wasn't hard to figure out that this would increase the 390 ppm of carbon in the atmosphere today by more than half. Indeed, it would increase the gap between the current level and the safe level of 350 ppm five-fold. He called the pipeline "a fifteen hundred mile fuse to the biggest carbon bomb on the planet." He quoted the leading NASA climate change specialist, Jim Hansen, saying that tar sands "must be left in the ground." Indeed, "if the tar sands are thrown into the mix it is essentially game over" for a viable planet.

The media rushed to portray the pipeline as a typical case of "jobs versus the environment," pitting the labour movement against the environmental movement; NPR proclaimed, "Pipeline Decision Pits Jobs Against Environment."[6] However, efforts began immediately to develop labour opposition to the pipeline. A series of articles by the Labor Network for Sustainability questioned whether KXL was really in labour's interest. A widely publicized study by the Cornell Global Labor Institute challenged the industry's job claims and indicated the pipeline could produce as few as fifty permanent jobs.[7]

The Transport Workers Union (TWU) and the Amalgamated Transit Union (ATU) issued a joint statement, saying, "We need jobs, but not ones based on increasing our reliance on Tar Sands Oil." It called for major "New Deal"–type public investments in infrastructure modernization and repair, energy conservation, and climate protection as a means of "putting people to work and laying the foundations of a green and sustainable economic future for the United States."[8] Terry O'Sullivan, president of the Laborers' International Union of North America (LIUNA), cracked back: "It's time for ATU and TWU to come out from under the skirts of delusional environmental groups which stand in the way of creating good, much needed American jobs."[9] LIUNA threatened to end support for legislation that benefits transit workers.

With its member unions divided, the AFL-CIO decided not to take a position on the pipeline. The BGA also took no position, even though more of its members opposed than supported the pipeline. Six unions and several environmental groups, most of them members of the BGA, issued a statement that was neutral on the pipeline but supported President Obama's decision not to give it an accelerated permit. Terry O'Sullivan responded, "We're repulsed by some of our supposed brothers and sisters lining up with job killers like the Sierra Club and the Natural Resources Defense Council to destroy the lives of working men and women."[10] LIUNA withdrew from the BGA, testified for some of the most anti-labour members of Congress, and even participated in events funded by the Koch brothers. Jack Gerard, president of the American Petroleum Institute, gleefully proclaimed, "We will stand shoulder to shoulder with labor unions that have backed the pipeline, including the Teamsters and the AFL-CIO's Building and Construction Trades Department."[11]

While the KXL issue illustrated tensions and conflicts both within organized labour and between labour and environmental movements, it opened up a conversation that needs to take place. If union support for KXL had not been challenged, the labour movement would simply have ignored the climate and environmental issues raised by the tar sands and the pipeline. Without the conflict, it is doubtful that the six unions would have supported Obama's permit decision or engaged with the issue in any other way. Such tensions are inescapable if the necessary change is to come. But those tensions can only be creative if labour and environmental groups focus on building relationships that keep tensions within limits and minimize lasting damage. Even more important, those tensions can lead to the recognition that labour and environmentalists must defuse "jobs versus the environment" with a jobs strategy based on protecting the environment. Ultimately, it is through honest differences of opinion that the labour movement can arrive at sound conclusions and correct judgments.

Job Alternatives on the Ground

The growing scarcity of fossil fuels is leading to efforts to utilize energy that is increasingly harmful to extract, transport, and use, such as tar sands oil, fracked natural gas, coal from mountaintop removal and ecologically fragile locations, oil from deepwater drilling, inappropriate biomass, and nuclear power. As with the tar sands pipeline, so in each of these cases proponents will dangle the promise of jobs; unions will be tempted to play the role the Laborers have played with KXL; the public will be told that the issue is "jobs versus the environment." Those who oppose such extreme energy will similarly be branded "job killers."

While advocates of renewable energy alternatives rightly point out that solar, wind, and energy conservation create far more jobs than fossil fuel and nuclear alternatives, that means little to workers whose current livelihoods or opportunities for a decent job are threatened by environmental campaigns. While critics can validly point out that claims about the numbers of jobs to be created by KXL and similar projects are often wildly inflated, that is largely irrelevant to desperate workers for whom any job is better than no job. And while critics can often show that most of the jobs created are temporary, the same can be said of many jobs in today's economy, including most union construction jobs. Even some union officials who strongly supported climate protection legislation simultaneously argued heatedly for the Keystone XL pipeline as a source of immediate jobs for their desperate members.

The solution for advocates of renewable energy in both the environmental and the labour movements is to develop our own jobs programs to provide workers and communities with a better alternative than destroying everyone's future through the extraction and use of extreme energy.

How is that possible? Some interesting examples come from recent campaigns to close coal-fired power plants, which we have analyzed in *Jobs Beyond Coal*.[12] In Centralia, Washington, for example, local environmentalists, religious leaders, and the Sierra Club campaigned to transition a coal-fired TransAlta power plant to cleaner energy. At first they met opposition from the union that represented workers at the plant. But in extended discussion with the union, the environmental coalition discovered that its real concern was not to prolong coal burning per se, but to protect the jobs of workers in the plant and provide an economic future for nearby communities. Thereupon, wrote journalist Mark Hertsgaard, the environmental coalition "insisted that the plant's workforce be retained throughout its closure and cleanup; that workers be trained in the technologies that would replace coal, especially energy efficiency; and that the company, not the taxpayers, subsidize the transition."[13] The result was an agreement between environmentalists, TransAlta, and the state of Washington that meant 40 per cent of the plant's 250 employees will reach retirement age before the closing, and the rest will have at least eight years in their current jobs. The company also agreed to provide $30 million to a community investment fund and $25 million for an energy-technology transition fund.[14] The union enthusiastically supported the deal.

While there is no single model for such work, there are numerous cases where unions and environmentalists have cooperated to transition beyond coal in ways that are acceptable to both.[15] Such on-the-ground cooperation around particular facilities—existing and proposed—can provide an alternative for protecting worker interests wherever the threat of an extreme energy project raises its head. Similar responses could be developed wherever extreme energy programs offer jobs destroying our future. But that will require commitment and proactive response, preferably from labour and environmental movements working in tandem.

Protecting Workers by Protecting the Climate

In a letter advocating KXL, trade union leaders acknowledged the criticism that "further development of Canada's oil sands puts in jeopardy U.S. efforts aimed at capping carbon emissions and greenhouse gasses." They answered, "Comprehensive energy and environmental policy should strive to address climate concerns while simultaneously ensuring adequate supplies of reliable energy and promoting energy independence and national security."[16] That expresses the official energy and climate policy of the American labour movement. It is similar to the "all of the above" energy policy advocated by President Obama.

Such a "balanced policy" sounds reasonable. But in practice, it means putting off the necessary sharp reductions in greenhouse gas emissions for further decades, guaranteeing that climate catastrophe will grow worse and worse. Indeed, the trade union letter backing KXL goes on to say, "Alternative energy sources are generally still in developmental stages; therefore it is likely the U.S. consumer will remain substantially dependent on carbon fuels for the next several decades." Any policy based on the assumption that the US will "remain substantially dependent on carbon fuels for the next several decades" is condemning American working people, all Americans, and indeed the entire world to a fate worse than humanity has ever known.

There are growing points in organized labour's position that could serve as the basis for a very different approach. AFL-CIO president Richard

Trumka has argued that "addressing climate risk is not a distraction" from solving our economic problems. Indeed, it is critical to the solution: "Every factory and power plant, every home and office, every rail line and highway, every vehicle, locomotive and plane, every school and hospital, must be modernized, upgraded, renovated or replaced with something cleaner, more efficient, less wasteful." That means "retooling our world." And that means there is plenty of work to be done. "If we are going to rebuild, restore, modernize or replace everything we inherited in just 30 years," we need "the skill and effort of all of us."

Trumka recognized that this would not happen simply through current market forces: "By themselves, capital markets will not properly incorporate climate risk and reward into pricing investment opportunities." Investors need "government policies to make sure that critical investments get made—investments in building retrofits, in high speed rail and the smart grid, in carbon capture and sequestration."[17]

Clean, renewable energy and energy conservation are cheaper than extreme fossil fuels and nuclear power. They are available right now. Many studies have shown that dollar for dollar, they produce far more jobs. If labour is to use its political clout to secure more jobs, the best way to do so is to fight for a new energy economy that rapidly phases out carbon-emitting fossil fuels and even more rapidly replaces them with renewable energy and conservation.

Fighting for "green jobs" is not enough. It must be combined with resisting the drive for extreme energy and a rapid phased transition beyond fossil fuels. (The trendy idea that extreme energy, like fracked natural gas or nuclear power, is the solution disregards the serious liabilities of each.) This will require an economic reorientation far beyond the labour-backed Waxman-Markey climate legislation. Just as the US phased out production of pleasure cars during the Second World War in the interest of national survival, we will have to phase out our greenhouse gas–emitting production and consumption in the interest of human survival. Every dollar we invest in fossil fuels is not only a dollar that goes to intensify the climate crisis; it is also a dollar that we should instead be spending on the transition to renewable energy.

Of course, such an approach raises the question of what will happen to the workers in the phased-out sectors. Although the global labour movement has strongly advocated for a "just transition" that protects current workers in the transition to a low-carbon economy, much of the American labour movement has resisted even talking about such an approach. When he was president of the Miners union, Richard Trumka maintained that such talk meant the elimination of his membership. As president of the AFL-CIO, however, he now advocates a "Just Transition to a low carbon-emissions economy."[18]

It is time for American labour to walk the walk. The climate crisis is here and now. To continue business as usual in the face of it is like ignoring the advance of an enemy army. If the labour movement is to have a future, it will have to be as part of a wider movement for a transition to sustainability. The goal of such a movement will have to be a new economy that protects the environment while it provides for the needs of the world's people.

Labour has been critical of corporate short-term thinking, maximizing profits on a quarterly basis and not looking to the future. Yet labour manifests similar short-term thinking when it comes to climate and sustainability. Of course, unions have to balance the immediate needs of their members with those of the future. But exclusively short-term thinking is bad for the planet and its people, and equally bad for the future of the labour movement. Indeed, helping to take the lead in a proactive response to climate change may provide labour's greatest opportunity to reconstruct our economy, thereby providing the context to rebuild the labour movement. That will inevitably involve tension within the labour movement—just like the transformations that challenged racism, immigrant exclusion, and kneejerk militarism.

III

Future Prospects

21

Ending the Age of Fossil Fuels and Building an Economics for the Seventh Generation

●

WINONA LaDUKE

●

Ojibwe prophecies speak of a time during the seventh fire when our people will have a choice between two paths. The first path is well worn and scorched. The second path is new and green. It is our choice as communities and as individuals how we will proceed.

A key part of the struggle to protect our Mother Earth, and renew our covenant with both the Creator and the generations to come, must be to keep fossil fuels in the ground. This means we must say no to tar sands oil, and no to fracking and dirty coal.

We've already raised the average temperature of the globe roughly 1°C since we started our economies based on fossil energy. The question is whether we can stop it from rising much more: *this is at the core of our survival*. It is essential for us to look at the world's economic and environmental realities in order to make critical decisions about our future. That means we must address issues such as climate change, peak oil, and food insecurity. This new millennium is a time when we are facing the joint challenges of an industrial food system and a centralized energy system, both of which are based on fossil fuels and are damaging the health of our peoples and the earth at an alarming rate. In the US—the largest and most inefficient energy economy in the world—tribal communities have long supplied the raw materials for nuclear and coal plants, huge dam projects, and oil and gas development. These resources have been exploited to power far-off cities and towns, while Indigenous peoples and people of colour live in the energy sacrifice zones.

All of this already has a big long-term price tag. For example, in 2011, fourteen weather-related disasters in the US (from Joplin's tornado to Grand Forks's flooding to New England's storms) are estimated to have cost the country around $14 billion, according to a study by the Natural Resources Defense Council, and these numbers were dwarfed by Hurricane Sandy the following year. These costs, and the frequency and severity of disasters, have increased every year since then. Disasters related to climate change cause immeasurable losses, such as the poisoning of the Athabasca River in the tar sands extraction zone, and present premature deaths and hospitalizations caused by climate change—related health issues, such as extreme heat and flooding. Climate change is expensive and deadly.

Tar Sands Pipelines

The expansion of the tar sands industry is rapidly destroying one of the largest and most pristine river systems on the continent, the Athabasca River Basin, as well as a huge carbon sink in the boreal forest. It is an understatement to say that environmental regulations in Alberta are very lax. This beautiful-land-turned-petro-chemical-state is governed by a virtual dictatorship that has been unresponsive to national and international outcry at the grave human rights violations being carried out at the behest of some of the largest, richest, and most powerful oil companies in the world. But First Nations voices are stronger, and we support our friends and relatives in their call for healing.

Tar sands production is licensed to use more water than Calgary and Edmonton combined, which are together home to almost two million people. Worse, tar sands wastewater is so laced with chemical sludge it is turned into poison. All of this is happening in a world that is increasingly water challenged. Every day, tar sands producers burn six hundred million cubic feet of natural gas to produce tar sands oil—enough natural gas to heat three million homes—and carbon emissions for the project surpass those of ninety-seven nations in the world combined. Accelerating this through seeking new markets for tar sands would only worsen the situation.

Some of the most important battles today are around the tar sands. Since the construction of new pipelines and the expansion of existing ones are central to the expansion of this destructive and wasteful industry, they are also key fronts of struggle—and I see this struggle to protect our lands uniting Native communities in the States with First Nations communities in the North in new ways. Idle No More in Canada was a catalyst for spreading that consciousness as well.

Clearly, the struggle to protect our lands is intensifying at both ends of the pipeline. Tar sands oil is sixteen times more likely to breach a pipeline than regular crude oil. Consider our landscape in Minnesota, which is full of lakes, rivers, and wetlands. Wetlands are like sponges—they soak up everything. In Minnesota alone, nearly one and a half million gallons of oil have spilled out of the Enbridge/Lakehead pipelines over the past thirty years.

In the northern US, our land and water are the lifeblood of the Anishinaabeg people, sustaining and nourishing us. A large share of the world's fresh surface water supply lies here, and it is worth protecting. Further, our sacred wild rice beds, lakes, and rivers are precious, and our regional fisheries generate $7.2 billion annually and support forty-nine thousand jobs. Our White Earth tribal chairman said, "When we signed those treaties, and secured protection for our wild rice, we weren't talking about getting some rice in a bag.... We meant a lake. We have a right to the land, water, and air that our food came from—and that needs to be protected by sovereign nations."

Our land and water are being threatened by Enbridge pipelines transporting ever-larger amounts of tar sands oil (and also toxic lighter "diluents") across Minnesota, and by permits sought by Calumet Refinery to ship oil on Lake Superior. Enbridge is responsible for the largest on-land spill in US history, and six Enbridge pipelines currently cross the territories of the Leech Lake and Fond du Lac Bands of Ojibwe. The Alberta Clipper pipeline was built through our land in 2009, over the opposition of many concerned people. At the same time, Enbridge built another pipeline—a "diluent" pipeline that transports toxic lighter hydrocarbons back into Canada. The two pipelines form a loop: the Clipper moves heavy Alberta tar sands diluted bitumen mixed with diluents southward to Chicago, while the diluent line returns the proprietary diluents northward for reuse. Enbridge's four older pipelines in the area have no easement across, yet they trespass on Red Lake–ceded land. The Leech Lake Ojibwe have suffered through one major spill already.

The Certificate of Need—Or Is It Greed?

Nearly two million barrels of oil already flow through and across Minnesota daily, but even this is not enough for Enbridge. It is now pushing to increase the amount of Alberta tar sands diluted bitumen in its Alberta Clipper pipeline. This pipeline—also known as Line 67—would be expanded from 440,000 barrels per day to a maximum of 880,000 barrels per day through hundreds of miles of Minnesota, and through the Red Lake, Leech Lake, and Fond du Lac reservations. To increase the amount of Alberta tar sands diluted bitumen through Minnesota would bring unacceptable risks of more oil spills.

Enbridge is also proposing a "Sandpiper" pipeline more than six hundred miles long in this region. The pipeline would run from Beaver Lodge Station, just south of Tioga, North Dakota, to Superior, Wisconsin. This project threatens our home community of White Earth. The proposed Sandpiper southern route would follow the Minnesota pipelines from Clearbrook to Park Rapids, running south of the Fond du Lac Reservation and invading several established tribal areas that provide tribal members hunting and gathering rights from the 1854 Treaty. Enbridge refers to "a minimum of 24-inch diameter"[1] pipeline in its proposal, but a 36-inch or larger pipeline could also be built instead to pump fuel from the development boom of the Bakken Oil play in North Dakota. This proposal is currently in the works, and Enbridge is promoting it across Minnesota. It would carry an estimated 375,000 barrels a day from Clearbrook, Minnesota, to Superior, Wisconsin.

Next to the Sandpiper, the second-biggest potential tar sands pipeline in the US is the Keystone XL expansion proposed by TransCanada Corporation, which would entail a twelve-hundred-mile-long pipeline ending in Steele City, Nebraska. This project is yet another sham, a money-making scheme for oil and pipeline companies, not the "'Good Fairy" for the American economy that the company's public relations team describes.

To think that anyone would consider approving such pointless projects pains me deeply, as I raise my family on the land the Sandpiper pipeline would cross, but it also pains me as an economist—which is to say that it makes no sense in terms of creating jobs, either. The reality is that the present $100 billion or so in US investments in the Canadian tar sands represents a waste of money for long-term US security. Keystone is just 7 per cent of that stupidity, but it opens a pipeline to an exponential expansion in waste. As the industry tries to deflect attention about the real impacts, costs, and risks of pipelines, companies are aggressively promoting them, using many exaggerations. The hype around Keystone XL has been particularly intense, so it is important to directly confront the claims from proponents. Across the board, the song and dance of the big corporations seeking to build more pipelines does not jive with the realities.

One of the biggest promises made by proponents of Keystone XL is that it will bring jobs and energy security, but the truth is that it will do neither. Even if the pipeline never spilled, even if the tar sands were not an environmental atrocity, this would still be a bad deal for the American public. Defenders of the project claim that Keystone XL will create 20,000 jobs for American workers, and as many as 120,000 "direct, indirect and induced"[2] jobs. Both are gross exaggerations that include overestimates of construction jobs and an outdated plan, which includes parts of the pipeline that have already been built. The Cornell Global Labor Institute published an assessment of the Keystone XL project that stands in stark contrast to the picture painted by oil companies and those in receipt of lobbying dollars in Washington. This report, which used TransCanada's own data, concluded that just 2,500 to 4,650 jobs will be created, most of them temporary and non-local. So much for putting America back to work.[3]

Further, even if all the Keystone fantasies were true, seasonally adjusted unemployment numbers would not budge from the current level of 9.1 per cent. American unemployment, it turns out, is a bit more complex than one pipeline dream. America's economic woes may have more to do with a trillion-dollar war, a trade deficit to China, and some serious systemic ineffi-ciencies and inequalities, rather than one pipeline.

Another misleading promise sold to Americans is that Keystone XL will keep domestic gas prices down, though it has been estimated that it actually would result in an increase in gas prices of twenty to thirty cents per gallon.

The existing Keystone pipeline delivers gas to refineries in the Midwest, and the Keystone XL expansion would route petroleum to the Gulf of Mexico, where it would be sold internationally at a higher price. This will hurt not only consumers, but also businesses, which will likely cut workers to cover (inelastic) costs.

This also relates to the false promise that Keystone XL will reduce our dependence on foreign oil. Keystone XL is intended to be an export pipeline, with contracts for export all signed, sealed, and delivered before it reaches the refineries in Port Arthur, Texas. For instance, research group OilChange reports that the Valero Energy Corporation, which has contracts for at least one hundred thousand barrels daily from the proposed Keystone XL pipeline, has a "publically [sic] disclosed business model [that] is focused on exporting crude oil."[4] The Valero Port Arthur Refinery in Texas is located in a foreign trade zone, where it joins corporate neighbours Motiva (a joint venture between Royal Dutch Shell and the Saudi government) and TOTAL of France in the complex of Gulf Coast refineries. Indeed, testimony at Canadian hearings had oil companies arguing that there is a present and pending glut in the US oil market, which requires the tar sands producers to ship outside the continent.

In short, the Keystone XL pipeline means a few jobs, higher gas prices, and a pretty good chance of contaminating the Ogallala aquifer—the big one in Nebraska (the risks to which may have stopped the project in the short term, at least).

Making a New Path

While the vast advertising and lobbying dollars of the big oil and pipeline companies have tried to present the expansion of tar sands pipelines as the Good Fairy for the American economy, activists have shown these promises to be a sham.

The battle against the Keystone XL pipeline has already shown the power of grassroots activism. There has been a huge groundswell of public resistance within North America, with the effect of delaying approval from the US secretary of state and President Obama. Resistance towards projects like Keystone XL will continue on multiple fronts. Much of my involvement in seeking these alternatives to tar sands is through my role as executive

HONOR THE EARTH

Spiritual horse rides to protect Mother Earth and the communities of the Plains and Great Lakes along the proposed KXL and Sandpiper/Alberta Clipper pipeline routes, 2013. The rides coincided with community meetings and nonviolent direct action trainings in stops along the route. Rides were organized by Honor the Earth, the Horse Spirit Society, Owe Aku International, and Moccasins on the Ground organizers.

director of Honor the Earth, in which I work nationally and internationally on the issues of climate change, renewable energy, and environmental justice with Indigenous communities.

In 2014, two of Honor the Earth's core priorities are to oppose the expansion of tar sands and fracking imports (in particular the Enbridge pipelines in Minnesota), and to support the Lakota nation in its opposition to the KXL pipeline (which crosses their territory). This work is done both through campaigns and through the re-granting of funds to Native-led initiatives. There is very little funding available for Native-led work on these issues, and we need to take initiative to address the reality that only 0.07 per cent of all foundation funding in the United States goes towards Native non-profits, and only a very small fraction of that goes towards initiatives that are actually led by Native peoples. We need to create the economic solutions for our own communities in ways that are aligned with our various cultural traditions, and we also need to organize our own people to protect our communities.

One of our previous responses to tar sands pipelines was the Ride for Mother Earth along the pipeline route of the Line 67 expansion. In September and October of 2013, my sister, friends, and I rode our horses along the Enbridge pipeline route in Minnesota, where it passes through our 1855 treaty area as it crosses near our precious lakes, rivers, wetlands, and towns—which are already burdened by high rates of cancer related to pesticides and oil. We did this in prayer, with our community leaders, to raise awareness of the devastation caused by the tar sands in Canada and fracking in North Dakota, and to protect our communities from the proposed Alberta Clipper expansion and the Enbridge Sandpiper pipelines.

We also rode to support our relatives of the Lakota nation in its opposition to the Keystone XL pipeline, which crosses their territory. Part of our journey was talking to people along the way, who need to have their voices heard. Another part was a spiritual ride, to send that power back. We also wanted to have an educational moment to inform landowners and towns, as well as our tribal nations, about the possible impacts and risks of these pipelines.

At the same time, our brothers and sisters of the Lakota Nation rode their horses from the Rosebud to the Cheyenne River, across land in Lakota territory that is still untarnished by a pipeline, in order to oppose the flow of dirty tar sands oil. This land is part of a vast prairie region that was once full of 250 species of grass and fifty million buffalo.

Our efforts have also involved a media campaign and public education efforts, including the rental of two billboards and a speaking tour, along with grassroots organizing and advocacy. We are collaborating with Indigenous Environmental Network, WaterLegacy, and Minnesota 350 to build a stronger campaign against the Alberta Clipper project.

Honor the Earth has also been involved in bringing community concerns about the Alberta Clipper project to the Minnesota Public Utilities Commission (MPUC). Enbridge is asking for a "certificate of need" from the MPUC to double the capacity of the present Alberta Clipper pipeline carrying tar sands diluted bitumen to the Superior refinery. The MPUC approved the first of two expansions to the Alberta Clipper in July of 2013. The second and larger expansion of up to 880,000 barrels a day has now been sidetracked into a "Contested Case Hearing" due to local citizen outcry and written comments contesting facts presented by Enbridge during their application to the MPUC. There will be public hearings during the second expansion, and an open written comment period in winter; we have been encouraging public participation.

Enbridge's Sandpiper is another project that will have to be opposed in coming years. Based on evidence of a history of spills and a lack of effective cleanup, I, along with many community members on White Earth, believe that this project should not be approved. Enbridge has failed to address the public's growing concerns over their pipelines' impacts on our lands.

There is no need for pipelines to be built or expanded. There is a need for safety, planning, and infrastructure for efficiency—not profit. This land, its people, and the animals that still inhabit it do not need pipelines. And the people who live in the North, in the Athabascan River Basin, do not want to see more mining done that is ravaging their land.

So, What Is the Solution?

This is the happy part. It turns out that our ancestors and my father had it right. My father used to say to me, "Winona, I don't want to hear your philosophy, if you can't grow corn." Now that's an interesting thing to say to your child. Well, I thought about it, and thought about it some more. And then, I decided to grow corn. Along the way, I became an economist who wanted to look at the systems that support sovereignty and self-determination, namely our economic system.

As tar sands projects bring localized impacts to many places, it is undeniable that climate change is happening, and that if we do not take action there will be serious financial, ecological, and cultural consequences—and Indigenous peoples will experience the disproportionate burden.

There are some basic choices ahead:

1) Do nothing, and allow governments and businesses to make market-based decisions at a pace that does not mirror the urgency of the problem;

2) Get involved in mitigation, or reduction of carbon, as communities and nations; and/or

3) Adapt for climate change and ultimately a climate-challenged world.

The second and third options provide real opportunities to make a better future. Jimisawaabandaaming, or how we envision our future, is a worldview of positive thinking. It's an Anishinaabe worldview, coming from a place and a cultural way of life that has been here, on the same land, for ten thousand years. To transform modern society into one based on survival, not conquest, we need to make some big changes. We need to actualize an economic and social transformation. Restoring an economics that makes sense for upcoming generations needs to be a priority. In our community, we think of this as economics for the seventh generation.

In our teachings, we have some clear direction: our intention is Minobimaatisiiwin, a spiritual, mental, physical, and emotional happiness—sort of an Anishinaabe version of Bhutan's Gross National Happiness Index. Within our cultural teachings lie these Indigenous Economic Principles: intergenerational thinking and equity (thinking for the seventh generation); inter- and intra-species equity (respect); and valuing those spiritual and intangible facets of the natural world and cultural practice (not all values and things can be monetized).

Consider what may be one of the largest follies in economic thinking from fossil fuel supporters: the opportunity forgone costs. What this means is that we waste $200 billion or so on tar sands oil and infrastructure, and do not create weatherized and energy-efficient houses, a smart grid, energy-efficient vehicles, a relocalized food system, and renewable energy. And, ten years from now, we will in fact be in worse economic shape.

Frankly, if we put that much money into weatherization, efficiency, relocalizing power production, and an energy-efficient grid powered by new renewables, as well as localized food and energy-efficient mass transportation systems, we would build a stronger economy and we would have a shot at lasting much longer than another fifty years. Money spent on efficiency and relocalizing food systems means that we do not need dirty oil. In the meantime, the average meal today travels fifteen hundred miles from farmer to table, and the transportation system on this continent is incredibly inefficient. Oil and auto companies continue to lobby against regulations on efficiency.

Renewable energy means that you pay for the infrastructure now, but can project the price of fuel into the future—given that the wind and sun are still free. Efficiency is the key to economic stability—consider, for instance, how we lose 57 per cent of our power between point of origin and point of consumption.

Now, all of that means money is being made by higher levels of consumption in an inefficient system. These inefficiencies and new pipelines are clearly in the interest of Suncor, ExxonMobil, TransCanada, Enbridge, and the like—but not the general public. In the end, there is a lot of destruction for corporate profits, something that those Occupying Wall Street have been saying pretty loudly and clearly. Tar sands oil is not intended to serve the long-term interests of us on this continent. As such, it will not only dirty our land, rivers, aquifers, and consciences, but it will waste billions of dollars that could be invested in mass transportation systems, localized food and energy, and efficiency, thereby eliminating the need for dirty oil. Rebooting America and Native America's infrastructure and employment opportunities would put tens of thousands of people to work in a renewable energy economy—which, it turns out, has a key economic stabilizer. That economics is durable, and will provide not only for 99 per cent of us, but also for our future generations.

Recovering and restoring local food and energy production requires a conscious transformation and set of technological and economic leaps for our communities. We need to restore our relationship to place, and we need to determine what an economy that is Indigenous looks like. Our focus has been on the traditional economy, which involves extensive subsistence agriculture and falls outside the definition of market economies.

The economy of the future is the green economy. The rising price of fossil fuels will create a mandate for efficiency, and the challenge of addressing climate change will require a reduction in carbon emissions from power generation, transportation, and agricultural sources. In Honor's work, we re-grant funds to Native-led initiatives across the continent. I can say that as Native peoples, we're leading in building some sense of economic stability for the future, while we get some control over our health, food, and energy systems—these are all interrelated.

We have a lot of work to do; Thomas Berry calls it the "great work."[5] We need to work and to clean up the toxic waste caused by the companies opposing us. No longer do we want to live in the shadow of their lethal pollution and without our own sources of heat or electricity. It is time for our communities to recognize the links between corporate profit and the earth's destruction.

When we destroy the earth, we destroy ourselves. So we must create sustainable energy and food economies for this millennium and for the generations yet to come. In my community on the White Earth reservation, we are choosing the green path. That is the work of restoring Indigenous ways of living and land-based economics for the seventh generation. What will your community choose?

22

The Rise of the Native Rights– Based Strategic Framework

Our Last Best Hope to Save Our Water, Air, and Earth

●

CLAYTON THOMAS-MULLER

●

Years ago, I was working for a well-known Indigenous environmental and economic justice organization known as the Indigenous Environmental Network (IEN). During my time there, I had the privilege of working with hundreds of Indigenous communities across the planet that have seen a sharp increase in the targeting of Native lands for mega-extractive industries and other toxic projects. The largest of these conflicts, of course, was the overrepresentation by Big Oil, which works to gain access to the valuable resources located in our territories—often in cahoots with state, provincial, First Nations, tribal, and federal governments both in the US and Canada. IEN hired me to work on very abstract ideas, under impossible conditions, with little or no resources to support grassroots peoples fighting oil companies, which had become, in the era of free-market economics, the most powerful and well-resourced entities of our time. My mission was to fight to protect the sacredness of Mother Earth from toxic contamination and corporate exploitation, and to support our Peoples to build sustainable local economies rooted in the sacred fire of our traditions.

My work took me to the Three Affiliated Tribes of Fort Berthold Reservation in the Great Plains to support a collective of mothers and grandmothers fighting a proposed oil refinery, which, if built, would process tar sands shipments. I spent time in Oklahoma working with Sac and Fox Tribal Environmental Protection Agency, under the tutelage of the late environmental justice warrior Jan Stevens, to learn about the legacy of one hundred years of oil and gas on America's Indian Country—Oklahoma being one of the end-up points of the shameful Indian relocation era. I joined grassroots peoples on the Bay of Fundy in an epic battle against the state of Maine and a liquefied natural gas (LNG) producer that wanted to build a massive LNG terminal on their community's sacred site, known as Split Rock. The terminal, had it been built, would have provided natural gas to the city of New York for their power plants.

I worked extensively with youth on the Navajo reservation in America's Southwest who were fighting the Peabody Energy coal mining company, to try to stop the mining of Black Mesa, a source of water and a known sacred site in the Navajo Nation. On the western side of the Navajo Nation, I worked to support Diné/Navajo who were fighting an attempt to lift the ban on uranium mining, which would have meant the introduction of a dangerous form of uranium mining called in situ, or "in place," extraction that could have poisoned precious groundwater resources in the desert region. Uranium had already left a devastating legacy on the Diné/Navajo in the 1940s and 50s.

In the Great Lakes region, I worked on Walpole Island (Bkejwanong First Nation) to stop an oil company from drilling in the community, where First Nations peoples harvest things such as wild rice, muskrat, and fowl, and rely on income from American duck hunters. Walpole Island is already forced to deal with the impacts of sixty petro-chemical facilities located within sixty kilometres of their nation. I worked to support groups in Montana's Northern Cheyenne and Crow Indian reservations, who were fighting against the massive expansion of coal bed methane in their region—encroachment that was decimating local groundwater resources. I worked in Alaska and was a co-founder of the powerful oil-busting network known as Resisting Environmental Destruction on Indigenous Lands (REDOIL). We created this network to take on the corrupt Alaska Native Corporations and Big Oil, which had been running roughshod to start development in fragile places like the Arctic National Wildlife Refuge. I worked with groups in British Columbia's Northeast, where natural gas companies were ripping apart the landscape with massive gas developments in the region. And this is only a partial picture; I have worked in many more places across the globe than I can mention in this story.

During my five years as an IEN Indigenous oil campaigner (2001-6), I learned that: these fights were all life-and-death situations, not just for local communities, but for the biosphere; organizing in Indian Country called for a very different strategic and tactical play than conventional campaigning; our grassroots movement for energy and climate justice was being led by our Native women and, as such, our movement was as much about fighting patriarchy and asserting as a core part of our struggle the sacred feminine creative principle; and a large part of the work of movement building was about defending the sacredness of our Mother Earth and helping our peoples decolonize our notions of government, land management, business, and social relations by going through a process of re-evaluating our connection to the sacred.

In the early years, I often struggled with the arms of the "non-profit industrial complex" and its inner workings, which have been heavily fortified with systems of power that reinforce racism, classism, and gender discrimination at the highest levels of both non-profit organizations and foundations (funders). It has been difficult to measure the success of environmental and economic justice organizing using the Western terms of quantitative versus qualitative analysis. Sure, our work had successfully kept many highly polluting fossil fuel projects at bay, but the attempts to take our land by agents of the fossil fuel industry—with their lobbyists pushing legislation loopholes and repackaging strategies—continued to pressure many uninformed or economically desperate tribal governments to grant access to our lands.

The most high-profile victory came during the twilight of the first Bush/Cheney administration, when our network collaborated with beltway groups like the Natural Resources Defense Council to effectively kill a harmful US energy bill containing provisions that would have kicked open the back door to fossil fuel companies and expanded their access into our lands. The Indian Energy Title V campaign identified the fact that if the energy bill passed, US tribes—under the guise of tribal sovereignty—would be able to administer their own environmental impact assessments and fast-track development in their lands. Now, this sounds like a good thing, right? Well, maybe it would be for tribal governments that had the legal and scientific capacity to do so, but for the hundreds of US tribes without the resources, it set up a highly imbalanced playing field that would give the advantage to corporations to exploit economically disadvantaged nations to enter into the industrialization game.

Through a massive education campaign and the highly negotiated and coordinated collaborative effort of grassroots, beltway, and international environmental NGOs—as well as multiple lobbying visits to Washington, DC, led by both elected and grassroots tribal leaders—we gained the support of the National Congress of American Indians, who agreed to write a letter opposing the energy bill to some of our champions in the US Senate, most notably the late Daniel Akaka, who was Hawaii's first Native senator. Under the guidance of America's oldest Indian Advocacy group, he led the vote to kill the energy bill in the Senate. This was my first view into the power of the Native rights–based strategic and tactical framework, and how it could bring the most powerful government on earth (and the Big Oil lobby) to their knees. Of course, upon the re-election of the Bush/Cheney administration, we lost the second reincarnation of the energy bill, and Title V was passed.

What I learned in those battles was that with our unique priority rights— the fiduciary obligation governments have to Native Americans, defined by our sacred treaties, trust relationships, and other unique legal instruments— Native American and First Nations peoples have an important tool. We are the keystones in a hemispheric social movement strategy that could end the era of Big Oil and eventually usher in another paradigm from this current destructive age of free-market economics.

The challenge would be to get the people who hold the most power (or pretensions to power) to understand this reality. It is a task not easily accomplished. For example, with the passing of the US energy bill under the second US Bush/Cheney administration, the US climate movement began to ramp up its attempts to have the administration pass a domestic climate bill, in the hope of forcing the country to start dramatically reducing emissions. This movement saw the rise of mega-labour/ENGO coalitions like the Blue-Green Alliance and the Apollo Alliance, and mega-ENGO groups like 1Sky.

Citizen groups like the US Public Interest Research Group received millions of dollars to try and organize people to put pressure on President Bush, and later President Obama, to adopt some form of climate policy. However, the strategy screamed that age-old saying, "What goes around comes around" ... again. There would be no climate bill under Bush, and, to the surprise of the people who voted for Obama, no climate bill under his administration (yet).

The groups that ended up receiving resources from the limited pot of climate funding did what they did best, which was to invest in top-heavy policy campaigns. They did not focus on mobilizing the masses to get out in the streets, to target and stop local climate criminals, or to build a bona fide social movement rooted in an anti-colonial, anti-racist, anti-oppressive foundation to combat the climate crisis. Instead, they kept the discourse focused on voluntary technological and market-based approaches to mitigating climate change—like carbon trading and carbon capture and storage. I argue that this frame has kept millions of Americans from marching into the streets to stop the greenhouse gangsters from wrecking Mother Earth. Groups like the Indigenous Environmental Network, the Southwest Workers' Union, and others fought tooth and nail to try and carve out pieces of these resources to go towards what we saw as the real carbon killers, which included local campaigns being led by Indigenous Nations and communities of colour to stop coal mining, coal-fired power, and Big Oil (including gas).

During the early hours of the Obama administration, there was a massive effort to "green" the economic stimulus, a package of job creation funding doled out by the Obama administration to counter the Great Recession that crippled the US economy. I had the opportunity to sit with some of the leaders of some of the biggest NGOs and foundations at a New York City roundtable, including members of the Obama White House team—high-profile individuals like former "green jobs czar" Van Jones and Energy Action/Mosaic Solar founder Billy Parish were also in attendance. At this table, I told a story.

In the 1980s and 1990s, America was in the grips of a recession. Groups rose up from all sectors to create a strategy to combat the crisis. Alliances were formed between the trade unionists and the NGOs and social justice groups. When the negotiated target of funding was in sight and Congress was about to write a cheque, groups became divided, and what was plentiful turned to scarcity. In the end, AmeriCorps was born. Unions, NGOs, and social justice groups, and more importantly the unity they had created, were shattered. There were political games, and those in power used race, class, and gender politics to divide a movement. I said that we were in the exact same moment in time: we were seeing Big Oil ram through an energy bill loaded with corporate welfare for the 1 per cent during the collapse of America's middle class, and the stalling of a US climate bill would affect the most vulnerable to our rapidly destabilizing climate—poor communities of colour and Native American communities.

America's wealth, and more directly, America's energy infrastructure, was built on our backs. Efforts should be made to invest locally first—from training green jobs workers locally to using local building materials to producing energy locally—which would close the financial loop and help revitalize Native America's strangled economies, making them less vulnerable to volatile external costs while maximizing the positive impact of the new green revolution.

A green jobs economy and a new, forward-thinking energy and climate policy would transform tribal and other rural economies, and provide the basis for an economic recovery in the United States. In order to make this possible, I argued, we had to encourage the Obama administration to provide incentives and assistance to actualize renewable energy development by tribes and Native organizations and our allies.

I made the argument that we could use the attributes of a predatory economic paradigm, which had disproportionately targeted our communities, to flip the script on our enemies, and recognize that Native Americans can have a unique rights-based and trust relationship with the US government. It could be a strategic and tactical asset to a diverse social movement trying to lobby for an economic stimulus bill that would actually help empower the most vulnerable while not exacerbating an ecological crisis. For this to work, we would have to make moral agreements and not be denied, under any circumstances. On the table was $750 million earmarked for green jobs, and the task at hand was to determine how to equitably share the pot. In the media, the number of jobs created versus the number of workers unemployed went from one million to five million and then back to one million and back again. Once we got to the point where Congress was ready to write a cheque, we saw the downfall of mega-groups like the Apollo Alliance and the complete dissolving of 1Sky (with some pieces of the latter getting absorbed by 350.org). Many groups that started off at the table fell, one by one, with the first groups representing racialized constituencies. Meanwhile, in Indian Country, tribes saw congressional allocations from this economic stimulus packaged in the billions (rightfully so), and kept on keeping on.

The point of the story was that if we could truly understand the aspects of our struggle that kept us united, and more importantly, if we could understand what were our unique contributions to a successful social movement paradigm, we could effectively expand the pot from $750 million to billions. By converging struggles in a solidarity framework rooted in anti-racism, anti-oppression, and anti-colonialism, and by creating economic and political initiatives uniting urban and rural centres, we could wield a power never seen by our oppressors and actually gain economic independence and community self-determination. We could develop economies that do not force people to have to choose between clean air, water, and earth, or putting food on the table. I did not attend this meeting to ask for handouts, but rather as an ambassador of a strategic framework that I had come to know as the Native rights–based approach, which could be used to bring to an end to what Native American activist, author, and vice-presidential candidate Winona LaDuke has described as "predator economics,"[1] and what activist and author Naomi Klein rightfully describes as "shock doctrine" economics.[2]

Little did I know that all of these experiences were preparing me for what would be one of the biggest battles of my life. During the IEN Protecting Mother Earth Summit in 2006 in northern Minnesota, three women from a small, mostly Native, village called Fort Chipewyan, Alberta, came to share their Dene peoples' struggle with what would soon be known as the most destructive industrial project on the face of the earth: the tar sands megaproject. These three women were related to each other and represented three generations of one prominent family in Fort Chip known as the Deranger clan. They listened to the dozens of stories told in the energy and climate group about the injustices happening because of oil companies and complicit governments across Turtle Island. They told us about a project so large, so devastating, that you had to see it to believe it. They spoke of a Wild West of sorts, one of the last bastions of earth where Big Oil was ramping up, and they spoke of the deaths in their community from rare cancers, auto-immune diseases, and boomtown economics that plagued people living downstream from the tar sands. They said that we needed to go up to Fort Chipewyan and help.

I was taking time off from organizing, living in Ottawa with my wife and newborn son, Felix. My lifelong mentor and friend Tom Goldtooth, executive director of the IEN, took this invitation from the Deranger matriarch, Rose Desjarlais, very seriously. IEN immediately organized a fact-finding mission in the Athabasca region of the tar sands with our Native energy and climate director, Jihan Gearon, and Rainforest Action Network campaigner Jocelyn Cheechoo, from the James Bay Cree in northern Quebec. I was invited because of my experience in fighting Big Oil across Turtle Island.

When we flew into Fort McMurray, the boomtown in the heart of the tar sands, I was immediately struck by how much it reminded me of Anchorage, Alaska. That was the only other city I had ever been to that also reeked of oil money. The town had an infrastructure to support 35,000 people, but was bursting at the seams with a population of 75,000. Most were men between the ages of 18 and 60, and all worked directly or indirectly for the tar sands sector. We took a tour of the infamous Highway 63 loop to Fort McKay Cree Nation that carves though man-made desert tailings ponds so big you could see them from outer space. We marvelled at the twenty-four-hour life of the city and the incredible traffic jams at shift change. I think what struck me most was the level of homelessness in a town where there was a six-figure salary for anyone who wanted it. To see the tar sands themselves was devastating; to fly over endless clear-cuts, open pit mines, and smokestacks surrounded by pristine Cree and Dene peoples' homelands was gut-wrenching. When we drove through and walked in the tar sands, the smell of bitumen filled our noses and added to the trauma that locals live with every day.

We got on a bush plane at the Fort McMurray airport and flew to Fort Chipewyan along the route of the Athabasca River—a critical life path of the people of that land, a source of water, fish, and transportation, and a spiritual connection to the past. We were told of how the river had changed, become poisoned, and was no longer safe, and how every year the water levels became lower due to industry use. When we got to Fort Chip, we were well taken care of, and we met many elders, the elected leadership, and youth, who all told the same stories of hardship—the untimely sickness and death, and the destruction of a subsistence way of life—all by the tar sands. We heard about the history of the peoples going out into the Athabasca Delta and onto Lake Athabasca for food and medicine, and how that was becoming impossible due to the massive regional contamination by industry. Again, we were told that we needed to help local grassroots people magnify this scandal to the world by amplifying their voices as the face of the issue.

After we took in the horrifying, science fiction–like landscape of the tar sands—and more importantly, the power, beauty, and resiliency of the people of this land they call Athabasca—Tom Goldtooth asked me to build the Canadian Indigenous Tar Sands Campaign. The first thing we did was raise funds for an action camp in Fort Chip, where we could do a proper power mapping and skill share with community members who were leading local campaigns and wanted to scale them up. Our first action camp had around fifteen community members, including tar sands warriors and climate movement folk heroes like former Mikisew Cree Nation Chief George Poitras, local Dene activists Mike Mercredi and Lionel Lepine, Melina Laboucan-Massimo, a Lubicon Cree activist, and Eriel Deranger, a Dene woman also of Fort Chipewyan.

We brought in resource people from the NGO sector, and with the direction of local Indigenous leaders, we organized a series of workshops on Aboriginal law, organizing, campaign planning, power mapping, and the Native rights–based approach. The outcome of the camp formed directives to launch a Native-led campaign to: stop the expansion of the tar sands; utilize a treaty- and Aboriginal rights–based framework; ensure that Indigenous peoples on the frontlines were the face of the campaign; raise the human health impacts as a moral issue; follow the money financing the tar sands; and target those controlling them. We also planned to advocate in the non-profit industrial complex that a meaningful proportion of funding and resources earmarked for tar sands work go directly to First Nations.

What came next would consume most of my waking time on Mother Earth for the next seven years. When IEN launched our tar sands campaign, we knew that this issue was about to become one of the most (if not the most) visible campaigns on the planet. The local grassroots peoples were engaging with the most ruthless, powerful, well-resourced, and just plain old evil corporate entities on the face of the planet. We knew that these companies had bought every level of colonial government, and many were in bed with our own First Nations governments. But we knew that if our campaign were executed properly, we would see victory. This multi-pronged campaign would contain elements of legal intervention, base building, policy intervention (at all levels of government, including the United Nations), narrative-based storytelling strategies in conventional and social media, civil disobedience, popular education, and a whole lot of prayer and ceremony.

Again, I found myself at a table of funders and ENGO directors, discussing a massive campaign that would affect every segment of our society, including our biosphere. I found myself viewed by my peers as being without power, as though I were at the table looking for handouts rather than with something to offer. The same old tricks of top-heavy, policy-focused pitches by the usual suspects happened again. And I found myself repeating the need to take the time to understand and work in solidarity with the Native rights–based strategic framework. I talked about how there had not been a major environmental victory won in Canada in the last thirty years without First Nations at the helm asserting their Aboriginal rights and title. This included many of the victories that those in the room counted in their own personal careers. I argued passionately that we should agree on the fact that we needed to dedicate meaningful resources to this approach, and the decision would mean the difference between a fight lasting years or decades. During that meeting, the facilitator representing the collective of foundations and donors that had contributed to a pot of money to fund anti–tar sands work became noticeably frustrated with our platform, and things escalated to a point where he was yelling and swearing that our IEN campaign was "in the way" of plausible strategies that were actually going to work. Once the chastising was over, I proceeded to say, "Well, now that I know where you're coming from and you know where IEN is at, how much of this funding are we going to get?" We walked out of that meeting with fifty thousand dollars in seed money to start our campaign.

From that moment to now, our Indigenous heroes—or "sheroes"—have successfully built an international movement to stop the Canadian tar sands. Supported by thousands of Native and non-Native allies, the campaign is now active in the United States, Canada, and Europe, with hundreds of First Nations, unions, NGOs, private-sector companies, municipalities, foundations, and individuals participating and elevating First Nations and our rights-based strategic approach as the keystone to the campaign. Part of this success was achieved through some seriously gutsy moves, one being a visit from high-profile Hollywood director James Cameron to tour the tar sands right when his blockbuster movie *Avatar* had become the highest-grossing film in history.

Cameron's tour was done at a time when IEN was pushing hard for our Keystone XL campaign to be funded. It was an uphill battle, since everyone knew that pipeline fights historically have usually been defeats. We had done an analysis on the viability of victory in a Keystone XL campaign for the funders, as we were one of the only groups that had taken on the first Keystone pipeline. Our analysis told us a few important things. In the US, we knew the Ogallala aquifer would be the primary ecological card, as millions depended on this source of water and the pipeline was right through the heart of it. We knew that the dozen or so US tribes in the area could be educated to use the power of their unique rights-based approach to fight the pipeline. We also knew that no one in the US, especially in the heartland of the Dakota states, Nebraska, Oklahoma, and Texas, knew what the tar sands were. We knew that bringing James Cameron to the tar sands, and having him talk about the human rights scandal unfolding in First Nations communities during a time when *Avatar* was on every theatre screen on the planet, would be huge boost to our cause.

Cameron came, he saw, he met with the tar sands industry, the Alberta government, and First Nations. He made a lot of promises about direct support of the legal strategies of First Nations against the oil sector and the government of Canada. As an avid supporter of technological remedies, he did not condemn the tar sands, and he spoke highly of nuclear energy as an alternative—as well as the theoretical role of carbon capture and storage technologies. What he did do was say in front of the international press, "I did not make *Avatar* until the technology was available for me to tell the story right, and the Canadian government should not develop the tar sands until they have the technology to not poison and kill First Nations people with cancers."[3]

Avatar 2 is set to come out in 2016, and *Avatar 3* in 2017, and I have a feeling that Cameron and his commitments to First Nations about directly funding the rights-based strategic framework are yet to be tested. The fallout from his visit was in every newspaper and on every television, computer, and smart phone in America, comparing the story of *Avatar* to the real-life situation unfolding between First Nations and the tar sands. This response was crucial to the emergence of the Keystone XL campaign as the lightning rod of the US environmental movement, and one that has involved a lens of human rights.

The tar sands campaign of IEN started at a time when direct community funding was in the tens of thousands, but, over time and through pressure, it is now in the millions. We are still dealing with a non-profit industrial complex that is its own worst enemy. But Stephen Harper's corrupt, totalitarian federal government, with their extremism, is pushing a larger base of non-Native allies to our side of the equation.

The Harper government's omnibus legislation meant that thirty years of environmental, social, and economic policy have been thrown out. In response, we have seen the rise of Idle No More, a catchy social media and education campaign launched again by First Nations women, and the result was a quickening of Canadian reconciliation with its own violent history of colonization, as well as the rapid politicization of tens of thousands of Indigenous peoples occurring not just in Canada, but in all occupied lands across Mother Earth. Left without a pot to piss in, the conventional non-profit industrial complex and their supporters are trying to figure out their next steps in dethroning Harper, a daunting task given the strength of his support from the wealthy and powerful within Canada.

The one area the Harper government has not been able to stack the cards is the courts, and a Native rights–based tactical and strategic framework—supported by labour, NGOs, students, and other social groups scaled up to the proportions of the 1960s US civil rights movement—could not only dethrone Harper, it also could be the last best effort save our resources from Canada's extractive industries sector and the banks that finance them. This rights-based approach has been tested time and time again: it is enshrined in Section 35 of the Canadian Constitution; it has been validated by more than 170 Supreme Court victories; it is validated by all of the Indian treaties; it is validated by the United Nations Declaration on the Rights of Indigenous Peoples; and it is validated by the International Labour Organization Convention 169, along with many, many other legal instruments.

The racism towards Native peoples that Idle No More has met in the media,[4] reminiscent of 1950s-era Mississippi, and our winning rights-based strategy has driven some of the most conservative Canadians to our side and toppled some of the biggest architects of the free market neo-liberal agenda, such as the infamous US-trained lawyer and mentor to Harper, Thomas Flanagan. We have come too far as Indigenous peoples to give up who we are; we have always been kind, and again we will share the wealth and abundance of our homelands with our relatives from across the pond. Instead of lessons on how to survive the harsh winters of our lands, today we are offering lessons on how to be resilient and overcome the oppression from the archaic oil sector and those in our own government who have lost their minds with power.

We are faced with tremendous odds: the end of the era of cheap energy, the loss of ecosystems that have sustained unfettered economic growth, and, of course, the global climate crisis. We must understand that these are all symptoms of a much larger problem called capitalism. This economic system was born from notions of manifest destiny, the papal bull, and the doctrines of discovery, and built up with the free labour of slaves, on stolen Indian lands. We have much to do in America and Canada to bring our peoples into a meaningful process of reconciliation.

I have learned that our movement is very much led by women; this is something I am very comfortable with, given that I am a Cree man and we are a matriarchal society. Conversely, there is a powerful similarity between the economic policies of Canada and the US and their treatment of our Indigenous women and girls. When you look at the extreme violence taking place against the sacredness of Mother Earth in the tar sands, for example, and the fact that this represents the greatest driver of both the Canadian and US economies, and then you look at the lack of action being taken on the thousands of First Nations women and girls who have been murdered or just disappeared, it all begins to all make sense. It is also why our women have been rising up and taking power back from the smothering forces of patriarchy dominating our economic, political, social, and, I would say, spiritual institutions. When we turn things around as a people, it will be the women who lead us, and it will be the creative feminine principle they carry that will give us the tools we need to build another world.

Indigenous peoples have been keeping a tab on what has been stolen from our lands, which the Creator put us on to protect, and there is a day coming soon when we will collect. Until then, we will keep our eyes on the prize, organize, and live our lives in a good way, and we welcome you to join us on this journey.

23

Pipelines and Resistance across Turtle Island

●

SÂKIHITOWIN AWÂSIS

●

Over the past few years, grassroots struggles to stop the spread of pipeline infrastructure have been central to conflicts over the fate of the Athabasca tar sands megaproject. Companies are proposing new pipeline systems, and are seeking to repurpose existing pipelines, to accommodate the transport of bitumen and the expansion of the industry. In the region where I reside, Enbridge is attempting to bring tar sands through Anishinaabek, Haudenosaunee, Lenape, and Michif territories in present-day Ontario and Quebec. This is one of several corporate projects to pump tar sands across Turtle Island (North America). In most cases, these moves are being met with determined resistance from members of frontline Indigenous communities, who are increasingly the leading sources of legal and practical barriers to tar sands expansion.

In this chapter, I will focus on Indigenous resistance and alternatives in the context of the anti-pipeline movement. I will begin by examining some of the impacts and threats of tar sands pipelines and their expansion. I will then explore how anti–tar sands mobilizing can include understandings of Indigenous peoples' relationships and responsibilities, as well as their rights to resources. This chapter explores some of the ways in which decolonization is interrelated with the resurgence of Indigenous traditions, and how this can transform the very notion of what it means to be human on a path to freedom. Some of the challenges that lie ahead in our struggle, as well as strategies for overcoming these, will also be discussed.

Threats and Impacts: Locally and Globally

Transporting diluted bitumen through pipelines that stretch across thousands of kilometres makes toxic spills a near inevitability. When spills occur, these produce long-term adverse effects on human communities, wildlife, marine animals, fish, and food webs. For instance, heavy metals, such as mercury and nickel, are released with diluted bitumen during spills, and can leak into groundwater.[1] Heavy metals and other contaminants also accumulate in the bodies of those who live nearby.[2] Human symptoms of exposure to diluted bitumen include headaches, nausea, memory loss, rashes, burning eyes, respiratory issues, and impacts on reproductive health.[3] Everyone living in proximity to Enbridge pipelines should be aware that on average, the company released seventy-three spills a year between 1999 and 2010, which totals approximately 25.67 million litres of hydrocarbons.[4]

The tar sands industry is a form of colonization, both in the sense that it disproportionately affects Indigenous communities and in the sense that it coercively plunders resources from Indigenous lands. The Mikisew Cree, Athabasca Chipewyan, and Métis Nations are some of the communities living among the tar sands themselves. As companies burden these peoples with industrial pollutants and adverse health impacts, their capacity to use the land and water as sources of food and as a basis for the resurgence of their vital traditions is severely compromised. If rare kinds of cancer and illness were as prevalent among predominantly white settler communities as they are among the people of Fort Chipewyan in northern Alberta, for instance, it would be considered an epidemic. This is not the case, however, because capitalism tremendously undervalues the lives of Indigenous people and people of colour. Meanwhile, the economic marginalization of these communities effectively forces Indigenous peoples to seek an income by participating in the very industry that so undermines their lives and traditions. There are physical, mental, emotional, and spiritual impacts as the industry intensifies experiences of disconnection from the land and each other. This feels different for everyone, but the more severe the feeling of alienation from the land and each other, the more violence that may be tolerated towards the land and each other.

The impacts on Indigenous peoples and on the lands intersect with systemic racism. In Toronto, a significant proportion of the population living along Enbridge Line 9 are recent immigrants, many of whom are racialized.[5] Low-income urban communities of colour and rural Native communities are the most at risk and heavily affected by the tar sands and accompanying pipelines. This is a typical case of environmental racism: people of colour and Indigenous peoples are disproportionately subject to increased environmental risks and substandard public health protection.

The tar sands boom in the Fort McMurray area of Alberta has been responsible for a range of oppressive and colonial impacts. There are links between the presence of the tar sands industry and heightened rates of missing and murdered Indigenous two-spirits,[6] women, and girls.[7] In Fort McMurray neighbourhoods the ratio of men to women is two to one, so there is an intensification of patriarchal culture, which is part of an ongoing colonial legacy that has normalized violence against Indigenous bodies and the land.[8] Across Turtle Island, Indigenous women in particular continue to be sexualized and stereotyped as victims lacking in agency, while systemic oppression and violence are ignored. This invisibility translates into a lack of services available to address violence against Indigenous women and children, and a general apathy towards the types of harm they face.

These attacks are one feature of an increase in rates of sexual, domestic, family, homophobic, and transphobic violence in northern Alberta, where the male-dominated industry has the strongest foothold. Associated reproductive health impacts include elevated rates of STIs, toxins in breast milk, and complications with childbearing. The tar sands industry treats women and gender non-conforming bodies in the same ways as the earth: with violence and disregard. Pollutants that make the land infertile and the waters undrinkable are also polluting the water that carries our children in the womb. Activists confronting the tar sands industry should recognize how hetero-patriarchy and the tar sands reinforce each other. Exploitation and environmental racism are exacerbated because the project was designed to profit the capitalist class, and not to benefit rural, Indigenous women and two-spirits, who generally are excluded from that class. Although some hope that communities will receive profits from the tar sands, the industry brings much more than paycheques.

Anti–tar sands mobilizing can only be effective if these efforts are part of a larger radical transformation, because the tar sands are a form of colonization, with intersecting impacts of racism and hetero-sexism.

Relations and Responsibilities

In the context of tar sands resistance, treaties are important because they are the basis of the Canadian state's Constitution and grant settler nations recognition within Turtle Island. Treaties are the foundations for nation-to-nation relationships between Indigenous nations and the colonial government that will hold "as long as the sun shines, the rivers flow, and the grass grows."[9] For many Indigenous peoples, these are sacred agreements—made in ceremony and the presence of the spiritual world—between independent nations with their own pre-existing laws, ways of being, and forms of governance.

Yet, tar sands projects are at odds with many treaty agreements. In the region now called the Province of Ontario, the treaties violated by Line 9 include the Nanfan Treaty, Kaswentha (also called the Two-Row Wampum) and the silver covenant chain, the Great Peace of Montreal treaty, the Royal Proclamation of 1763, the 24 Nations Treaty of 1764, and the Haldimand Proclamation.

In previous centuries, treaties were established when nations and peoples agreed to live in peaceful coexistence and non-interference with one another. The international status of treaties entails honouring the self-determination of Indigenous nations, with respect and full recognition of the authority of each nation's traditional government. We would have the right to live according to Indigenous laws and the right to an equitable distribution of land and resources necessary for our sovereign nations' ability to govern ourselves.

Treaties cannot be upheld singlehandedly by the Crown (the Canadian government), given that Indigenous peoples are not its subjects. The Royal Proclamation Treaty holds that the Government of Canada is not entitled to make unilateral decisions in regards to the implementation of other treaties. Instead, the spirit and intent of the treaties are supposed to be upheld. This would involve continually honouring evolving principles of consent and Indigenous traditions that respect all of creation.

Free, prior, and informed consent (FPIC) is an important moral and legal principle that guides some of the opposition towards tar sands destruction. The principle of FPIC is included in the United Nations Declaration on the Rights of Indigenous Peoples, which the Canadian government initially refused to endorse. But fulfilling FPIC would entail empowering Indigenous peoples to uphold these responsibilities. In this context, "free" implies that consultation happens without coercion, intimidation, or manipulation, with as little colonial power dynamics as possible. The term "prior" implies that consent is obtained in advance of any activity associated with the proposal, and includes the time necessary for Indigenous peoples to engage in their own decision-making processes. "Informed" implies that Indigenous peoples have been provided all information relevant to the project in an accessible manner. Finally, "consent" means that Indigenous peoples have the right to say "no" to proposed and ongoing activities on their traditional territories, while subjecting that activity to conditions decided by the affected community.

In reality, settlers and the colonial state have rarely sought consent, and settler treaty responsibilities have been largely ignored as land theft and dispossession have occurred. For centuries, Canada has illegally occupied Indigenous lands, inflicting eco-genocide on all peoples through the continued industrialization of Native territories. Historically, the Canadian government has not only breached the conditions of land surrender, but has also created those conditions in unfair circumstances (such as under the threat of expropriation). The colonial government has also outright stolen unsurrendered land. Such is the case with the attempts of government officials and their partners in industry to make way for the Northern Gateway pipeline within the borders of British Columbia, and a much more extensive pipeline corridor that also would support fracking on the West Coast.

In many ways, the tar sands industry is in direct violation of the Canadian Constitution and treaties with Indigenous nations. The implementation of a Native rights strategic framework (NRF), as outlined by Clayton Thomas-Muller in the previous chapter of this book, would pose important legal challenges to tar sands pipelines by providing ways to delay or stop construction necessary for expansion. Referring to the documents of a genocidal state for strategic purposes may help our movements restore land to Indigenous peoples, stop corporate land theft, and end capitalist control of resources.

Sometimes we have to set aside some of our principles temporarily for limited strategic victories. Yet, even as we make these pragmatic choices, it is crucial to recognize and emphasize how the right to Indigenous self-determination exceeds nation-to-nation treaties. This sovereignty should be central to any NRF.

The Inuit, the Métis, and most of the Indigenous peoples in the territory claimed by British Columbia did not sign treaties with the British or Canadian governments. The Canadian Constitution is not the source of these rights, nor has it adequately protected them. An NRF that strictly adheres to Canadian law puts the onus on the colonial powers to give us our rights, instead of encouraging Indigenous people and our supporters to reclaim land and exercise our inherent rights. So it is important in anti–tar sands mobilizing to emphasize our responsibilities to uphold balanced relationships between Indigenous nations and settler nations. Operating within an NRF that is defined in relation to Canadian law alone entails the risk of taking energy away from actual land reclamation and work with the land to create more balanced ways of living.

Victories confined to Canadian legal instruments risk further formalizing the colonial system of oppression and exploitation. The Canadian government refuses First Nations the right to a shared decision-making process in nation-to-nation negotiations. Instead, colonial institutions, such as the National Energy Board and the Supreme Court of Canada, conduct hearings and trials in which they make decisions unilaterally. By limiting the negotiations to Canadian jurisdiction only, traditional Indigenous governments are denied power and legitimacy. Such an approach does not recognize how legal processes are spatially, temporally, and culturally unique. Each distinct Indigenous nation has its own laws that determine whether the tar sands and tar sands pipelines are prohibited on their land. These laws should be central to any NRF.

Native and treaty rights within a colonial framework are exclusionary, and employ a "divide and conquer" tactic. Mainstream media and the colonial government also operate within the colonial framework when they misrepresent band councils as representative of entire communities. Through the imposition of the electoral process on a traditional system, the colonial government engages in an act of political and cultural colonialism by continuing to try to replace hereditary chiefs with elected band councils, and traditional territories with *Indian Act* reserves. This limited approach to an NRF risks reproducing spiritually impoverishing limitations on our consciousness.

The Importance of Indigenous Resurgence

While versions of the NRF that only base Native rights in Canadian law are problematic, Indigenous understandings of the basis for these rights can and should be a key part of resistance to the tar sands. I will begin to indicate how traditional understandings are relevant to a deeper NRF. From a Michif perspective, the most basic social unit is not the individual, but the community in a universal sense. Rights are not created by humans, but by gichi manidoo (the Great Spirit). Inherent rights have existed since time immemorial, long before human beings did, and connect us to our responsibilities to protect the land, water, and future generations. Mino bimaadiziwin (a good way of life) is a central part of spiritual liberation.

In preparation for the reoccupation of our ancestral lands across Turtle Island, grassroots Indigenous peoples and traditional governments are attempting to embody the resurgence of political and economic traditions to recreate balanced relationships and viable alternatives to the colonial regime that supports the tar sands. Taiaiake Alfred has described the relationship between Indigeneity and resurgence:

> We are dedicated to recasting the identity and image of Indigenous people in terms that are authentic and meaningful, to regenerating and organizing a radical political consciousness, to reoccupying land and gaining restitution, to protecting the natural environment, and to restoring the Nation-to-Nation relationship between Indigenous nations and Settlers.
>
> This reframing of Indigeneity as Resurgence provides the ethical, cultural and political bases for a transformative movement that has the potential to remove the stain of colonialism from the land and to liberate the spirits of Original Peoples and Newcomers alike.[10]

This is a strategy to reimagine not only human relationships, but also what it means to be human. Anti-colonial campaigning against tar sands pipelines is very much rooted in Indigenous epistemologies and responsibilities to restore healthy relationships. These continuously evolving, community-based, reciprocal relationships can regenerate Indigenous unity and renew a commitment to defending the land. Through the resurgent actions of Indigenous families and communities, our ancestors and future generations will know the land and thrive.

For instance, in present-day Ontario, the Haudenosaunee Development Institute (HDI) provides the Haudenosaunee confederacy council with historical reviews of projects and updates about the status of negotiations, including the non-relinquishment of treaty rights. However, as discussed, the colonial government does not honour these sacred agreements, and negotiations are almost entirely one sided and abusive. The HDI develops a compensation model to address treaty violations and mitigate adverse impacts on the land and rights of the Haudenosaunee people. It looks at how specific projects, including Enbridge Line 9, will affect traditional medicines, the treaty area, harvesting, and hunting. Indigenous peoples have the inalienable and inherent right to free and undisturbed hunting, harvesting, trapping, and fishing throughout our traditional territories, in whatever way we choose.

Another example is the grassroots Wet'suwet'en, who are reasserting their traditional laws and practices on unceded territory. The Unist'ot'en (Big Frog Clan) are against all pipelines proposed to cross their territories, including Enbridge Northern Gateway, Pacific Trail, Coastal GasLink, Kinder Morgan's northern proposal, and additional projects. Drawing on their ancestral knowledge of the land, the Unist'ot'en have built a cabin and pit house and have organized a resistance camp along the Wedzin Kwah (Morice River), directly in the pathway of the Pacific Trail pipeline. These are healers, warriors, elders, hunters, fishers, and knowledge keepers who are living their responsibilities to reverse the impacts of colonization and spiritual poverty. Everyone comes from the earth, and she sustains us. We can regenerate these relations by upholding responsibilities in and through our resistance movements.

Anti-colonial Organizing

An anti-colonial pipeline campaign is accountable to treaty relationships and responsible for creating space for Indigenous resurgence to occur. Although treaties are not necessary for the right to self-determination, they can be symbolic of a balanced relationship. All people need to ask themselves: how are our relationships transformed through treaty? How are our thoughts and actions transformed by treaty? How are we going to protect the water and food now that it is contaminated? In order to survive, how will future generations understand and value their relationships with the land? These considerations are particularly important for non-Indigenous peoples because they can result in creating shared relationships. For example, some of the dialogue surrounding Idle No More has involved recognition of the obligations of settlers and the Canadian state to fulfill its end of the treaty agreements. The slogan "we are all treaty people" was brought into Idle No More's messaging to highlight these treaty responsibilities.

Settlers intending to uphold their treaty responsibilities by supporting Indigenous-led movements must base their mobilizations and education work on Indigenous peoples' inherent right to self-determination. As Thomas-Muller and Coats argue in this collection, mobilizing towards Indigenous autonomy can be, and should be, fundamental to tar sands resistance. Other chapters in this collection provide more direct accounts of Indigenous efforts to confront the tar sands. These efforts are part of Indigenous resurgence, which is based on the inherent rights, responsibilities, and relationships that exist from the moment Indigenous peoples are born with ancestral connections to Turtle Island.

Anti-colonial organizing can include ceremonies, songs, storytelling, tobacco offerings, healing circles, and Native-only spaces, as well as physical support for Indigenous people reclaiming their ancestral lands. This is solidarity through difference, and in some ways, it is already happening. Some of us are constantly working to ensure that anti–tar sands and anti-pipeline messaging and campaign objectives are consistent with an NRF, which can be crucial to our struggles. Yet, an anti-colonial approach to organizing requires space, time, and energy above and beyond what is needed to create social, economic, and political initiatives that unite urban, rural, and reserve communities.

A pipeline campaign rooted in an anti-colonial framework brings together converging anti-racist, anti-sexist, anti-colonial, and environmental struggles. This means that the strategies of our grassroots anti–tar sands movements entail leadership from Native peoples defending the sacred land. This work is already being led by women, girls, and two-spirits, sometimes called okichidaakwewag—the Anishinaabe word for Warrior Women. For instance, a warrior woman who lived during the mid-1800s was known as Aazhawigiizhigokwe (hanging cloud, or goes across the sky woman). She participated in battles, raids, hunting parties, war council, war dances, and all warrior ceremonies. Aazhawigiizhigokwe was a biological woman who had a vision that revealed she was destined to fulfill responsibilities; it did not matter that those responsibilities were often considered to be a male's. All individuals have gifts that are valuable to their community; everyone is a sacred bundle that has a rightful place in creation. The concept of okichidaakwewag is part of a traditional way of life that can inform anti–tar sands organizing. Okichidaakwewag demonstrates how women, children, and two-spirits can transform our cultures and the nature of our relationships through visions and dreams.

Our communities can facilitate spiritual fulfillment by encouraging individuals to develop a meaningful vision of their role in the universe. As well, nibi (water) walkers, okichidaakwewag, women, children, youth, and two-spirits have important roles in the healing of the earth and our peoples that will pose significant obstacles for further tar sands destruction.

Decolonizing ourselves and our anti–tar sands organizing means actively cultivating respect and spaces for Indigenous ways of being. More space is needed for Indigenous peoples to have meaningful involvement in directing the planning and facilitating of actions and gatherings.

Moccasins on the Ground frontline activist training on the Pine Ridge Homeland, in collaboration with Great Plains Tar Sands Resistance and Tar Sands Blockade, 2013.

Spaces for Indigenous women, two-spirits, and youth have been particularly scarce. Indigenous people can unite to define our own roles and representation in movement-related media and social movement organizations, ensuring that the anti–tar sands and anti-pipeline resistance is rooted in anti-colonial principles.

The proper acknowledgement of the land you are on, as well as learning or re-learning the history of it and the peoples that came before us, is important. This kind of self-education means that the burden of creating anti-colonial organizing spaces that enable settlers to work and act in solidarity does not continuously fall on Indigenous peoples. We can address the social norms that allow for some bodies and lives to be more valued than others by fully embodying resistance and actively confronting all forms of colonization and oppression. A thoroughly anti-colonial approach entails challenging all forms of oppression. And an anti-oppressive pipeline campaign would be accountable to treaty relationships, and responsible for supporting resurgence and decolonization.

Challenges Ahead

Working anti-colonial principles into our movements is a process. Not everyone who opposes a pipeline that crosses a river upstream from their home will oppose oppression, capitalism, or mining in general. At the same time, many people have no idea that there is already a pipeline so close to their homes. It is best to communicate with people by meeting them where they are at and mobilizing with them around their concerns. This makes them less likely to emotionally shut down or become defensive.

If someone's reason to fight is to protect where their children play or where their food comes from, we should validate those feelings as we educate people about systemic violence, including ecological destruction. While campaigning against pipeline projects like the Line 9 reversal, we can start to engage and mobilize a wider range of people by actively listening, thereby validating the ways in which people are legitimately at risk and frustrated by their circumstances. From there, it is also easier to explain how a system of privilege and oppression hurts everyone, and what kinds of actions can undermine this system. It is often the case that if we have been told about environmental racism, sexism, or oppression at all, we have only been taught about how it puts people at a disadvantage, not about how it also puts some at an advantage. This is why, when we have conversations about pipelines, it is important to take the opportunity to explain how oppression stems from the privilege of others. In the context of anti-pipeline struggles, it is crucial to address that the tar sands disproportionately affect Indigenous peoples because of ongoing colonialism. This includes the residential school system and experiments, the *Indian Act*, and the separation of children from their parents during the 1960s and millennium scoops. These are reasons settlers and Indigenous peoples are not affected by the tar sands in the same ways.

In campaigns around pipelines, there are further complications in how we relate to colonial governments. I have discussed strategic considerations concerning treaties. There are also difficult questions around whether we should attempt to lobby federal bodies that assess pipeline applications. In Canada, some campaigners are bringing their concerns to the National Energy Board (NEB). It is important to remember that colonial, capitalist government entities cannot be the focus of a truly anti-oppressive campaign. Too much focus on the NEB hearings not only will limit the scope and ultimately the effectiveness of our movement building, but also makes it exclusive, inaccessible, and undemocratic.

The structure of the NEB's process is a major reason for the lack of participation. For instance, it can cost about fifty thousand dollars in legal fees to even participate in a hearing. People who wanted to send a letter to the NEB to state their concerns with Line 9 first had to apply for permission to send in a letter, and fill out a ten-page questionnaire that asked for a resumé and references. (The window for these formal responses has long since closed, however.)

These are among the concerns that have prompted debate about whether to intervene in or disrupt the NEB hearings. One thing to consider about intervening in these hearings is the restrictions on what is discussed there: there can be no talk of the tar sands, capitalism, or the impact of resource extraction on future generations. This is what led the Lax Kw'alaams Nation on the West Coast to boycott the NEB Joint Review Panel for the Northern Gateway pipeline.

In September 2011, when the Haudenosaunee Development Institute sent a letter of comment to the NEB informing Enbridge of the treaty rights that apply to the proposed Line 9 project area, they were completely ignored.

In response, a group of activists, led by grassroots Haudenosaunee people, shut down the hearing (temporarily) and commenced a People's Hearing across the street from the NEB. Ultimately, the official hearing process is a mere formality. A key part of this movement is going to be maintaining momentum long after the NEB hearings cease.

Regarding Enbridge's proposal for the reversal of Line 9, the principle of free, prior, and informed consent has been breached during the National Energy Board's decision-making process. Indigenous people have been arrested at "public" hearings that the public was later barred from and that were then held exclusively for registered interveners. Additional construction on the western section of the pipeline (Line 9A) started to occur before the full reversal was approved. All communities were not adequately informed of risks, and the hearings were repeatedly fast-tracked.

Moving forward, it will be important to clarify for the public what it means to actually implement FPIC, and to point out how this did not happen with Line 9. The NEB will try to make it seem as though FPIC occurred and was attained, which is not the case. A concern about the most recent NEB hearing in Toronto in October 2013 was the traditional song in honour of the Elsipogtog Warriors being recorded in the official transcript. Out of context, this risks adding legitimacy to the corrupt colonial process. However, at the same hearing, Ononodowa'ga (Seneca) land defender Amanda Lickers made it clear "this application is an invitation to social conflict. It is an invitation to self-defence and a beckoning to land defence."[11]

Concluding Thoughts

We cannot expect the ongoing process of confronting normalized racism and colonialism to be comfortable. Often, white supremacy and colonialism are reproduced through settlers' insistence that decolonization be a comfortable process for them. Settlers need to be cognizant of when and how they are speaking, listening, and taking up space. It is important to not act defensively when called out for colonial behaviour, whether intentional or not; it is the impacts that count. Anti-colonial efforts cannot try to justify the behaviour or undermine people's experiences. Instead, look for actions with decolonizing potential. It is important to realize that right now, it is impossible to create a completely safe space, because our lives are in conflict with systems of oppression that we cannot yet exist outside of. By embodying a commitment to dismantling oppression in our everyday lives and interpersonal relationships, we can transform into more relational selves with a meaningful connection to the land and each other.

24

What Does It Mean to Be a Movement?

A Proposal for a Coherent, Powerful, Indigenous-Led Movement

●

EMILY COATS

•

Introduction

The tar sands industry has an exorbitant amount of power, wealth, and political influence. Every day, the well-oiled PR machine sells a story of "clean, green, and ethical" tar sands. The Canadian government more or less does everything in its power to support the industry, having repeatedly demonstrated its willingness to abolish environmental legislation, override its own Constitution, and break UN conventions. But neither the tar sands industry nor the government propping it up exists in a vacuum. These are dimensions of a neo-liberal economic system that is powering a frenzy of overconsumption, environmental destruction, and seemingly endless growth while serving the interests of only the wealthiest citizens, with devastating consequences for the rest.

Yet, there is a movement of dedicated people who are working hard to confront the tar sands industry and slow its expansion, so that we might ultimately leave the remaining tar sands in the ground and clean up the environmental devastation. The question is how this movement can be effective with the limited resources at hand. I believe that to be successful in confronting the tar sands industry, the movement needs to do two somewhat contradictory things: create change within the existing economic and political system, but also completely change this system.[1] Neither approach will succeed alone. Nor, given the limited resources available, will either method succeed unless these two approaches work in harmony, rather than against each other.

I also believe that although the effects of the tar sands will ultimately affect everyone in the world through climate change, this struggle cannot be observed abstractly. The people who live in northern Alberta's rich boreal forest are primarily Indigenous communities, for whom industrial projects and pollution are only the latest in a series of injustices they have experienced at the hands of Canada's ruling elite.[2] Indigenous communities in northern Alberta suffer from polluted water and food, rare illnesses, and the loss of traditional medicines and cultural practices. As a result, many are forced to make the entirely unreasonable choice between accepting jobs with the tar sands industry, or attempting to campaign against it to protect their subsistence ways of life—and thus facing unemployment.[3]

However, Indigenous rights are technically enshrined in the Constitution, the highest form of Canadian law, from treaties signed with the Crown in the late 1700s and afterwards. Treaties 6 and 8 govern much of the land now sought after by the tar sands industry. These were negotiated by the Crown to give the government the right to settle on land and use resources. In return, the government and settlers were required to not impinge on First Nations' traditional subsistence lifestyle. The right to "hunt, fish, and trap" was to be honoured "for as long as the sun shines, grass grows and the rivers flow."[4] As Huseman and Short argue, the government negotiators' primary task was "to reassure the Indians that their way of life would remain intact," whether or not they believed this to be true.[5] Nonetheless, Treaties 6 and 8 are enshrined in Canadian law, and technically limit what the government can accept or do on this land.

Moreover, the Canadian government, after refusing for three years, finally endorsed the UN Declaration on the Rights of Indigenous People in 2010. This document recognizes Indigenous peoples' right to free, prior, and informed consent (FPIC), which would amount to the ability of communities to say "no" to a development on their land. Yet, Indigenous peoples in Canada enjoy neither FPIC nor much of their treaty rights, as tar sands operations continue to go ahead without adequate consultation, let alone consent.

Tar sands projects would likely have suffered the fate of the UK's unbuilt wind farms had they happened to lie under the land of gentrified, country-dwelling Tories. Instead, the tar sands struggle is another phase of Indigenous resistance against colonialism, and this context is integral to understanding it and finding ways forward.

In this chapter, I will begin to take stock of the current movement against the tar sands by exploring the different types of actors involved, and the three broad positions they take. I will look critically at the distribution of resources and opportunities across the different groups, and explore some of the strategies currently employed. Then, I will suggest a different strategy the movement could take—one that would not only echo the world we would ultimately like to create, but would be the most strategic way to get there.

Who or What Is the Movement?

Social movements are typically made up of campaigns, networks, and groups. These have varying degrees of organizational capacity, as well as differing and sometimes competing goals that are aimed, broadly, at creating sweeping change and challenging the current order.[6] Although I obviously could not survey everyone in the movement against the tar sands, I have spoken to a cross-section, and have made some generalizations about the composition of the movement.

While the tar sands industry is highly polarizing, with most people either staunchly against it or impatient to accelerate it, there are of course a whole spectrum of views in between. In this analysis of the movement against the tar sands, I focus on those who broadly oppose the status quo—who, for a variety of reasons, see the rate of development as too fast, and advocate for a slower pace, eventual decline, or immediate halt to operations.

Many people in the movement believe that, in an ideal world, the bitumen would be left in the ground. Among those who agree, there are nevertheless a variety of approaches or frames to what the underlying problem is, and how to go about solving it. Of course, these discrete positions I identify exist on a sliding scale, and many groups, individuals, and campaigns would straddle the categories as they are labelled here, yet they serve as a useful analytical frame nonetheless.[7]

The Conservationist Approach

This approach views the tar sands as a polluting industry that needs to be stopped and cleaned up to prevent further destruction of forests, habitats, and freshwater, and to prevent further climate change. It advocates the use of technological and market-based approaches to protect the local environment, and encourages governments and businesses to address climate change.

Campaigning activities include: lobbying various levels of government for stricter emissions reductions targets and measures; awareness raising, especially on the climate and environmental impacts of tar sands; convincing businesses to take tar sands oil out of supply chains; conserving the boreal forest and its inhabitants through legislation or court cases (e.g., to save the caribou); and public campaigns that focus on how tar sands pipelines threaten waters, lands, and wildlife.

Examples include large NGOs, such as World Wildlife Fund and Sierra Club, as well as smaller grassroots groups that focus on wildlife conservation or mitigating climate change without challenging its underlying causes. These groups often have relatively substantial resources and paid staff, as well as a large reach of local networks and groups and a number of sympathetic funders to draw on.

The Climate Justice Approach

This approach sees the underlying problem as the neo-liberal or capitalist economic system that recklessly promotes resource extraction, including the tar sands, while exacerbating climate change, at the expense of the poorest communities and the planet. Their way forward is usually to work towards ending the oil-fuelled, growth-focused economic system or to seek to create a new one around it, or both, while in the meantime using existing measures to push for change. Equity is central to their goals: the rich should pay for the mess they have created.

Campaigns usually include raising awareness about the climatic and human rights impacts of tar sands and divestment campaigns, as well as public mobilization, protest, and direct action to embarrass and disgrace tar sands companies and remove their "social licence to operate," while preventing particular tar sands pipelines or projects. Examples include grassroots direct action and climate justice groups such as Rising Tide, and NGOs such as the Council of Canadians. Some of these groups or organizations have much less funding, staff, and time available to them.

The Indigenous Rights Approach

This overall approach holds that the colonial system in Canada and abroad fails to protect Indigenous peoples' rights. The disproportionate effects of tar sands pollution on Indigenous communities are only the latest in a string of injustices they are challenging. Their way forward is to assert Indigenous treaty rights, improve living standards, exercise their right to self-determination, and heal Mother Earth.

Their campaigning against the tar sands may include: participating in consultation and review panels; taking legal action against companies and/ or federal or provincial governments; raising awareness about tar sands, especially the impacts on Indigenous peoples and their land; building alliances with other groups; and actions to conserve the boreal forest and its inhabitants.

Examples include communities affected by tar sands extraction, such as the Athabasca Chipewyan First Nation and the Beaver Lake Cree Nation, as well as peoples along pipeline pathways, such as the Yinka Dene Alliance, and advocacy groups focused on Indigenous rights, such as the Indigenous Environmental Network and the Canadian Indigenous Tar Sands Campaign. While monetary resources have been very limited, there is great potential to engage and enlist people.

Why We Need to Change the Whole System

These three different positions tend to overlap considerably, and they generally do not interfere directly with one another. However, they often pull in different directions, which can dissipate energy, so that the overall resources expended on tar sands campaigning are not being used efficiently.

As I implied already, I reject the conservationist approach, which views the problem of tar sands—and climate change more generally—as an environmental issue that can be solved by working solely within existing power

structures. Tar sands have to be thought of simultaneously as a climate justice issue and an Indigenous rights issue. These systemic problems cannot be
solved without substantial redistribution of power and resources globally, yet
the Athabasca tar sands are also situated in a specific place, and the industry
disproportionately affects local people. Merely using campaigning tools that
tweak the current order will not suffice, for several reasons.

First, the current political environment prioritizes climate change denial-
ism, fossil fuel "independence," and ever-increasing resources for the richest
segment of society. These patterns do not set a good scene for making change
within the system. We are not in a functioning democracy that could slow
down the tar sands industry through legislative, electoral, and legal means.
Working within the system will also never be enough on its own, given how
this system is designed to recreate the injustices that drive it. Power structures
will continue to adapt to serve the needs of those who have the most economic
wealth, so any victories will be temporary. For instance, the massive gains in
gender and racial equality in the Global North over the past centuries are put
to shame by its increasing exploitation of the majority of the world.

Furthermore, activities within the current order are not only likely to fail;
they also often further entrench the system that is the cause of the problem
in the first place. Take, for example, the Forest Ethics campaign to encourage
large corporations to take tar sands oil out of their supply chains.[8] While
this has the potential to decrease the market value of the tar sands and raise
its profile publicly, this campaign also endorses transnational corporate
control and allows companies to greenwash themselves, and even co-opt the
movement.[9] Furthermore, as Indigenous environmental justice campaigner
Clayton Thomas-Muller argues in chapter 22, large non-profit organizations
and funders, especially when working closely with transnational corporations, have the potential to reinforce disparities on the basis of race, class,
or gender.

At the same time, short-term victories certainly invigorate the movement
and provide regular reminders to the industry, the government, and the
public that people with alternative agendas are taking action. But more confrontational activities are needed as well. Isolated acts of direct action and
civil disobedience go some way towards moving beyond the shortcomings
of reformist conservationism, as does including messaging around climate
justice, equity, and systemic change.

Yet, while these strategies can open up space for new debates, on their own they will also fall short of achieving sufficient transformation. Direct action may alienate the public, who see it as extreme and counterproductive. Messaging calling for systemic change can be perceived as unrealistic and unhelpful. Moreover, even anti-capitalist groups can fall into recreating oppression (such as racism) or colonialism in their methods of organizing.

To move beyond this catch-22, it is essential to have a strategy that involves acting within conventional political structures to achieve small victories and captivate the broader public imagination, while devoting the majority of our energy to challenging the economic structures and oppressive tendencies of the established order.

A Suggested Way Forward

Some have already begun to combine the strategic and inclusive Indigenous rights frame with the broader perspective of the climate justice approach. By continuing to bring these strands of the movement together, we will gain further opportunities to create a coherent, powerful, Indigenous-led movement that would both leverage and change the system. Unlike other campaigners, members of First Nations in Canada are in a unique position: if treaties are upheld, they "hold the balance of power in deciding the fate of Canada's resource projects."[10]

In recent years, Canada has seen a surge in Indigenous-led activism under the Idle No More banner. The scope of issues covered within the variety of protests, roadblocks,[11] teach-ins, and solidarity actions has been epic, and we saw international support for an Indigenous-led movement in North America.

How an Indigenous-Led Movement Would Be a More Effective Way to Work within the Current Political Order

The Harper government has shown no fear in abolishing its opposition, while allowing the oil industry to rewrite the rules[12] as it forges ahead with a pro–tar sands agenda. Thus, taking action through most traditional political routes, such as voting, lobbying local members, and so on, has become all but impossible. In early 2012, the Harper government effectively wiped out decades of environmental legislation by passing a package of laws critics have dubbed the "Environmental Destruction Act."[13] Later that year, there was a decision to uproot another law that protected water bodies across the country.[14] This move was seen as an affront to Indigenous communities across Canada, and it proved to be the catalyst for the Idle No More movement.

One area that has remained relatively free of the Harper government's interference is the court system, which is a valuable avenue for challenging the tar sands industry, particularly for Indigenous communities in the affected regions. If Indigenous communities continue to address violated agreements, inadequate consultation, and infringed treaty rights by taking individual companies, or the federal or Alberta governments, or both, to court, these exertions of constitutionally enshrined Indigenous rights could have profound effects on the industry. In chapter 22, Thomas-Muller argues that over the past thirty years, Indigenous assertions of rights and title have been at the forefront of all of the major environmentalist victories in Canada.

In many communities, there are potential cases that could be heard, but putting together a lawsuit is an expensive and time-consuming process.[15] Currently, the Beaver Lake Cree Nation is asking the Alberta courts to declare that the cumulative effects of approximately seventeen thousand tar sands projects in their territory are a fundamental violation of their treaty rights (see chapter 11). This is the first time that Canada's courts are allowing litigation against large-scale industrial operations—including tar sands activity—in response to the cumulative effects these activities may have on constitutionally protected treaty rights.[16] If this case is successful, it could set a further precedent in the legal system, making thousands of other leases void. This is one of the most useful cases the movement can support.

The judicial system is not without problems, including the ways it drains time and money. Nonetheless, it is a very powerful and underexplored avenue that remains one of the most promising options—at least while the Harper government is in power, and environmental legislation is being eroded while politicians remain very open to oil industry lobbying.

Empowered, educated, proactive communities, supported by the rest of the movement, would also be better placed to assert their rights within the consultation process, thereby preventing destructive projects in the first place instead of taking companies to court after the damage has been done. Yet, consultation procedures are currently lengthy and complicated, and they can easily be misunderstood, or misconstrued. For example, the

Athabasca Chipewyan First Nation attempted to present their concerns to a Joint Review Panel about one of the two huge open pit mines that Shell has proposed to build on their land. The community found it difficult to have their concerns heard by the panel. Not only were they told that the panel could not assess the adequacy of Shell's "consultation"—which was one of the community's biggest complaints[17]—but dozens of First Nations peoples were denied the right to participate at all. Official technicalities were cited as their applications were denied.[18] The panel eventually acknowledged that the project was "likely to cause significant adverse environmental effects" to the land, but, demonstrating the inadequacy of the consultation process, the federal government gave the mine the go-ahead anyway. Athabasca Chipewyan First Nation is now considering legal action.[19]

How an Indigenous-Led Movement Could Bring Systemic Change

For centuries, Indigenous peoples in Canada have suffered repeated assaults on their autonomy, including the forced dispossession of their lands and resources, the suppression of their governments and laws, and the erasure of their traditional cultures and identities.[20] North American energy extraction and infrastructure has been yet another form of colonization. As Huseman and Short state, "Many people in indigenous communities feel that they are in the final stages of a battle for survival that began in North America in the seventeenth century."[21] Even today, First Nations communities continue to experience some of the worst living conditions in the world, some having no access to running water, and the lowest education, employment, and income levels in Canada.[22] But a rights-based approach could turn this around, as Thomas-Muller also argues.

An Indigenous-led campaign would diminish racism, oppression, and colonialism within the movement, and across Canada more broadly, by addressing centuries of injustices towards First Nations peoples. It would also encourage systemic change in the ways people treat each other more broadly. If we want to live in a world where the human and environmental costs of tar sands are considered too high to justify whatever profit may be made, then we need to begin to iron out inequalities at every level. A more democratic economic and energy system that would draw the line at the tar sands despite its short-term profit potential would have to be founded on respect for human rights and the earth. It is these standards that we need to create, and recreate, at every stage of the campaign. Social movement theorists point out how the aim of a social movement is not only to advocate alternative visions, but also to build social relations conducive to realizing these visions.[23]

An Indigenous-led movement would also promote traditional values of protecting Mother Earth and living within the means of our planet, rather than beyond them. Over thousands of years, First Nations have developed a variety of deep understandings of how humanity can live on the Earth in harmony with its other inhabitants.[24] The idea that the land owns us, rather than vice versa, as well as the imperative to be stewards rather than conquerors of the planet and a concern not just for our children but also for our descendants in twenty generations' time[25]—these are some of the very ideas that we should be emphasizing when addressing climate change.

Finally, elevating the struggles of Indigenous communities in Canada could inspire other frontline communities around the world to take action against other carbon-intensive industries. It is no coincidence that the dirtiest developments consistently take place in close proximity to Indigenous communities, people of colour, and the poorest socio-economic groups. Witnessing a powerful, Indigenous-led movement in Canada could bring phenomenal encouragement to others who feel similar impacts.

What Would "Indigenous-Led" Mean in Practice?

There is currently a clear disparity of resources within the movement. Most of these resources are held by those who are the least willing to change the system—as is true in the world generally. The tar sands movement is not overtly racist, but it does, like any movement, have the potential to recreate outside hierarchies and oppressions. As the Declaration of non-Indigenous Support for Defenders of the Lands communicates, being allies to an Indigenous struggle involves us committing "to doing our part to actively decolonize ourselves by recognizing our own complicity and taking responsibility to change this society that privileges us." Supporters must recognize Indigenous self-determination, and reckon with the "racist and genocidal" history of Canada.[26]

Therefore, we need a shift of culture within the movement to one that prioritizes mutual education and skill-sharing. There are more than five hundred years of First Nations' struggles, which have both commonalities and differences. There are many rich, complex cultures to understand. Non-Indigenous campaigners need to be genuinely willing to learn about and engage with the issues Indigenous peoples face, rather than making token gestures, such as including the term "treaty rights" as footnotes in their campaigning materials.[27]

Thomas-Muller has pointed out how NGOs and grassroots networks should work with grassroots community voices, especially women, rather than only with Chiefs and band councils. Not only does this ensure that the Chief and council are held to account and are genuinely representing the community, but this can inspire other members of the community to act in the way of their peers.[28]

We can expect that some of the movement would want to campaign on various aspects of the tar sands issue, such as preventing pipelines, and any campaigning should be done in solidarity with First Nations struggles. Doing so would mean using campaign messaging that acknowledges the importance of Indigenous rights, while consulting Indigenous groups about campaigning ideas and messaging and having a willingness to direct energy and resources towards court cases, review panels, and other important events at key points.[29] Without this respect, Lameman argues, First Nations communities will continue to be dictated to by outsiders, as they have been for centuries, rather than being treated as equal partners.[30]

This solidarity would entail channelling significant amounts of resources towards Indigenous groups to lead their own campaigns. Ideally, funding would not be funnelled through one central group. Communities would be encouraged to seek funding from a variety of different sources, including foundations and individual donations. Better-resourced groups should be willing to support Indigenous-led campaigns, by splitting funding and sharing fundraising contacts or skills, rather than handing out funds only when this is deemed "strategic." New opportunities for funding would open up, attracting funders with a greater interest in Indigenous rights, as opposed to climate change and the environment.

Conclusion

The tar sands resistance movement is made up of a number of different struggles around different facets, but the overarching issues behind them are all familiar: capitalism, colonialism, oppression, inequality, greed, and short-termism. The solutions, therefore, will ultimately be rooted in people finding better ways to relate to each other, and the earth. Justice must start within the movement. Creating a strong, Indigenous-led movement therefore needs to begin with education. Non-Indigenous campaigners need to open their doors to communication, and their minds to new ways of working.

Climate change is one of the gravest threats in our time, and Indigenous peoples may be threatened more than anyone else on earth. Nevertheless, climate change sometimes may not be the immediate priority of Indigenous communities struggling to assert their treaty rights. Yet, an Indigenous-led tar sands campaign would have the potential to genuinely rock the boat, by disrupting Canada's legal and political inertia and creating severe waves for the tar sands industry.

25

Expanding the Fossil Fuel Resistance

●

BILL McKIBBEN

•

After decades of scant organized response to climate change, a movement is quickly emerging in the United States, Canada, and around the world, building on the work of frontline organizers who have been fighting the fossil fuel industry for decades. It has no great charismatic leader and no central organization; it battles on a thousand fronts. But taken together, it's now big enough to matter, and it seems to be growing fast.

Americans got to see some of this movement spread out across the Mall in Washington, DC, on a bitter-cold day in February 2013. Press accounts put the crowd at upwards of forty thousand—by far the largest climate rally in the country's history. They were there to oppose the Keystone XL pipeline proposal, which would run south from Canada's tar sands to the Gulf of Mexico, a fight that *Time* magazine referred to as the Selma and the Stonewall of the climate movement.[1] This enormous pipeline battle is also entangled with a wider fossil fuel resistance, reflected in the fact that there were thousands in the rally at the Mall also working to block fracking wells across the Appalachians and proposed Pacific Coast deepwater ports that would send coal to China. Students from most of the 323 campuses where the fight for fossil fuel divestment is underway mingled with veterans of the battles to shut down mountaintop-removal coal mining in West Virginia and Kentucky and with earnest members of the Citizens Climate Lobby, there to demand that Congress enact a serious price on carbon.[2]

A few days earlier, forty-eight leaders had been arrested outside the White House. They included ranchers from Nebraska who didn't want a giant pipeline across their land, and leaders from Texas refinery towns who didn't want more crude oil spilling into their communities. Even famed investor Jeremy Grantham was on hand, urging scientists to accompany their research with civil disobedience, as were solar entrepreneurs quickly figuring out how to deploy panels on rooftops across the country. The original Americans were well represented; Indigenous groups are core leaders of the fight, since their communities have been devastated by mines and cheated by oil companies. Reverend Lennox Yearwood Jr. of the Hip Hop Caucus was handcuffed next to Julian Bond, former head of the NAACP, who recounted stories of being arrested for integrating Atlanta lunch counters in the 1960s.

It's a sprawling, diverse, and remarkably united movement, marked by its active opposition to the richest and most powerful industry on earth. The fossil fuel resistance has already won some serious victories, blocking dozens of new coal plants and closing down existing ones—ask the folks at Little Village Environmental Justice Organization, who helped shutter a pair of coal plants in Chicago, or the Asian Pacific Environmental Network, which fought to stop Chevron from expanding its refinery in Richmond, California. "Up to this point, grassroots organizing has kept more industrial carbon out of the atmosphere than state or federal policy," says Gopal Dayaneni of the Movement Generation Justice and Ecology Project, a group that combines struggles for economic and environmental justice in communities of colour in the San Francisco Bay Area.[3]

The fossil fuel resistance is an economic resistance movement, too, and it's well aware that renewable energy creates three times as many jobs as coal and gas and oil.[4] Further, these are good, skilled jobs that can't be outsourced, because the sun and the wind are close to home. Renewable energy creates a future, in other words. These are serious people: you're not a member of the resistance just because you drive a Prius. You don't need to go to jail, but you do need to do more than change your light bulbs. You need to try to change the system that is raising the temperature, the sea level, the extinction rate— even raising the question of how well civilization will survive this century.

Soon after the big DC rally, the US State Department issued a report downplaying Keystone XL's environmental impact, thus advancing the pipeline proposal another step. Following this, at the urging of the remarkable cellphone-company-cum-activist-group Credo, nearly sixty thousand people have signed a pledge promising to resist, peacefully but firmly, if the pipeline is ever approved. By March 2013, even establishment commentators like Thomas Friedman had noticed—he used his *New York Times* column to ask activists to "go crazy" with civil disobedience.[5] Forty-eight hours later, twenty-five students and clergy members were locked down inside a pipeline company office outside Boston. It's not a one-sided fight anymore.

No movement this diverse is going to agree on a manifesto, but any reckoning begins with the idea that fossil fuel is dirty at every stage, and we need to put it behind us as fast as we can. For those of us in affluent countries, small shifts in lifestyle won't be enough; we'll also need to alter the policies that keep this industry fat and happy. For the poor world, the much harder goal is to leapfrog the fossil fuel age and go straight to renewables—a task that those of us who prospered by filling the atmosphere with carbon must help with, for reasons both moral and practical. And for all of us, it means standing with communities from the coalfields of Appalachia to the oil-soaked Niger Delta as they fight for their homes. They've fought longest and hardest, and too often by themselves. Now that global warming is starting to pour seawater into subways, the frontlines are expanding, and the reinforcements are finally beginning to arrive.

Right now, the fossil fuel industry is mostly winning. Peak oil theory has led many to hope that we'd run out of fossil fuel soon enough to force the switch to renewables—but though oil and gas may get more expensive, new discoveries show there's more than enough accessible carbon left underground to wreck the climate. As the price rose for hydrocarbons, companies found lots of new sources, though mostly by scraping the bottom of the barrel, spending even more money to get even cruddier energy. The tar sands are a classic example of this, as the high price of oil has made it economical for the industry to take the sludgy bitumen and heat it with natural gas (and copious amounts of water) until the oil flows. Another major new dimension is the expansion of fracking for shale oil and gas, essentially by exploding a pipe bomb a few thousand feet beneath the surface to release the fossil fuels from the surrounding rock. They've also managed to drill miles beneath the ocean's surface. As with the tar sands in Canada, the hyperbolic enthusiasm for fracking in the US has gushed even higher than the oil. *The Wall Street Journal* has declared North Dakota a new Saudi Arabia, and *The New York Times* described a new shale-oil find in California as more than four times as large as North Dakota's.[6]

But all that fossil fuel will only get pumped and mined and burned if we decide to ignore the climate issue; were we to ever take it seriously, the math would quickly change. The world's fossil fuel companies, even before these new finds, apparently have five times more carbon in their reserves than we could burn if we hope to stay below a 2°C rise in global temperatures.[7] That's the red line almost every government in the world has agreed to (at least on paper) as the "safe" upper limit for warming, but the coal, oil, and natural gas companies, propelled by record profits, just keep looking for more—and ignoring reality. An anonymous group of industry billionaires has secretly poured more than $100 million into anti-environmental front groups like Americans for Prosperity and the Heartland Institute in recent years, and weeks before the 2012 US election, Chevron gave the largest corporate Super PAC contribution of the post–Citizens United era in order to ensure that Congress stayed in the hands of climate deniers.[8]

But every flood erodes their position, and every heat wave fuels the resistance. When the Keystone XL pipeline first became controversial, in 2011, a poll of DC "energy insiders" showed that more than 70 per cent of them thought they'd have permits to build it by the end of the year.[9] Big Oil, of course, may end up getting its way, but so far its money hasn't overwhelmed the passion, spirit, and creativity its foes have brought to the battle. And this is not just playing defence anymore: the rapidly spreading divestment movement may be the single biggest face of the resistance. It's no longer confined to campuses; city governments and religious denominations have begun to unload their stakes in oil companies, and the movement is even spreading to self-interested investors now that HSBC has calculated that taking climate change seriously could cut share prices of oil companies by up to 60 per cent.[10]

With each passing month, something else weakens the industry's hand: the steady rise of renewable energy, a technology that's gone from pie-in-the-sky to panel-on-the-roof in remarkably short order. In the few countries where governments have really gotten behind renewables, the results are staggering. For instance, there were days in the spring of 2012 when Germany (pale, northern Germany) managed to generate half its power from solar panels. Even in the United States, much of the generating capacity added in 2012 came from renewables, and research in the *Journal of Power Sources* showed that by 2030, the nation could be affordably powered 99.9 per cent of the time on renewable energy.[11] In other words, logic, physics, and technology work against the fossil fuel industry. For the moment, it has the political power it needs—but political power shifts perhaps more easily than physics.

This is where the resistance comes in. In 1970, the first anarchic Earth Day drew twenty million Americans into the streets. That surge helped push through all kinds of US legislation—the *Clean Air Act*, the *Endangered Species Act*—and spurred the growth of organizations like the Natural Resources Defense Council (NRDC) and the Environmental Defense Fund. As these organizations became the face of the environmental movement, they grew adept at playing an inside-the-Beltway lobbying game. But that strategy got harder as the power of the right wing grew, and for twenty-five years they've been unable to win significant progress on climate change.

Now, energized by the Keystone protests, some strides have been made. The NRDC, for example, has done yeoman's work against the pipeline. The Sierra Club, which just a few years ago was taking millions from the fracking industry to shill for natural gas, has been reinvented, to an extent that the club dropped a 120-year ban on civil disobedience in January 2013 and its executive director, Michael Brune, was led away from the White House in handcuffs the following month.

While we might see these as encouraging changes, there can be little doubt that the centre of gravity within environmentalism is shifting from big, established groups to more local, grassroots, and distributed efforts. In the Internet age, direct mail and a big headquarters aren't the only bases for outreach; there is also Facebook and Twitter. There are many other encouraging movements appearing all over the place. In Texas and Oklahoma, hundreds have joined actions led by the Tar Sands Blockade, which has used daredevil tactics and lots of courage to get between the industry and the pipeline it needs to move oil overseas. In Montana, author Rick Bass and others sat in to stop the export of millions of tons of coal from ports on the West Coast. And all across the Marcellus and Utica shale formations in the Northeast, people have been standing up for their communities, often by sitting down in front of the fracking industry. The fossil fuel resistance looks more and more like Occupy. In fact, they've overlapped from the beginning, since the elite's running oil companies are in the 1 per cent of the 1 per cent. The movements often share a political analysis, too, favouring decentralized and democratic alternatives. A grid with a million solar rooftops feels more like the Internet than ConEd (the energy company); it's a farmers' market in electrons, with the local control that implies.

Like Occupy, this new resistance is not obsessed with winning over political party leaders. The approach US environmental activists have taken towards President Obama is telling. While Obama was once viewed by many with some hope that climate change would begin to be taken seriously by the US government, environmentalists have increasingly turned from quietly lobbying to loudly protesting, culminating with the 2011 Keystone arrests outside the White House and the great rally at the Mall, which may have been the most militant protests outside the White House during Obama's first term. Van Jones, who once worked for the president, began to call Keystone the "Obama pipeline."[12] Used to dealing with the established green groups, the administration thinks in terms of deals—"We'll approve the pipeline but give you something else you want"—the kind of logic that gains the approval of op-ed columnists and talking heads.

But given how fast the Arctic is melting, we don't have room for easy compromises. Obama's insistence that he favours an "all of the above" energy system, where oil and gas are as welcome as solar and wind, seems increasingly like a classic political hedge (only somewhat more nuanced than Stephen Harper's all-out advocacy for the tar sands). In fact, Obama's campaign trail rhetoric in 2012 would have made Harper proud, posing in front of a stack of oil pipe in Oklahoma and bragging about adding enough new pipelines to encircle the earth. Following the 2012 election, the president began talking green again, promising that now climate change would be a priority—but this growing resistance is, I think, unconvinced. As Naomi Klein has warned, Obama's first term must be a lesson to all activists that the appearance of a progressive leader should not lull us into a false sense of accomplishment; there is simply no room for a honeymoon or hero worship, as though we only need to elect the right leader.

Only grit and hard work will do. There have been some great cultural shifts and organizing successes in the US in recent years, like the marriage equality and immigration reform movements. But breaking the power of oil companies may be even harder, because the sums of the money on the other side are so fantastic—there are trillions of dollars' worth of oil in Canada's tar sands alone, and the people who own these resources will spend what they need to assure their victories. In March 2013, Rex Tillerson, Exxon's $100,000-a-day CEO, said that environmentalists were "obtuse" for opposing new pipelines, while announcing that the company planned to more than double the acreage on which it was exploring for new hydrocarbons—and projecting that renewables would account for just 1 per cent of the total US energy supply in 2040. Noting that "my philosophy is to make money," he was essentially declaring that the war to save the climate was over before it started.[13]

That same day, scientists announced that the earth was now warming fifty times faster than it ever has in the history of human civilization, and that atmospheric CO_2 levels had set a perilous new record at Mauna Loa's measuring station. Right now, we're losing. But as the planet runs its spiking fever, the antibodies are starting to kick in. We know what the future holds unless we resist. And so resist we will.

26

Secondary Targeting

A Strategic Approach to Tar Sands Resistance

●

STEPHEN D'ARCY

•

I do not ask that you place hands upon the tyrant to topple him over,
but simply that you support him no longer; then you will behold him,
like a great Colossus whose pedestal has been pulled away, fall of his
own weight and break in pieces.
—Étienne de La Boétie, *Discourse on Voluntary Servitude*

Like the megaproject it opposes, the movement to shut down the tar sands is remarkably ambitious. Its aim is to bring the world's largest energy project grinding to a halt. As other chapters in this book make clear, the forces arrayed against this movement are powerful indeed: not only the fossil fuel industry, but also the network of investors and financiers that bankroll the project, and the provincial and national governments that have placed the industry's expansion at the centre of their economic development strategies. Further, the general view that tar sands expansion is both inevitable and, on balance, beneficial is embraced by all of Canada's major political parties and most of its leading media outlets. In short, it is hard to exaggerate the political and economic might of the movement's adversary.

In comparison, the political and economic resources behind the movement to shut down the tar sands seem almost insignificant. While it draws together an assemblage of Indigenous communities, environmental NGOs, trade unions, and community defence organizations, the movement lacks the support of any major political party in Canada or the US, is confined to the margins of public debate, and is widely viewed as incapable of posing a serious threat to the industry.

In the face of this uneven conflict, the question that I address in this chapter is one that haunts many anti–tar sands activists: can we really win? Can we actually keep the bitumen in the ground? Or do we have to accept, however grudgingly, the ultimate futility of our efforts, while contenting ourselves with "fighting the good fight" and perhaps mitigating the scale of the disasters to come?

I argue that the movement *can* indeed prevail, and that in spite of the relative weakness of the resistance in its current forms, there is a plausible path to victory. To that end, I focus on one strategic element in this struggle: *secondary targeting*. Much of the movement's potency, I suggest, derives not from its capacity to directly influence the tar sands industry itself, but from its capacity to disrupt the system of financial, political, and ideological support on which the industry depends.

Grappling with Asymmetry

The struggle to shut down the tar sands, like so many other struggles for social and environmental justice, is an "asymmetrical" conflict, in the sense that a relatively weak force is pitted against an extremely strong one.[1] Yet, while such asymmetry clearly poses difficult strategic challenges, historical experience shows that there are tactical resources on which grassroots movements can draw that make victory possible, even against imposing odds.[2]

In order to grapple with asymmetry, it is especially important for a movement to focus its limited capacities on attacking vulnerable yet important targets. There is little to be gained by attacking a "hard" or invulnerable target, or a target that is not vulnerable to the particular types of action that a grassroots social movement can carry out. Conversely, there is also little to be gained by attacking a "soft" or vulnerable target if that target is relatively unimportant to the outcome of the conflict. What a movement needs to do is focus its attacks on *strategic vulnerabilities*: soft targets that crucially bear upon conflict outcomes.

This poses a special problem for the movement to shut down the tar sands. The problem is that the tar sands industry itself—made up of very large fossil fuel extraction, processing, and pipeline infrastructure firms like Suncor, Syncrude, Royal Dutch Shell, TransCanada, and Enbridge—is not a very soft target for grassroots activists. I do not mean that the movement cannot target the industry directly. It can and it does, as it must—it is symbolically indispensable to do so. What I mean is that when activists attack it directly, these actions have only a very limited capacity to affect its vital interests; put simply, the industry has limited material vulnerability to these attacks.

To see why, recall that corporations are purely *self-interest-motivated* institutions, in the sense that what they do depends on their economic calculations of costs and benefits. Their options are evaluated in terms of how they positively or negatively affect the organization's vital interests, which centre on growth, the maximization of profits, and shareholder returns.[3] As a result, if activists want to influence corporate behaviour, the only way to do so is to threaten the corporation's vital interest in profit maximization.

Can the movement to shut down the tar sands carry out actions that directly threaten the profitability of firms like Suncor, Syncrude, TransCanada, and Enbridge? In my view, it can do so only to a very limited degree. Consider the kinds of threats that grassroots activism can pose for these corporations when relying on popular education, public protest, and confrontational disruption or defiance. These include:

- relentless, long-term campaigns of negative publicity and vilification or shaming, in order to discredit or delegitimize corporations;[4]
- sit-ins, blockades, lockdowns, and other forms of civil disobedience and direct action to disrupt their day-to-day functioning;[5]
- community-based, public-interest infrastructure disassembly or dismantling (so-called "sabotage") to protect the environment, public health, or human rights;[6]
- attention-getting acts of legal defiance or civil disorder to heighten levels of public scrutiny for business practices that would otherwise remain hidden from public view;[7]
- approaching small-scale, narrowly framed, or single-issue disputes as opportunities to convert specific grievances into incubators of more radical opposition to large-scale systems of exploitation; and

- establishing alternative economic or political practices and institutions that draw people out of mainstream institutions into oppositional ones (e.g., popular assemblies and workers' cooperatives), as a means of weakening integration into the existing society and bolstering counter-institutions that are apart from and opposed to mainstream society.

Should any of these grassroots-activist capabilities worry the tar sands industry? Most of them have been used against firms like Enbridge and Suncor in the past few years, and none seems to have seriously weakened the megaproject. Of course, to have their full effect, tactics have to be implemented *relentlessly*, on an *escalating* trajectory, with an *ever-broadening base* of participation. But even if we imagine a marked scaling-up of these tactics, it is hard to imagine the tar sands industry itself caving in due to pressure of this type, given the magnitude of the resource and the potential for long-term profits, as well as the massive upfront investments that are the price of entry into the industry.

But we have to exercise caution in drawing conclusions at this stage. If we conclude that these grassroots-activist capabilities pose no real threat to the tar sands industry *at all*, then the movement seems destined to fail, and we can only despair. On the other hand, if we overestimate their likely direct impact on the industry itself, we risk pouring all our energy into fruitless confrontations with a "hard target" that is largely invulnerable to the kinds of challenges that grassroots activism can bring to bear.

From Primary to Secondary Targeting

The way out of this impasse, I suggest, is to pay careful attention to the distinction between *primary* and *secondary targeting*. Primary targeting deploys movement capabilities to directly attack the adversary's vital interests. For example, if a group of people want to target a certain clothing retailer, they might picket its stores, or try to orchestrate a consumer boycott, or use direct action to disrupt the company's business on a busy shopping day. This sort of primary targeting (assuming it is relentless and escalating) might work to effectively pressure the firm into making certain concessions, for the simple reason that a retailer is a soft target for tactics of delegitimization and disruption due to their reliance on positive public perceptions and the reproduction of "brand loyalty" among customers. A company that supplies ladders to construction firms, by contrast, would be a harder target because it markets to *other companies*, and not to the general public. These other companies are unlikely to be influenced by negative publicity directed against the supplier, as long as the ladders are cost effective for them. In cases where primary targeting is largely ineffective, activists have the option of resorting to *secondary targeting*, attacking an adversary *indirectly* by trying to penalize businesses or politicians that support or collaborate with it.

The classic example of secondary targeting is the use of boycott and divestment campaigns by the anti-apartheid movement of South Africa, led by the African National Congress (ANC).[8] The ANC had tried to target the apartheid regime for decades with a range of tactics, including armed struggle, but with apparently diminishing returns over time. As one way to strengthen the struggle, they introduced new campaigns geared at promoting economic sanctions and financial divestment from South Africa, along with cultural boycotts by artists, athletes, academics, and tourists. This strategy assumed that the apartheid regime could not be effectively shamed, defied, or disrupted internally—any more than it already was—given its siege mentality, intense commitment to white supremacy, and the vastly superior military and economic power it had at its disposal. It was, in short, a very hard target.

But the apartheid regime was not self-sufficient, as it relied on a *support system* of transnational corporations and foreign governments, which gave it both a certain amount of legitimacy and, above all, access to export markets, essential imports, and international capital. This made the regime *indirectly* vulnerable, to the extent that many of the participants in the regime's transnational support system were themselves vulnerable to targeting by ANC and anti-apartheid solidarity activists. Governments that offered assistance to the regime could be shamed or confronted *at home* for their role in lending support to injustice; corporations or institutional investors, notably university endowment funds, could be shamed into divesting from the South African economy and boycotting South African businesses and cultural products and exchanges. These secondary targets were much softer than the regime itself for two notable reasons: first, because the tools available to grassroots activism could effectively threaten these targets with real burdens, since association with racism was more socially disapproved of in Europe or the Americas than it was in white South Africa itself; and second, because the burdens associated with defecting from the apartheid support system were, for these targets, relatively minimal, since secondary targets could easily shift capital investment to other sectors of the global economy. The object of the cultural boycott was to cut off any source of legitimacy for the regime and turn it into a pariah state, while the object of the economic divestment and sanctions campaign was to choke off the sources of financial and economic support that provided the regime with the material lifeline it needed, notably for its crucial mining industry. In the end, these tactics enhanced the impacts of others the ANC pursued, and helped to provoke elite defections from the regime's support system (notably many transnational banks and corporations, and even the US Congress), until apartheid was defeated and majority rule was instituted.[9]

This example helps to demonstrate the basic logic behind secondary targeting. In essence, when the primary targeting of an adversary brings diminishing returns or is altogether self-defeating, movements can magnify their impact by shifting towards an *indirect* attack upon their adversary. In practical terms, that means redirecting some of the movement's focus away from the main adversary and fixing it on the support system upon which the adversary relies. If the movement can find suitable secondary targets within this support system that are both vulnerable to activist interventions (such as disruption, shaming, and public protest) and strategically crucial in political and economic terms, then the movement will be well positioned to trigger elite defections.

In the case of the movement to shut down the tar sands, this means that elites in both allied businesses and allied governments—many of which are softer targets than pipeline infrastructure and bitumen mining or processing firms—can be effectively targeted to the point where it becomes more costly for them to participate in the tar sands support system than to defect from it. It remains to be shown how the secondary targeting approach to tar sands resistance would look in practice, and how it might differ from the movement as it is currently constituted.

Tactical Implications of the Secondary Targeting Approach

Tactically, a secondary targeting approach does not propose anything entirely new. For instance, chapter 19 shows how secondary targeting strategies have been important in the campaigning of the UK Tar Sands Network and their collaborators, and many similar tactics that are now widely used to oppose the tar sands fit nicely into a secondary targeting approach. What would be new is that the *focus* of the movement's energy would shift, to a considerable extent, away from efforts to target the corporations directly involved in the extraction, refining, and shipping of bitumen, and towards efforts to impose burdens on elites in allied businesses, governments, and the news media that constitute the industry's support system, with the overriding strategic objective of provoking elite defections from that system.

If the tar sands industry is to operate successfully, it fundamentally depends upon the supportive context established by industry-friendly public policy (e.g., subsidies, weak environmental regulations, the ability to externalize myriad costs), the ideological legitimacy that informs public debates, the availability of project and corporate financing, and so on. That is, it would not be possible without the financing of banks and institutional investors, the extensive government support both in Canada and abroad, and the general tone in the news media that serves to normalize the industry and treat it as an acceptable (or at worst, inevitable) part of the wider economy. In short, the support system serves to effectively insulate the tar sands industry from the consequences of its devastating impacts on Indigenous communities, public health, ecosystems and other species, and climate change. It is crucial for activists to find ways of making the industry as toxic in public perception as it is in reality—that is, a pariah industry that is no more acceptable than other pariah industries like the slave trade or trade in human organs.

What makes the secondary targeting approach promising is the fact that key elements of the tar sands industry's support system are soft targets that are directly vulnerable to the kinds of threats that activist intervention can generate. For instance, there is potential to disrupt public events or retail business activities; generate negative publicity and critical public scrutiny; undermine claims to legitimacy and authority; spread localized conflicts into generalized controversy and radicalization; and so on. If these soft targets in the industry's support system can be threatened by such interventions, with relentless and escalating pressure, it becomes very plausible to anticipate large-scale elite defections from the system of enablers that supports the tar sands industry.

There are at least four avenues for applying such pressure to the industry support system. I call them institutional disruption, delegitimization, anti-systemic escalation, and jurisdictional contestation. Each of these would serve to raise the cost of participating in the system, or at the very least, decrease the benefits of continuing that participation.

Institutional Disruption

Disruptive direct action is a central resource in the toolbox of any social movement. Frances Fox Piven, a noted social movement scholar, suggests that the potency of any popular protest is rooted in the capacity of people to disrupt social practices and institutions. Organized social systems provide a source of strength for elites, because they coordinate social action. However, these systems are also sources of vulnerability, because they depend on cooperation that could potentially be withdrawn. Piven highlights what she calls "the leverage inherent in interdependencies," which essentially means that the dominance of elites also involves a kind of dependence on non-elites, and hence a kind of vulnerability to resistance.[10] When people act to withdraw their cooperation from systems of interdependent power, they acquire what Piven calls "disruptive power": the power to bring systems to a stop, so that the institutions and practices that elites depend upon for their privileges come grinding to a halt, at least temporarily.

In the movement to shut down the tar sands, this sort of institutional disruption has been used extensively. At times, it has been used in primary targeting against leading corporations in the industry, such as in the Unist'ot'en Camp blockade, which has been attempting to protect Wet'suwet'en territory from the proposed Pacific Trail Pipeline, or the blockade of Enbridge's North Westover pump station (part of Enbridge's Line 9 Reversal pipeline project) near Hamilton, Ontario, in the summer of 2013—to name only two prominent examples. This disruption has also been used in the context of secondary targeting, as when Climate Justice London (Ontario) and other groups disrupted business in retail bank branches as part of the Indigenous Environmental Network and Rainforest Action Network's secondary targeting campaign against the Royal Bank of Canada, a leading financier of tar sands projects. My contention here is that the disruption of soft targets in the support system is both easier to carry out and, in many cases, likely to be more effective than disrupting pipeline and bitumen mining firms because it targets retailers like banks and gas stations, who court favourable brand images, and politicians holding campaign or public speaking events designed to reach out to the broader public. For these reasons, disruptive secondary targeting of support-system soft targets is, generally speaking, a more efficient use of scarce movement energies than disruptive primary targeting of the tar sands industry firms, even if at times the latter is also necessary or helpful.

Delegitimization

Delegitimization campaigns are a second tactical avenue in secondary targeting, and are also already in use in the movement to shut down the tar sands. To some extent, *any* public education campaign that tries to raise awareness of the adverse ecological, public health, or human and Indigenous rights impacts of the industry could be described as a delegitimization campaign. In the context of the secondary targeting approach, the most notable use of delegitimization in anti–tar sands activism is the launching of a campus-based divestment campaign in late 2012, which was modelled explicitly on the anti-apartheid campaign discussed above. Within a few months of being launched in the United States, students at over one hundred college and university campuses had embarked on divestment campaigns, demanding that school endowment and pension funds pull out of tar sands firms and projects. In the long run, these campaigns can pose a material threat to tar sands financing, as occurred in South Africa in the mid-1980s, while also having the immediate effect of calling the legitimacy of the entire industry into question. Other secondary targeting forms of delegitimization include attempts to expose and denounce any newspaper editorialist or news media pundit who promotes the industry as complicit in the industry's social and ecological crimes. Aggressive public denunciation campaigns, backed up by rigorous information and analysis, can help to ensure that the ideological promotion of the tar sands by key figures who influence public opinion carries a reputational cost, much the way support for apartheid did in the 1980s.

Anti-systemic Escalation

A third tactical avenue for secondary targeting is anti-systemic escalation, which is the attempt to take the outrage associated with a specific grievance and use it to encourage critical thinking about the wider system it is embedded in, and thus to promote a more generalized radicalization of the people involved. Many people may find themselves initially politicized by concern about the negative social or ecological impacts of the industry, such as pipeline projects that threaten public health or wildlife habitats. These concerns, which some might ridicule as simply Nimbyism (i.e., the famous "not in my backyard" mentality, questioning only the location and not the infrastructure), in fact have the potential to steer people towards a wider opposition to the industry itself.

This is possible if activists can effectively situate immediate issues in the context of an anti-systemic analysis. For instance, people who are concerned with things like pipelines, tailings ponds, or tanker transit routes should be encouraged to see these as mere symptoms of larger, systemic problems, like colonial domination and dispossession, capitalist exploitation, and the ecocide associated with economies built on fossil fuels. In so doing, the movement "raises the stakes" for support-system participants by using the conflict as an incubator of anti-systemic radicals who oppose not only the tar sands industry itself (which does not much care), but also *other* industries and the wider system they operate within. As with the previous tactics, the goal here is to simultaneously add material costs (and affect the cost/benefit calculus that determines the behaviour of elites) and foment popular disaffection and unrest.

Jurisdictional Contestation

The fourth avenue for secondary targeting I suggest is jurisdictional contestation, which is sometimes called "dual power." Generally speaking, jurisdictional contestation is the attempt to establish or assert the authority of institutions of popular autonomy, outside the framework of official systems of law and governance. Indigenous communities opposed to the tar sands have often, and quite rightly, contested the unilateral jurisdiction of the legislative, judicial, and regulatory institutions of the Canadian state to make decisions and rulings that crucially affect the welfare and rights of their communities. In contrast, they highlight their own traditional systems of governance and legal decision-making, which should have either shared or sole jurisdiction over key decisions, such as the approval of pipelines that cross their territories.

As important as the Indigenous form of jurisdictional contestation is, it is not the only form. People's Assemblies on Climate Justice have been held in dozens of cities and in several countries. These grassroots, community-based assemblies have brought together a wide range of stakeholders to engage in deliberations about the public interest as it relates to climate justice, including the struggle to shut down the tar sands. These assemblies *should* claim jurisdiction, along with Indigenous governance and legal systems, over crucial decisions that affect nothing less than the future of life on earth and that are now being made unilaterally by business and government elites. In particular, People's Assemblies on Climate Justice can be used to declare neighbourhoods or cities and towns to be tar sands–free zones, prohibiting pipeline projects, processing, or the sale and distribution of its products. The role of jurisdictional contestation in secondary targeting is analogous to that of anti-systemic escalation, in that it raises the stakes of various tar sands struggles by using them to launch more far-reaching challenges, not only to the industry but also to elite governance and unaccountable decision-making. Large-scale jurisdictional contestation can create a perception of uncertainty and unpredictability that weakens the appeal of the megaproject for would-be investors, thereby weakening the project's support system.

Conclusion

A secondary targeting approach, applied in a relentless and escalating way, with a gradually broadening base of public participation, has a chance to prevail against the tar sands industry because it would pose a serious threat to its most vulnerable aspect, which is its support system of elite enablers in government, business, and the media. Probably the most difficult aspect of this project is the one that I have emphasized the least: the need to broaden the base of participation. But one of the crucial elements in this is not only to convince people of the importance of the issues, but to give them reason to believe that the movement might actually win.

Ultimately, our ability to map out the path to stopping the tar sands will remain partial and limited until movement participants and allies have engaged in the necessary process of in-depth, multi-stakeholder dialogue over a period of months and even years, while drawing in thousands of people from all walks of life. What I offer here is a preliminary contribution to these indispensable discussions, which are already underway,[11] in the belief that the process of tactical planning is itself a necessary precondition for winning. Serious conversations about how we can win are by their very nature steps along the path to possible victory.

From the Tar Sands to "Green Jobs"?

Work and Ecological Justice

●

GREG ALBO AND LILIAN YAP

•

The ecological and social implications of climate change have—or should—become a central parameter for all discussions of work and capitalism. It is generally agreed that reliance on the burning of fossil fuels as the pre-eminent energy source for production and consumption over the history of capitalism is the critical factor in the ruinous greenhouse gas emissions triggering global warming, which would become irreversible if the earth's atmosphere were brought to a "tipping point," typically set at 2°C.[1] The unrelenting build-up of greenhouse gases has led to the jarring conclusion, drawn by climatologists, ecological militants, and union activists, that an exit from reliance on fossil fuels for energy needs to occur with some urgency.

In Canada, the hyper-development of the Alberta tar sands, as well as the intensifying exploitation of both conventional and unconventional fossil fuel deposits across the country, has opened a major political divide over climate change strategies and their implications for work.[2] On the one side, the oil industry, governments, and many workers in the oil and gas sectors have sought to lock in further tar sands development. They have argued that this could be done through a strategy of carbon intensity (more output per unit of carbon emitted from fossil fuels burned), by "green growth" and a range of "market ecology" measures to shift consumer behaviour towards energy saving. On the other side, many Aboriginal nations and ecological and labour organizations have pushed for a transition to an "ecologically sustainable" economy built around "green" technologies, a renewable energy regime, and "green jobs" that would "de-carbonize" production processes. (For the Aboriginal nations, this also could involve reclamation, if on an entirely different foundation, of traditional territories and economies.) This could be accomplished, it is argued, through "Keynesian-style" public policies that build non-market institutions that embed and guide capitalist markets along a more sustainable and equitable growth path—in effect, an "institutional ecology."[3]

For reasons of both theoretical clarity and the political injunction to address climate change, the varied strategies for "greening work" need dissection. If levels of carbon emissions are to be stabilized, it will be necessary to not be limited by plans acceptable to the capitalist classes and their interest in endless accumulation. An ambitious vision of possible eco-socialist alternatives for Canada needs, we argue, to connect the restructuring of work to wider transformations in the socio-ecological system. This is a key task of the growing movement, in Canada and globally, to stop the tar sands and stand for climate justice.

Work and Capitalism

To make earth an object of huckstering—the earth which is our one and all, the first condition of our existence—was the last step towards making oneself an object of huckstering.[4]

—Friedrich Engels

The current societal addiction to fossil fuels is intimately tied to the dynamics of capitalist production and the exploitative nature of work. Although it is true that humans have always had to labour, and through this interact with and transform nature in order to reproduce themselves as social, cultural, and natural beings, these interactions take on particular characteristics in capitalist society. What, then, are these characteristics? Historically, the loss of direct access to nature—in particular, land—as a means for producers to gain their subsistence for reproducing their households has had important consequences for labour and social life. Understanding some of these peculiar dynamics of capitalism will help us evaluate the possibilities and limits of green work.

Capitalist social relations are characterized by a general situation in which the producing class is stripped of all non-market means of reproduction. That is, workers are market dependent and must sell their labour-power to a capitalist for a wage, with the earnings then used to buy the necessities of life now sold as commodities in the market. Labouring has become the forced commodified labour—or work—of capitalist societies. In turn, capitalists appropriate all of the products and the value realized from the sale of commodities, including any surplus they can earn in the form of profits after their costs are met.

Here, the market mediates the collective interaction and metabolism with nature that occurs with capitalist production. For each individual capitalist, the primary goal of investment and production is to realize profits, rather than satisfying human needs consistent with ecological sustainability. In this sense, both workers and nature are brought into the production process simply as input—as a means to another's end.[5] In this process, workers lose control over the products of their labour, the labour process itself, and the interaction with nature that this entails. In short, work within capitalism is, at its core, an experience of exploitation and alienation. As the social surplus that results from production is owned privately, decisions on the direction of investment (say, to move from fossil fuels to solar power) also lie in private hands, rather than involving the workers affected or being democratically decided.

The intrinsic character of capitalism means that "competitive imperatives" compel capitalist firms to constantly attempt to lower the costs of production to earn the profits necessary for the accumulation of capital that ensures their survival. To do so, and to increase the value they appropriate, firms try to increase the length and intensity of the workday, lower wages, and increase the productivity of labour through technological development. This last implies using less labour for the same or more output. To maintain or even increase employment with technological advancement, then, the market must grow (or, for an individual firm, at least its market share must increase).[6] Fossil fuels have been decisive: they have been the key energy enabler of the machinery necessary for the continual, 24/7 production and consumption cycles characteristic of capitalism. Indeed, it is in this fusion that the particular "space-time" dynamic of capitalist production consolidates in the unremitting effort to unhinge accumulation from nature and the constraints of material time and space, in the pursuit of abstract exchange-value in the form of money.[7]

Similarly, demands for better wages, working conditions, or environmental quality all increase the costs of production. Within capitalist social relations, these demands can only be met through lowering profits or—wait for it—more technological change and growth. What we see, then, is that the pursuit of growth becomes the preferred way of mediating social and distributional conflicts necessarily engendered in capitalist production without also changing its underlying social property relationships. This apparent solution, however, raises further contradictions. The unrelenting quest for economic growth causes the unsustainable deployment of fossil fuels, leading to climate change, the degradation of wildlife habitats, mountains of waste, and a host of other socio-ecological issues. In this sense, capitalist growth displaces the conflicts over work and income through time into nature, via the build-up of ecological crises, and into space, in the form of the unequal relations between states and peoples in the world market.

It is this context of the capitalist growth imperative, with all of its social and ecological impacts, that proposals for "green growth" through policies of "market ecology," and for "green jobs" by an "institutional ecology," can best be understood. Each has stood for an alternate path—within capitalism—out of both the climate crisis and the economic stagnation that has gripped the world market since 2008.

Green Growth and Market Ecology

Some may be surprised to see how the economic crisis has reinvigorated neo-liberal politics (of freer markets to increase the profits and power of capital) in the form of a strategy of "permanent austerity" imposed on the public sector and workers. An agenda of "green growth" to address climate change, best laid out in the United Nations Environment Programme's (UNEP) *Towards a Green Economy,* and the UN report for the 2012 Rio+20 summit, *Working*

Towards a Balanced and Inclusive Green Economy,[8] has emerged as a core feature of neo-liberal renewal.

The environmental crisis, the reports contend, is fundamentally a problem of a "gross misallocation of capital."[9] The full suite of neo-liberal proposals, now with a "market ecology" twist, are offered: removal of subsidies in agriculture; privatization of public utilities to impose market discipline and prices; public-private partnerships with full-cost recovery in the guise of "polluter pays" pricing; leveraging "green" private investment to rebuild with carbon-reducing public infrastructure; and the promotion of free trade and intellectual property rights to encourage trade and growth in "green" products and technology transfer, to name but a few. Remarkably, in light of the financial crisis, they propose to encourage more financialization—that is, the predominance of financial markets in driving carbon reduction investments through the development of "green" financial instruments. For instance, the insurance industry, given its experience with managing risks in general, is now touted as the best driver of the "green economy," given its capacity to "price in" environmental risks. This will, so the market logic goes, encourage preventative measures and shift relative prices favourably towards "green" production.

In a striking example of market fetishism, more prices and more markets are proposed. Nature and pollution are put forward as new zones of accumulation, with the state facilitating the creation of markets and property rights where none existed before. With more complete and transparent markets, capitalist growth will be "greener," and an energy transition from fossil fuels towards renewables will "naturally" occur via firm responses to more efficient price signals. "Green jobs" will follow in due course. The market imperatives that drive capital accumulation and carbon emissions are now offered up, without any sense of paradox or doubt, as the solution to the climate crisis.

"Green Jobs" and Institutional Ecology

The long-standing failure of "protecting the environment through privatizing it" has led many environmental and labour organizations to take a different tack. Instead, they have focused on "green jobs" resulting from a "green" restructuring of the capital stock (not the ownership or control of industry) and a change in government policies (not a democratization of the state). The landmark UN report *Green Jobs: Towards Decent Work in a Sustainable, Low-Carbon World* defines "green jobs" as "work in agricultural, manufacturing, research and development (R&D), administrative, and service activities that contribute substantially to preserving or restoring environmental quality."[10] The criterion of being a "decent" job also needs to be met to be considered a "green job." Like other such reports, *Green Jobs* urges a mix of stronger public investment and regulation with market-based policy instruments: carbon markets; payment for ecosystem services schemes; eco-taxes; and redirection of incentives and subsidies from "dirty" to "green" industries.

Since the economic crisis, this "institutional ecology" project is associated with the idea of a "Green New Deal," as part of a Keynesian stimulus package to tackle economic stagnation.[11] Government stimulus funds, for example, could be mobilized to build the infrastructure for a transition to renewable—solar, wind, biofuels—energy and other "green" sectors rather than further lock in a high-carbon infrastructure. The Green New Deal also commonly includes: support for research and development into energy- and resource-efficient technologies; upgrading public infrastructure and building "smart grids"; retrofitting buildings; and expanding public transportation. Such "green" sectors, moreover, will tend to be relatively labour intensive and thus create more jobs than investment in "traditional" sectors. The basic idea is encouraging "green jobs" via "green growth" (as with the "market ecology" project of the neo-liberals) as a central means of transitioning to a low-carbon economy.

These policies certainly modify some of the most ecologically abusive features of capitalist production. For the most part, they merit support for at least "doing something." But there are also serious limitations. Note, for example, that according to the UNEP definition, oil spills from pipelines carrying diluted bitumen (or "dilbit") from the tar sands could lead to a *rise* in "green jobs," because employment in environmental remediation counts as "green" employment. The quantitative growth in "green jobs" may not be a proxy for anything more than coping with the ecological consequences of capitalist production—the so-called "shades of green" jobs problem—and the inability to actually address climate change.

Although the *Green Jobs* report argues that investment in "green" sectors would lead to a net gain in employment, a low-carbon economy would have an adverse effect on employment in industries such as oil and gas extraction.

Workers displaced by climate change mitigation policies would thus require the support of "active labour market policies," such as skills retraining, education upgrades, temporary income support, and the like. Such a "just transition" would help workers in carbon-based industries to gain employment in emerging "green" sectors. A number of the "green jobs" reports also suggest that revenues from imposing various eco-taxes might be used to reduce payroll taxes (such as the employer contribution to social security) in order to boost employment. This would produce, they suggest, a "double dividend" of achieving both employment and environmental gains.[12]

It is clearly suspect for a "just transition" to cut taxes on employers and then fund income support out of "pollution," and to adhere to neo-liberal fallacies that unemployment is a result of the high cost of labour (and thus workers can be "priced" back into employment). Indeed, the initial *Green Jobs* report even took up the concept of "flexicurity," implicitly accepting the neo-liberal push for labour flexibility with its intent on increasing the precariousness of work and weakening unions.

To add to the confusion of the meaning of "green jobs," there is often a recognition in these reports that a significant portion of the jobs found within "green" sectors are informal, non-unionized jobs with poor working conditions. They cannot meet the test of decent work. This is particularly true of the recycling industry in the Global South—for instance, the informal work of waste pickers, or electronics recycling in China. A recent World Bank report circumvents the issue by simply arguing that the requirement of decent work should not be applied to the developing world when planning for "green jobs," as even near-subsistence wages might contribute to "poverty reduction."[13] The International Labour Organization, in contrast, tends to consider how low wages and poor working conditions are actually what constitute the poverty of these workers. They call for the formalization of these "green" sectors so as to improve working conditions and transform these into decent jobs.[14] Similar problems are, in fact, common to "green jobs" in core capitalist zones.

In any case, efforts to improve workers' rights, wages, and ecological sustainability run up against the competitive imperatives to lower the costs of production. Without substantial, long-term, extra-market institutional (or state) coordination, it is quite unclear what can be achieved, beyond stimulating initial modest investments in renewable energy and adjustments in regulatory rules. This has been the case even in something as basic as the informal recycling sector. If the transition to decent and "green" jobs cannot be achieved through market mechanisms, then the entire "institutional ecology" project of leveraging the private sector for an exit from the climate crisis will fail. Even with a fundamental break with austerity-friendly fiscal policies and new eco-taxes, substantial collective investments and non-market interventions would be necessary to generate and maintain decent "green jobs."

In this sense, the "institutional ecology" path to "green jobs" shares a great deal with the "market ecology" agenda in depending upon capitalist sector–led growth. If the "only" problem is environmental impact, so the logic of both goes, then it is possible to continue to encourage growth as long as the ecological footprint is reduced. And capital accumulation can be "decoupled" from more intensive resource use through more efficient markets and technological improvement, *including the burning of fossil fuels*. Yet more growth within capitalism has consistently resulted in greater aggregate resource use and carbon emissions, even when relative gains in resource and energy efficiency are achieved.[15] And even the most optimistic scenarios raise serious doubts that, in a long phase of stagnation, continued capitalist growth can be consistent with greenhouse gas reductions. In short, these are technical "solutions" to a broader social problem. These "solutions" to climate change are, to be sure, also *political* strategies defending particular interests.[16]

Carbon Reduction and Environmental Justice Alternatives

The energy sector poses, in the starkest terms, the limits of the "green economy" within capitalism. Rather than lead a transition towards renewable energy as "price signals" register peak oil, the market has increased supply in "extreme energy," with a systemic market failure to register carbon emission constraints. Indeed, the International Energy Agency now refers to a new "golden age of gas" as reported fossil fuel supplies swell.[17] Under current usage patterns, even by 2040, up to 75 per cent of all energy could still be supplied by fossil fuels,[18] provided that the industry overcomes obstacles such as finite freshwater supplies. Canadian oil and gas companies would, of course, be central contributors to the supply. At some 173 billion barrels of recoverable oil (and an ultimate potential of 343 billion barrels), the Alberta tar sands are generally considered to be the second-largest deposit in the world.[19] With conventional oil production in decline, tar sands bitumen now constitutes more than half of production and will continue to increase (and, of course, serves as the single largest source of carbon emissions in Canada). In other words, the projected burning of these reserves for energy would easily breach the 2°C global warming distress threshold that many organizations have highlighted.

The massive capital investment in fossil fuel extraction, further intensified with extreme energy, means that employment in these operations is slight—the lowest of any sector in Canada—relative to output and emissions. Estimates for global employment in the sector are only at about ten million jobs worldwide. In Canada, employment is about 120,000 jobs, including fossil fuel extraction, coal, and petroleum manufacturing products and support activities, or well less than 1 per cent of total employment, with tar sands employment assessed at around 20,000 jobs (with totals expected to increase with new developments).[20] The numbers employed directly in extraction are even less: a large portion of employment occurs in planning and development, construction, and servicing sites. If many of these jobs are well paid, they are also surprisingly precarious and insecure, as projects and output volumes wind up and down, and they have come to include a "second tier" of migrant workers with limited rights. The shift to renewables is likely, in almost all forecasts, to have a positive impact on employment during both construction and steady-state operations due to the lower capital intensity. But this should not be exaggerated (as renewables producers do), as this is still quite capital-intensive production. A shift to renewable energy is a solution to neither the general problem of unemployment in capitalism, nor to the employment instability resulting from climate change.

The political imaginary of a climate justice movement cannot be confined, therefore, to a market-led energy transition, whether spurred by further institutional coordination or not. It can become a vital example of societal political alliances co-joining in programmatic alternatives. At the scale of the workplace, this struggle has formed around the notion of a just transition. As noted above, this is set narrowly as retraining policies for workers as fossil fuel extraction is phased down and workers shift to indeterminate prospects elsewhere in the economy. Workers and communities adjust as the capitalist classes shift to value extraction in new "green" sectors. A more ambitious just transition would extend workers' collective rights and point towards new socio-ecological relations[21]—that is, a militant rejection of the quantitative commodification of nature and life, for a transition to qualitative growth in de-carbonized and de-commodified sectors of production and work.

Such an "eco-imaginary" is a rupture with the chase after "green jobs" in a thoroughly commodified society. It could inform specific interventions at the scale of workplaces and building workers' collective capacities, such as:

- the incorporation of carbon-reduction strategies within collective agreements through clauses on reductions of the carbon footprint, energy committees, and adjustment plans for jobs affected by climate change;
- workers' plans forged to extend best practices for carbon reduction in labour processes and between workplaces;
- building democratic planning capacities for plant conversion to sustain capital equipment, workers' skills, and community infrastructure as ecologically responsible production norms are internalized; and
- participatory planning structures built at the level of local wards for carbon reduction and ecological clean-up in neighbourhoods.

An energy transition extends beyond particular labour processes, and the fossil fuel branches of production, to the energy sector as a whole.[22] In providing the general conditions facilitating production and consumption, the energy sector tends to be both highly concentrated and monopolistic, as well as highly decentralized and diversified. An energy transition entails concerns not only with the phasing out of fossil fuel production (and immediate limits on extreme energy, such as the tar sands) and the reversal of the neo-liberal privatization of power supplies. It also needs to be conceived in terms of "*energy democracy*": public ownership and control; diversity, decentralization, and localization in production and control; and transparency and accountability in ecological impacts.[23] For the most part, renewable energy production also fails miserably on all these accounts.

Here, energy conservation and renewable technological conversion need to link to "structural reforms" that push beyond capital,[24] such as:

- the democratization and participatory planning over centralized energy production and supply systems;

- a reduction in the massive capital intensity involved in fossil fuel and nuclear production to give developmental preference to a diversity of direct and local production;
- redistributive energy supply and pricing strategies; and
- publicly supported technological transfer to equalize renewable energy access globally.

If it is quite wrong to expect climate change to be resolved by more markets and more technology, it also cannot be limited to an energy transition. Some have recognized and challenged these limitations, however. In its response to climate change, the International Transport Workers' Federation put out a remarkable statement advising that "there is no alternative but to progressively liberate key sectors of economic life from the imperatives of profit and consumption ... [and to expand] social and democratic ownership of industries that produce emissions ... to prevent further damage to people and the environment and to plan an equitable and orderly transition to a low carbon economy."[25] This ecological directive is consistent with the long-standing socialist case for de-commodified production in an egalitarian world order. The core left program is also strikingly carbon reducing in its implications:

- a sharp reduction in standard work time, to share out work and increase the time for democracy and self-management of workplaces;
- a shift from private to public transit in electrified systems tied to "transit justice" and "free fares";
- the extension of de-commodified public spaces in terms of parks, museums, galleries, and other cultural and recreational spaces;
- the mass public expansion of the caring sectors;
- the universalization of free post-secondary education for all age groups;
- the dismantling of military production and mobilization of civil brigades for ecological restoration.

These demands could easily be extended.[26] They should be at the centre of any ecological justice movement. In practical outline, they present a possible future directly connecting a de-carbonized energy regime to quality-intensive, democratized work, and from there to the provisions of everyday life as social need. They are essential to overcoming the claims the neo-liberal period has had on our political imaginary, even in activist circles, and the claptrap of carbon markets and "greening growth."

Beyond Green Jobs

An alternate agenda for the democratization of work, and over the production and supply of energy, is ecologically necessary and economically feasible. Significant political hurdles exist, however.

The fossil fuel energy regime has been integral, we have argued, to capitalist development and is embedded in the entire economic structure, from energy to transportation to plastics to agro-industry and all else. In Canada, the entire spectrum of energy corporations is a central component of the power structure, with the financial industry intricately linked to the financing, insurance, and speculative interests of the oil and gas sector. The Canadian state, moreover, has had a central strategic objective for over three decades of turning Canada into the pre-eminent twenty-first-century energy superpower, steadily building the Canadian accumulation regime around this prospect. This strategy entails running down conventional oil and gas resources and increasing the exploitation of "extreme energy" via drilling in the Arctic and deep seas, fracking for shale gas, "tight oil" recovery, and, of course, the mass mining of the tar sands. As a result, climate change policies in Canada have been all but completely absent. Alternate decentralized energy development, on the one hand, and democratically controlled public power provision, on the other, have been wholly lacking in coordinated state support.

Divestment from fossil fuels is a necessary condition for stabilizing greenhouse gas emissions, and thus a core demand of the climate justice movement. It is politically inconceivable to isolate a transition out of fossil fuels from a project of democratizing the state and a vision of a post-capitalist society. The ecological crisis is deeply intertwined with the modes of energy usage internal to the production and consumption patterns of contemporary capitalism—endless accumulation and overconsumption alongside hideous inequalities, the environment served up as a dumping ground for industrial waste, the ceaseless commodification of agriculture spaces and wetlands. The massive destruction of the boreal forest for the toxic mines of the Alberta tar sands is only the most visible and violent landscape produced by this mode of development.

Anti–fossil fuel campaigns, however, too often remain confined within the market logic of the "green economy," trading off a measure of ecological remediation for more capital accumulation. Any number of the market-based policies to address global warming commit this folly—through carbon emissions trading, feed-in tariffs, conversion tax incentives, and so forth. The notion of shifting "brown work" into "green jobs" suffers from the equally debilitating illusion that climate change might be technocratically managed by supplementing market pricing with a few "green" institutional supports, without any rupture in the existing matrix of political institutions and social forces. These ideological confusions about markets and technological fixes too often provide cover for further tar sands development, as deftly utilized in the propaganda bombardment from the Canadian oil and gas industry.

It is *capitalism as a system* that is the central obstacle in the transition to ecologically responsible production, work, and energy regimes.[27] Marx pointed out in the *Grundrisse* that capitalism has a general disdain for nature apart from the use-values it can appropriate (and the accumulation regime in Canada particularly commits this sin). And this contempt extends to workers apart from the value their labour produces: "For the first time, nature becomes purely an object for humankind, purely a matter of utility ... whether as an object of consumption or as a means of production."[28] This arises not from whim or malice on the part of individual capitalists, even if overt scheming and greed have always characterized the oil industry. It emerges from the competitive imperatives to maximize profits and thus to continually annihilate space (as both natural and built environments) by the acceleration of time through productivity enhancement (enabled by the energy from fossil fuels).[29] The accumulation of capital is, historically and to this day, the accumulation of carbon in the earth's atmosphere.

In the urgency to tackle climate change and to halt the extraction of the most destructive fossil fuel source on the planet, there is a normal inclination to take the detour of "market ecology" and "green work" in the hope of preventing further damage. But the political calculation of ecologists, unionists, and socialists needs to be as ambitious as the challenges at hand are large. This is to insist that a rupture with the existing paradigm of production and work is needed—"ways of living" as the early ecology and socialist movements envisioned. Solar communism, anyone?

Tar Sands, Extreme Energy, and the Future of the Climate Movement

●

BRIAN TOKAR

●

Efforts by TransCanada and Enbridge to transport increasing quantities of tar sands bitumen across North America emerged at a crucial juncture in the evolution of our movements to confront the global climate crisis. For activists in both the US and Canada, the further development of the Alberta tar sands represents an unusually clear convergence of environmental and social justice concerns, and the popular response shows how today's actions may help halt the destabilization of the climate. Campaigns to stop the tar sands pipelines have highlighted the wider significance of an array of local organizing efforts and reignited hopes for a more unified movement for climate justice. Perhaps most remarkably, organizing around the tar sands has helped reverse the trend towards increasing despair among climate activists that had emerged following the diplomatic failure of the 2009 Copenhagen climate conference.

Public actions for the climate had reached an initial peak in 2009, as large numbers of people demonstrated their hopes for a positive outcome to the UN climate negotiations in Copenhagen in December of that year. In the United States, large environmental NGOs launched a wave of outreach efforts and public actions aimed at convincing the Obama administration to play a constructive role in Copenhagen. The group 350.org, launched by Bill McKibben and several of his former students from Middlebury College, held the first in a series of coordinated worldwide demonstrations aimed at dramatizing the need to reduce atmospheric carbon dioxide to a concentration of 350 parts per million. A flawed but politically significant climate bill—establishing a "cap-and-trade" carbon market to nominally reduce greenhouse emissions—passed the US House of Representatives, and a counterpart bill was being drafted by prominent senators.

Additionally, a loose alliance of grassroots groups—many of which were highly critical of the proposed cap-and-trade legislation—mounted a series of demonstrations across the US and Canada highlighting a justice-centred approach to the climate crisis, focused on the widely disparate impacts of global climate disruptions on communities marginalized by factors of race and class. North American activists took the first steps towards forging a homegrown movement inspired by the global outlook of "climate justice" that was beginning to unite a disparate but politically significant alliance of civil society movements from around the world. These included Indigenous and other land-based peoples from the Global South, racial and environmental justice activists in North America, and explicitly anti-capitalist formations, mainly European, which had emerged from mobilizations challenging global institutions such as the World Trade Organization, NATO, and the annual G8 summits.[1]

By the middle of 2010, however, many of these efforts had reached a point of impasse. The Copenhagen conference only produced a three-page "accord" urging countries to submit voluntary pledges to reduce their emissions, and the US delegation had played a central role in promoting this inadequate substitute for binding emissions reductions.[2] The climate debate in the US Senate was aborted as soon as it became clear that even the most extravagant corporate exemptions and giveaways would not break the political deadlock around "cap-and-trade."[3] 350 continued to organize numerous simultaneous symbolic events each year, but had not yet articulated a strategy for challenging the fossil fuel interests mainly responsible for rising emissions. And the fledgling North American Mobilization for Climate Justice ceased to operate once it was apparent that various community groups struggling with the daily impacts of political and economic marginalization lacked the capacity—and perhaps the inclination—to help lead a unified national effort. On a global scale, the development of a comprehensive climate justice movement after Copenhagen "remained something more of a potential than a reality," in the words of two prominent European activists.[4]

In the shadow of these political and organizational disappointments, proposals for new tar sands pipelines soon shattered North American activists' temporary malaise and rekindled a sense of urgency and outrage. The tar sands issue drove thousands of people back into action, and began to reawaken the potential for a more unified and assertive climate movement, driven in part by a new wave of corporate assaults on the integrity of ecosystems and human communities all across the continent.

By early 2013, tens of thousands of people had demonstrated in Washington, DC, against the proposed tar sands pipelines, including twelve hundred people arrested for civil disobedience in front of the White House and nearly forty thousand people at the largest Washington climate rally so far. Nearly thirty towns in Vermont and other states across the region were on record against the Eastern Access pipeline option, which would pump tar sands bitumen out of Montreal and across northern New England to be shipped out of Portland, Maine. Indigenous opposition to the proposed Northern Gateway pipeline in British Columbia helped galvanize a nationwide popular uprising of First Nations peoples across Canada. And an improbable alliance of conservative landowners and autonomous direct actionists had dramatically escalated the movement to halt the construction of TransCanada's Keystone XL pipeline through Kansas, Oklahoma, and Texas.

Extreme Energy

Central to all these developments was the growing continent-wide movement to stop further development of the tar sands. Activists across the continent are drawn to the tar sands issue for a variety of reasons. First and foremost are the uniquely severe climate consequences. Mining and extracting oil from the tar sands releases three to four and a half times more carbon dioxide into the atmosphere than conventional oil extraction, and the eminent climatologist James Hansen estimates that Alberta's tar sands contain as much as 240 gigatons of carbon, enough to raise the atmospheric CO_2 concentration by an additional 120 parts per million.[5] A close second is the destruction of the land, waterways, and livelihoods of First Nations peoples in the Athabasca region of Alberta, the focus of numerous inspiring efforts of Indigenous nations throughout western Canada to challenge new extraction and pipeline developments.

Another factor, perhaps less directly apparent but of profound economic and political significance, is the understanding that the tar sands are one central aspect of a larger trend towards "extreme energy" developments throughout North America. As author Michael Klare, a long-time analyst of energy geopolitics, points out, most current efforts to tap new sources of oil and gas require energy companies "to drill in extreme temperatures or extreme weather, or use extreme pressures, or operate under extreme danger—or some combination of all of these."[6] With readily accessible sources of oil and gas reaching their limits worldwide, industry projections for the future of fossil fuels are increasingly tied to so-called "unconventional" sources, such as tar sands, shale gas, and oil drilled from miles beneath the oceans, including the far reaches of the Arctic.

Now that oil prices have reached eighty to one hundred dollars per barrel, technologies such as hydro-fracturing (also known as fracking), horizontal drilling, deepwater drilling, and oil extraction from tar sands—once seen as hypothetically possible but economically prohibitive—have become central to the fossil fuel industry's plans for the future. Each of these has profound implications for the people and ecosystems affected by new energy developments, and each has sparked determined opposition from frontline communities. Just as the scale of destruction in Alberta today provides an important lens on one possible future for energy in North America and worldwide, the breadth of organizing efforts to halt tar sands development helps us envision the potential for a renewed climate justice movement.

A few short years ago, many climate activists and advocates for local self-reliance looked to the arrival of "peak oil" as a reason for confidence that the fossil fuel era might end before reaching its maximum impact on the climate. Now, however, an unexpected North American energy boom threatens to extend the Age of Oil far past the point of total destabilization of the climate system. With known worldwide fossil fuel reserves already containing at least five times as much CO_2 as can be burned without exceeding the long-term carbon budget projected by climate scientists, it is clear why James Hansen has described the further development of the tar sands as a "game over" scenario for the earth's climate system.[7]

The current oil boom, which is entirely driven by "extreme energy" technologies, has made the United States a net exporter of refined petroleum for
the first time in at least six decades. Not only has the US begun exporting oil
to Canada, but so many Gulf of Mexico refineries have retooled their facilities
to accommodate tar sands bitumen and other sources of heavy oil that much
of the light crude unearthed by hydro-fracking and horizontal drilling operations could end up being exported. North Dakota alone is currently producing 85 per cent as much oil—of significantly higher quality—as the volume
of material that would be piped from Canada by Keystone XL.[8] Further,
prices for natural gas have plunged to near-record lows due to the massive
increase in gas supplies from the Marcellus Shale formation in the East and
several other major shale basins across the US. Not only has this discouraged
US utilities from investing in new coal and nuclear power plants, as the sheer
quantity of fracked gas overturns the traditional economics of the electric
power industry, but it could threaten continuing investments in solar- and
wind-powered generation as well.[9]

Resisting Extreme Energy

Over the past couple of years, campaigns to resist new "extreme energy"
developments have arisen all across the US and Canada. The movement to
resist the continued exploitation of the tar sands is one primary source of
inspiration. Another is the movement in the coal-mining regions of southern
Appalachia to resist the most extreme form of strip mining for coal, whereby
some five hundred mountaintops have literally been blasted away to expose
the coal seams below.

As the practice of "mountaintop-removal" coal mining has expanded
over the past decade, the region has experienced an unprecedented alliance
between long-time local residents—many from families that have worked
in the coal mines for generations—and youthful forest activists from across
the country. Organizations such as Coal River Mountain Watch, Rising Tide,
Climate Ground Zero, and Mountain Justice have transcended long-standing
cultural, political, and even religious divides, and brought hundreds of new
activists into coal-mining regions of West Virginia and neighbouring states
for summer action camps, days-long marches, and other creative actions.[10]
The coal campaigns have helped revive the tactic of long-term tree-sits,

pioneered by Earth First activists in Oregon and northern California, and more recently adopted, with some new twists, by those seeking to block the construction of the Keystone XL pipeline in Texas and Oklahoma.[11] A national campaign launched by the Sierra Club has helped halt the construction of at least 174 new coal-fired power plants, and activists in the US Northwest are working to stop the construction of several proposed new coal export terminals.[12]

People in rural areas of Pennsylvania and New York State have been organizing to challenge the practice of fracking for shale gas, which has expanded rapidly throughout the Marcellus Shale region. For many years, representatives of gas drilling companies were able to pressure individual landowners into signing leases, exploiting a lack of public awareness of the consequences of gas fracking. But as drilling rigs have sprouted throughout much of the region, and reports of severe water and land contamination have followed, the resistance has begun to assume the character of a growing regional movement.[13] In New York, efforts to protect drinking-water supplies for major cities led to a temporary moratorium on fracking, and the issue has brought thousands of people to demonstrate at the state capitol in Albany to demand a complete ban. In 2012, the Vermont legislature approved a ban on fracking, an idea that activists hope to extend throughout the region.

Fracking and horizontal drilling for oil and gas have also provoked increasing opposition in many western US states. People in Utah, Colorado, and central California have challenged the opening of previously protected public lands for drilling, and one campaign successfully delayed plans to auction off leases to drill for gas on more than twenty thousand acres in Colorado. The federal Bureau of Land Management withdrew plans to drill in several environmentally sensitive areas in Colorado following protests, including locations near Dinosaur National Monument and Mesa Verde National Park.[14] Iñupiat communities in Alaska have been at the forefront of opposition to oil drilling in newly navigable but uniquely hazardous Arctic waters, and environmentalists across the continent breathed a sigh of relief when Shell Oil withdrew its damaged drilling vessels from Alaskan waters in early 2013.[15]

First Nations communities have also been at the forefront of challenging plans to expand uranium mining in the US Southwest and across Canada. With an estimated 70 per cent of world uranium supplies located underneath

Indigenous lands, many communities are still experiencing health effects from radiation released during the first uranium boom of the 1970s and have vowed not to let it happen again. There are reportedly over a thousand abandoned uranium mines on Native lands in the American Southwest, where communities faced epidemics of cancer following the earlier wave of mining.[16] In Canada, plans to expand uranium mining have united opponents from Cree, Dene, Inuit, and other Indigenous peoples, from Quebec all the way to Nunavut in the Far North.[17]

It remains to be seen whether these efforts contain the seeds of a more unified opposition to extreme energy projects throughout North America. Each struggle has its distinctive qualities and unique challenges, and all of the legal, political, and personal issues faced by these campaigners can make it difficult to focus on broader alliance-building efforts. But it is clear that their stories are already having an essential catalytic effect on the broader climate movement, whose centres of gravity are often more urban and historically removed from the day-to-day realities of crucial resource-centred struggles.

Looking Forward

In an illuminating 2008 paper, political scientist John M. Meyer highlighted the chronic divide between traditionally paternalistic approaches to environmental issues—mobilizing expert knowledge to intervene to prevent harm—and a more populist outlook rooted in the experiences of those most affected by various forms of pollution.[18] Conventional climate discourses, with their emphasis on atmospheric modelling, the sensitivity of future climates to varying levels of greenhouse gas emissions, and relatively distant effects—whether in space or in time—tend to weigh towards the paternalist side of the spectrum. In contrast, many past environmental successes were firmly rooted in particular local experiences of air and water contamination, among other problems, which ultimately shaped state and national policies. The most effective campaigns for environmental justice rely on scientific analyses of various environmental hazards—as well as of the disproportionate exposures that are experienced as a function of race and class—but they are fundamentally populist in their campaign structures and organizing methods.

The emergence of struggles against extreme new energy developments throughout North America raises the potential for a transformed climate movement that similarly transcends this divide. Climate discourses that are wholly science- and policy-centred can raise the spectre of elitism and are often more readily defused in the public media by those who deny the reality of human-caused climate disruptions. In contrast, movements of people on the frontlines of extreme energy development give voice to the immediate human consequences of corporate practices that most threaten the climate. Just as earlier climate justice campaigns highlighted the voices of people around the world whose lives have been catastrophically altered by climate change, current movements help sustain a focus on the direct human consequences of new energy developments.

People everywhere are now seeing their lives upturned by extreme weather events, such as droughts, wildfires, floods, and more intense coastal storms. While marginalized communities continue to experience the most severe impacts, nearly everyone can now identify ways in which their lives are affected by climate change. In northern California, home of some of the most determined and inspired alliance-building work with environmental justice communities during the lead-up to Copenhagen, organizers have proposed a strategy of "finding your frontline"—in other words, highlighting the ways we are each personally affected as a means for aligning our activism with those who are affected the most. Reaching beyond traditional, sometimes paternalistic, modes of alliance building, they are striving to create relationships of mutual aid that challenge barriers of power, privilege, and trust, and strategically align climate activists' worldviews with those of the most affected communities.[19] Oakland's Movement Generation and other groups behind this approach challenge all who identify with climate justice to reach past their established organizing models and personal comfort zones to raise their solidarity work to an entirely new level.

A further dilemma still remains, however. While local organizing is central to movement building, how can it actually help curtail excess greenhouse pollution and prevent a slide into extreme global climate chaos? It may be too soon to tell, but we do know from the early history of the environmental movement that the most successful policy interventions are rarely orchestrated entirely from above. In the US, the federal government only began to consider meaningful environmental regulations in the early 1970s, after states and municipalities began to implement far-reaching programs of environmental monitoring and enforcement, and an unprecedented wave of environmental lawsuits challenged business as usual. It was only at that point, reported *Fortune* magazine on the eve of the first Earth Day in 1970, that elite business interests "strongly desire[d] the federal government to step in, set the standards, regulate all activities pertaining to the environment, and help finance the job with tax incentives."[20]

Indeed, the environmental regulations that are now frequently denounced as "bad for business" were once viewed in elite circles as a way to allay public concerns while offering corporations a menu of uniform and relatively predictable environmental rules. Two scholarly analyses of the failure of US climate legislation during Obama's first term correctly placed much of the blame on the alliance between business-friendly environmentalists and polluting corporations that crafted the first wave of "cap-and-trade" legislation.[21] Perhaps more adequate climate policies, like the first generation of anti-pollution rules, will emerge in response to local and regional campaigns that directly challenge corporate practices, rather than through a false compromise that largely neglects the interests of those most threatened by environmental hazards.

Of course, a successful social movement cannot be wholly defined by what it opposes. While people are coming forward in solidarity with communities affected by extreme weather and extreme energy developments, the movement is still a long way from convincing most North Americans of the depth of social transformation needed to prevent climate chaos. A variety of studies suggest that reductions in greenhouse pollution on the order of 2 to 3 per cent or more per year are necessary to avoid irreversible climate tipping points.[22] While energy use has been successfully decoupled from economic growth for limited periods of time, especially in the aftermath of the 1970s Arab oil embargo, it is highly unlikely that a successful climate mitigation strategy will be compatible with the levels of growth that are historically associated with economic prosperity and rising employment.[23]

This remains a significant obstacle to engaging those who remain wedded to the economics of growth. While promising proposals for "green jobs," a Green New Deal, and a just transition away from fossil fuels have been advanced by labour, business, and environmental groups alike, it is increasingly doubtful that we can reduce carbon dioxide emissions quickly enough without more fundamentally overturning the capitalist growth paradigm. It is also increasingly apparent that fears of impending crisis and catastrophe can

SHADIA FAYNE WOOD AND PROJECT SURVIVAL MEDIA

Five hundred youth from 138 countries express solidarity with the tar sands struggle during the Global Power Shift convergence in Istanbul, Turkey, 2013.

serve to increase many people's resistance to fundamental change. Indeed, a timely book by four US and Canadian authors shows how predictions of impending catastrophe throughout history have tended to derail the political left, empower right-wing scapegoating and militarism, and generally limit the potential of progressive social movements.[24]

During the first large wave of activism against nuclear power in North America, many activists merged an uncompromising call for "No Nukes" with a long-range vision of an entirely new social order, rooted in decentralized, solar-powered communities with the ability to decide both their energy future and their political future. Not only did that movement help end the 1970s wave of nuclear power development, but it developed a continent-wide network of decentralized, grassroots anti-nuclear alliances, committed to nonviolent direct action, bottom-up forms of internal organization, and a sophisticated understanding of the relationship between technological and social changes. The movement also helped facilitate the first significant wave of solar energy development, which was only derailed by the sudden withdrawal of public funds for renewable energy at the beginning of the Reagan administration in the US.

Similarly, today's climate activists need to find ways to dramatize the positive, even utopian, potentialities for a post-petroleum, post-suburban world. We know that the technical means exist, but also that private investors have expressed relatively little enthusiasm for renewable energy, despite numerous studies demonstrating its economic advantages.[25] We can't deny the potentially dire consequences of a chaotic, out-of-control climate regime, but it is also clear that today's movements will not be able to prevent a worst-case scenario unless we can also demonstrate a compelling vision of an enhanced quality of life, not dominated by competition and consumerism, that may be possible in a world of declining energy consumption.

Ernst Bloch, the eminent mid-twentieth-century chronicler of the utopian tradition, authored an exhaustive and free-ranging three-volume work, *The Principle of Hope*, which takes readers on an epic journey through Western history's myriad expressions of the urge to transform society. Bloch explores the role of folktales, the arts, and literature, along with political and social activists' perennial search for a better world. "Fraudulent hope is one of the greatest malefactors, even enervators of the human race," he wrote, while "concretely genuine hope its most dedicated benefactor."[26] As we further our strategies to raise climate awareness, resist extreme energy, forge new alliances, and challenge the inordinate political influence of the fossil fuel industry, the future of the climate movement may also depend on how well we can embody a forward-looking and even hopeful vision for the future.

Acknowledgements

Our deep gratitude to Amanda Crocker and Between the Lines for their tremendous support throughout the entire course of this project. We are also grateful to Jessie Hale for her meticulous editorial work. Finally, we wish to thank all of our comrades and friends who patiently gave feedback and advice in the shaping of this book and the writing within it, and the organizers who held us accountable to our stated vision.

The following chapters have been adapted from previous publications:

"Assembling Consent in Alberta: Hegemony and the Tar Sands" by Randolph Haluza-DeLay has been revised from an article in the *Journal for Activism in Science & Technology Education*, 4(1), 2012.

"Canadian Diplomatic Efforts to Sell the Tar Sands" by Yves Engler has been revised from an excerpt from his book *The Ugly Canadian: Stephen Harper's Foreign Policy* (RED/Fernwood, 2012).

"Canada's Eastward Pipelines: A Corporate Export Swindle, Confronted by Cross-Country Resistance" by Martin Lukacs has been revised and expanded from an article that appeared in *The Guardian* in August 2013.

"Awaiting Justice: The Ceaseless Struggle of the Lubicon Cree" by Melina Laboucan-Massimo has been revised from an article that appeared in *Briarpatch Magazine* in February 2012.

"Culture Works" by Christine Leclerc and Rex Weyler has been adapted from the introduction to *The Enpipe Line: 70,000+ kilometres of poetry written in resistance to the Enbridge Northern Gateway Pipelines proposal* (Creekstone Press, 2012).

"Labour Faces Keystone XL and Climate Change" by Jeremy Brecher and the Labor Network for Sustainability has been revised from an article that appeared in *New Labor Forum* in January/February 2013.

"The Rise of the Native Rights–Based Strategic Framework" by Clayton Thomas-Muller has been revised from an article that appeared in *Canadian Dimension* in May 2013.

"Expanding the Fossil Fuel Resistance" by Bill McKibben has been revised from an article that appeared in *Rolling Stone* in April 2013.

Notes

Klein and McKibben, Foreword

1 Oil Sands Truth, oilsandstruth.org.
2 James Hansen, "Game Over for the Climate," *New York Times*, May 9, 2012, accessed July 20, 2013, www.nytimes.com/2012/05/10/opinion/game-over-for-the-climate.html.

Weis, Black, D'Arcy, and Russell, Introduction

1 In this context, "frontline" means people and communities who are the most impacted by injustice, and who are self-organized and engaged in struggles to improve their conditions. Because capital tends to locate the burden of pollution in highly inequitable ways—among politically marginalized populations—it means that the frontlines of environmental injustice tend to have racial, class, and international dimensions.
2 The environmental justice movement produced a historically important statement of principles during the First National People of Color Environmental Leadership Summit. See "Principles of Environmental Justice," www.ejnet.org/ej/principles.html.
3 Some of our primary political commitments include organizing with grassroots networks and movement servicing groups like Rising Tide North America and the Wildfire Project, in addition to our "day jobs" working in academia and for non-profits.
4 Industry and governments prefer to call bituminous reserves "oil sands" in an attempt to make them sound less different from conventional oil, but the term "tar sands" better reflects their physical character, and gives some indication of the additional resources and risks involved in transporting and refining this substance.
5 Christopher Hatch and Matt Price, *Canada's Toxic Tar Sands: The Most Destructive Project on Earth* (Toronto: Environmental Defence, 2008).
6 Tim McDonnell, "There's No Hiding From Tar Sands Oil," *Mother Jones*, December 15, 2011, accessed June 15, 2013, www.motherjones.com/environment/2011/12/theres-no-hiding-tar-sands-oil.
7 Greg Quinn, "Liepert Says Alberta Needs Many Outlets for Landlocked Oil," *Bloomberg News*, February 15, 2012, accessed October 31, 2013, www.businessweek.com/news/2012-02-15/liepert-says-alberta-needs-many-outlets-for-landlocked-oil.html.
8 Chris Turner, *The War on Science: Muzzled Scientists and Wilful Blindness in Stephen Harper's Canada* (Vancouver: Greystone, 2011); Andrew Nikiforuk, *Tar Sands: Dirty Oil and the Future of a Continent* (Vancouver: Greystone, 2010); William Marsden, *Stupid to the Last Drop: How Alberta Is Bringing Environmental Armageddon to Canada (And Doesn't Seem to Care)* (Toronto: Vintage, 2008).

9   Two recent and potentially influential agreements in this regard could be the Foreign
    Investment Promotion and Protection Agreement with the Chinese government, and the
    Comprehensive Economic Trade Agreement with the European Union.

10 Around 1980, annual consumption of oil came to dramatically outpace annual discoveries
    on a world scale. By the late 2000s it was widely recognized that the world had consumed
    roughly half of all conventional oil supplies since the late nineteenth century, and that the
    second half would be consumed a lot faster than the first. See Richard Heinberg, *Peak
    Everything* (Gabriola, BC: New Society Publishers, 2007).

11 International Energy Agency (IEA), *World Energy Outlook 2012* (Paris: OECD/IEA, 2012).

12 Michael T. Klare, *The Race for What's Left* (New York: Metropolitan Books, 2012).

13 The environmental impacts of the tar sands have been extensively detailed elsewhere. Some
    prominent examples include: Hatch and Price, *Canada's Toxic Tar Sands*; Tony Clarke, *Tar
    Sands Showdown* (Toronto: Lorimer, 2008); Nikiforuk, *Tar Sands*; and Marsden, *Stupid to
    the Last Drop*.

14 None more famously than Maude Barlow, who used this analogy while serving as senior
    water advisor to the United Nations. The tar sands landscape also famously inspired James
    Cameron's depiction of the rapacious resource extraction on the planet of Pandora in the
    blockbuster movie *Avatar*.

15 D'Arcy Hande and Mark Bigland-Pritchard, "Green Bitumen?!" *The Dominion*, August 27,
    2012, accessed January 13, 2014, www.dominionpaper.ca/articles/4570.

16 Andrew Nikiforuk, "Next Oil Sands Threat: Cracking Caprock," *The Tyee*, October 7, 2012,
    accessed January 12, 2014, thetyee.ca/News/2013/10/07/Next-Oil-Sands-Threat/.

17 This can be seen in the very powerful set of images provided by *National Geographic* in
    2011: news.nationalgeographic.com/news/energy/2011/12/pictures/111222-canada-oil-
    sands-satellite-images/.

18 Erin N. Kelly et al., "Oil sands development contributes elements toxic at low concentrations
    to the Athabasca River and its tributaries," *Proceedings of the National Academy of
    Sciences*, 107,37 (2010), 16178–83; Erin N. Kelly et al., "Oil sands development contributes
    polycyclic aromatic compounds to the Athabasca River and its tributaries," *Proceedings of
    the National Academy of Sciences*, 106 (2009), 22346–51.

19 Abha Parajulee and Frank Wania, "Evaluating officially reported polycyclic aromatic
    hydrocarbon emissions in the Athabasca oil sands region with a multimedia fate model,"
    Proceedings of the National Academy of Sciences, 111,9 (2014), 3344–49.

20 Joshua Kurek, "Legacy of a half century of Athabasca oil sands development recorded by
    lake ecosystems," *Proceedings of the National Academy of Sciences*, 110,5 (2013), 1761–66;
    Peter V. Hodson, "History of environmental contamination by oil sands extraction,"
    Proceedings of the National Academy of Sciences, 110,5 (2013), 1569–70.

21 Clayton Thomas-Muller, "The world's biggest climate crime," *Left Turn*, January 2010,
    endofcapitalism.com/2010/07/14/tar-sands-worlds-biggest-climate-crime/.

22 Anthony Swift, Susuan Casey-Lefkotiz, and Elizabeth Shope, *Tar Sands Pipelines Safety
    Risks*, joint report prepared by Natural Resources Defense Council, National Wildlife
    Federation, Pipeline Safety Trust, and the Sierra Club, 2011, www.nrdc.org/energy/files/
    tarsandssafetyrisks.pdf.

23 ForestEthics, "Tar Sands Refineries: Communities at Risk," September 2012,
    forestethics.org/sites/forestethics.huang.radicaldesigns.org/files/ForestEthics-Refineries-
    Report-Sept2012.pdf.

24 Mike Soraghan, "Oil Spills: Crude mishaps on trains spike as rail carries more oil," *Energy-Wire*, July 17, 2013, accessed January 9, 2014, www.eenews.net/stories/1059984505.

25 Opponents of megaload shipments have also emphasized how these huge and slow-moving shipments are likely to obstruct traffic, including emergency vehicles.

26 Turner, *The War on Science*.

27 Emma Pullman, "The Harper government, Ethical Oil and Sun Media connection," *Rabble.ca*, January 20, 2012, accessed January 12, 2014, rabble.ca/blogs/bloggers/alex/2012/01/harper-government-ethical-oil-and-sun-media-connection.

28 In contrast, a mere $237,000 was allocated for Natural Resources Canada's advertising budget in 2010-11. See Bruce Cheadle, "Ottawa spending $40-million to pitch Canada's natural resources," *The Globe and Mail*, November 27, 2013, www.theglobeandmail.com/news/politics/ottawa-spending-40-million-to-pitch-canadas-natural-resources/article15641360/.

29 Matthew Millar, "Breaking: Chief spy watchdog working for Enbridge since 2011," *Vancouver Observer*, January 6, 2014, www.vancouverobserver.com/environment/chief-spy-watchdog-working-enbridge-2011; Jenny Uechi, "Ethics Commissioner shrugs off conflict of interest in spy watchdog's Enbridge lobbying," *Vancouver Observer*, January 8, 2014, www.vancouverobserver.com/news/ethics-commissioner-shrugs-conflict-interest-spy-watchdogs-enbridge-lobbying.

30 David Campanella and Shannon Stunden Bower, *Taking the Reins: The Case for Slowing Alberta's Bitumen Production* (Calgary: Parkland Institute, 2013).

31 Alberta Federation of Labour, "Exploitation of foreign workers continues unabated," January 9, 2014, www.afl.org/index.php/Temporary-Foreign-Workers/overview.html.

32 Bob Barnetson and Jason Foster, "Foreign Migrant Workers in Alberta" (paper presented at the Canadian Political Science Association 84th Annual Conference, 2013).

33 CO_2, methane, and nitrous oxide are described as greenhouse gases (GHG) because of their heat-trapping capacity, and CO_2 is the most important GHG affecting global warming. Paleoclimatic records show that atmospheric CO_2 varied between roughly 180 and 310 ppm for most of the past 200,000 years that humans have been on earth. Since the early 1970s, atmospheric concentrations of CO_2 have risen by roughly 2 ppm per year, and in 2013 they surpassed 400 ppm for the first time in millions of years.

34 Two major examples are how declining sea and glacial ice means declining albedo and increasing thermal absorption in the Arctic Ocean and across high-latitude land masses, and how thawing permafrost threatens to release vast stores of methane.

35 Intergovernmental Panel on Climate Change, *5th Assessment Report*, 2013; James Hansen, *Storms of My Grandchildren: The Truth about the Coming Climate Catastrophe and Our Last Chance to Save Humanity* (New York: Bloomsbury, 2009).

36 David Biello, "'Greenhouse Goo,'" *Scientific American*, 308,7 (2013), 56–61; see also Neil C. Swart and Andrew J. Weaver, "The Alberta Oil Sands and Climate" in *Nature Climate Change*, Vol. 2, 134–136, February 19, 2012.

37 Energy Resources Conservation Board, *Alberta's Energy Reserves 2012 and Supply/Demand Outlook 2013–2022*, 2013, www.aer.ca/documents/sts/ST98/ST98-2013.pdf.

38 Petroleum coke wastes are not new to refineries, but the processing of tar sands has greatly increased their output. These wastes are increasingly being exported to countries like China, India, and Mexico for use as a cheap fuel source. See Oil Change International, *Petroleum Coke: The coal hiding in the tar sands* (Washington), 2013.

39 Barry Saxifrage, "Climate pollution: 140 nations vs Alberta's tar sands," *Visual Carbon*, November 21, 2013, accessed January 9, 2014, www.saxifrages.org/eco/show64a/ Climate_pollution_140_nations_vs_Albertas_tar_sands_.

40 Rebecca C. Rooney, Suzanne Bayley, and David Schindler, "Oil sands mining and reclamation cause massive loss of peatland and stored carbon," *Proceedings of the National Academy of Sciences* (2012), 1–10.

41 James Hansen., "Game Over for the Climate," *New York Times*, May 9, 2012, accessed October 31, 2013, www.nytimes.com/2012/05/10/opinion/game-over-for-the-climate.html.

42 Toghestiy, Mel Bazil, and Freda Huson, "Grassroots Wet'suwet'en," in *Undoing Border Imperialism*, Harsha Walia (Oakland: AK Press, 2013).

43 Idle No More has included tar sands struggles but extended to social and environmental injustices far beyond them, with the tipping point being the huge cuts to the Canadian government's monitoring and regulatory capacity contained in the Harper government's omnibus bill in 2012.

44 In 2013, companies sometimes were receiving half or less of the global price of oil when it is processed in the Midwest, instead of further afield.

45 Jeff Lewis, "Oil sands upstarts face tough decisions as growth prospects stall," *Financial Post*, December 20, 2013, accessed January 8, 2014, business.financialpost.com/2013/12/ 20/oil-sands-upstarts-face-tough-decisions-as-growth-prospects-stall.

46 Protestors succeeded in temporarily shutting down Utah's first tar sands mine in 2013, but the US government has approved this project (as well as shale extraction) across 800,000 acres in the state, so a challenging battle is in store.

47 Robert Bullard, ed., *The Quest for Environmental Justice* (San Francisco: Sierra Club Books, 2005).

48 The notion of drawing a line in the tar sands had seemed original when we initially discussed the title for this book, but it is hardly original now. Its aptness is reflected in the fact that it has recently been used in a series of events, media projects, and call-outs for protests and fundraising.

1. Carter, Petro-Capitalism and the Tar Sands

1 Social Sciences and Humanities Research Council funding supported this research. I would also like to acknowledge that this work draws on the advice of Laurie Adkin and builds from co-authored work with Randy Haluza-Delay, Philippe Le Billon, and Anna Zalik. Thanks to John Peters and the editors of this book for comments and revisions, which greatly improved the chapter.

2 Stephen Harper, "Address by the Prime Minister at the Canada-UK Chamber of Commerce" (speech, London, July 14, 2006), pm.gc.ca/eng/media.asp?id=1247.

3 Elmar Altvater, "The Social and Natural Environment of Fossil Capitalism," in *Socialist Register 2007: Coming to Terms with Nature*, ed. Leo Panitch et al. (London: Merlin Press, 2006), 39.

4 Matthew Huber, "Energizing Historical Materialism: Fossil Fuels, Space and the Capitalist Mode of Production," *Geoforum*, 40,1 (2008).

5 Altvater, "The Social and Natural Environment of Fossil Capitalism."

6 Ibid., 50.

7 Terry Lynn Karl, *The Paradox of Plenty: Oil Booms and Petro-States* (Berkeley: University of California Press, 1997), 16.

8 Minqi Li, "The 21st Century Crisis: Climate Catastrophe or Socialism," *Review of Radical Political* Economics, 43 (2011); Servass Storm, "Capitalism and Climate Change: Can the Invisible Hand Adjust the Natural Thermostat?" *Development and Change*, 40 (2009).

9 International Energy Agency (IEA), "World Energy Outlook 2010" (2010).

10 IEA, "Oil Market Report" (2013).

11 Li, "The 21st Century Crisis."

12 Stephen Harper, "Reviving Canadian Leadership in the World" (speech, Ottawa, October 5, 2006), pm.gc.ca/eng/media.asp?category=2&pageId=46&id=1343 [emphasis added].

13 OECD, *Inventory of Estimated Budgetary Support and Tax Expenditures for Fossil Fuels* (2011), 67.

14 IEA, "Medium-Term Oil & Gas Markets" (Paris, 2011), 60.

15 Natural Resources Canada, "Important Facts on Canada's Natural Resources" (2010).

16 P. Cross, "The Role of Natural Resources in Canada's Economy," *Canadian Economic Observer* (November 2008), 3.1–3.10.

17 IEA et al., "The Scope of Fossil-Fuel Subsidies in 2009 and a Roadmap for Phasing Out Fossil-Fuel Subsidies" (2010).

18 Bruce Campbell, "The Petro-Path Not Taken: Comparing Norway with Canada and Alberta's Management of Petroleum Wealth" (Ottawa: Canadian Centre for Policy Alternatives, 2013).

19 Ramzi Issa et al., "The Turning Black Tide: Energy Prices and the Canadian Dollar," *Canadian Journal of Economics*, 41 (2008), 756.

20 Michael Burt et al., "Fuel for Thought: The Economic Benefits of Oil Sands Investment for Canada's Regions" (Ottawa: Conference Board of Canada, 2012).

21 Doer is cited in Jonathan Kay, "United at Last," *National Post*, December 15, 2011, A20.

22 National Energy Policy Development Group, "National Energy Policy," (2001), 8.

23 Jon Rozhon, "Foreign Investment in the Oil Sands and British Columbia Shale Gas" (Calgary: Canadian Energy Research Institute, 2012).

24 Natural Resources Canada, "Important Facts on Canada's Natural Resources" (2010).

25 Gordon Laxer, "Freezing in the Dark: Why Canada Needs Strategic Petroleum Reserves" (Edmonton: Parkland Institute and Polaris Institute, 2008).

26 IEA, "Energy Policies of IEA Countries: Canada 2009 Review" (Paris, 2009), 25.

27 Canadian Association of Petroleum Producers (CAPP), "Crude Oil: Forecast, Markets and Pipeline" (2010).

28 CAPP, "Statistical Handbook for Canada's Upstream Petroleum Industry" (Calgary, 2011), Table 3.2a.

29 Dan Woynillowicz et al., *Oil Sands Fever: The Environmental Implications of Canada's Oil Sands Rush* (Drayton Valley, AB: Pembina Institute, 2005).

30 Robert Mansell and Ron Schlenker, "Energy and the Alberta Economy: Past and Future Impacts and Implications," in *Alberta Energy Future Project* (Calgary: Institute for Sustainable Energy, Environment and Economy, 2006).

31 Joshua Kurek et al., "Legacy of a Half Century of Athabasca Oil Sands Development Recorded by Lake Ecosystems," *Proceedings of the National Academy of Sciences*, 110 (2013); Kevin Timoney et al., "Does the Alberta Tar Sands Industry Pollute? The Scientific Evidence," *Open Conservation Biology Journal*, 3 (2009).

32 Quoted in Alberta Energy, *Oil Sands Consultations: Multistakeholder Committee Final Report* (2007), 18.

33 Mary Griffiths and Dan Woynillowicz, *Heating Up in Alberta: Climate Change, Energy Development and Water* (Drayton Valley, AB: Pembina Institute, 2009); Simon Dyer et al., *Under-Mining the Environment: The Oil Sands Report Card* (Drayton Valley, AB: Pembina Institute, 2008).

34 Matt Price, *The Tar Sands' Leaking Legacy* (Toronto: Environmental Defence, 2008).

35 Jennifer Grant et al, *Beneath the Surface: A Review of Key Facts in the Oilsands Debate* (Drayton Valley, AB: Pembina Institute, 2013), 11.

36 Erin Kelly et al., "Oil sands development contributes polycyclic aromatic compounds to the Athabasca River and its tributaries," *Proceedings of the National Academy of Sciences*, 106 (2009).

37 Andrzej Bytnerowicz et al., "Spatial and Temporal Distribution of Ambient Nitric Acid and Ammonia in the Athabasca Oil Sands Region," *Alberta Journal of Limnology*, 69 (2010); Dean Jeffries et al, "Recently Surveyed Lakes in Northern Manitoba and Saskatchewan, Canada: Characteristics and Critical Loads of Acidity," *Journal of Limnology*, 69 (2010).

38 OECD, *Inventory of Estimated Budgetary Support and Tax Expenditures for Fossil Fuels* (2013).

39 EnviroEconomics Inc. et al., *Fossil Fuels—At What Cost?: Government Support for Upstream Oil Activities in Three Canadian Provinces* (Geneva: Global Subsidies Initiative and International Institute for Sustainable Development, 2010).

40 William Hunter et al., *Our Fair Share: Report of the Alberta Royalty Review Panel* (2007).

41 Philippe Le Billon and Angela Carter, "Securing Alberta's Tar Sands: Resistance and Criminalization on a New Energy Frontier," in *Natural Resources and Social Conflict: Towards Critical Environmental Security*, ed. Matthew A. Schnurr and Larry A. Swatuk (London: Palgrave MacMillan, 2012).

42 Laura Payton, "Radicals Working Against the Oilsands, Ottawa Says," *CBC News*, January 9, 2012.

43 Royal Canadian Mounted Police, "Creation of an RCMP-led INSET in Alberta," June 6, 2012, www.rcmp-grc.gc.ca/news-nouvelles/2012/06-06-inset-eisn-eng.htm.

44 Andrew Nikiforuk, "The Republican Who Dared Tell the Truth About Oil," *The Tyee*, August 30, 2010.

45 Altvater, "The Social and Natural Environment of Fossil Capitalism," 54, original emphasis.

2. Haluza-DeLay, Assembling Consent in Alberta

1 David Campanella, *Misplaced Generosity Update 2012: Extraordinary profits in Alberta's oil and gas industry* (Edmonton: Parkland Institute, 2012).

2 Kate A. F. Crehan, *Gramsci, Culture and Anthropology* (Berkeley: University of California Press, 2002), 71.

3 The quotations in this paragraph were collected by the author and assistants during a research project that ran from 2008 to 2012. This CAPP campaign has since been removed from the Internet.

4 Bill Kaufmann, "Ralph Klein remembered at public ceremony in Calgary," *Calgary Sun*, April 5, 2013.

5 Dean W. Manders, *The Hegemony of Common Sense: Wisdom and Mystification in Everyday Life* (New York: Peter Lang, 2006); Deb J. Hill, *Hegemony and Education: Gramsci, Post-Marxism and Radical Democracy Revisited* (Lanham, MD: Rowman and Littlefield, 2007).

6   Raymond Williams, *Marxism and Literature* (Oxford, UK: Oxford University Press, 1977), 107.

7   Jennifer Earl, "The Cultural Consequences of Social Movements," in *The Blackwell Companion to Social Movements*, eds. David A. Snow, Sarah A. Soule, and Hanspeter Kriesi (London: Blackwell, 2004), 508–30; Stephen Hart, *Cultural Dilemmas of Progressive Politics: Styles of Engagement among Grassroots Activists* (Chicago: University of Chicago Press, 2001).

8   Crehan, *Gramsci, Culture and Anthropology.*

9   Nathan Kowalsky and Randolph Haluza-DeLay, "Homo Energeticus: Technological Rationality in the Alberta Tar Sands," in *Jacques Ellul and the Technological Society in the 21st Century*, eds. Helena Mateus Jeronimo, Jose Luis Garcia, and Carl Mitcham (Berlin: Springer, 2013), 159–75, link.springer.com/chapter/10.1007/978-94-007-6658-7_12. This chapter represents a small piece of a much bigger set of research projects on the tar sands, which draw on a variety of methods, including: ethnographic participant-observation; interviews with key informants; participatory action research; content analysis of media responses to social movements' actions; and focus groups with citizens of Alberta. See: Randolph Haluza-DeLay and Angela Carter, "Social Movements Scaling Up: Strategies and Opportunities in Opposing the Oilsands Status Quo," in *Political Ecology and Governance in Alberta*, eds. L. Adkin, N. Krogman, and B. Miller (Toronto: University of Toronto Press, forthcoming); Randolph Haluza-DeLay, Michael P. Ferber, and Tim Wiebe-Neufeld, "Watching Avatar from 'AvaTar Sands' Land," in *Avatar and Nature Spirituality*, ed. Bron Taylor (Waterloo, ON: Wilfred Laurier University Press, 2013), 123–40.

10   Campanella, *Misplaced Generosity Update 2012.*

11   See www.albertaenterprisegroup.com/.

12   Barbara Yaffe, "'In Fact, Every Canadian Has a Stake in This'; Alberta Oilsands Industry Fights a Public Relations War in Advance of a New Energy Policy in the U.S.," *Vancouver Sun*, November 25, 2008.

13   See the extensive Wikipedia page on Leduc #1 (en.wikipedia.org/wiki/Leduc_No._1), and the historic site's interpretive centre (www.leducnumber1.com/).

14   There have been recent revisions to the social science curriculum.

15   See oilsands.alberta.ca.

16   The original URL for this advertisement (from 2009) is now a dead link.

17   Kevin Timoney and Peter Lee, "Does the Alberta Tar Sands Industry Pollute? The Scientific Evidence," *The Open Conservation Biology Journal*, 3 (2009), 65–81; "Scientist apologizes to oilsands researchers," *CBC News*, June 21, 2010, www.cbc.ca/news/canada/edmonton/story/2010/06/21/edmonton-mceachern-defamatory-apology.html.

18   Alice Woolley, "Enemies of the State? The Alberta Energy and Utilities Board, Landowners, Spies, a 500kV Transmission Line and Why Procedure Matters," *Journal of Energy and Resource Law* 26,2 (2008), 234–66.

19   Jeffrey R. Masuda, Tara K. McGee, and Theresa D. Garvin, "Power, Knowledge, and Public Engagement: Constructing 'Citizenship' in Alberta's Industrial Heartland," *Journal of Environmental Policy & Planning*, 10,4 (2008), 359–80; John Parkins, "De-Centering Environmental Governance: A Short History and Analysis of Democratic Processes in the Forest Sector of Alberta, Canada," *Policy Sciences*, 39,2 (2006), 183–202.

20   Julian Agyeman et al., eds., *Speaking for Ourselves: Environmental Justice in Canada* (Vancouver: University of British Columbia Press, 2009).

21 L. Bouchard, "The Integrity of Creation and the Athabasca Tar Sands," Pastoral Letter
    on The Integrity of Creation and the Athabasca Oil Sands to The Faithful of the Diocese
    of St. Paul on the Occasion of the Jubilee Year in Honour of St. Paul, January 25, 2009;
    Richard Warnica, "Bishop assesses fallout from letter," *Edmonton Journal*, February
    28, 2010.

22 Author's notes from a speech given by Bouchard at the Social Justice Institute in 2010.

23 Maarten A. Hajer, "Ecological Modernisation As Cultural Politics," in *The Ecological
    Modernisation Reader: Environmental Reform in Theory and Practice*, eds. Arthur P. J.
    Mol, David A. Sonnenfeld, and Gert Spaargaren (London: Routledge, 2009), 80–100.

24 Margaret E. Keck and Kathryn Sikkink, *Activists Beyond Borders: Advocacy Networks in
    International Politics* (Ithaca, NY: Cornell University Press, 1999).

25 Kowalsky and Haluza-DeLay, "Homo Energeticus."

3. Katz-Rosene, The Rise of Reactionary Environmentalism in the Tar Sands

1   Paul Koring, "Ottawa Pitches the Oil Sands as 'Green'," *The Globe and Mail*, March 5, 2013,
    www.theglobeandmail.com/news/politics/ottawa-pitches-the-oil-sands-as-green/
    article9306257/.

2   The Honourable Joe Oliver, "An Open Letter from the Honourable Joe Oliver, Minister of
    Natural Resources, on Canada's Commitment to Diversify Our Energy Markets and the Need
    to Further Streamline the Regulatory Process in Order to Advance Canada's National
    Economic Interest," Natural Resources Canada, January 9, 2012, www.nrcan.gc.ca/
    media-room/news-release/2012/1/3520.

3   Government of Canada, "Responsible Resource Development," *Canada's Economic Action
    Plan*, 2013, actionplan.gc.ca/en/content/r2d-dr2; Ezra Levant, *Ethical Oil: The Case for
    Canada's Oil Sands* (Toronto: McClelland & Stewart, 2010); Canadian Association of
    Petroleum Producers, "Environment & Community," *Canadian Association of Petroleum
    Producers*, 2012, www.capp.ca/environmentCommunity/Pages/default.aspx.

4   Richard York and Eugene A. Rosa, "Key Challenges to Ecological Modernization Theory,"
    Organization & Environment 16,3 (2003), 273–88; Gregory Albo, "The Limits of Eco-
    Localism: Scale, Strategy, Socialism," in *Socialist Register 2007*, eds. Leo Panitch and
    Colin Leys (London: Merlin Press, 2007), 337–63; Noel Castree, "Neoliberalising Nature:
    The Logics of Deregulation and Reregulation," *Environment and Planning A*, 40
    (2008), 131–52.

5   Dan Woynillowicz, Chris Severson-Baker, and Marlo Reynolds, *Oil Sands Fever: The
    Environmental Implications of Canada's Oil Sands Rush* (Drayton Valley, AB: Pembina
    Institute, November 2005).

6   Kevin Carmichael, "Redford Stumps for Oil Sands, Keystone XL in Washington," *The Globe
    and Mail*, February 23, 2013, www.theglobeandmail.com/report-on-business/industry-
    news/energy-and-resources/redford-stumps-for-oil-sands-keystone-xl-in-washington/
    article9007811/.

7   National Task Force on Oil Sands Strategies of the Alberta Chamber of Resources [NTOSS],
    The Oil Sands: A New Energy Vision for Canada (Edmonton: Alberta Chamber of
    Resources, Spring 1995), 16.

8   Chris Severson-Baker and Simon Dyer, "Environmental Groups Pull Out of Multi-
    stakeholder Oilsands Process," *Pembina.org*, August 18, 2008, /media-release/1678.

9   Canadian Press, "Time to Review Oilsands: Prentice," *Red Deer Advocate*, July 15, 2009.

10 As quoted in Carol Christian, "Province Defends Oilsands Management Plan," *Fort McMurray Today*, August 15, 2009.

11 Marlo Reynolds, "Canadian Environmental Groups Issue Declaration on Oilsands Development," *Pembina.org*, December 1, 2005, /media-release/1166.

12 Debra J. Davidson and Norah A. MacKendrick, "All Dressed Up with Nowhere to Go: The Discourse of Ecological Modernization in Alberta, Canada," *The Canadian Review of Sociology and Anthropology*, 41,1 (2004), 62.

13 See, for example, NTOSS, *The Oil Sands*.

14 House of Commons Standing Committee on Natural Resources, *The Oil Sands: Toward Sustainable Development* (Ottawa: Parliament of Canada, March 2007).

15 See Damian Carrington, "UK Secretly Helping Canada Push Its Oil Sands Project," *The Guardian*, November 27, 2011, www.guardian.co.uk/environment/2011/nov/27/canada-oil-sands-uk-backing.

16 Levant, *Ethical Oil*; "EthicalOil.org," accessed March 11, 2013, www.ethicaloil.org.

17 Andrew Nikiforuk, *Tar Sands: Dirty Oil and the Future of a Continent* (Vancouver: Greystone Books, 2008).

18 See *The New Internationalist*, "Ralph Klein," *NewInt.org*, November 1, 2002, newint.org/columns/worldbeaters/2002/11/01/ralph-klein/.

19 Levant, *Ethical Oil*, 231.

20 Ibid., 107.

21 See Douglas Macdonald, *Business and Environmental Politics in Canada* (Toronto: Broadview Press, 2007); Matthew McClearn, "Shifting Sands: How Shell Lost the Goodwill of Stakeholders," *Canadian Business Magazine*, July 20, 2009; Environmental Defense, "Tar Sands Tailings Leakage Subject of NAFTA Complaint," *Environmental Defense*, April 14, 2010, www.environmentaldefence.ca/pressroom/viewnews.php?id=764.

22 Government of Canada, "Responsible Resource Development: Environmental Protection and Safety," *Canada's Economic Action Plan*, October 1, 2012, actionplan.gc.ca/en/video-vault?page=1.

23 "Kyoto Views Get Medical Officer Fired," *CBC News*, October 5, 2002.

24 Andrew Nikiforuk, "A Public Tarring in Saudi Canada," *The Toronto Star*, June 28, 2009, www.thestar.com/opinion/2009/06/28/a_public_tarring_in_saudi_canada.html.

25 Florence Loyie, "Doctor O'Connor Cleared Once and for All," *The Edmonton Journal*, November 7, 2009.

26 "Kyoto Views Get Medical Officer Fired."

27 Adam Albright, "Tar Sand Dreams," *Onearth*, June 18, 2010, www.onearth.org/node/2243.

4. Engler, Canadian Diplomatic Efforts to Sell the Tar Sands

1 People and Planet, with Greenpeace UK, the UK Tar Sands Network and The Co-operative's Toxic Fuels campaign, "A First Nations' view on keeping tar sands oil out of Europe," Facebook event page, November 9, 2011, www.facebook.com/events/133749866729835/?source=1

2 UK Tar Sands Network, "Canada poses as 'Friendly, Green Oil Giant' to win over UK universities," October 20, 2011, www.no-tar-sands.org/2011/10/canada-poses-as-%E2%80%9Cfriendly-green-oil-giant%E2%80%9D-to-win-over-uk-universities/.

3 David Chivers, "A tarred reputation," *New Internationalist*, October 16, 2012, newint.org/blog/2012/10/16/tar-sands-chatham-house/.

4 This ran on November 30, 2011.

5 Allan Woods, "'Dirty oil' anger shocked Tories, leaked documents show," *Toronto Star*, December 23, 2012, www.thestar.com/news/canada/2010/12/23/dirty_oil_anger_ shocked_tories_leaked_documents_show.html.

6 Martin Lukacs, "The Harper Offensive: Selling Tar Sands to Europe and the USA," *Canadian Dimension*, November 29, 2011, canadiandimension.com/articles/4344/.

7 Martin Lukacs, "Canada's PR work for tar sands: Dirty, crude and oily," *The Guardian*, August 14, 2011, www.guardian.co.uk/commentisfree/cifamerica/2011/aug/14/ canada-tar-sands-keystonexl.

8 Martin Lukacs, "Canada on Secret Oil Offensive: Documents," *The Dominion*, May 25, 2011, www.dominionpaper.ca/articles/3991.

9 Mike De Souza, "Feds list First Nations, green groups as oilsands 'adversaries'," *Canada.com*, January 26, 2012, www2.canada.com/story.html?id=6055184.

10 Lukacs, "The Harper Offensive."

11 Barbara Lewis, David Ljunggren, and Jeffrey Jones, "Canada's oil sand battle with Europe," *Reuters*, May 10, 2012, www.reuters.com/article/2012/05/10/canada-oil-sands-idUSL4E8GAAXW20120510.

12 Ibid.

13 Mike De Souza, "Pro-oil lobby urges feds to deliver on climate change," *The StarPhoenix*, February 13, 2012, www2.canada.com/saskatoonstarphoenix/news/story.html ?id=8004a8df-d138-4e39-9e60-f2ef000a0326.

14 Mike De Souza, "Taxpayers Paying for Pro-Oilsands Lobbying in Europe," *Alberta Surface Rights*, February 12, 2012, www.albertasurfacerights.com/articles/?id=1621.

15 Mike De Souza, "Feds downplay oilsands lobbying," *Winnipeg Free Press*, January 27, 2012, www.winnipegfreepress.com/business/feds-downplay-oilsands-lobbying-138186319.html?.

16 De Souza, "Feds list First Nations, green groups as oilsands 'adversaries.'"

17 Andy Rowell, *Keeping their head in the sands: Canada's* EU *Fuel Quality Directive lobby diary* (Brussels, Belgium: Friends of the Earth Europe, January 2013), www.foeeurope.org/sites/default/files/publications/keeping_their_head_in_the_sand_ january_2013.pdf.

18 Lewis, Ljunggren, and Jones, "Canada's oil sand battle with Europe."

19 Jason Feteke, "Canada threatens trade war with EU ahead of oil sands vote," *Financial Post*, February 21, 2012, business.financialpost.com/2012/02/21/canada-threatens-trade-war-with-eu-ahead-of-oil-sands-vote/.

20 Ibid.

21 Shawn McCarthy, "France, Netherlands key to EU oil sands decision," *The Globe and Mail*, February 23, 2012, www.theglobeandmail.com/report-on-business/industry-news/ energy-and-resources/france-netherlands-key-to-eu-oil-sands-decision/article548563/.

22 Damian Carrington, "EU tar sands pollution vote ends in deadlock," *The Guardian*, February 23, 2012, www.guardian.co.uk/environment/2012/feb/23/eu-tar-sands-pollution-vote.

23 Ros Donald, "Carbon Briefing: Who killed the EU's transport fuel standards," *The Carbon Brief*, January 30, 2014, www.carbonbrief.org/blog/2014/01/who-killed-the-fuel-quality-directive/.

24 *National Post*, "Ottawa targets oil-sands opponents," *Canada.com*, November 22, 2010, www.canada.com/story_print.html?id=95643ba5-91da-4112-8618-beec30a62db4&sponsor; Lukacs, "The Harper Offensive."

25 Carl Meyer, "Too bad it doesn't have a national energy policy yet: Former diplomat," *Embassy of Mexico in Canada*, August 4, 2010, embamex.sre.gob.mx/canada_eng/index. php?option=com_content&view=article&id=914:canadas-high-powered-energy-advocates-embassy&catid=107:miercoles-4-agosto-2010.

26 Ibid.

27 Geoff Dembicki, "Gary Doer's Startling Embrace of the Oil Sands," *The Tyee*, April 4, 2011, thetyee.ca/News/2011/04/04/GaryDoer/.

28 Geoff Dembicki, "Breakfast with the Oil Sands' Top Salesman," *The Tyee*, March 15, 2011, thetyee.ca/News/2011/03/15/OilSandsTopSalesman/print.html.

29 Ibid.

30 Geoff Dembicki, "The Battle to Block Low Carbon Fuel Standards," *The Tyee*, March 17, 2011, thetyee.ca/News/2011/03/17/LowCarbonFuelFight/.

31 Geoff Dembicki, "Climate Group Says Washington's Oil Sands War Is 'David vs. Goliath'," *The Tyee*, March 28, 2011, thetyee.ca/News/2011/03/28/DavidVsGoliath/.

32 Geoff Dembicki, "Big oil and Canada thwarted U.S. carbon standards," *Salon.com*, December 15, 2011, www.salon.com/2011/12/15/ big_oil_and_canada_thwarted_u_s_carbon_standards/.

33 Geoff Dembicki, "Canada trying 'to kill' global warming laws: report," *The Tyee*, November 22, 2010, thetyee.ca/Blogs/TheHook/Environment/2010/11/22/canada-alberta-oilsands-lobby/.

34 Lisa Raitt, letter to Governor Arnold Schwarzenegger, April 21, 2009, climateactionnetwork.ca/wp-content/attachments/09-04-21-raitt-letter-to-schwarzenegger-lcfs.pdf.

35 Terry Macalister, "Oil groups mount legal challenge to Schwarzenegger's tar sands ban," *The Guardian*, February 14, 2010, www.guardian.co.uk/business/2010/feb/14/oil-sands-ban-legal-challenge.

36 Mary Lazich, "Global warming bill could shut off a major source of Wisconsin's energy" (legislative column), legis.wisconsin.gov/senate/lazich/Pages/pa-show.aspx? id=Global+Warming+Bill+Could+Shut+Off+a+Major+Source+of+ Wisconsin%26rsquo%3Bs+Energy.

37 Communications, Energy and Paperworkers Union of Canada, "Tories spend on Keystone XL ads, while cutting environmental funding," news release, May 27, 2013, www.newswire.ca/en/story/1172403/tories-spend-on-keystone-xl-ads-while-cutting-environment-funding.

38 "Parties hold budget debate on Natural Resources main estimates," *Environmental Hansard*, May 21, 2013, envirohansard.ca/2013/05/parties-hold-budget-debate-over-natural-resources-main-estimates/.

39 Andrew Mayeda and Rebecca Penty, "Canada's latest Keystone headache—a spat with diplomats that could hurt lobbying efforts," *Financial Post*, April 25, 2013, business.financialpost.com/2013/04/25/keystone-xl-lobbying/?__lsa=cc31-b6ba.

40 Geoff Dembicki, "TransCanada to Ambassador Doer: 'Thank you'," *The Tyee*, November 26, 2012, thetyee.ca/Blogs/TheHook/Federal-Politics/2012/11/26/keystone-xl-transcanada-doer-emails/.

41 Geoff Dembicki, "Canadian Officials 'Aggressive' in Selling Congress on Oil Sands," *The Tyee*, March 23, 2011, thetyee.ca/News/2011/03/23/OilSandsSell/.

5. Vasey, The Environmental NGO Industry and Frontline Communities

1   See, for example, Dawn Paley, "Are green groups ready for tarsands deal?" *Georgia Straight*, November 20, 2013.

2   Macdonald Stainsby and Dru Oja Jay, *Offsetting Resistance: The effects of foundation funding and corporate fronts from the Great Bear Rainforest to the Athabasca River*, s3.amazonaws.com/offsettingresistance/offsettingresistance.pdf.

3   Dorceta E. Taylor, "The Rise of the Environmental Justice Paradigm: Injustice Framing and the Social Construction of Environmental Discourses," *American Behavioral Scientist*, 43,4 (2000), 508–80.

4   Robert D. Bullard, ed., *Confronting Environmental Racism: Voices from the Grassroots* (Cambridge, MA: South End Press, 1993).

5   Ibid.

6   United Church of Christ, *Fauntroy Report* (1983); United Church of Christ, *Toxic Wastes and Race in the United States* (1987).

7   *Environmental Justice Principles*, adopted at the First National People of Color Environmental Leadership Summit (Washington, DC, 1991). Retrieved from www.toxicspot.com/env_justice/env_principles.html.

8   Southwest Organizing Project Letter to Big Ten Environmental Groups, 1990, www.ejnet.org/ej.

9   Dylan Rodriguez, "The Political Logic of the Non-Profit Industrial Complex," in *The Revolution Will Not Be Funded: Beyond the Non-Profit Industrial Complex*, eds. Incite: Women of Color Against Violence (Cambridge, MA: South End Press, 2007), 21–40; Philip McMichael, *Development and Social Change: A Global Perspective*, 4th ed. (New York: Sage Publications, 2008).

10 Gary Gereffi, Ronie Garcia-Johnson, and Erika Sasser, "The NGO-Industrial Complex," *Foreign Policy*, 125 (2001), 56–65.

11 Assembly of First Nations (AFN), *First Nations Issues Paper Executive Summary*, 2001, accessed October 2010, www.afn.ca/current%20Events/first_nations_issues. Note: An updated statistic could not be found at the time of writing.

12 Ibid.

13 Randolph Haluza-Delay, "Introduction: Speaking for Ourselves, Speaking Together: Environmental Justice in Canada," in *Speaking for Ourselves: Environmental Justice in Canada*, eds. Julian Agyeman et al. (Vancouver: UBC Press, 2009), 1–26.

14 Ibid., 12.

15 Stainsby and Oja Jay, *Offsetting Resistance*.

16 Roger Hayter, "'War in the Woods': Post-Fordist restructuring, globalization, and the contested remapping of British Columbia's forest economy," *Annals of the Association of American Geographers,* 93,3 (2003), 706–29.

17 David Rossiter, "The nature of protest: Constructing the spaces of British Columbia's rainforests," *Cultural Geographies*, 11 (2004), 139–164.

18 Stainsby and Oja Jay, *Offsetting Resistance*.

19 Holly Spiro Mabee and George Hoberg, "Equal Partners? Assessing Comanagement of Forest Resources in Clayoquot Sound," *Society & Natural Resources*, 19,10 (2006), 875–88.

20 Haluza-Delay et al., "Introduction: Speaking for Ourselves, Speaking Together."

21 Mabee and Hoberg, "Equal Partners?"

22 "Rainforest agreement a done deal," *CBC News*, February 7, 2006, accessed September 14, 2013, www.cbc.ca/news/canada/british-columbia/rainforest-agreement-a-done-deal-1.612845.

23 Stainsby and Oja Jay, *Offsetting Resistance*.

24 Larry Pratt, *The Tar Sands: Syncrude and the Politics of Oil* (Edmonton: Hurtig Publishers, 1976).

25 David Suzuki, "The fundamental failure of environmentalism," *Science Matters*, March 6, 2012, accessed September 14, 2013, www.davidsuzuki.org/blogs/science-matters/2012/05/the-fundamental-failure-of-environmentalism/.

26 Clayton Thomas-Muller, personal correspondence, September 7, 2013.

27 A major example is Bill Clinton, "Federal Actions to Address Environmental Justice in Minority Populations and Low-Income Populations," Executive Order 12898, February 11, 1994, www.archives.gov/federal-register/executive-orders/pdf/12898.pdf.

28 Antonio Machado, "Proverbios y cantares XXIX [Proverbs and Songs 29]," in *Selected Poems of Antonio Machado*, trans. Betty Jean Craige (Baton Rouge: Louisiana State University Press, 1979), accessed March 14, 2014, en.wikiquote.org/wiki/Antonio_Machado.

6. Lukacs, Canada's Eastward Pipelines

1. Allan Lisner, *Dunham Climate Camp*, YouTube video, 3:05, September 4, 2010, www.youtube.com/watch?v=mbZk9_BaPok.

2 See "Line 9B Reversal (Phase II) and Line 9 Capacity Expansion Project Overview," www.enbridge.com/ECRAI/Line9BReversalProject.aspx.

3 Lauren Krugel, "TransCanada pipeline to connect Alta., Quebec," *Winnipeg Free Press*, August 2, 2013.

4 Jeff Lewis, "A 'nation-building' pipeline in the plans," *Financial Post*, August 2, 2013.

5 Shawn McCarthy and Jeffrey Jones, "The promise and the perils of a pipe to Saint John," *The Globe and Mail*, August 1, 2013.

6 Jeff Rubin, "Canada's race to build pipelines won't spell relief at the pumps," *The Globe and Mail*, August 19, 2013, www.theglobeandmail.com/report-on-business/industry-news/energy-and-resources/why-gasoline-prices-will-rise-along-with-canadas-race-to-build-pipelines/article13837648/.

7 Équiterre, "Pipeline safety expert finds "high risk of Line 9 rupture" if National Energy Board approves Enbridge's reversal plan," news release, August 9, 2013, www.newswire.ca/en/story/1208821/pipeline-safety-expert-finds-high-risk-of-line-9-rupture-if-national-energy-board-approves-enbridge-s-reversal-plan.

8 Tony Clarke, Jim Stanford, Diana Gibson, and Brendan Haley, "The Bitumen Cliff: Lessons and Challenges of Bitumen Mega-Developments for Canada's Economy in an Age of Climate Change," *Canadian Centre for Policy Alternatives*, February 21, 2013, www.policyalternatives.ca/publications/reports/bitumen-cliff.

9 "Study: 20 jobs from Keystone XL," *UPI.com*, March 20, 2012, www.upi.com/Business_News/Energy-Resources/2012/03/20/Study-20-jobs-from-Keystone-XL/UPI-58381332244550/.

10 Adam Carter, "Group protests Enbridge donations to Hamilton police," *CBC News*, June 5, 2013, www.cbc.ca/hamilton/news/story/2013/06/05/hamilton-enbridge-police-

line-9.html; www.lapresse.ca/actualites/national/201308/16/01-4680400-energie-est-transcanada-augmente-la-pression.php.

11 Nicolas Van Praet, "'No economic development possible in Quebec' if Enbridge's Line 9 plan crushed, business lobby says," *Financial Post*, May 29, 2013, www.ottawacitizen.com/business/fp/economic+development+possible+Quebec+Enbridge+Line+plan+crushed+business/8451978/story.html.

12 Jeff Lewis, "Energy workers' union backs Line 9 project, calls for stricter oil-by-rail regulation," *Financial Post*, online edition, July 9, 2013, business.financialpost.com/2013/07/09/energy-workers-union-backs-line-9-project-calls-for-stricter-oil-by-rail-regulation/?__lsa=318a-0c8a.

13 The International Labour Organization, for example, has argued that a worldwide transition to a "green economy" could yield "up to 60 million additional jobs globally over the next two decades." See the ILO's Green Jobs Initiative report, *Working Towards Sustainable Development: Opportunities for Decent Work and Social Inclusion in a Green Economy* (Geneva: ILO, 2012), www.ilo.org/wcmsp5/groups/public/---dgreports/---dcomm/---publ/documents/publication/wcms_181836.pdf.

14 Jane McAlevy, "Unions and Environmentalists: Get It Together!" *The Nation*, May 7, 2012, www.thenation.com/article/167460/blues-and-greens-get-it-together#; Marc Lee, "Enbridge Pipe Dreams and Nightmares: The Economic Costs and Benefits of the Proposed Northern Gateway Pipeline," *Canadian Centre for Policy Alternatives*, March 21, 2012, www.policyalternatives.ca/sites/default/files/uploads/publications/BC%20Office/2012/03/CCPA-BC_Enbridge_Pipe_Dreams_2012_SUMMARY.pdf.

15 "Anti-pipeline Organizing Across Turtle Island," *Upping the Anti*, Issue 15 (2013).

16 "Keep 'world's dirtiest fuel' out of Quebec, green groups say," *Montreal Gazette*, November 6, 2008, www.canada.com/montrealgazette/news/story.html?id=b9e1b9cb-b54e-427d-bf6f-f74213d741cc.

17 Martin Croteau, "Pipeline Ontario-Montréal: Enbridge dépose sa demande," *La Presse*, November 30, 2012, www.lapresse.ca/actualites/national/201211/29/01-4599216-pipeline-ontario-montreal-enbridge-depose-sa-demande.php.

18 Diana Mehta, "National Energy Board approves Enbridge's Line 9 reversal plan," *CTV News*, March 6, 2014, www.ctvnews.ca/business/national-energy-board-approves-enbridge-s-line-9-reversal-plan-1.1716611#ixzz2wKhooBkW.

19 Quebec nationalists and sovereigntists seek independence from the rest of Canada.

20 Philippe Duhamel, "Civil resistance as deterrent to fracking: Part One, They shale not pass," *Open Democracy*, September 26, 2013, www.opendemocracy.net/civilresistance/philippe-duhamel/civil-resistance-as-deterrent-to-fracking-part-one-they-shale-not-0. There have since been plans in the works for a similar 700-km walk alongside the path of TransCanada's proposed Energy East pipeline in the summer of 2014.

7. Walia, Migrant Justice and the Tar Sands Industry

1 Dave Dean, "75% of the World's Mining Companies are Based in Canada," *Vice News*, July 9, 2013, www.vice.com/en_ca/read/75-of-the-worlds-mining-companies-are-based-in-canada.

2 Greenpeace, "Tar Sands and Social Costs," www.greenpeace.org/canada/Global/canada/report/2010/4/SocialCosts_FS_Footnotes_rev_4.pdf.

3   Alberta Federation of Labour, "Alberta hit with 800 complaints from foreign workers: Accommodation, unfair wage deductions cited," April 1, 2008, afl.org/index.php/AFL-in-the-News/alberta-hit-with-800-complaints-from-foreign-workers-accommodation-unfair-wage-deductions-cited.html.

4   Jeff Gray, "Sinopec, the oil sands and justice delayed," *The Globe and Mail*, September 27, 2011, www.theglobeandmail.com/report-on-business/industry-news/the-law-page/sinopec-the-oil-sands-and-justice-delayed/article595935/.

5   Canadian Press, "Oil sands workers complain they were laid off and replaced by foreigners making half the wage," *Financial Post*, February 7, 2014, business.financialpost.com/2014/02/07/oil-sands-workers-foreigners-imperial-2014/?__lsa=7124-f905; Alberta Federation of Labour, "Temporary Foreign Worker Program Displacing Canadians," October 10, 2013, www.afl.org/index.php/Press-Release/temporary-foreign-worker-program-displacing-canadians.html.

6   Joanna Zelman, "50 Million Environmental Refugees by 2020, Experts Predict," *Huffington Post*, February 22, 2011, www.huffingtonpost.com/2011/02/22/environmental-refugees-50_n_826488.html.

8. Grewal, Responding to Chinese Investments in the Tar Sands

1   Tom Steyer is an investment fund manager with the equity firm Hellman & Friedman.

2   Reuters, "Public opinion 'crystallizing' against Nexen deal, NDP says," *The Globe and Mail*, October 2, 2012, www.theglobeandmail.com/news/politics/public-opinion-crystallizing-against-nexen-deal-ndp-says/article4582176/.

3   Jessica Hume, "Feds should heed CSIS warnings of security threat in foreign takeovers: Critics," *Toronto Sun*, September 21, 2012, www.torontosun.com/2012/09/21/feds-should-heed-csis-warnings-of-security-threat-in-foreign-takeovers-critics/.

4   Green Party of Canada, "Stand up to the sellout to China," October 2013, www.greenparty.ca/stop-the-sellout.

5   Andrew Nikiforuk, "Chairman Harper and the Chinese Sell-Out," *The Tyee*, October 11, 2012, thetyee.ca/Opinion/2012/10/11/Chairman-Harper/print.html/.

6   Maude Barlow, letter to the editor, *The Globe and Mail*, February 11, 2012, www.theglobeandmail.com/globe-debate/letters/feb-11-letters-to-the-editor/article545421/.

7   Prime Minister Stephen Harper, "Canada-Tanzania Foreign Investment Promotion and Protection Agreement (FIPA)," news release, October 4, 2012, pm.gc.ca/eng/news/2012/10/04/canada-tanzania-foreign-investment-promotion-and-protection-agreement-fipa.

8   It is well documented that these tar sands products fuel the US military industrial complex.

9   Andrew Jacobs, "Harassment and Evictions Bedevil Even China's Well-Off," *New York Times*, October 27, 2011, www.nytimes.com/2011/10/28/world/asia/harassment-and-house-evictions-bedevil-even-chinas-well-off.html?_r=0.

10 Todd Gordon, *Imperialist Canada* (Winnipeg: Arbeiter Ring Publishing, 2010).

11 bilaterals.org and GRAIN, "Colonisation redux: New agreements, old games," *bilaterals.org*, September 2007, www.bilaterals.org/?colonisation-redux-new-agreements.

12 Kent Wong and Elaine Bernard, "Rethinking the China Campaign," *New Labor Forum*, Fall/Winter 2000, www.coloursofresistance.org/304/rethinking-the-china-campaign/.

9. Stainsby, New Beginnings

1 This term implies that natural gas has lower CO_2 emissions than oil or coal, such that some advocates believe it can help wean industrial economies off of the latter while reducing emissions.

2 Francisco Toro, "Blast from the Past Chronicles: Orimulsion Edition," *Caracas Chronicles*, August 8, 2012, caracaschronicles.com/2012/08/08/blast-from-the-past-chronicles-orimulsion-edition/.

3 Embassy of the Bolivarian Republic of Venezuela, "Venezuela's Orinoco Oil Belt Nationalized Five Years Ago," May 1, 2012, venezuela-us.org/2012/05/01/venezuela%E2%80%99s-orinoco-oil-belt-nationalized-five-years-ago-today/.

4 For further information on the PDVSA's operations, see the company's website: www.pdvsa.com.

5 PDVSA, www.pdvsa.com.

6 "For T&T oil sands, talks before threats," *Trinidad Express Newspapers*, April 23, 2012, www.trinidadexpress.com/commentaries/For_T_T_oil_sands___talks_before_threats-148616925.html.

7 Government of Alberta, "Facts and Statistics," *Alberta Energy*, www.energy.alberta.ca/OilSands/791.asp.

8 Business Day Staff, "Green issues and banking do mix," *Trinidad and Tobago Newsday*, March 31, 2011, www.newsday.co.tt/businessday/0,138127.html.

9 The Office of the Prime Minister, "Prime Minister holds bilateral discussions with Canadian Prime Minister," news release, April 14, 2012, www.opm.gov.tt/media_centre.php?mid=14&eid=171.

10 Jamie Ashcroft, "Madagascar Oil begins steam injection at Tsimiroro," *Proactiveinvestors*, May 15, 2013, www.proactiveinvestors.com/companies/news/43892/madagascar-oil-begins-steam-injection-at-tsimiroro-43892.html.

11 Macdonald Stainsby, "Devastation, Madagascar," *The Media Co-op*, December 27, 2010, www.mediacoop.ca/story/devastation-madagascar/5524.

12 Israel Energy Initiatives, www.iei-energy.com.

13 "Shfela Oil Shale Pilot," Israel Energy Initiatives, October 2010, www.iei-energy.com/pdfs/Oil-production-from-oil-shale---Addendum-to-the-env--doc.pdf.

14 Joshua Hammer, "Israel: IEI's Land Of Oil And Money," *Fast Company*, August 8, 2011, www.fastcompany.com/1769210/israel-ieis-land-oil-and-money.

15 Arwa Aburawa, "JNF plants trees to uproot Bedouin," *The Electronic Intifada*, October 18, 2010, electronicintifada.net/content/jnf-plants-trees-uproot-bedouin/9072.

16 Macdonald Stainsby, "Apartheid Oil," *The Media Co-op*, November 10, 2011, www.mediacoop.ca/story/apartheid-oil/8906.

17 Yves Engler, *Canada and Israel: Building Apartheid* (Black Point, NS: Fernwood and RED, 2010).

18 "Canada, Israel discuss energy ties," *UPI*, May 2, 2013, www.upi.comBusiness_News/Energy-Resources/2013/05/02/Canada-Israel-discuss-energy-ties/UPI-71801367490476/.

19 Royal Dutch Shell PLC, royaldutchshellplc.com/tag/jordan/.

20 "Extending the world's oil supply," Karak International Oil, www.kio.jo/en/.

21 Toomas Hõbemägi, "Jordan awards Eesti Energia a permit to build an oil shale plant," *BBN*, June 13, 2013, balticbusinessnews.com/article/2013/6/13/jordan-awards-eesti-energia-a-permit-to-build-an-oil-shale-plant.

22 Abdul Jalil Mustafa I, "Jordan signs MoU with Total and Petrobras," *Arab News*, September 11, 2008, www.arabnews.com/node/316054.

23 "Our Portfolio," Global Oil Shale Holdings, www.goshjordan.com/portfolio.php.

10. Laboucan-Massimo, Awaiting Justice

1 Ross Harvey, "Transcript of Statement made during House of Commons 'Late Show' for private Members' business," December 19, 1989, bcgreen.com/~samuel/lubicon/1989/ROSS.DOS.txt.

11. Lameman, Kihci Pikiskwewin

The title of this chapter has been set in the Cree syllabary as well as in the English alphabet.

1 Winona LaDuke and Sean Aaron Cruz, *The Militarization of Indian Country* (East Lansing, MI: Makwa Enewed, 2013).

2 See Article 32 of the United Nations Declaration on the Rights of Indigenous Peoples, www.un.org/esa/socdev/unpfii/documents/DRIPS_en.pdf.

3 Stan Boutin, *Expert report on woodland caribou [*Rangifer tarandus caribou*] in the Traditional Territory of the Beaver Lake Cree Nation*, report prepared for Raven Trust, July 5, 2010, www.raventrust.com/media/beaverlakecree/BLCTT___-_Stan_Boutin_Report_-_5_July_2010_final.pdf.

4 "A to Z Species Index," Species at Risk Public Registry, last modified July 10, 2012, www.sararegistry.gc.ca/sar/index/default_e.cfm.

5 Alberta Wilderness Association, "Canadians Can Stop Massive Wolf Kill," news release, February 16, 2012, albertawilderness.ca/news/2012/2012-02-16-awa-news-release-canadians-can-stop-massive-wolf-kill.

6 Beaver Lake Cree Nation, *Kétuskéno Declaration*, May 14, 2008, www.beaverlakecreenation.ca/upload/documents/declaration.pdf.

7 Erin Hanson, "Constitution Act, 1982 Section 35," *Indigenous Foundations*, 2009, indigenousfoundations.arts.ubc.ca/?id=1050.

8 Carol Linnitt, "The Beaver Lake Cree Judgment: The Most Important Tar Sands Case You've Never Heard Of," *DeSmog Blog*, May 24, 2013, accessed December 2, 2013, desmog.ca/2013/05/23/beaver-lake-cree-judgment-most-important-tar-sands-case-you-ve-never-heard.

9 Bill C-45 introduces the ability to lease land reserved for Indians, without consulting the citizen-members of those communities.

10 Office of the Prime Minister, "Prime Minister Stephen Harper Announces Meeting with First Nations Leadership," news release, January 4, 2013, pm.gc.ca/eng/news/2013/01/04/prime-minister-stephen-harper-announces-meeting-first-nations-leadership.

11 Linnitt, "The Beaver Lake Cree Judgment."

12. Cardinal, The Tar Sands Healing Walk

1 These translations are in Cree, my ancestors' first language.

2 Many simply show up in hope of getting work in the oil industry, some with quads, Ski-Doos, and big boats, but some with just the clothes on their backs and a backpack. Since getting work is not always as easy as it is made to seem, sometimes it falls to the communities, the Alberta government, and the taxpayers to take care of the newcomers.

3 Greenpeace, *Deep Trouble: The reality of insitu tar sands operations*, report, April 7, 2011, www.greenpeace.org/canada/en/campaigns/Energy/tarsands/Resources/Reports/

DEEP-TROUBLE-THE-REALITY-OF-IN-SITU-TAR-SANDS-OPERATIONS/; William Donahue, "In Situ oil sands—get ready for massive water demands in northern and central Alberta," *Water Matters*, August 26, 2010, www.water-matters.org/story/401.

4 Andrew Nikiforuk, "Scientists Doubt Fix to Wetlands Damaged by Oil Sands," *The Tyee*, March 14, 2012, thetyee.ca/News/2012/03/14/Wetlands-Damage/.

5 Eriel Deranger is a member of Athabasca Chipewyan First Nation, and its communications director. Cleo Reece is a band councillor for the Fort McMurray First Nation, and a member of Keepers of the Athabasca. Sheila Muxlow formerly worked with Sierra Club Prairie Chapter and now works with Living Oceans. The late Roland Woodward was a member of the Fort McMurray First Nation and Anzac Métis Community, and for many years served as chair for Keepers of the Athabasca.

13. Black, Petro-Chemical Legacies and Tar Sands Frontiers

1 "Bitumen—Adding Value," accessed June 7, 2013, canadabitumen.com.

2 Vanessa Gray, personal communication with the author, May 21, 2013.

3 In Sarnia-Lambton, Nova Chemicals has also begun to import fracked gas from the Marcellus Shale in the United States.

4 Researchers have begun to measure the extent of the toxins in the bodies of residents in the area. See Nil Basu and Diana Cryderman, *Biomarkers of Chemical Exposure at Aamjiwnaang*, 2013, sitemaker.umich.edu/aamjiwnaang/files/report-aamjiwnaang_biomonitoring_2013-v4-final.pdf.

5 Constanze A. Mackenzie, Ada Lockridge, and Margaret Keith, "Declining Sex Ratio in a First Nation Community," *Environmental Health Perspectives*, 113 (2005), 1295.

6 This figure is from 2005, but the basic situation remains the same. Petro-chemical facilities continue to surround the reserve. For additional background, see EcoJustice, "Exposing Canada's Chemical Valley," 2007, www.ecojustice.ca/publications/reports/report-exposing-canadas-chemical-valley/attachment.

7 Sarnia-Lambton Environmental Association, www.sarniaenvironment.com.

8 Enbridge's Line 7 pipeline runs beside the western section of Line 9, and Enbridge has received permission to pump 180,000 barrels per day through this pipeline—a 22 per cent increase in the flow of oil through Line 7.

9 Bakken shale deposits extend across North Dakota, Montana, and Saskatchewan.

10 Court of Appeal for Ontario, DOCKET: C32170, C32188, C32202 (2000), www.usask.ca/nativelaw/factums/view.php?id=99.

11 Ibid.

12 Suncor, "Suncor Energy's Sarnia refinery completes project to improve environmental performance and strengthen integration with oil sands operation," news release, accessed June 16, 2013, www.suncor.com/en/newsroom/2418.aspx?id=1088437.

13 Richard J. Marceau and Clement W. Bowman, *Canada: Winning as a Sustainable Energy Superpower,* Volume II (2012), www.clembowman.info/CanadaEnergySuperpower/VolumeII-HR.pdf.

14 ForestEthics, *Tar Sands Refineries: Communities at Risk* (2012), forestethics.org//sites/forestethics.huang.radicaldesigns.org/files/ForestEthics-Refineries-Report-Sept2012.pdf.

15 EcoJustice. "Exposing Canada's Chemical Valley."

16 Ibid.

17 In 1919, a tract was surrendered after federal officials threatened to expropriate Aamjiwnaang land. See Monica Virtue, "The Steel Company and the 1,184 acres stolen from Aamjiwnaang," accessed June 14, 2013, monicavirtue.com/portfolio-items/the-steel-company-and-the-1184-acres-stolen-from-aamjiwnaang/.

18 EcoJustice, "Exposing Canada's Chemical Valley."

19 Between 2009 and 2014, the fines for environmental violations from the industry in Sarnia-Lambton were less than an one-eighth of the amount collected for parking fines in Sarnia. See Zak Nicholls, "Demand More from Your Ministry of the Environment," Facebook post,March3,2014,www.facebook.com/notes/zak-nicholls/demand-more-from-your-ministry-of-the-environment/10152272863568293.

20 Dayna Nadine Scott, "Confronting Chronic Pollution: A Socio-Legal Analysis of Risk and Precaution," *Osgoode Hall Journal*, 46 (2008), 293.

21 Ibid.

22 Robert M. VanWynsberghe, *AlterNatives: Community, identity, and environmental justice on Walpole Island* (Toronto: Allyn and Bacon, 2002).

14. McCreary, Beyond Token Recognition

1 I thank the editors, as well as Richard Milligan, who helped me think through colonialism in Canada, and Nikki Skuce, who provided valuable feedback on an early draft of this chapter. This research was supported by funding from the Social Sciences and Humanities Research Council.

2 Enbridge Northern Gateway Project, Sec. 52 Application—Volume 1: Overview and General Information (Submitted to the JRP for the Northern Gateway Project, May 27, 2010).

3 Enbridge Northern Gateway Project, Sec. 52 Application—Volume 2: Economics, Commercial and Financing (Submitted to the JRP for the Northern Gateway Project, May 27, 2010), www.northerngateway.ca/project-details/regulatory-consultation-and-application/, accessed Jan. 31, 2013.

4 Greg Brown, Jeremy Moorhouse, and Jennifer Grant, *Opening the Door for Oil Sands Expansion: The Hidden Environmental Impacts of the Enbridge Northern Gateway Pipeline* (Drayton Valley, AB: Pembina Institute, 2009); David A. Levy, *Pipelines and Salmon in Northern British Columbia: Potential Impacts* (Drayton Valley, AB: Pembina Institute, 2009); Anthony Swift et al., *Pipeline and Tanker Trouble: The Impact to British Columbia's Communities, Rivers, and Pacific Coastline from Tar Sands Oil Transport* (New York and Drayton Valley, AB: Natural Resources Defense Council and Pembina Institute, 2011); Anthony Swift, Susan Casey-Lefkowitz, and Elizabeth Shope, *Tar Sands Pipelines Safety Risks* (New York: Natural Resources Defense Council, 2011); Kirsten Zickfeld, "Greenhouse Gas Emission and Climate Impacts of the Enbridge Northern Gateway Pipeline" (Submitted to the JRP for the Northern Gateway Project, Dec. 21, 2011), Marc Lee and Amanda Card, *Peddling GHGs: What is the Carbon Footprint of Canada's Fossil Fuel Exports?* (Ottawa: Canadian Centre for Policy Alternatives, 2011).

5 Sheila Leggett, Kenneth Bateman, and Hans Matthews, *Connections: Report of the Joint Review Panel for the Enbridge Northern Gateway Project* (Calgary: National Energy Board, 2013).

6 Gateway Pipeline, *Preliminary Information Package* (submitted to CEAA and NEB, October 31, 2005).

7   Gordon Jaremko, "Ambrose Named in Enbridge Pipeline Suit," *Calgary Herald*, October 27, 2006; Tyler McCreary and Richard Milligan, "Pipelines, Permits, and Protests: Carrier Sekani Encounters with the Enbridge Northern Gateway Project," *Cultural Geographies*, 21 (2014), 115–29.

8   Andrew Nikiforuk, *Tar Sands: Dirty Oil and the Future of a Continent* (Vancouver: Greystone Books and the David Suzuki Foundation, 2010), 11.

9   Canadian Environmental Assessment Agency, *Scope of the Factors — Northern Gateway Pipeline Project: Guidance for the Assessment of the Environmental Effects of the Northern Gateway Pipeline Project* (Ottawa: CEAA, 2009), 10.

10 Joe Oliver, "An Open Letter from Natural Resources Minister Joe Oliver," *The Globe and Mail*, January 9, 2012, accessed January 22, 2012, www.theglobeandmail.com/news/politics/an-open-letter-from-natural-resources-minister-joe-oliver/article2295599/.

11 Ibid.

12 *An Act to Implement Certain Provisions of the Budget Tabled in Parliament on March 29, 2012 and Other Measures* (*Jobs, Growth and Long-term Prosperity Act*), 154.

13 Martin Lukacs and Tim Groves, "RCMP Spying on First Nations Group; B.C. Natives at Enbridge Meeting in Toronto Are Being Tracked for 'Civil Disobedience'," *The Toronto Star*, May 10, 2012.

14 Paul Nadasdy, "The Anti-Politics of TEK: The Internationalization of Co-Management Discourse and Practice," *Anthropologica*, 47 (2005), 224.

15 James Youngblood Henderson, *First Nations Jurisprudence and Aboriginal Rights: Defining the Just Society* (Saskatoon: Native Law Centre, 2006).

16 Brian Slattery, "The Generative Structure of Aboriginal Rights," *Supreme Court Law Review*, 38 (2007), 595–628; Dwight G. Newman, *The Duty to Consult: New Relationships with Aboriginal Peoples* (Saskatoon: Purich, 2009).

17 McCreary and Milligan, "Pipelines, Permits, and Protests."

18 Enbridge Northern Gateway Project, *Sec. 52 Application — Volume 5A: Aboriginal Engagement* (Submitted to the JRP for the Northern Gateway Project, May 27, 2010), 5–73.

19 Carrier Sekani Tribal Council, *Aboriginal Interest and Use Study on the Enbridge Gateway Pipeline* (Prince George, BC: Carrier Sekani Tribal Council, 2006).

20 Enbridge Northern Gateway Project, *Sec. 52 Application — Volume 5B: Aboriginal Traditional Knowledge* (Submitted to the JRP for the Northern Gateway Project, May 27, 2010).

21 Jim Munroe, Joint Review Panel for the Enbridge Northern Gateway Project, Hearing Order OH-4-2011, Volume 19, Transcript of Hearing at Royal Canadian Legion Branch no. 268, 330 4th Avenue East, Fort St James, British Columbia, February 2, 31–32.

22 Ibid., front matter. This quote is included in the front matter of all the hearing transcripts of the JRP.

23 Henry Amos (Gupsalupus), Joint Review Panel for the Enbridge Northern Gateway Project, Hearing Order OH-4-2011, Volume 8, Transcript of Hearing at Haisla Recreation Centre, 1538 Jassee, Kitamaat Village, British Columbia, January 10, 2012, 52.

24 Oliver, "An Open Letter."

25 Sheila Leggett, Joint Review Panel for the Enbridge Northern Gateway Project, Hearing Order OH-4-2011, Volume 8, Transcript of Hearing at Haisla Recreation Centre, 1538 Jassee, Kitamaat Village, British Columbia, January 10, 2012, 53.

26 Ibid.

27 Ellis Ross, Joint Review Panel for the Enbridge Northern Gateway Project, Hearing Order OH-4-2011, Volume 8, Transcript of Hearing at Haisla Recreation Centre, 1538 Jassee, Kitamaat Village, British Columbia, January 10, 2012, 58.

28 Ibid., 59.

29 Gathering of Nations, "Save the Fraser Declaration" (Declared at T'exelc (Williams Lake), Secwepemc Territory, and Vancouver, Coast Salish Territories, December 1, 2010).

30 Quoted in Yinka Dene Alliance, "First Nations Gain Powerful New Allies in Fight Against Enbridge Northern Gateway Pipeline and Tankers," news release, December 5, 2013.

31 For more discussion of the contemporary political dynamism of tradition among the Carrier Sekani, see, McCreary and Milligan, "Pipelines, Permits, and Protests."

15. Leclerc and Weyler, Culture Works

1 Interviews with some artists who have collaborated on works to oppose the Enbridge tar sands proposal can be found at christineleclerc.com/blog.

2 Shauna Lewis, "Gitxsan steps back from pipeline agreement," *Raven's Eye*, 15 (2012), www.ammsa.com/publications/ravens-eye/gitxsan-steps-back-pipeline-agreement.

3 The poems submitted were put into 12-point Times New Roman font. The poems were then hand-measured in centimetres. Sometimes we used handmade rulers. Next, the poem lengths were converted from centimetres to kilometres to reflect the fact that *The Enpipe Line*'s actual height is one kilometre. Why so big? Because the height of the text is intended to match the width of the right-of-way requested by Enbridge to build their proposed pipelines.

4 The printed form of *The Enpipe Line* is a fraction of its actual size. At 72,129 kilometres long, it would be almost impossible to print the poem in full scale.

5 The editorial collective includes Jen Currin, Jordan Hall, Ray Hsu, Nikki Reimer, Melissa Sawatsky, and Daniel Zomparelli.

6 "Enbridge offering $1B to groups to push pipeline though," *The Canadian Business Journal*, February 10, 2011, www.cbj.ca/mobile/business_news/canadian_business_news/10_02_enbridge_offering_1b_to_groups_to_push_pipeline_though_11.html.

16. Russell et al., Lessons from Direct Action at the White House

1 For more background, see "An Open Letter to 1Sky from the Grassroots" in *Grist*, October 23, 2010, grist.org/article/2010-10-23-open-letter-to-1-sky-from-the-grassroots/.

2 By "movement moments," we mean an event that cross-pollinates multiple movement sectors and efforts and thus helps to change the landscape for organizing.

3 This phrase is commonly used by our friend Gopal Dayaneni of Movement Generation, usually in reference to organizing, though the spirit applies to public calls to action as well.

4 Interestingly, George W. Bush also made similar statements warning that "America is addicted to oil"—while some activists bemoan the disingenuous rhetoric from politicians, we can use that same rhetoric as a tool to campaign against them. en.wikipedia.org/wiki/North_American_energy_independence#Bush.27s_2006_.22Addicted_to_oil.22_speech.

5 Obama made this statement in the speech that announced his run for president. Barack Obama, "Presidential Announcement" (speech, Springfield, IL, February 10, 2007), chicago.about.com/od/chicagopeople/a/ObamaRunSpeech_2.htm.

6 Obama made this statement in his acceptance speech for the Presidential Nomination. Barack Obama, "Remarks" (speech, St. Paul, MN, June 3, 2008), www.huffingtonpost.com/2008/06/03/obamas-nomination-victory_n_105028.html.

7   *Newsmax,* "Romney Vows Immediate Approval of Keystone XL on First Day in White House," May 18, 2002, www.newsmax.com/Newsfront/romney-keysteon-pipeline-approval/2012/05/18/id/439519/.

8   For more on this, see a great reflection from Maya Lemon, "The Climate Movement Needs to Stop 'Winning'," *Huffington Post,* November 24, 2013, www.huffingtonpost.com/maya-lemon/to-the-leaders-of-the-cli_b_4305189.html.

17. Foytlin et al., Gulf Coast Resistance and the Southern Leg of the Keystone XL Pipeline

1   For more on this technique, see "Rachel Maddow's Mayflower Oil Spill Coverage Criticizes Exxon's 'Paper Towel' Cleanup Efforts," *Huffington Post,* September 4, 2013, www.huffingtonpost.com/2013/04/09/rachel-maddow-mayflower-oil-spill-exxon_n_3047331.html.

2   In this chapter, we refer to efforts of specific actions, including "blockades" as a direct action tactic that is used to oppose destruction. To clarify, Tar Sands Blockade (TSB) does not refer to a specific action; Tar Sands Blockade is an organizing collective of affected Texas residents and climate justice organizers.

3   Dina Cappiello, "Chronicle cross-country study reveals risky load of 'air toxics'," *Houston Chronicle,* January 16, 2005, www.chron.com/news/article/Chronicle-cross-county-study-reveals-risky-load-1643020.php.

4   Ingrid Lobet, "Testing what's in the air one Houston neighborhood at a time," *Houston Chronicle,* August 31, 2013, environmentalintegrity.org/news_reports/documents/TestingwhatsintheaironeHoustonneighborhoodatatime-HoustonChronicle_000.pdf.

5   "Frequently Asked Questions Concerning Pipeline Easements," West Harbour, www.westharbour.org/documents/PipelineFAQ.pdf.

6   By *anti-oppression,* we are referring to attempts to lessen disparities in power and privilege held by different members of our group based on their gender identity, sexuality, race, ethnicity, immigration status, class background, able-bodiedness, age, and other dividing lines within our society.

7   "Pipeline Eminent Domain and Condemnation Frequently Asked Questions (FAQs)," Railroad Commission of Texas, www.rrc.state.tx.us/about/faqs/eminentdomain.php.

18. Grant, The Enbridge Pipeline Disaster and Accidental Activism along the Kalamazoo River

1   I am extremely grateful to informants in Michigan who taught me about the burdens of toxins and the Kalamazoo River spill. Many thanks to Emily Gilbert for her mentorship and support, and to the editors of this book for productive feedback on earlier drafts of this chapter.

2   Enbridge, "Liquids Pipelines," last modified 2012, www.enbridge.com/DeliveringEnergy/OurPipelines/LiquidsPipelines.aspxwebsite; Elizabeth McGowan, "Timeline: How the Dilbit Disaster Unfolded," *Inside Climate News,* June 26, 2012, insideclimatenews.org/news/20120626/timeline-dilbit-diluted-bitumen-marshall-michigan-kalamazoo-enbridge-pipeline-6b-oil-spill.

3   National Oceanic and Atmospheric Administration (NOAA), NOAA/Hazardous Materials Response Division, *NOAA oil spill trajectory analysis, August 4, 2010,* Seattle, WA, 2010.

4   Personal communication, July 10, 2013. See also HRCTI (2010), below.

5 House of Representatives Committee on Transportation and Infrastructure (HRCTI), *Enbridge Pipeline Oil Spill in Marshall, Michigan: Hearing: 111th Cong., 2d. sess.* (Washington, DC: US Government Printing Office, 2010).

6 National Transportation and Safety Board (NTSB), *Pipeline accident report: Enbridge Incorporated Hazardous Liquid Pipeline Rupture and Release Marshall, Michigan, July 25, 2010*, Washington, DC, July 10, 2012.

7 Personal communication, May 14, 2013.

8 Personal communication, May 29, 2013.

9 Environmental Protection Agency (EPA), *Dredging Begins on Kalamazoo River*, August 2013, www.epa.gov/enbridgespill/pdfs/enbridge_fs_201308.pdf.

10 Pipeline and Hazardous Materials Safety Administration (PHMSA), US Department of Transportation, *Notice of Probable Violation and Proposed Civil Penalty* (Kansas City, MO, July 2, 2012); NTSB, *Pipeline accident report.*

11 PHMSA, *Notice of Probable Violation.*

12 NTSB, *Pipeline accident report.*

13 Personal communications with a number of key officials from agencies involved in the NRDA, May 28, June 5, July 3, July 18, 2013.

14 Todd Heywood provides an important overview of how the companies subcontracted by Enbridge hired mostly out-of-state workers—and in one case, undocumented workers—who were employed in unsafe working conditions. Todd Heywood, "Michigan Oil Spill Contractors Convicted on Immigration Crimes Linked to Cleanup Work," *American Independent*, August 23, 2013, americanindependent.com/220389/michigan-oil-spill-contractors-convicted-on-immigration-crimes-linked-to-cleanup-work.

15 Personal communication, July 8, 2013.

16 Fritz Klug, "Health studies cited in decision to reopen Kalamazoo River to public nearly 2 years after Enbridge oil spill," *MLive*, June 22, 2012, www.mlive.com/news/kalamazoo/index.ssf/2012/06/health_reports.html.

17 Fritz Klug, "Kalamazoo River Oil Spill Health Questions Go Unanswered Without Long-term Study," *MLive*, December 12, 2011, www.mlive.com/news/kalamazoo/index.ssf/2011/12/kalamazoo_oil_spill_health_que.html. This petition was made by the Calhoun County Community Health Department.

18 Personal communication, July 8, 2013.

19 Personal communications, May 14, May 31, June 5, June 8, June 10, June 12, June 26, 2013. See also HRCTI, *Enbridge Pipeline.*

20 Personal communication, May 17, 2013.

21 Personal communication, June 10, 2013.

22 HRCTI, *Enbridge Pipeline.*

23 Francisco Aguilera et al., "Review on the effects of exposure to spilled oils on human health," *Journal of Applied Toxicology*, 30, (2010), 291–301; Beatriz Perez-Cadahia et al., "Biomonitoring of Human Exposure to Prestige Oil: Effects on DNA and Endocrine Parameters," *Environmental Health Insights*, 2 (2008), 83–92.

24 National Toxicology Program, *12th report on carcinoge,* 2012, ntp.niehs.nih.gov/?objectid=03C9AF75-E1BF-FF40-DBA9EC0928DF8B15; Lisa Song, "What Sickens People in Oil Spills, and How Badly, is Anybody's Guess," *InsideClimate News,* June 18, 2013, insideclimatenews.org/news/20130618/what-sickens-people-oil-spills-and-how-badly-anybodys-guess?page=show.

25 Personal communication, June 11, 2013.

26 Personal communication, May 29, 2013.

27 Ibid.

28 Scott Frickel et al., "Undone Science: Charting Social Movement and Civil Society Challenges to Research Agenda Setting," *Science, Technology, & Human Values* 35,4 (2010), 445.

29 Personal communication, July 8, 2013.

30 Personal communication, June 26, 2013.

31 Personal communication, July 8, 2013.

32 Personal communication, June 12, 2013.

33 The analysis of the data collected via these community-led studies was still underway at the time this chapter was written.

34 PHMSA, "Letter Re: Restart Plan for Line 6B: CPF 3-2010-5008H," September 22, 2010, phmsa.dot.gov/staticfiles/PHMSA/DownloadableFiles/Files/Pipeline/320105008H_Approve%20Restart%20Plan_09222010.pdf.

35 Michigan Public Service Commission, "Order Approving Application, Case No. U-17020," January 31, 2013, efile.mpsc.state.mi.us/efile/docs/17020/0209.pdf; Michigan Public Service Commission, "Order adopting Proposal for Decision and Approving Application, Case No. U-16838," May 24, 2012, efile.mpsc.state.mi.us/efile/docs/16838/0092.pdf.

36 Personal communications, June 24, July 19, July 22, 2013. See also the MICATS website: www.michigancats.org. Three members of the MICATS were convicted of felonies for participating in a nonviolent direct action in July 2013. These MICATS had locked themselves to construction equipment along the Line 6B replacement route, stopping work on the pipeline for one day. They served 36 days in prison, were sentenced to 13 months of probation, and were each fined $47,600. See Ken Palmer, "3 Enbridge Protesters Get Time Served," *Lansing State Journal,* March 6, 2014, www.lansingstatejournal.com/article/20140305/NEWS01/303050036/3-Enbridge-protestors-sentenced-time-served-probation?nclick_check=1.

37 Lisa Song, "Map: Another Major Tar Sands Pipeline Seeking U.S. Permit," *InsideClimate News,* June 3, 2013, insideclimatenews.org/news/20130603/map-another-major-tar-sands-pipeline-seeking-us-permit.

19. Worth, Getting Europe Out of the Tar Sands

1 Zoe Cormier, "Not really a green country anymore," *The Globe and Mail,* September 4, 2009, www.theglobeandmail.com/news/politics/not-really-a-green-country-any-more/article4286820/.

2 Tar Sands in Focus (the UKTSN's original blog), "Indigenous Canadians deliver message to RBS and the Treasury: stop funding bloody oil!," November 16, 2009, tarsandsinfocus.wordpress.com/2009/11/16/indigenous-canadians-deliver-message-to-rbs-and-the-treasury-%E2%80%9Cstop-funding-bloody-oil%E2%80%9D/. See also "Speaker tour follow-up," November 27, 2009, tarsandsinfocus.wordpress.com/2009/11/27/speaker-tour-follow-up/.

3 Liberal Democrats, "Taxpayer must not support tar sands extraction—Hughes," November 17, 2009, www.libdems.org.uk/news_detail.aspx?title=Taxpayer_must_not_support_tar_sands_extraction_%E2%80%93_Hughes&pPK=e840c72d-e4e1-40d4-a2c1-dcf187316a1b.

4 Tar Sands in Focus, "Climate protesters scale Canadian embassy and deface flag," December 16, 2009, tarsandsinfocus.wordpress.com/2009/12/16/climate-protestors-scale-canadian-embassy-and-deface-flag/.

5   Jess Worth, "Brazen Posturing," *New Internationalist*, April 20, 2010, newint.org/blog/editors/2010/04/20/brazen-posturing/.

6   For the Olympics sponsorship campaign, see Owen Gibson, "Protest groups target Olympics sponsors with new campaign," *The Guardian*, April 15, 2012, www.guardian.co.uk/sport/2012/apr/15/protest-groups-olympics-sponsors-campaign, as well as the campaign website, www.greenwashgold.org; for the Reclaim Shakespeare Company's onstage anti-BP sponsorship interventions, see www.bp-or-not-bp.org.

7   "Valero: no tar sands in the UK," October 2012, UK Tar Sands Network, www.no-tar-sands.org/campaigns/valero/.

8   "Dirty diplomacy: tar sands lobbying and the Fuel Quality Directive," UK Tar Sands Network, www.no-tar-sands.org/campaigns/dirty-diplomacy-tar-sands-lobbying-and-the-fuel-quality-directive/.

9   For 2012's BP AGM, see "Protesters dragged out of BP AGM as board avoids uncomfortable questions," UKTSN, April 12, 2012, www.no-tar-sands.org/2012/04/protesters-dragged-out-of-bp-agm-after-board-avoids-uncomfortable-questions/; for 2012's Shell AGM, see "Shell shocked at AGM," UKTSN, May 30, 2012, www.no-tar-sands.org/2012/05/shell-shocked-at-agm/.

10 See, for example, "Activists disrupt speeches by Canadian Minister and Shell Chairman," UKTSN, October 15, 2012, www.no-tar-sands.org/2012/10/activists-disrupt-speeches-by-canadian-minister-and-shell-chairman/; "Stop Harper!: Canadian PM met by multiple tar sands protests in London," UKTSN, June 13, 2012, www.no-tar-sands.org/2013/06/stop-harper-canadian-pm-met-by-multiple-tar-sands-protests-in-london/.

11 Rob Edwards, "Royal Bank of Scotland cancels climate change campaign sponsorship," *The Guardian*, November 28, 2011, www.guardian.co.uk/business/2011/nov/28/royal-bank-scotland-climate-sponsorship.

12 Kiran Stacey, "Winners and losers from BP AGM," *Financial Times*, April 14, 2011, blogs.ft.com/energy-source/2011/04/14/winners-and-losers-from-bp-agm/#axzz2JeZryfBu.

13 "Athabasca Chipewyan First Nation's Case against Shell," *ACFN Challenge*, November 28, 2011, acfnchallenge.wordpress.com/2011/11/28/acfncase/

14 Pan European Oil Sands Team, "Pan European Oil Sands Team Mid-Year Report (20 August 2010)," climateactionnetwork.ca/2010/08/20/pan-european-oil-sands-team-mid-year-report-20-august-2010.

15 Zoe Cormier, "I'll die doing this," *New Internationalist*, April 1, 2010, newint.org/features/2010/04/01/first-nations/.

16 For example, see "Tar sands oil orgy blockades Canada House in London," UKTSN, November 20, 2012, www.no-tar-sands.org/2012/11/tar-sands-oil-orgy-blockades-canada-house-in-london/.

17 You and I Films, "'Oil orgy' invades energy summit," 1:35, October 11, 2001, vimeo.com/30373841#.

18 You and I Films, "Reverend Billy and & The Church of Earthalujah—An exorcism of the evil spirit of BP," 7:12, July 18, 2011, vimeo.com/45436933.

19 You and I Films, "Keep Europe out of the tar sands," 6:59, January 14, 2011, vimeo.com/18793439.

20 Arthur Neslen, "Canada's tar sands charm offensive hits the rocks," *Euractiv*, January 25, 2013, www.euractiv.com/climate-environment/canada-tar-sands-charm-offensive-news-517338.

20. Brecher et al., Labour Faces Keystone XL and Climate Change

1   AFL-CIO Energy Task Force, *Jobs and Energy for the 21st Century* (n.d.), www.workingforamerica.org/documents/PDF/1agexecutivealert.pdf.

2   "Remarks by AFL-CIO President Richard Trumka," AFL-CIO, January 12, 2012, www.aflcio.org/Press-Room/Speeches/Remarks-by-AFL-CIO-President-Richard-Trumka-UN-Investor-Summit-on-Climate-Risk.

3   Jane McAlevey, "Unions and Environmentalists: Get It Together!," *The Nation*, May 7, 2012.

4   Letter to the Honorable Hilary Clinton, Secretary of State, October 22, 2010, www.transcanada.com/docs/Key_Projects/Labour_Union_Signatures_22October2010.pdf.

5   Bill McKibben et al., "Join Us in Civil Disobedience to Stop the KXL Tar-Sands Pipeline," *Grist*, June 23, 2011, grist.org/climate-change/2011-06-23-join-us-in-civil-disobedience-to-stop-the-keystone-xl-tar-sands/.

6   Ari Shapiro, "Pipeline Decision Pits Jobs Against Environment," NPR, November 3, 2011.

7   Lara Skinner and Sean Sweeney, *Pipe Dreams? Jobs Gained, Jobs Lost by the Construction of Keystone XL*, Cornell University Global Labor Institute, January 2012, www.ilr.cornell.edu/globallaborinstitute/research/upload/GLI_KeystoneXL_012312_FIN.pdf.

8   Amalgamated Transit Union, "ATU & TWU Oppose Approval of the Keystone XL Pipeline and Call for End of Increased Use of Tar Sands Oil," news release, August 19, 2011, www.atu.org/media/releases/atu-twu-oppose-approval-of-the-keystone-xl-pipeline-and-call-for-end-of-increased-use-of-tar-sands-oil.

9   McAlevey, "Unions and Environmentalists."

10 Ibid.

11 Ibid.

12 Jeremy Brecher, *Jobs Beyond Coal: A Manual for Communities, Workers, and Environmentalists* (Washington, DC: Labor Network for Sustainability, 2012), report.labor4sustainability.org.

13 Mark Hertsgaard, "How a Grassroots Rebellion Won the Nation's Biggest Climate Victory," *Mother Jones*, April 2, 2012. www.motherjones.com/environment/2012/04/beyond-coal-plant-activism?page=1.

14 Brecher, *Jobs Beyond Coal.*

15 Brecher, *Jobs Beyond Coal*, analyzes numerous such cases.

16 Letter to Honorable Secretary Clinton.

17 Trumka, "Remarks."

18 Ibid.

21. LaDuke, Ending the Age of Fossil Fuels and Building an Economics for the Seventh Generation

1   Enbridge, Sandpiper Pipeline Project, 2013, enbridge.com/~/media/www/Site%20Documents/Delivering%20Energy/Projects/Sandpiper/ENB2013-Sandpiper-L19.pdf.

2   Andy Newbold, "Fox Wildly Inflates the Number of jobs Keystone XL Pipeline Might Create," *Media Matters*, November 9, 2011, mediamatters.org/research/2011/11/09/fox-wildly-inflates-the-number-of-jobs-keystone/182345

3   Cornell University Global Labor Institute, *Pipe Dreams? Jobs Gained, Jobs Lost by the Construction of Keystone XL*, September 2011, www.ilr.cornell.edu/globallaborinstitute/research/upload/GLI_keystoneXL_Reportpdf.pdf.

4   Oil Change International, *Exporting Energy Security: Keystone* XL *Exposed*, September 2011, priceofoil.org/content/uploads/2011/09/OCIkeystoneXL_2011R.pdf.

5   Thomas Berry, *The Great Work: Our Way into the Future* (New York: Broadway Books, 2000).

22. Thomas-Muller, The Rise of the Native Rights–Based Strategic Framework

1   Winona LaDuke, 20th Annual Sheinberg Lecture on "Predator Economics, Human Rights, and Indigenous Peoples" at NYU, November 13, 2013, www.law.nyu.edu/news/winona-laduke-delivers-the-20th-annual-sheinberg-lecture.

2   Naomi Klein, *The Shock Doctrine: The Rise of Disaster Capitalism* (Toronto: Knopf Canada, 2007).

3   James Cameron, Tar Sands Press Conference, September 29, 2010, www.youtube.com/channel/UCV2gfWXslNkAoOdtgibts5g.

4   Leanne Simpson, "Idle No More: Where the Mainstream Media Went Wrong," *The Media Co-op*, February 27, 2013, dominion.mediacoop.ca/story/idle-no-more-and-mainstream-media/16023.

23. Awâsis, Pipelines and Resistance across Turtle Island

1. Mason Inman, "Will Tar Sands Pipeline Threaten Groundwater?," *National Geographic News*, September 19, 2011, news.nationalgeographic.com/news/2011/09/110919-keystone-xl-tar-sands-pipeline-groundwater/.

2   These and other adverse health impacts affecting frontline communities in the vicinity of the Athabasca tar sands are documented in a report produced by the Sierra Club. See Gabriel DeRita and Tom Valtin, *Toxic Tar Sands: Profiles from the Front Lines* (2010).

3   World Health Organization, "Asphalt (Bitumen)," 2004, www.who.int/ipcs/publications/cicad/cicad59_rev_1.pdf.

4   See Enbridge's Environmental, Health and Safety and Corporate Social Responsibility Reports: csr.enbridge.com.

5   Statistics regarding the number of recent immigrants in Toronto census tracts are available from Stuart Thompson of York University. See Anna Mehler Paperny, "Interactive Map: Explore the data behind Toronto's working poor," *The Globe and Mail*, February 10, 2012, www.theglobeandmail.com/news/toronto/interactive-map-explore-the-data-behind-torontos-working-poor/article545650/.

6   For the purposes of this chapter, the term "two-spirit" is used to refer to Indigenous people who embrace the fluid, non-linear, and interrelated nature of all aspects of their identity, including their gender, sexuality, community, culture, and spirituality.

7   Native Youth Sexual Health Network, "Native Youth Sexual Health Network statement in support of 4th Annual Tar Sands Healing Walk," www.nativeyouthsexualhealth.com/tarsandshealingwalk.pdf.

8   "Recent Migration Trends in Census Divisions: Fort McMurray, Calgary and Edmonton," Alberta Demographic Spotlight, March 2011, www.finance.alberta.ca/aboutalberta/demographic_spotlights/2011-0311-migration-trends-fort-mcmurray-calgary-edmonton.pdf.

9   These Nation-to-Nation relationships are complicated by the fact that some consider Quebec to be a separate nation in itself.

10 Taiaiake Alfred, "What Does the Land Mean to Us?," *Indigenous Nationhood Movement*, November 19, 2013, nationsrising.org/what-does-the-land-mean-to-us/.

11 Quoted in Jonathan Goldsbie, "The Line Stops Here," *Now Magazine*, 33,8, October 24–31, 2013.

24. Coats, What Does It Mean to Be a Movement?

1 This approach is taken from Kenrick (2013), who argues that there are in fact three prongs to combatting climate change: confronting the system, working for change within the system, and building a new system. While I refer to the third prong implicitly in this discussion, it is the first two that are most relevant to the tar sands subset of the climate change battle. See Justin Kenrick, "Emerging from the Shadow of Climate Change Denial," *ACME: An International E-Journal for Critical Geographies*, 12,1 (2013), 102–30, www.acme-journal.org/vol12/Kenrick2013.pdf.

2 For more information on the centuries of injustice experienced by Indigenous peoples in Alberta, see Jennifer Huseman and Damien Short, "'A slow industrial genocide': Tar sands and the Indigenous Peoples of northern Alberta," *The International Journal of Human Rights*, 16,1 (2012), 216–37.

3 From "The 17 Principles of Environmental Justice," *EJnet.org:* Web Resources for Environmental Justice Activists: "Environmental Justice affirms the right of all workers to a safe and healthy work environment without being forced to choose between an unsafe livelihood and unemployment. It also affirms the right of those who work at home to be free from environmental hazards." See www.ejnet.org/ej/principles.html.

4 See "Articles of Treaty 8," Treaty 8 First Nations of Alberta, www.treaty8.ca/About-Us/ Articles-of-Treaty-8/.

5 Huseman and Short, "'A slow industrial genocide'," 218.

6 Paraphrased from Leslie Sklair, *Globalization: Capitalism and its Alternatives* (Oxford: Oxford University Press, 2002), 272.

7 These are incidentally similar to the three frames of social movements identified by Carroll and Ratner, "Master Framing and Cross-Movement Networking," 609–10: liberal frame, political-economy frame, and identity politics frame. See W. Carroll and R. Ratner, "Master Framing and Cross-Movement Networking in Contemporary Social Movements," *The Sociological Quarterly,* 37,4 (1996), 601–25.

8 See "19 Major Companies (and Two Important US Cities) Act to Clean Up Their Transporta-tion Footprints," ForestEthics, www.forestethics.org/major-companies-act-to-clean-up-their-transportation-footprints.

9 Leslie Sklair has a detailed discussion of attempts by the "Transnational Capitalist Class" to co-opt the green movement. Leslie Sklair, *The Transnational Capitalist Class* (Oxford: Blackwell, 2001), 200–10.

10 See Claudia Cattaneo, "170 legal victories empower First Nations in fight over resource development," *Financial Post*, December 14, 2010, business.financialpost.com/2012/ 12/14/170-legal-victories-empower-first-nations-in-fight-over-resource-development/ ?__lsa=d4ae-dd40.

11 Most Idle No More blockades have not centred on tar sands, but Chief Allan Adam of the Athabasca Chipewyan First Nation has shown that his community will consider blocking Highway 63 to the tar sands if their concerns remain unheard. See Athabasca Chipewyan First Nation and the Tar Sands, "Press Statement from Chief Allan Adam regarding Highway

63 Roadblocks," news release, January 15, 2013, acfnchallenge.wordpress.com/2013/01/15/for-immediate-release-press-statement-from-chief-allan-adam-regarding-highway-63-roadblocks/.

12 An important case of oil industry lobbying in 2013 was their influence on the package of environment-destroying laws; see Keith Stewart, "What the oil industry wants, the Harper government gives," *Greenpeace Canada* (blog), January 9, 2013, www.greenpeace.org/canada/en/Blog/what-the-oil-industry-wants-the-harper-govern/blog/43617/.

13 Elizabeth May, "Bill C-38: the Environmental Destruction Act," *The Tyee,* May 10, 2012, thetyee.ca/Opinion/2012/05/10/Bill-C38/.

14 Mike de Souza, "Feds remove water protection from historic law," *Postmedia News*, October 18, 2012, o.canada.com/2012/10/18/historic-water-protection-law-no-longer-to-protect-water-under-stephen-harper-budget-bill/.

15 Over the past decades, many communities have tried, with varying amounts of success, to sue tar sands companies. See Indigenous Environmental Network, *Tar Sands and Indigenous Rights* (Bemidji, MN: 2010), 7, www.no-tar-sands.org/wp-content/uploads/2011/05/NEW-IEN-BRIEFING-SMALL.pdf.

16 See "Beaver Lake Cree," RAVEN (Respecting Aboriginal Values and Environmental Needs), raventrust.com/beaverlakecree.html.

17 Marty Klinkenberg, "First Nations upset after Alberta appeal court rejects argument over Jackpine Mine," *Edmonton Journal,* November 26, 2012, www.edmontonjournal.com/First+Nations+upset+after+Alberta+appeal+court+rejects+argument+over+Jackpine+Mine/7611963/story.html.

18 Kristen E. Courtney, "First Nations shut out of Jackpine oil sands hearing," *Financial Post,* October 26, 2012, business.financialpost.com/2012/10/26/first-nations-shut-out-of-jackpine-oil-sands-hearing/.

19 Lauren Krugel and Bob Weber, "Shell's Jackpine Mine Gets Nod From Ottawa, Despite Environmental Effects," *Huffington Post*, December 12, 2013, www.huffingtonpost.ca/2013/12/06/shell-jackpine-oilsands-mine-approval_n_4401259.html.

20 See "Declaration of non-Indigenous Support for Defenders of the Land," Defenders of the Land, www.defendersoftheland.org/supporters.

21 Huseman and Short, "'A slow industrial genocide'," 230.

22 Daniel Wilson and David Macdonald, *The income gap between Aboriginal Peoples and the rest of Canada* (Toronto: Canadian Centre for Policy Alternatives, April 2010), www.policyalternatives.ca/sites/default/files/uploads/publications/reports/docs/Aboriginal%20Income%20Gap.pdf.

23 Carroll & Ratner, "Master Framing and Cross-Movement Networking in Contemporary Social Movements," 602.

24 One summary of these values can be found on the "About" page of Defenders of the Land: www.defendersoftheland.org/about/. "The rapport and relationship between Indigenous peoples and the lands and waters we have inhabited since time immemorial is fundamental and cannot be broken. The wealth of our nations must not only be measured in economic terms, but rather through the strength of our cultural knowledge and traditions, which are bound up with our relations to the land. The health and well-being of our peoples depends on our relations to the land, and the health of the land depends on its relation to our peoples."

25 Crystal Lameman, "Powershift 2012 Keynote Presentation" (speech).

26 "Declaration of non-Indigenous Support for Defenders of the Land."

27 Crystal Lameman, interview with the author, December 12, 2012.

28 Clayton Thomas-Muller, interview with the author, January 18, 2013.

29 This model has been pioneered by UK Tar Sands Network, among others.

30 Lameman, interview.

25. McKibben, Expanding the Fossil Fuel Resistance

1 Michael Grunwald, "I'm with the Tree Huggers: If we're in a war to stop global warming, then we need to fight it on the beaches, the landing zones, and the carbon-spewing tar sands of Alberta," *Time Magazine*, February 28, 2013, swampland.time.com/2013/02/28/im-with-the-tree-huggers/#ixzz2bCc6mwLT.

2 See Fossil Free Campaign (gofossilfree.org/) and Citizens Climate Lobby (citizensclimatelobby.org).

3 This movement combines struggles for economic and environmental justice in communities of colour in the San Francisco Bay Area. See: www.movementgeneration.org.

4 Union of Concerned Scientists, "Benefits of Renewable Energy Use," 2013, www.ucsusa.org/clean_energy/our-energy-choices/renewable-energy/public-benefits-of-renewable.html.

5 Thomas Friedmann, "No to Keystone, Yes to Crazy," *New York Times*, March 9, 2013.

6 Stephen Moore, "How North Dakota Became Saudi Arabia," *The Wall Street Journal*, October 1, 2011; Norimitsu Onishi, "Vast Oil Reserve May Now Be Within Reach, and Battle Heats Up." The International Energy Agency in Paris has also made massive upward revisions in the scale of fossil energy reserves as a result of the rise of fracking.

7 These issues are discussed further in Bill McKibben, "Global Warming's Terrifying New Math," *Rolling Stone*, July 19, 2012.

8 Polluter Watch, a project of Greenpeace, provides some valuable details on the extent of corporate lobbying for anti-environmental lobbying. See: www.polluterwatch.com/; Paul Blumenthal, "Chevron Gives $2.5 Million to House Republican Super PAC," *Huffington Post*, October 26, 2012, www.huffingtonpost.com/2012/10/26/chevron-super-pac_n_2023842.html.

9 Olga Belogolova, "Insiders: Obama Will Approve Keystone XL Pipeline This Year," *National Journal*, October 11, 2011, www.nationaljournal.com/energy/insiders-obama-will-approve-keystone-xl-pipeline-this-year-20111011.

10 David Roberts, "Attention investors: Climate policy could knock off half the value of fossil fuel companies," *Grist*, February 8, 2013, grist.org/business-technology/attention-investors-climate-policy-could-knock-off-half-the-value-of-fossil-fuel-companies/.

11 Cory Budischak et al., "Cost-minimized combinations of wind power, solar power and electrochemical storage, powering the grid up to 99.9% of the time," *Journal of Power Sources*, 225 (2013), 60–74.

12 Lisa Hymas, "Van Jones: Keystone XL would be 'the Obama Pipeline," *Grist*, March 2, 2013, grist.org/news/van-jones-keystone-xl-would-be-the-obama-pipeline/.

13 Charlie Rose, "Charlie Rose Talks to ExxonMobil's Rex Tillerson," *Bloomberg Business Week*, March 7, 2013, www.businessweek.com/articles/2013-03-07/charlie-rose-talks-to-exxonmobils-rex-tillerson.

26. D'Arcy, Secondary Targeting

1 For a theory of asymmetry in the military context, see Ivan Arreguin-Toft, "How the Weak Win Wars: A Theory of Asymmetric Conflict," *International Security*, 26,1 (Summer 2001),

93–128. For a discussion of asymmetry in the context of anti-capitalist activism, see Stephen D'Arcy, "Strategy, Meta-Strategy and Anti-Capitalist Activism," *Socialist Studies*, 5,2 (2009), 64–89. For an analysis of the implications of asymmetry for contemporary anti-colonialism in the Canadian state, see Taiaiake Alfred, *Wasáse: Indigenous Pathways of Action and Freedom* (Toronto: University of Toronto Press, 2005). For important anthropological analyses of the strategic logic of asymmetry, see James C. Scott, *Weapons of the Weak: Everyday Forms of Peasant Resistance* (New Haven, CT: Yale University Press, 1985) and *Domination and the Arts of Resistance: Hidden Transcripts* (New Haven, CT: Yale University Press, 1990).

2   See Frances Fox Piven and Richard Cloward, *Poor People's Movements: Why They Succeed, How They Fail* (New York: Vintage, 1979).

3   Joel Bakan, *The Corporation: The Pathological Pursuit of Profit and Power* (New York: Free Press, 2005).

4   See Michael John Bloomfield, "Shame Campaigns and Environmental Justice: Corporate Shaming as Activist Strategy," *Environmental Politics* (2013), 1–19.

5   Frances Fox Piven, *Challenging Authority: How Ordinary People Change America* (New York: Rowman and Littlefield, 2008).

6   Dave Foreman, ed., *Ecodefense: A Field Guide to Monkeywrenching*, 3rd Edition (Chico, CA: Abzug Press, 1993). For a detailed examination of sabotage, see Stephen D'Arcy, *Languages of the Unheard: Why Militant Protest is Good for Democracy* (Toronto: Between the Lines, 2013), 103–18.

7   D.L. Spar, "The Spotlight on the Bottom Line," *Foreign Affairs*, 77,2 (March-April 1998), 7, draws attention to the corporate vulnerability to adverse brand-image effects from negative publicity in the wake of human rights protest.

8   For a good account that is sensitive to the dynamic of the regime's vulnerability to support system targeting, see Richard Knight, "Sanctions, Divestment, and U.S. Corporations in South Africa," in Robert D. Edgar, ed., *Sanctioning Apartheid* (Trenton, NJ: Africa World Press, 1990).

9   As many readers will know, the same approach has been adopted in recent years by the Palestinian anti-colonial movement, to considerable effect. See Omar Barghouti, *Boycott, Divestment, Sanctions: The Global Struggle for Palestinian Rights* (Chicago: Haymarket Books, 2011).

10   Piven, *Challenging*, 20. For more detail on disruptive direct action, see D'Arcy, *Languages*, 89–102.

11   Some of the chapters of this book touch directly on questions of movement strategy. These include the contributions by Coats, Tokar, Thomas-Müller, and Brecher. But there have also been important discussions in the Global South, notably in the context of the First Peoples' World Conference on Climate Change and the Rights of Mother Earth, held in Bolivia in 2010, discussed by eco-socialist Terisa Turner in her article, "From Cochabamba, a New Internationale and Manifesto for Mother Earth," *Capitalism, Nature, Socialism*, 21 (September 2010), 56–74.

27. Albo and Yap, From the Tar Sands to "Green Jobs"?

1   The leading scientific estimates project that a rise in average global temperatures of 2°C is the threshold for irreversible climate change; that this can be expected from an accumulation of one trillion metric tons of carbon in the atmosphere; that we are approaching six

hundred million tons; and that the carbon "tipping point" may well be reached in thirty years unless carbon emissions can be reduced by 2 to 5 per cent per year. See: J.B. Foster, "James Hansen and the Climate Change Exit Strategy," *Monthly Review*, 64,9 (2013), 1–19; John Carey, "Global Warming: Faster than Expected?," *Scientific American*, 307,5 (November 2012), 50–55.

2   Tony Clarke, *Tar Sands Showdown* (Toronto: James Lorimer, 2008); Andrew Nikiforuk, *Tar Sands: Dirty Oil and the Future of a Continent* (Vancouver: Greystone Books, 2010).

3   We refer here to "institutional ecology" to underline the extra-market foundations seen as necessary for offsetting structural market failures, as with Keynesian political economy in this perspective. In the ecology literature, this is often associated with "ecological modern-ization." See Arthur Mol, David Sonnenfeld, and Gert Spaargaren, eds., *The Ecological Modernisation Reader: Environmental Reform in Theory and Practice* (London: Routledge, 2009); Maarten Hajer, *The Politics of Environmental Discourse: Ecological Modernization and the Policy Process* (Oxford: Oxford University Press, 1995). For a critique: John Bellamy Foster, Brett Clark, and Richard York, *The Ecological Rift: Capitalism's War on the Earth* (New York: Monthly Review Press, 2010), 41–43.

4   Friedrich Engels, "Outlines of a Critique of Political Economy," in *The Economic and Philosophical Manuscripts of 1844* (New York: International Publishers, 1964[1844]), 221.

5   On the metabolic relations of nature in capitalism, see John Bellamy Foster, *Marx's Ecology: Materialism and Nature* (New York: Monthly Review Press, 2000), chapter 5.

6   See: Karl Marx, *Capital*, Vol. 1 (London: Penguin Books, 1976 [1867]).

7   Elmar Altvater, *The Future of the Market* (London: Verso, 1993); Andrea Malm, "The Origins of Fossil Capital," *Historical Materialism*, 21,1 (2013).

8   UNEP, *Towards a Green Economy: Pathways to Sustainable Development and Poverty Eradication* (Nairobi: UNEP, 2011); UN, *Working Towards a Balanced and Inclusive Green Economy: A United Nations System-wide Perspective* (Geneva: United Nations, 2011). For "market ecology" strategies in Canada, see "CAPP on Climate," Canadian Association of Petroleum Producers, 2013, www.capp.ca/environmentCommunity/Climate/; Clare Demerse, *Reducing Pollution, Creating Jobs: The Employment Effects of Climate Change and Environmental Policies* (Drayton Valley, AB: Pembina Institute, 2011); Chris Bataille, Benjamin Dachis, and Nic Rivers, *Pricing Greenhouse Gas Emis-sions: The Impact on Canada's Competitiveness*, C.D. Howe Institute Commentary, N. 280, 2009.

9   UNEP, *Towards a Green Economy*, 14.

10 UNEP, *Green Jobs: Towards Decent Work in a Sustainable, Low-carbon World* (Nairobi: UNEP, September 2008), 3. The report was drafted by the Worldwatch Institute, but circulated by UNEP, and ILO and differs from the UNEP report a few years later. A few key Canadian interventions are Tony Clarke, Jim Stanford, Diana Gibson, and Brendan Haley, *The Bitumen Cliff: Lessons and Challenges of Bitumen Mega-Developments for Canada's Economy in an Age of Climate Change* (Ottawa: CCPA, 2013); *Making the Shift to a Green Economy: A Common Platform of the Green Economy Network* (Ottawa: GEN, 2011); Andrea Harden-Donahue and Andrea Peart, *Green, Decent and Public* (Ottawa: Canadian Labour Congress/Council of Canadians, 2009).

11 A few prominent examples: UNEP, *Global Green New Deal Policy Brief* (Geneva: UNEP, 2009); Robert Pollin et al., *Green Recovery: A Program to Create Good Jobs and Start Building a Low-carbon Economy* (PERI and Centre for American Progress, 2008); *A Green*

New Deal: Joined-up Policies to Solve the Triple Crunch of the Credit Crisis, Climate Change and High Oil Prices (London: New Economics Foundation, 2008).

12 ILO, *Building a Sustainable, Job-Rich Recovery* (Geneva: ILO, 2011); ILO, *Towards a Greener Economy: The Social Dimensions* (Geneva: ILO, 2011); OECD, *The Jobs Potential of a Shift Towards a Low-Carbon Economy* (Paris: OECD, 2012).

13 Alex Bowen, *'Green' Growth, 'Green' Jobs and Labor Markets*, Policy Research Working Paper N. 5990 (Washington: The World Bank, 2012), 4–5.

14 Green Jobs Initiative, *Working Towards Sustainable Development: Opportunities for Decent Work and Social Inclusion in a Green Economy* (Geneva: ILO, 2012), chapter 7.

15 For a discussion of the environmental contradictions of the multiplier effect and other green Keynesian propositions, see: Bill Blackwater, "Two Cheers for Environmental Keynesianism," *Capitalism, Nature, Socialism*, 23,2 (2012), 51–74.

16 Romain Felli, "An Alternative Socio-Ecological Strategy? International Trade Unions' Engagement with Climate Change," *Review of International Political Economy* (2013), 14–18.

17 IEA, *World Energy Outlook 2011: Are We Entering a Golden Age of Gas?* (Paris: IEA, 2011).

18 US Department of Energy, *International Energy Outlook 2013* (Washington: DOE, 2013), reference table A2.

19 National Energy Board, *Canada's Energy Future: Energy Supply and Projections to 2035* (Ottawa: NEB, 2011); Gavin Bridge and Philippe, *Oil* (Oxford: Policy, 2013), chapter 1.

20 Sean Sweeney, *Resist, Reclaim, Restructure: Unions and the Struggle for Energy Democracy* (New York: Rosa Luxemburg Stiftung/Cornell Global Labour Institute, 2012), 11–12; Statistics Canada, *Employment (SEPH)*, Table 281-0024; Petroleum Human Resources Council of Canada, *The Decade Ahead: Oil Sands Labour Market Outlook to 2021*, Spring 2012, at www.petrohrsc.ca.

21 Thomas Mann, *Some Responses to the Challenges of Climate Change by North American Labour*, York University, Work in a Warming World, Working Paper N. 2011-01, 2011; Carla Lipsig-Mumme, ed., *Climate @ Work* (Halifax: Fernwood, 2013).

22 The International Energy Agency cautions on the slow growth of renewable energy and thus the slowdown in carbon emissions: *World Energy Outlook 2012* (Paris: IEA, 2012).

23 Mario Candeias, "Energy Struggles for Energy Democracy," Rosa Luxemburg Stiftung, 2012, www.alternativen.blog.rosalux.de; Sweeney, *Resist, Reclaim, Restructure*, part 3.

24 We follow Andre Gorz in using *structural reforms* to mean the struggle for reforms that are anti-capitalist in their logic and capacity-building in their democratic content. See his "Reform and Revolution," in *Socialist Register 1968*, eds. Ralph Miliband and John Saville (London: Merlin Press, 1968); *Ecology as Politics* (Montreal: Black Rose Press, 1980).

25 International Transport Workers' Federation, *Transport Workers and Climate Change: Towards Sustainable, Low-Carbon Mobility* (London: ITF, 2010), 42–43.

26 Andre Gorz, *Capitalism, Socialism, Ecology* (London: Verso, 1994); David Rosnick, "Reduced Work Hours as a Means of Slowing Climate Change," *Real-World Economics Review*, 63 (2013); Climate Space/World Social Forum, "Change the System, Not the Climate," *The Bullet*, 810, (2013).

27 Greg Albo, "The Limits of Eco-Localism: Scale, Strategy, Socialism," in *Socialist Register 2007: Coming to Terms with Nature*, eds. Leo Panitch and Colin Leys (London: Merlin Press, 2007).

28 Karl Marx, *Grundrisse* (New York: Vintage, 1973 [1858]), 410.

29 Neil Smith, *Uneven Development: Nature, Capital and the Production of Space* (London: Verso, 2010).

28. Tokar, Tar Sands, Extreme Energy, and the Future of the Climate Movement

1 For a more detailed review of the emergence of climate justice, see Brian Tokar, *Toward Climate Justice: Perspectives on the Climate Crisis and Social Change* (Porsgrunn, Norway: New Compass Press, 2010), and Brian Tokar, "Movements for Climate Justice," in *Routledge Handbook of the Climate Change Movement*, eds. M. Dietz and H. Garrelts (London and New York: Routledge, 2013).

2 An analysis of the US strategy in Copenhagen appears in Tokar, *Toward Climate Justice*, chapter 3; an influential defence of the shift towards voluntary emissions reductions in Copenhagen is Michael A. Levi, "Copenhagen's Inconvenient Truth: How to Salvage the Climate Conference," *Foreign Affairs*, 88,5 (September/October 2009), 92–104.

3 See Tokar, *Toward Climate Justice*, chapter 2; for an "insider" account of the US Senate negotiations on the climate bill, see Ryan Lizza, "As the World Burns: How the Senate and the White House missed their best chance to deal with climate change," *The New Yorker*, October 11, 2010.

4 Nicola Bullard & Tadzio Mueller, "Beyond the 'Green Economy': System change, not climate change?" *Development*, 55,1 (2012), 57.

5 James Hansen, "Game Over for the Climate," *New York Times*, May 9, 2012; US Department of Energy data, cited in Marc Huot et al., *Oilsands and Climate Change: How Canada's oilsands are standing in the way of effective climate action* (Calgary: Pembina Institute, 2011), 4.

6 Michael T. Klare, "The New 'Golden Age of Oil' That Wasn't," *TomDispatch.com*, www.tomdispatch.com/blog/175601/klare_the_new_golden_age_of_oil_that_wasn.

7 Hansen, "Game Over for the Climate"; Carbon Tracker Initiative, "Unburnable Carbon—Are the world's financial markets carrying a carbon bubble?," *Carbon Tracker*, August 2012, www.carbontracker.org/wp-content/uploads/downloads/2012/08/Unburnable-Carbon-Full1.pdf.

8 Elizabeth Douglass, "Need for Keystone XL Shrinking as Industry Looks to Export U.S. Crude Oil," *InsideClimate News*, October 25, 2012.

9 Peter Schwartz, "Abundant Natural Gas and Oil Are Putting the Kibosh on Clean Energy," *Wired*, August 21, 2012, www.wired.com/business/2012/08/mf_naturalgas/all.

10 For an in-depth profile of many of these campaigns, see Tricia Shapiro, *Mountain Justice* (Oakland, CA: AK Press, 2010).

11 For frequent updates, see www.tarsandsblockade.org.

12 Mark Hertsgaard, "Climate Activists Put the Heat on Obama," *The Nation*, February 18, 2013.

13 Tom Wilber, *Under the Surface: Fracking, Fortunes and the Fate of the Marcellus Shale* (Ithaca, NY: Cornell University Press, 2012).

14 Jack Healy, "Colorado: Contested Gas Leases Are Delayed," *New York Times*, February 7, 2013; "Colorado Communities Take On Fight Against Energy Land Leases," *New York Times*, February 3, 2013.

15 Subhankar Banerjee, "Shell Game in the Arctic," *TomDispatch.com*, August 2, 2012, www.tomdispatch.com/post/175577/subhankar_banerjee_arctic_shell_game; Clifford

Krauss, "Shell Vessels Sidelined, Imperiling Arctic Plans," *New York Times*, February 11, 2013.

16 Winona LaDuke, "Navajos ban uranium mining," *Earth Island Journal*, www.earthisland.org/journal/index.php/eij/article/navajos_ban_uranium_mining.

17 "Uranium Hype Hits Indigenous Opposition Globally, Provokes Conflict in the North," Mining Watch Canada, www.miningwatch.ca/uranium-hype-hits-indigenous-opposition-globally-provokes-conflict-north; Ramsey Hart, "Indigenous Rights and Mining—Recent Developments, Opportunities and Challenges," Mining Watch Canada, www.miningwatch.ca/article/indigenous-rights-and-mining-recent-developments-opportunities-and-challenges.

18 John M. Meyer, "Populism, paternalism and the state of environmentalism in the US," *Environmental Politics*, 17,2 (2008), 219–36.

19 Hilary Moore and Joshua Kahn Russell, *Organizing Cools the Planet: Tools and Reflections to Navigate the Climate Crisis* (Oakland, CA: PM Press, 2011).

20 Robert S. Diamond, "What Business Thinks: The Fortune 500 Yankelovich Survey," *Fortune*, February 1970, 119.

21 Theda Skocpol, *Naming the Problem: What It Will Take to Counter Extremism and Engage Americans in the Fight against Global Warming* (Cambridge, MA: Harvard University, January 2013); Petra Bartosiewicz and Marissa Miley, *The Too Polite Revolution: Why the Recent Campaign to Pass Comprehensive Climate Legislation in the United States Failed* (New York: Columbia University, 2013), both available from www.scholarsstrategynetwork.org/node/2815.

22 Kevin Anderson, "Climate change going beyond dangerous: Brutal numbers and tenuous hope," *Development Dialogue*, 61 (Uppsala: Dag Hammarskjold Foundation, 2012).

23 Fred Magdoff has demonstrated that since World War II, unemployment in the US has only reliably fallen during years of greater than 5 per cent growth. See Fred Magdoff and John Bellamy Foster, *What Every Environmentalist Needs to Know about Capitalism* (New York: Monthly Review Press, 2011), 57–58.

24 Sasha Lilley et al., *Catastrophism: The Apocalyptic Politics of Collapse and Rebirth* (Oakland, CA: PM Press, 2012).

25 Since the 1980s, Amory Lovins and his colleagues at Colorado's Rocky Mountain Institute have documented the economic benefits and low relative cost of large investments in energy efficiency and renewable sources of generation, but only some US businesses have followed their recommendations. See, for example, Amory Lovins, et al., *Winning the Oil Endgame: Innovation for Profits, Jobs, and Security* (Snowmass, CO: Rocky Mountain Institute, 2005). One study showed that businesses demand a two-year payback for significant efficiency investments: reported in Matthew L. Wald, "Efficiency, Not Just Alternatives, Is Promoted as an Energy Saver," *New York Times*, May 29, 2007. Another in-depth feasibility study is Mark Z. Jacobson and Mark A. Delucchi, "Providing all global energy with wind, water, and solar power, Part I: Technologies, energy resources, quantities and areas of infrastructure, and materials," and "Part II: Reliability, system and transmission costs, and policies," *Energy Policy*, 39 (2011), 1154–69, 1170–90.

26 Ernst Bloch, *The Principle of Hope*, vol. 1 (Cambridge, MA: MIT Press, 1995), 5.

Index

ABOUT PM PRESS

PM Press was founded at the end of 2007 by a small collection of folks with decades of publishing, media, and organizing experience. PM Press co-conspirators have published and distributed hundreds of books, pamphlets, CDs, and DVDs. Members of PM have founded enduring book fairs, spearheaded victorious tenant organizing campaigns, and worked closely with bookstores, academic conferences, and even rock bands to deliver political and challenging ideas to all walks of life. We're old enough to know what we're doing and young enough to know what's at stake.

We seek to create radical and stimulating fiction and non-fiction books, pamphlets, T-shirts, visual and audio materials to entertain, educate and inspire you. We aim to distribute these through every available channel with every available technology — whether that means you are seeing anarchist classics at our bookfair stalls; reading our latest vegan cookbook at the café; downloading geeky fiction e-books; or digging new music and timely videos from our website.

PM Press is always on the lookout for talented and skilled volunteers, artists, activists and writers to work with. If you have a great idea for a project or can contribute in some way, please get in touch.

PM Press
PO Box 23912
Oakland, CA 94623
www.pmpress.org

BTL

About Between the Lines

FOUNDED IN 1977, Between the Lines publishes books that support social change and justice. Our goal is not private gain, nor are we owned by a faceless conglomerate. We are cooperatively run by our employees and a small band of volunteers who share a tenacious belief in books, authors, and ideas that break new ground.

Between the Lines books present new ideas and challenge readers to rethink the world around them. Our authors offer analysis of historical events and contemporary issues not often found in the mainstream. We specialize in informative, non-fiction books on politics and public policy, social issues, history, international development, gender and sexuality, critical race issues, culture, adult and popular education, labour and work, environment, technology, and media.

"Who is your leader?"
We create high-quality books that promote equitable social change, and we reflect our mission in the way our organization is structured. BTL has no bosses, no owners. It's the product of what some would likely describe as "sixties idealism"—what we call political principles. Our small office staff and Editorial Committee make decisions—from what to publish to how to run the place—by consensus. Our Editorial Committee includes a number of original and long-time members, as well as several younger academics and community activists eager to carry on the publishing work started by the generation before them.

www.btlbooks.com